Green Finance and Investment

Inventory of Energy Subsidies in the EU's Eastern Partnership Countries

OECD
BETTER POLICIES FOR BETTER LIVES

Please cite this publication as:
OECD (2018), *Inventory of Energy Subsidies in the EU's Eastern Partnership Countries*, Green Finance and Investment, OECD Publishing, Paris.
http://dx.doi.org/10.1787/9789264284319-en

ISBN 978-92-64-28430-2 (print)
ISBN 978-92-64-28431-9 (PDF)

Series: Green Finance and Investment
ISSN 2409-0336 (print)
ISSN 2409-0344 (online)

Revised version, October 2018
Details of revisions available at:
http://www.oecd.org/about/publishing/Corrigendum_Energy_Subsidies_EU_Eastern_Partnership_Countries.pdf

Foreword

In order to help governments in the European Union (EU)'s Eastern Partnership (EaP) countries develop a better understanding of existing energy-subsidy schemes and their economic, social and environmental impacts, the Organisation for Economic Co-operation and Development (OECD) has conducted a regional study of such subsidies in the EaP region. The study aims to provide the first comprehensive and consistent record of energy subsidies in these countries, with a view to improving transparency and establishing a solid analytical basis that can help build the case for reforms in the EaP region.

This study includes the six EU EaP countries, Azerbaijan, Armenia, Belarus, Georgia, Moldova and Ukraine. The analysis makes use of the method the OECD has been using to identify and quantify government support for fossil-fuel consumption and production in the Organisation's 35 member countries and a number of large emerging G20 economies (Brazil, China, India, Indonesia, the Russian Federation and South Africa). The study also uses the price-gap approach developed by the International Energy Agency (IEA).

The analysis presented in this study covers subsidies to consumers and producers of coal, oil and related petroleum products, natural gas, and electricity and heat generated on the basis of these fossil fuels. It also briefly looks at the subsidies benefiting energy-efficiency measures and renewable energy sources. In addition, the study discusses pricing and tax policies in the energy sector in the EaP countries. The analysis draws on a diverse body of publicly available sources and summarises the context, the state of play, and the mechanics of the complex and evolving landscape of energy subsidies in this region. The cut-off date for the data and information used in the analysis in this report is the end of 2015 unless otherwise indicated.

The study relies on publicly available sources of information, such as public accounts, official documents related to subsidy monitoring and budget planning and reporting, tariff calculation methodologies, academic literature and media items. It also draws upon feedback received from stakeholder consultations in each of the EaP countries conducted in the course of 2016.

In addition to individual country reports, the report contains a regional comparative overview chapter that summarises the main findings and conclusions from the country analyses. The report has been translated into Russian and the individual studies into the national languages of each of the countries, which are all available on the OECD website.

The study was prepared within the framework of the project on "Greening Economies in the Eastern Neighbourhood" (EaP GREEN) Project, funded by the European Union and co-ordinated with governments of the EaP countries. EaP GREEN is implemented by the OECD in partnership with United Nations partners: the UN Economic Commission for Europe (UNECE), United Nations Environment and UN Industrial Development Organisation (UNIDO). The work on Moldova was also financially supported by the government of Norway, through its Ministry of Foreign Affairs.

The views expressed here are in no way intended to reflect the official opinion of the European Union.

Acknowledgements

This report is a product of the collaborative efforts of many people. Given the complexity of the analysis, it would not have been possible without the dedicated and unwavering work of the project's core team. The project was carried out by the Global Subsidies Initiative (GSI) of the International Institute of Sustainable Development (IISD), with support from Sigra Group (Norway). Ivetta Gerasimchuk managed the project on the GSI/IISD side and assembled a team of experts, who are due special thanks. The country studies were drafted and edited by:

- **Armenia** – prepared by Tigran Sekoyan (Armenia) and Daniel Fjaertoft (Sigra Group), edited by Vibhuti Garg and Ivetta Gerasimchuk (GSI/IISD)
- **Azerbaijan** – prepared by Ahmad Alili and Vugar Bayramov (Center for Economic and Social Development, Azerbaijan) and Daniel Fjaertoft (Sigra Group), edited by Ivetta Gerasimchuk (GSI/IISD)
- **Belarus** – prepared by Andrei Malochka (Belarusian Heat-Energy Institute, or BELTEI) and Yuliia Oharenko (GSI/IISD), edited by Ivetta Gerasimchuk (GSI/IISD)
- **Georgia** – prepared by Giorgi Mukhigulishvili and Murman Margvelashvili (World Experience for Georgia) and Daniel Fjaertoft (Sigra Group), edited by Vibhuti Garg and Ivetta Gerasimchuk (GSI/IISD)
- **Moldova** – prepared by Mihai Roscovan (Business Consulting Institute, Moldova) and Rafal Stanek (SST-Consult, Poland), with support by Olga Driga, edited by Nelly Petkova (OECD)
- **Ukraine** – prepared by Yuliia Oharenko (GSI/IISD), edited by Ivetta Gerasimchuk (GSI/IISD).

Lars Lunden and Martin Jaer, Senior Research Fellows of the Sigra Group, provided methodological support in applying the price-gap approach in the country analyses. Oleksiy Shapovalov provided input on the Eurasian Economic Union and its implications for energy markets particularly in Armenia and Belarus.

The project was designed and its implementation overseen by Nelly Petkova of the OECD Environment Directorate, Green Growth and Global Relations Division (GGGR) who also put together the final report and prepared it for publishing.

The authors are particularly grateful to our colleagues from the OECD Trade and Agriculture Directorate (TAD) who inspired our work and paved the way for this analysis. Our work follows the OECD methodology for analysing government support for the production and consumption of fossil fuels in the OECD countries developed by our TAD colleagues. The TAD group, led by Ronald Steenblik, and including Jehan Sauvage, Christina Timiliotis and Federico de Luca, provided input on early drafts of the report, and their support has been invaluable.

The first drafts of the individual country chapters were discussed at stakeholder consultations in each of the countries over the course of 2016. These discussions were held in:

- **Yerevan, Armenia,** in April 2016, hosted by the Ministry of Energy and Natural Resources (since then renamed Ministry of Energy Infrastructure and Natural Resources)
- **Baku, Azerbaijan,** in October 2016, through individual consultations with key government stakeholders
- **Minsk, Belarus,** in April 2016, hosted by the Ministry of Economy
- **Tbilisi, Georgia,** in May 2016, hosted by the then Ministry of Energy
- **Chisinau, Moldova,** in November 2016, organised by the State Chancellery of Moldova
- **Kyiv, Ukraine,** in April 2016, hosted by the Committee on Fuel and the Energy Complex, Nuclear Policy and Nuclear Safety of the Parliament of Ukraine.

These debates were attended by representatives of key government offices, from the ministries of energy, economy, finance, environment, labour and national energy regulators, as well as parliamentarians and significant actors in the energy markets in these countries. Representatives of academia, research institutions and civil society also joined the discussions. Officials from international institutions, such as the Asian Development Bank, the European Bank for Reconstruction and Development (EBRD), European Union (EU) delegations to the countries, the International Monetary Fund (IMF), Islamic Development Bank, UN Environment, United Nations Industrial Development Organization (UNIDO), United States Agency for International Development (USAID) and the World Bank, also participated. The project team is grateful for their insightful comments in discussions, for their openness and their willingness to debate such politically sensitive issues as energy subsidies.

The team is indebted to many people for their contributions to this report. It is not possible to mention all of them, but their assistance was greatly appreciated. Key contributors from each of the countries are listed below. In Armenia, thanks go to Emil Zalinyan (Consultant to the World Bank), Ludovic Ciechanowski (EU Delegation to Armenia), Amalya Hambardzumyan (President of the "Khazer" Ecological NGO) and Aram Gabrielyan (UN Framework Convention on Climate Change, UNFCCC, Focal Point for Armenia). In Azerbaijan, the team worked closely with Asaf Rzayev (Ministry of Energy), Rauf Gurbanov and his colleagues (State Agency of Alternative and Renewable Energy Sources) and Elchin Mamedov (Ministry of Ecology and Natural Resources) and is very grateful for their support. In Belarus, Vyacheslav Čekurov (Head of the Economic Department, Ministry of Energy), Andrey Zorich (Head of the Department of Strategic Development and External Investment Co-operation, Ministry of Energy) and Vladimir Rak (Head of the Strategy Department of the State Enterprise Institute of Power Engineering of the Academy of Sciences of Belarus) provided thoughtful comments on the study. In Georgia, Deputy Minister of Energy Mariam Valishvili provided invaluable support, sharing her insights on how the energy market works. In Moldova, the contributions of Lilia Palii and her colleagues of the State Chancellery, Alexandru Ursu (National Agency for Energy Regulation, or ANRE) and Alexandre Darras (EU Delegation to Moldova) are much appreciated. In Ukraine, the authors are grateful to the staff of the Committee on Fuel and the Energy Complex, Nuclear Policy and Nuclear Safety of the Parliament of Ukraine and particularly to Oleksandr Dombrovsky (MP, Acting Head of the Committee), Oleksiy Ryabchyn (MP, Head of the Subcommittee on Energy Saving and Energy Efficiency of the Committee) and Olena Baida (Assistant-Consultant to MP Oleksiy Ryabchyn) for their support. Special thanks go to colleagues from NJSC Naftogaz of Ukraine for their openness, provision of data and information and for their constructive feedback on the draft report. Sergiy Konovets (Deputy Chairman of the Board of Naftogaz), Yurii Voytovych (Head of the Energy Efficiency Department), and Oleksii Khabatiuk (Deputy Head of the Energy Efficiency Department), worked closely with the OECD team on this analysis.

At the OECD, many people were involved at different stages of the project's implementation. The authors would like to thank Kumi Kitamori (Head, GGGR Division, Environment Directorate) and Krzysztof Michalak (Senior Programme Manager, GGGR Division) for their support and patience. Inmaculada Valencia provided overall administrative support for the project, Irina Belkahia helped with data collection, creating figures and preparing other elements of the report, while Jane Kynaston prepared the report for typesetting. The report was translated into Russian by Vadim Vinichenko and edited by Yuliia Oharenko (GSI/IISD). The authors would also like to thank Victoria Elliott for editing the report in English and Peter Vogelpogel for his help with typesetting and layout, as well as Janine Treves and Lupita Johanson, who assisted with the processing of the publication.

The financial support provided by the European Commission through the EaP GREEN project and by Norway was vital for the implementation of the project.

All these contributions are gratefully acknowledged.

Table of contents

Figures

Tables

Boxes

Boxes

Abbreviations and acronyms

ADB	Asian Development Bank
APEC	Asia-Pacific Economic Cooperation
ASCM	Agreement on Subsidies and Countervailing Measures
BAU	Business-as-usual scenario
BP	British Petroleum
BTC	Baku-Tbilisi-Ceyhan (oil pipeline)
CAPEX	Capital expenditure
CCGT	Combined cycle gas turbine
CHP	Combined heat and power
CIF	Climate Investment Funds
CNG	Compressed natural gas
COP	Conferences of the Parties
CSE	Consumer Support Estimate
DH	District heating
DSO	Distribution system operator
EABR	Eurasian Development Bank
EAEU	Eurasian Economic Union
EaP	Eastern Partnership
EaP GREEN	The "Greening Economies in the EU's Eastern Neighbourhood" Project
EBRD	European Bank for Reconstruction and Development
EC	European Commission
ECS	Energy Charter Secretariat
EE	Energy efficiency
EEA	Energy Efficiency Agency
EEF	Energy Efficiency Fund
EECCA	Eastern Europe, Caucasus and Central Asia
EFF	Extended Fund Facility
EU	European Union

FDA	French Development Agency
FIT	Feed-in tariff
G20	Group of 20, an international forum for the governments and central bank governors from 20 major economies
GDP	Gross domestic product
GEF	Global Environment Facility
GHG	Greenhouse gas
GIZ	*Deutsche Gesellschaft für Internationale Zusammenarbeit* (German Development Cooperation)
GRC	Guaranteed reserve capacity
GSI	Global Subsidies Initiative
GSI/IISD	Global Subsidies Initiative of the International Institute for Sustainable Development
GST	Goods and services tax
HGA	Host government agreement
HPP	Hydro power plant
IEA	International Energy Agency
IGU	International Gas Union
IFC	International Finance Corporation
IFI	International Finance Institution
IISD	International Institute for Sustainable Development
IMF	International Monetary Fund
INDC	Intended Nationally Determined Contribution
JSC	Joint stock company
LCOE	Levelised cost of electricity
LEDS	Low-emission development strategy
LPG	Liquefied petroleum gas
LULUCF	Land use, land-use change and forestry
MOU	Memorandum of understanding
n.a.	Not applicable
n.c.	Not calculated
n.d.	Not dated
NIF	Neighbourhood Investment Facility
NJSC	National joint stock company
NPP	Nuclear power plant

O&M	Operation and maintenance
OECD	Organisation for Economic Co-operation and Development
PPP	Purchasing power parity
PSA	Production sharing agreement
PSE	Producer Support Estimate
PSO	Public Service Obligation
RE	Renewable energy
RES	Renewable energy source
RROR	Real rate of return
RSP	Regional Sector Programme
SCMA	Subsidies and Countervailing Measures Agreement
SDG	Sustainable development goal
sLCOE	Simple levelised cost of energy
SME	Small and medium-sized enterprise
TFC	Total final consumption
TFEC	Total final energy consumption
TIC	Total installed capacity
TPES	Total primary energy supply
TPP	Thermal power plant
TSO	Transmission system operator
UNDP	United Nations Development Programme
UNECE	United Nations Economic Commission for Europe
UNFCCC	United Nations Framework Convention on Climate Change
UNIDO	United Nations Industrial Development Organization
USAID	United States Agency for International Development
USD	United States dollar
VAT	Value-added tax
WACC	Weighted average cost of capital
WDI	World Development Indicators
WEM	Wholesale electricity market
WHT	Withholding tax
WTO	World Trade Organization
yoy	Year-on-year/Year over year

Units of measure

bcm	billion cubic metres
bln	billion
btu	British Thermal Unit
Gcal	gigacalorie
GW	gigawatt
GWh	gigawatt hour
km	kilometre
koe	kilogramme of oil equivalent
ktoe	kilotonne of oil equivalent
kV	kilovolt
kVA	kilovoltampere
kW	kilowatt
kWh	kilowatt hour
l	litre
m^3	cubic metre
mbtu	million British thermal units
mln	million
Mt	million tonnes
Mt of CO_2	million tonnes of CO_2
Mtoe/mtoe	million tonnes of oil equivalent
MW	megawatt
MWh	megawatt hour
PJ	petajoule
t	tonne
toe	tonne of oil equivalent
TWh	terawatt hour

Pollutants

CO	Carbon monoxide
CO_2	Carbon dioxide
NO_2	Nitrogen dioxide
SO_2	Sulphur dioxide

Country-specific abbreviations

Armenia

AERC	Armenian Energy Regulatory Commission
AMD	Armenian Dram
ENA	Electric Networks of Armenia
PSRC	Public Services Regulatory Commission of Armenia
RA	Republic of Armenia

Azerbaijan

ACG	Azeri-Chirag-Gunashli (a complex of oil fields in Azerbaijan)
AZN	Azerbaijani manat
SOCAR	State Oil Company of the Azerbaijan Republic
SOFAZ	State Oil Fund of Azerbaijan
TAP-AG	Trans Adriatic Pipeline
USGS	(Russian) Unified system of gas supply

Belarus

BYR	Belarusian ruble
SPA	State Production Association
ZhKH	Housing and communal service organisation

Georgia

ESCO	Electricity System Commercial Operator
FGS UES	Federal Grid Company of Unified Energy System (of the Russian Federation)
GEL	Georgian lari
GEOSTAT	National Statistics Office of Georgia
GGTC	Georgian Gas Transportation Company
GNERC	Georgian National Energy and Water Supply Regulatory Commission
GOGC	Georgian Oil and Gas Corporation
GSE	Georgian State Electrosystem
MoE	Ministry of Energy of Georgia
MoENRP	Ministry of Environment and Natural Resources Protection of Georgia
NAOG	National Oil and Gas Agency
SCP	South Caucasus pipeline
SGGAS	SOCAR Georgia Gas
WEG	World Experience for Georgia

Moldova

ANRE	Moldovan National Energy Regulatory Agency
FISM	Social Investment Fund of Moldova
GoM	Government of Moldova
MDL	Moldovan leu
MEBP	Moldova Biomass and Energy Project
MLPS	Modernisation of Local Public Services (GIZ project)
MoREEF	Moldovan Residential Energy Efficiency Financing Facility
MoSEFF	Moldovan Sustainable Energy Financing Facility
MRDC	Ministry of Regional Development and Construction of Moldova
NBS	National Bureau of Statistics of Moldova
SCADA	Supervisory Control and Data Acquisition (system)

Ukraine

NCSREPU	National Commission for State Regulation of Energy and Public Utilities of Ukraine
TKEs	Teplokomunenerhos (local heat supply companies)
UAH	Ukrainian hryvnia

Executive summary

Background

Governments have long relied on energy subsidies to advance specific development goals or address market failures. The most common argument for introducing and maintaining energy subsidies is that they support important domestic policy objectives, such as rural and industrial development, job creation, improved energy access, energy security and independence, and poverty alleviation.

However, the economic cost of energy subsidies can represent a significant burden on a country's finances, weaken its growth potential and encourage wasteful energy consumption. Analysis shows that energy subsidies tend to accrue not to those with the lowest income, but rather to the largest and most economically powerful recipients, thus increasing profits for well-connected investors or industries. By encouraging use of fossil fuels and discouraging production of low-carbon fuels, energy subsidies can lead to increased emissions of carbon dioxide and other greenhouse gas emissions.

To help governments in the European Union (EU)'s Eastern Partnership (EaP) countries (Armenia, Azerbaijan, Belarus, Georgia, the Republic of Moldova and Ukraine) develop a better understanding of existing energy-subsidy schemes and their economic, social and environmental impact, the Organisation for Economic Co-operation and Development (OECD) conducted a regional study of such subsidies. The analysis was carried out as part of the EU-funded project "Greening Economies in the European Union's Eastern Neighbourhood" (EaP GREEN) which has assisted the six EaP countries to strengthen the analysis, policy instruments and capacities needed to make the transition to a green economy.

The analysis presented in this report covers both subsidies to consumers and to producers of coal, oil and petroleum products (particularly in the transport sector), natural gas and electricity and heat generated on the basis of these fossil fuels. It also reviews subsidies to energy efficiency and renewable energy sources. The analysis makes use of the OECD methodology for quantifying government support to fossil-fuel consumption and production. Over the years, the OECD has done extensive work on analysing government support measures in both OECD countries and key emerging G20 economies (Brazil, China, India, Indonesia, the Russian Federation and South Africa).

This study is the first comprehensive and consistent record of energy subsidies in the EaP region. It was prepared with a view to improving transparency and establishing a solid analytical basis that can help build the case for further reforms in the EaP countries. The information included in the report can be used by both policy makers and the general public.

Approaches to subsidy quantification: price-gap and inventory

There are two main approaches for quantifying subsidies: top-down estimates based on price-gap assumptions, and bottom-up inventories that consider each government support measure individually. Both were used in this study. Each approach has strengths and limitations, and the two can complement each other. This complementarity is especially useful if access to data and subsidy reporting are restricted. As with all inventories, analyses of energy support measures are always a mixture of subsidies that have been assigned a monetary value and those that are identified, but not quantified. The research team participating in the study found enough data to apply the inventory approach in sufficient detail in Armenia, Georgia, Moldova and Ukraine.

Main findings and conclusions of the study

This study found subsidies to fossil fuel production and consumption in all EaP countries. These subsidies are discussed in more detail in the individual country chapters. By combining the inventory and the price-gap approach, the research team could identify a number of subsidies but due to data limitations not all of them were quantified.

The main findings from the analysis in this study are:

- Since independence, the EaP countries have undergone significant energy sector and energy subsidy reforms (better known as energy pricing reforms). Natural gas, electricity and heat sectors remain subject to price regulation in all EaP countries for consumers and often for producers. The most deregulated segment is the market of liquid petroleum products. Pricing policies, including pricing methodologies, tariff structures and regulatory procedures continue to evolve. The tax system has been rationalised and simplified, which has led to increased tax collection.
- In **absolute terms**, the amount of government support that goes to fossil fuels is the highest in Ukraine. In 2015, fossil-fuel subsidies in Ukraine amounted to about USD 7 bln, down from about USD 17 bln in 2014 (about 13% of the country's GDP). This significant decrease was a result of a number of reforms that the government of Ukraine has put in place over the past couple of years. Fossil-fuel subsidies in Belarus steadily increased since 2010, reaching USD 1.6 bln and were approaching the level of subsidies in Azerbaijan in 2014 (USD 1.7 bln). Energy subsidies in Georgia and Moldova were much smaller but increased over the review period to the levels of USD 228 and 182 mln, respectively. The annual amount of subsidies in Armenia was significantly lower than in the other five countries and fluctuated between USD 37 and 42 mln during the review period.
- In **relative terms**, the analysis shows that as a share of GDP, in 2014, the quantified fossil-fuel subsidies in Azerbaijan, Moldova and Ukraine were larger than the general government deficit in these countries. This points to the possibility to further streamline these subsidies and raise additional revenue for the government which can be redistributed more efficiently and to better social causes.
- The **bulk of subsidies** goes to natural gas, heat and electricity, which is not surprising given that natural gas dominates the energy mix in these countries and is used in generating heat and electricity.
- Most of the **fossil-fuel subsidies aim to benefit residential consumers**. Regulated energy prices set at below-market rates that benefit consumers are the most

important form of subsidisation in the EaP region. Cross-subsidisation still exists in Belarus, Georgia and Ukraine. Often, such subsidies are seen as social measures by the governments and the population.

- At the same time, government support to **energy efficiency** and **renewables** is **negligible** compared to support that goes to the production and consumption of fossil fuels.

The analysis shows that several countries in the region have reformed their fossil-fuel subsidies in 2015-16, seizing the opportunity of low energy prices on the international market. These reforms continue to evolve and they can be observed in almost all countries in the region.

In analysing experience with energy-subsidy reform one message stands out above all others: countries should be prepared. This may seem obvious. But all too often countries implement reform because of a sudden crisis or an international requirement, and find themselves missing internal co-ordination and research and public support that would allow for effective and decisive change.

Governments should prepare for energy subsidy reform holistically. Energy subsidies are usually a long term, structural, problem – and they need structural solutions. Energy subsidy reform always requires research, consultations and efforts across many agencies within the government and groups of stakeholders. This is particularly true in terms of anticipating and managing the reform's impact that can be both direct and indirect.

In this context and with the aim of improving transparency of energy subsidies (who benefits, what is the cost of these subsidies on the public budget, what is their impact on the environment), the EaP governments could consider implementing the following actions:

- Review and improve the definition of subsidy in national legislation and budgetary documents. A clear definition in line with internationally-recognised practices is the building block for further adequate analysis.
- Regularly estimate tax expenditure that result from various tax breaks and tax advantages provided to individual groups and industries and prepare tax expenditure reports which will inform the legislature and society on fiscal losses from such policies. OECD countries prepare such reports on an annual basis and these reports are available in the public domain.
- Regularly analyse the evolution of energy subsidies in the sector and maintain a database which can be particularly useful in the decision-making process on energy subsidy reforms.

Chapter 1

Overview of energy subsidies in the EaP countries

This chapter summarises the main findings of the analyses of existing energy subsidy schemes in the six EU Eastern Partnership countries. It introduces the methodology used to identify and estimate government support for fossil-fuel production and consumption, as well as support for energy-efficiency and renewable measures. The chapter also discusses the main energy pricing and taxation policies in each country, which underpin government support in the energy sector. It also offers a discussion of the potential benefits of energy subsidy reform and the challenges related to its implementation.

Why do energy subsidies matter?

Governments have long relied on energy subsidies to advance specific development goals or address market failures. The most common argument for introducing and maintaining energy subsidies is that they support important domestic policy objectives, such as rural and industrial development, job creation, improved energy access, energy security and independence, and poverty alleviation.

However, the economic cost of energy subsidies can represent a significant burden on a country's finances, weaken its growth potential and encourage wasteful energy consumption. Analysis shows that energy subsidies tend to accrue not to those with the lowest income, but rather to the largest and most economically powerful recipients, thus increasing profits for well-connected investors or industries. By encouraging use of fossil fuels and discouraging production of low-carbon fuels, energy subsidies can lead to increased emissions of carbon dioxide and other greenhouse gas emissions.

Empirical studies suggest that removing subsidies that promote wasteful energy consumption could yield substantial emission reductions, as well as major environmental, economic and social benefits. In 2009, leaders of both G20 and the Asia-Pacific Economic Co-operation (APEC) committed to "phase out, over the medium-term, inefficient fossil-fuel subsidies that encourage wasteful consumption of energy" while protecting the vulnerable groups from possible negative impacts of such reforms (G20, 2009; APEC, 2009). Since then, G20 and APEC leaders have reiterated this commitment every year and have started the process of voluntary peer reviews (Gerasimchuk et al., 2017). This language was further used in the Fossil Fuel Subsidy Communiqué signed by over 40 countries, including Moldova (FFFSR, 2015).

Energy subsidies in the European Union's Eastern Partnership countries

The EU's Eastern Partnership (EaP) countries – Armenia, Azerbaijan, Belarus, Georgia, Moldova and Ukraine – are no exception to the global experience of energy subsidies and their reform. However, there is relatively little transparency over energy subsidies reform in the EaP region, and also little public discussion on the negative implications of government support to fossil fuels and possible benefits of its reform.

To help governments in the EaP countries develop a better understanding of existing energy-subsidy schemes and their economic, social and environmental impact, the Organisation for Economic Co-operation and Development (OECD) conducted a regional study of such subsidies. The analysis was carried out as part of the EU-funded project "Greening Economies in the European Union's Eastern Neighbourhood" (EaP GREEN) which has assisted the six EaP countries to strengthen the analysis, policy instruments and capacities needed to make the transition to a green economy.

The analysis presented in this report (this overview and six country chapters) covers both subsidies to consumers and to producers of coal, oil and petroleum products (particularly in the transport sector), natural gas and electricity and heat generated on the basis of these fossil fuels. It also reviews subsidies to energy efficiency and renewable energy sources. The analysis makes use of the OECD methodology for quantifying government support to fossil-fuel consumption and production. Over the years, the OECD has done extensive work on analysing government support measures in both OECD countries and key emerging G20 economies (Brazil, China, India, Indonesia, the Russian Federation and South Africa).

This study is the first comprehensive and consistent record of energy subsidies in the EaP region, with a view to improving transparency and establishing a solid analytical basis that can help build the case for further reforms in the EaP countries. This information can be used by both policy makers and the general public. The study aims to assist the EaP governments to consider complying with the best international practice, which consists of:

- Systematic reporting on energy subsidies as part of the preparation of tax expenditure budgets and notifications to the World Trade Organization (WTO)
- Participation in voluntary peer reviews of fossil-fuel subsidies such as those conducted within G-20 and APEC, but potentially not limited to the members of these organisations
- Open communication and stakeholder consultations over the effectiveness and impacts of energy subsidies, and government's plans of their reform.

Fossil-fuel subsidies are also subject to reporting under the UN Sustainable Development Goals (SDGs). This reporting requirement is applicable to all, including the EaP countries, since SDG 12 target C calls all countries to "Rationalise inefficient fossil-fuel subsidies that encourage wasteful consumption by removing market distortions, in accordance with national circumstances, including by restructuring taxation and phasing out those harmful subsidies, where they exist, to reflect their environmental impacts, taking fully into account the specific needs and conditions of developing countries and minimising the possible adverse impacts on their development in a manner that protects the poor and the affected communities" (UN SDKP, 2015).

Subsidy identification and estimation methodology

Energy subsidies have always been complex and large. The OECD's *Inventory of Support Measures for Fossil Fuels* released in 2015 found that governments in the OECD and the emerging BRIICS countries (Brazil, the Russian Federation, India, Indonesia, the People's Republic of China and South Africa) collectively support the production and consumption of fossil fuels to the tune of USD 160-200 bln a year. With most of that support coming in the form of budgetary transfers and tax breaks – the OECD inventory identifies about 800 such measures – this effectively means that governments today still spend billions to encourage the extraction and burning of fossil fuels at taxpayers' expense. Adding in the consumer price subsidies measured by the International Energy Agency (IEA), this makes total subsidies and other forms of support for fossil fuels in the vicinity of USD 500-600 bln a year (OECD, 2015a).

But how well energy subsidies are understood, and how large they are estimated to be, depends on the definition and analysis methodology. The sections below sketch out what distinguishes different approaches to subsidy identification and estimation, and outline the methodology followed in this study.

Definition and classification of subsidies

Definitions

For energy subsidy identification purposes, this study relies on the most widely recognised definition of a subsidy, formulated in the Agreement on Subsidies and Countervailing Measures (ASCM) (WTO, 1996) of the World Trade Organization. The ASCM has been signed by 164 countries, including Armenia, Georgia, Moldova and Ukraine (Azerbaijan and Belarus are at different stages of joining the WTO at the time of writing this report).

Under Article 1, the ASCM determines that for all types of economic activities (energy is just one area), four types of subsidies exist, where:

i. Government provides direct transfer of funds or potential direct transfer of funds or liabilities.

ii. Government revenue is foregone or not collected.

iii. Government provides goods or services or purchases goods on terms that confer a benefit compared to market terms.

iv. Government provides income or price support.

Article 2 of the ASCM further stipulates that in order to be considered a subsidy, the benefit has to be specific to the company or industry. The specificity criterion is important for screening policies and identifying them as subsidies. For instance, in Georgia, a value-added tax (VAT) exemption is granted for natural gas consumed by electricity generators, but not for other natural gas consumers, which distinguishes this policy as a subsidy in this study's relevant country chapter.

However, the ASCM subsidy definition is by no means the only one. It has also not been developed to address the issues specific to the energy industry, such as, for instance, different taxation benchmarks in different countries, as well as the natural resource rent that governments seek or fail to capture from the extractive companies, especially in the oil and gas sector.

For instance, the International Energy Agency has defined energy subsidies as "any government action that lowers the cost of energy production, raises the price received by energy producers or lowers the price paid by energy consumers" (IEA, 2006). This includes direct and indirect transfer of funds and liabilities, tax breaks, price and market support measures, as well as other regulations giving an advantage to fossil fuels. Using the price-gap approach, the IEA provides a global estimate of subsidies to fossil fuels at USD 325 bln in 2015, a figure that is limited only to consumer subsidies, and only to developing countries (IEA, 2016b, p. 97). The IEA also estimates worldwide subsidies for renewables at USD 150 bln in the same year (IEA, 2016b, p. 97).

Relying on a much broader definition, the International Monetary Fund (IMF) considers that the failure to impose an adequate tax on carbon, congestion and negative health externalities essentially constitutes a subsidy to fossil fuels (IMF, 2013; IMF, 2015). Thus, the IMF's post-tax estimate of global fossil-fuel subsidies in both developing and developed countries stands at USD 5.3 trillion in 2015, or USD 10 mln per minute (IMF, 2015). Other global and national estimates of fossil-fuel subsidies have also been made, although estimates of fossil-fuel subsidies on the production side require much more work and transparency.

The agreements and disagreements on the definition of subsidies are easiest to explain through concentric circles (OECD, 2010a). At the centre of the definition are ideas that are generally accepted, but as the definition expands to include other layers, it becomes more complicated and more controversial. This lends itself to an analogy with a *matryoshka* nesting doll, as presented in Figure 1.1.

At the centre of the definition are direct **budgetary transfers** to producers and consumers of energy. This category also includes liabilities for such direct transfers as a result of **transfer of risks** from energy producers or consumers to governments. Such cases include, for instance, provision of loan and loan guarantees at below-market rates or governments' assuming the costs of preventing and remediating environmental damage.

The second biggest *matryoshka* encompasses all **government revenue foregone** in terms of uncollected or under-collected levies on energy production and consumption. In other words, the value of this support equals the deviations from the national benchmarks of the respective corporate profit tax, property and land tax, royalties, fees on infrastructure use for producers, and reduced rates and exemptions with respect to VAT, excise and other possible taxes on energy sold to consumers.

Figure 1.1. **The nesting doll of subsidy definitions and scope of this study**

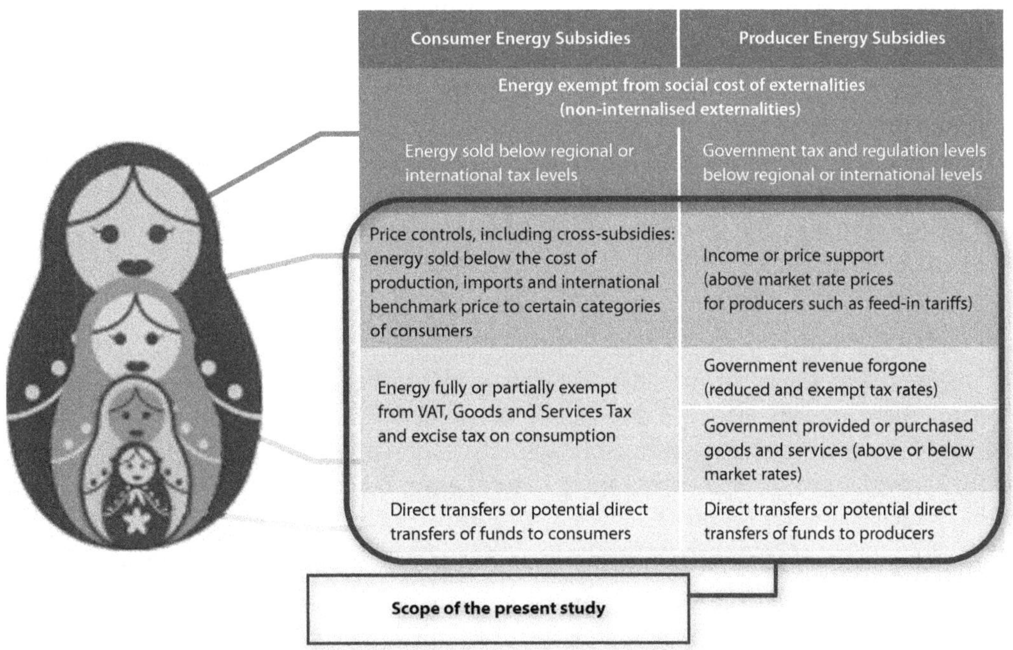

Sources: Gerasimchuk et al. (2012), Gerasimchuk (2014), OECD (2013a), IMF (2015).

These two inner "nesting dolls" capture the types of subsidies that have been subject to recent reforms in many countries and that are also the focus of the G20 and Asia-Pacific Economic Cooperation (APEC) commitments. These have been singled out because of the obvious cost of such measures for the budget. These two inner components – direct budgetary transfers and government revenue that has been foregone as a result – are also the subject of quantification of OECD's renowned *Inventory of Support Measures for Fossil Fuels* (OECD, 2015a).

The third "nesting doll" includes **induced transfers** to producers or consumers of energy through price or market regulations. In this case, there is no direct transfer from government budgets, and the cost of subsidies is pushed on to energy-supplying companies (though the latter can also be compensated by the government for the losses they incur this way). This is by far the largest category in the IEA estimates of consumer subsidies granted as a result of selling energy at below-market rates. However, this category can also include cross-subsidies, whereby one category of consumers (for instance, industry) pays a premium on the price of energy, which pays off the losses that suppliers incur by selling energy at below cost-recovery rates to a different category of consumers (for example, households).

The outer concentric circle is subject to most debate, as it compares the national taxation benchmarks with those in other countries, or those that attempt to reflect externalities and the social cost of energy, for example, a normative carbon tax. International organisations such as the IEA and the IMF have come up with certain regional and global benchmarks, in particular for fossil-fuel consumer taxes. The OECD has also discussed these issues in its flagship publication *Taxing Energy Use* (OECD, 2015b). However, when it comes to externalities, determining the benchmarks becomes more challenging. The OECD has largely excluded externalities from its subsidy quantification work, with the exception of the non-imposition of carbon tax legislated for other industries. The IMF, on the other hand, argues that governments' failure to internalise externalities confers a subsidy, and it is the inclusion of this fourth nesting doll that explains why the IMF consumer post-tax subsidy estimate of USD 5.3 trillion in 2015 is so much higher than the IEA's estimate of USD 325 bln, or the IMF's own estimate of pre-tax subsidies at USD 333 bln for the same year (IEA, 2016b; IMF, 2015).

This study focuses on the inner three nesting dolls: direct budgetary transfers and liabilities, government revenue foregone and induced transfers. Discussion of externalities and comparisons with international tax benchmarks is excluded from the scope of this study, given the challenges of benchmarking and other methodological disagreements among the key expert organisations. This fourth "nesting doll" can, however, be subject to follow-up activities.

Classifications

Different typologies of subsidies can be distinguished. The most commonly used approach distinguishes subsidies that benefit consumers from those benefitting producers of energy. Another straightforward approach breaks down subsidies by fuel. For example, the IEA provides subsidy estimates for oil, natural gas, coal and electricity, although it does not have such estimates for heat.

Another classification builds off the type of the subsidy mechanism, which is largely analogous to the discussion of "nesting dolls" above. This study follows the OECD classification grouping subsidies in 4 categories (OECD, 2013a): These groups are listed below. Table 1.1 spells out each of these categories.

- **direct transfers** of funds from the budget to energy producers and consumers (e.g. grants, support of energy purchases by low-income households)
- **tax expenditure and other government revenue foregone** (e.g. reduction or exemptions of certain taxes, such as VAT or excise taxes on fuel consumption)
- **induced transfers** (import tariffs, below-market electricity/heat prices, cross-subsidies in the electricity sector)
- **transfer of risk** to government (e.g. low-interest loans, loan guarantees).

Finally, the term **"government support"** is being used more widely, including by the OECD. It does not have the negative connotation of the word "subsidy", sometimes interpreted as government handouts. "Government support" also has a broader scope and defines a variety of government policies that benefit various types of energy. This report uses the terms "subsidies" and "government support" interchangeably.

Table 1.1. **Typology of subsidies**

	Types of subsidies	Examples
Direct transfer of funds	Direct spending	• **Earmarks and agency appropriations**: Targeted spending on the sector through government budgets of different levels and budgets of individual government agencies • **Research and development support**: Funding for research and development programmes • **Contracts and government procurement of energy at above-market rates**
	Government ownership of energy-related enterprises if on terms and conditions more favourable for business than in case of private ownership	• **Equity injection in the energy sector from government budgets** • **Government ownership of strategic and other energy assets that otherwise would not be viable:** e.g. strategic petroleum reserve, fossil-fuel exploration and extraction companies, electricity plants, transmission and distribution systems for gas, electric power and heat, energy import and export companies
Tax expenditure and other government revenue foregone	Tax breaks	• **Tax expenditures:** Tax expenditures are foregone tax revenues, due to special exemptions, deductions, rate reductions, rebates, credits and deferrals that reduce the amount of tax that would otherwise be payable • **Reduced overall tax burden by industry:** Marginal tax rates are lower than for other industries, for instance non-application of VAT or Goods and services tax (GST) • **Exemptions from excise taxes/special taxes:** Non-application of excise taxes on fuels; special targeted taxes on energy industry (e.g. based on environmental concerns or "windfall" profits)
	Foregone revenue from government-owned energy resources	• **Process for energy resource leasing:** Auctions for larger sites; sole-source for many smaller sites • **Royalty relief or reductions in other taxes due on extraction:** Reduced, delayed or eliminated royalties • **Process of paying royalties due:** Allowable methods to estimate and pay public owners for energy minerals extracted from public lands
	Foregone revenue from non-energy government-owned natural resources or land	• **Access to government-owned natural resources such as water and land:** At no charge or for below fair-market rate
	Foregone revenue from government-owned infrastructure	• **Use of government-provided infrastructure:** At no charge or below fair-market rate
	Foregone revenue from other government-provided goods or services	• **Government-provided goods or services at below-market rates**
Induced transfers (income or price support)	Income or price support and market regulation	• **Consumption mandates and mandated feed-in tariffs: fixed consumption shares for use of a specific energy type** • **Border protection or restrictions: controls (tariff and non-tariff measures) on imports or exports leading to unfair advantages** • **Regulated prices set at below-market rates:** For consumers (including where there is no financial contribution by government) • **Regulated prices set at above-market rates:** For producers • **Cross-subsidies in the electricity sector**
Transfer of risk to government	Credit support	• **Government loans:** Below-market lending to energy-related enterprises, including loans to energy exporters • **Loan guarantees:** At below-market rates
	Insurance and indemnification	• **Government insurance/indemnification:** Market or below-market risk management/risk shifting services • **Statutory caps on commercial liability:** Can confer substantial subsidies if set well below plausible damage scenarios
	Occupational health and accidents	• **Assumption of occupational health and accident liabilities**
	Environmental costs	• **Responsibility for closure and post-closure risks:** Facility decommissioning and clean-up; long-term monitoring; remediation of contaminated sites; litigation • **Waste management and environmental damages:** Avoidance of fees payable to deal with waste, avoidance of liability and remediation to make the environment whole

Source: Adapted from Lang (2010), Gerasimchuk (2012), OECD (2013a).

National subsidy definitions in the EaP countries

In correspondence with the state of international concepts on subsidies, each of the EaP countries has its own national legal and conceptual framework for energy pricing and taxation. These national contexts determine how the term "subsidy" is formally defined and understood in each country.

The country chapters explore the cases where the concept of a subsidy has been defined or left undefined in national legislation of each country. Regardless of the legislated definition or its absence, the use of the term "subsidy" and its synonyms can be quite loose in documents released by governments and other stakeholders. Subsidies are often narrowly understood as budgetary transfers that are unrequited and irrevocable ("freebies" or "handouts" in the public mind). Meanwhile, without defining the terms in the legislation, officials can also make use of subsidy-related notions that are translations of equivalents of international terms: government revenues foregone (выпадающие доходы бюджета), budget revenue shortfall (бюджетные потери), tax expenditures (налоговые расходы), etc. (Gerasimchuk, 2012).

Stakeholders in energy policy and expert circles in the EaP countries are well aware of the cost-recovery issues in the energy system, tariff calculation methodologies and existing cross-subsidies. However, defining these policies as subsidies is not typical in the region.

As the EaP countries harmonise their legislation with the European Union, a related term – "state aid" or "state support" – can also be applied to some of the types of subsidy. Table 1.2 summarises the commonalities and discrepancies in the national definitions of subsidies across the EaP countries. Whereas direct budget transfers are commonly understood as subsidies in every country, induced transfers that result from regulated prices are not legally defined as government support.

Table 1.2. **What do EaP countries include in the national definition of subsidies?**

■ Covered by the national definition of both "subsidy" and "state support"

▒ Covered only by the national definition of "state support"

□ Not covered by the national definitions of either "subsidy" or "state support""

EaP country	Direct budget transfers	Tax revenue foregone	Induced transfers (regulated prices)	Transfer of risk to government
Armenia	■			
Azerbaijan	■	■		
Belarus	■	▒		
Georgia	▒	▒		■
Moldova	■			
Ukraine	■	▒		

Source: Based on information provided in the individual country chapters in this report.

Two approaches to subsidy quantification: price-gap and inventory

There are two main approaches for quantifying subsidies: top-down estimates based on price-gap assumptions, and bottom-up inventories that consider each government support measure individually. Each approach has strengths and limitations, and the two approaches can complement each other. This complementarity is especially useful if access to data and subsidy reporting are restricted. The use of both approaches in this study has helped quantify energy subsidies in all EaP countries. Using both methods has helped to triangulate the obtained estimates.

However, in many cases, subsidy values are not reported by government agencies. In this case, quantification will rely on a number of methods mostly derived from the Producer Support Estimate and Consumer Support Estimate (PSE-CSE) framework that OECD initially developed for the agricultural sector. In each case, guidance can be taken from the manuals and publications dedicated to this work (OECD, 2010b, OECD 2013a; Jones and Steenblik, 2010). In practice, inventories of energy support measures are always a mixture of subsidies that have been assigned a monetary value and those that are identified, but not quantified. Overall, the research team has found enough data to apply the inventory approach in sufficient detail in Armenia, Georgia, Moldova and Ukraine.

Box 1.1. Main approaches to subsidy quantification

The **price-gap approach** is a default method for subsidy quantification for both the IEA and the IMF. This method estimates the gap between domestic energy prices and reference prices. If the domestic price is lower, a consumption subsidy is deemed to exist. For net importers of fossil fuels, the IEA and the IMF base reference prices of fossil fuels on the import parity price: the price of a product at the nearest international hub, adjusted for fuel quality differences if necessary, plus the cost of freight and insurance to the net importer, plus the cost of internal distribution and marketing and any value-added tax. Other taxes, including excise duties, are not included in the reference price. For net exporters of fossil fuels, reference prices are based on the export parity price: the price of a product at the nearest international hub, adjusted for quality differences if necessary, minus the cost of freight and insurance back to the net exporter, plus the cost of internal distribution and marketing and any VAT. For energy exporters, the quantified subsidy represents the opportunity cost of selling fuels at below-market prices domestically, rather than a measure of direct expenditure. The calculation of reference prices for electricity is based on the cost of production, transmission and distribution of electricity in individual countries.

Using the price-gap approach is useful to make comparisons possible across countries where the main form of support is through administrative pricing or export restrictions, but it does have some drawbacks (Koplow, 2009). In particular, assumptions underlying reference prices can often be challenged. For example, some governments of net energy-exporting countries assert that the opportunity cost of exporting fuels to the world market cannot be used as a reference price, and that if domestic prices cover production costs, there is no subsidy. For net importers of fossil fuels, VAT rates, costs of freight, insurance, distribution and marketing in the reference price assumptions can all be challenged. Cost-recovery assumptions for electricity can also be subject to debate. Further, a price-gap analysis will not reveal producer subsidies that arise when energy producers are inefficient and make losses at benchmark prices, nor consumption subsidies provided through, for example, fuel vouchers or other payments made directly to low-income households (Koplow, 2009). Similarly, if applied at the level of the entire market rather than individual groups of consumers, the price-gap approach can fail to capture the value of possible cross-subsidies among, for example, industry and households.

This study uses the price-gap approach for estimating the subsidy to natural gas consumption in each of the EaP countries, as well as for quantifying the value of a number of individual subsidies, especially fossil-fuel subsidies in Azerbaijan and Belarus, as well as subsidies to renewables conferred via feed-in tariffs in several EaP countries.

The **inventory approach** is a go-to method for subsidy quantification for both the OECD and the International Institute of Sustainable Development (IISD)'s Global Subsidies Initiative (GSI). This bottom-up approach to subsidy quantification involves constructing an inventory of

Box 1.1. **Main approaches to subsidy quantification** *(continued)*

policies supporting the production and consumption of energy, quantifying the value of support under each of them, and then aggregating the numbers.

The first step in bottom-up subsidy analysis and quantification is always filling in a template with key subsidy characteristics (such templates are used in the annexes to each of the individual country chapters). For subsidy quantification in inventories, the first-choice and most straightforward way is deriving an estimate from the values reported by governments themselves. Such estimates can be found in budget laws and reports on budget execution, tax expenditure budgets, explanatory notes of ministries of finance, and documents of other government agencies.

Source: Authors' summary.

Government support for fossil-fuel production and consumption

This study found subsidies to fossil fuels in all EaP countries, which are discussed in more detail in the individual country chapters. By combining the inventory and the price-gap approach, the research team could also quantify a subset of those fossil-fuel subsidies that were identified in the analysis, while the others were not quantified, due to data limitations.

Quantified fossil-fuel subsidies in the EaP countries

Although it was not possible to quantify all subsidies that were identified in all EaP countries in each year due to challenges with data availability, the estimates show that Ukraine is the country where the subsidies have been the largest. About USD 17 bln was provided in 2014 though the amount was significantly reduced in 2015 as part of the subsidy reform. Fossil-fuel subsidies in Belarus steadily increased since 2010, reaching USD 1.6 bln and were approaching the level of subsidies in Azerbaijan in 2014 (USD 1.7 bln). Energy subsidies in Georgia and Moldova were much smaller but increased over the review period to the levels of USD 228 and 182 mln, respectively. The annual amount of subsidies in Armenia was significantly lower than in the other five countries and fluctuated between USD 37 and 42 mln during the review period. Table 1.3 summarises the values of those fossil-fuel subsidies that lent themselves to quantification, over the period 2010-15.

These findings can provide an additional insight to the analysis carried out by the IEA which estimated subsidies to consumers of fossil fuels in 2014 in Azerbaijan at USD 1.5 bln (equivalent to 2% of GDP) and, in Ukraine at USD 6.4 bln (4.9% of GDP) (IEA 2016a). IEA estimates include subsidies to gas, oil, coal and electricity, but exclude subsidies to heat. IEA has not identified and quantified fossil-fuel subsidies in other EaP countries.

Apart from the data availability, the estimates in Table 1.3 only tell part of the story since USD value was sensitive to exchange rate fluctuations, and most EaP countries saw significant currency depreciation in the recent years. Finally, it should be noted that the value of the quantified fossil-fuel subsidies are not directly comparable across countries, since each country has its own tax benchmarks (OECD, 2013a).

Figure 1.2 presents quantified fossil-fuel subsidies as a share of GDP and compares these annual values with the national budget deficits in the EaP countries in 2014, the latest year for which the estimates were available for all countries. The data show that fossil-fuel subsidies reached the stunning 12.8% of GDP in Ukraine while equalling 2.1-2.3% in Belarus, Azerbaijan and Moldova and 1.4% in Georgia. In Azerbaijan, Moldova and Ukraine, fossil-fuel subsidies were larger than the national budget deficits. In Armenia the subsidies accounted for a much smaller share of GDP (0.4%) as compared to the budget deficit (1.9%).

Table 1.3. **Quantified fossil-fuel subsidies in the EaP countries, USD million**

	2010	2011	2012	2013	2014	2015
Armenia	n.c.	37	41	42	42	37
Azerbaijan	n.c.	n.c.	n.c.	n.c.	1 700	1 700
Belarus	1 039	1 117	1 469	1 384	1 562	n.c.
Georgia	122	218	233	205	228	n.c.
Moldova	n.c.	141	175	165	182	48
Ukraine	n.c.	n.c.	15 626	14 379	17 064	7 041

Note: These estimates are affected by data availability for different years, currency exchange rates and international fuel prices underlying price-gap estimates.

Source: Summary tables in the country chapters.

Figure 1.2. **General government deficit and quantified fossil-fuel subsidies as % of GDP in 2014**

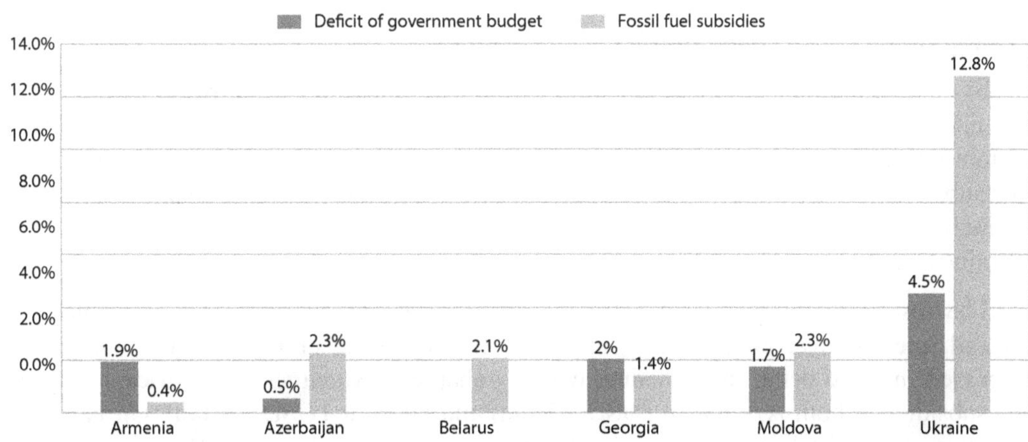

Source: Authors' presentation based on the summary tables in the country chapters and Eurostat (2016).

All EaP countries continued pricing reforms throughout 2016-17, and thus 2014 and 2015 subsidy estimates do not precisely describe the most recent situation in the EaP countries that keeps evolving. For instance, Belarus cancelled its VAT exemption for heat, electricity and natural gas for households starting in January 2016, ending a subsidy worth of USD 200 mln per year. Armenia eliminated its excise exemption for compressed natural gas (CNG) in May 2016, worth around USD 9 mln per year. Due to the conflict in eastern Ukraine, coal subsidies were stopped *de facto* and the country government made the decision in April 2016 to increase natural gas tariffs towards cost-recovery levels. This has led to a significant reduction of the value of Ukraine's fossil fuel subsidies most recently.

Natural gas is the most subsidised fossil fuel in the region and so are heat and electricity. This is not surprising given that natural gas dominates the energy mix and is a staple feedstock for electricity and heat generation in the EaP countries. Prices for petroleum products are regulated only in Belarus and Azerbaijan. During the reviewed period, coal subsidies were significant only in Ukraine. Figure 1.3 further breaks down the 2014 values of the quantified fossil-fuel subsidies by fuel in the EaP countries.

Figure 1.3. **Quantified fossil-fuel subsidies in the EaP countries by fuel in 2014, USD million**

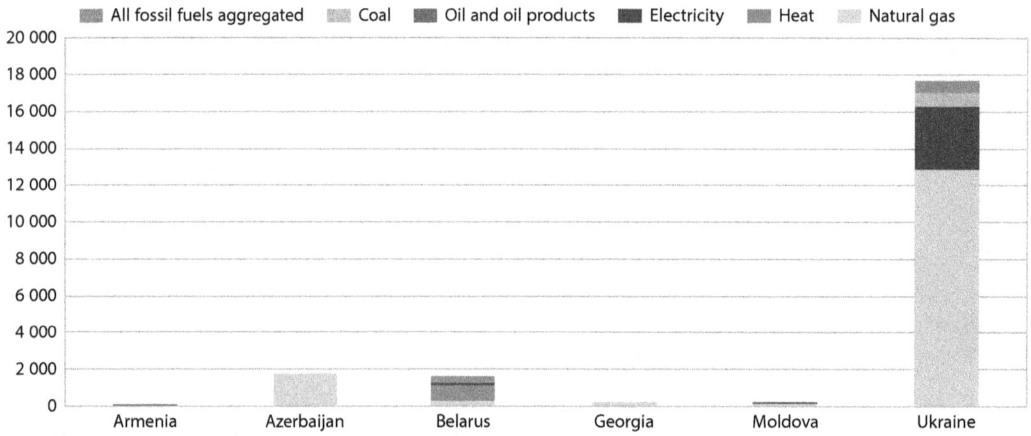

Source: Authors' presentation based on the summary tables in the country chapters.

Price-gap approach to estimating gas subsidies

In view of the importance of natural gas subsidies in the region, a price-gap analysis was undertaken of natural gas subsidies in all EaP countries in 2015 in order to triangulate bottom-up inventory findings. This exercise follows the logic of IEA estimates of fossil-fuel subsidies and enables a direct comparison across the EaP countries. In particular, IEA estimates subsidies to gas at the level of USD 0.7 bln and USD 3.7 bln in Azerbaijan and Ukraine in 2014, respectively.

The results of the price-gap estimates for natural gas are presented in Table 1.4. Overall, the findings point in the same direction as those of the IEA (calculation is discussed in more detail in individual country chapters) which show significant natural gas subsidies in both Azerbaijan (USD 1.7 bln) and Ukraine (USD 3.1 bln). On balance, the price-gap method does not reveal natural gas subsidies in Armenia, Belarus, Georgia and Moldova. But in the case of Belarus and Georgia below-market prices for natural gas supplied to households are covered by cross-subsidies from commercial users.

Taking account of mechanisms and beneficiaries, regulated energy prices that are set at below-market rates and benefit consumers are by far the most significant form of subsidisation in the EaP countries. Cross-subsidies for both energy producers and consumers are another widespread mechanism. In Georgia, for instance, electricity producers sell electricity to the grid at differentiated tariffs that ensure lower costs to end consumers, but in practice provide cross-subsidies from cheap hydropower generation to higher-cost natural gas generation. Another example is Belarus, where commercial consumers of natural gas, electricity and heat pay a premium in the tariff put in place to cross-subsidise the tariff for households. Furthermore, heat tariff for households is cross-subsidised not just through the higher heat tariffs for commercial users, but also through tariff for electricity, since Belarus co-generates a lot of its heat and electricity. Quantification of such cross-subsidies presents a methodological challenge, however the obtained estimates provide enough evidence to suggest that cross-subsidies add another level of complexity in distorting the level-playing field for competing energy sources in the EaP region.

Table 1.4. **Price-gap estimates of subsidies to natural gas consumers in the EaP countries in 2015**

	Price-gap estimate, total, USD million	Reference price, USD per 1 000 m³ (including VAT, but excluding transportation and distribution costs)	VAT exemptions	Weighted average domestic price (incl. VAT, adjusted for VAT exemptions if any)	Notes
Armenia	-204 (no subsidy)	198 (import cost USD 165 + 20% VAT)	none	295	All natural gas imported from Russia. Differentiated tariff for different categories of users.
Azerbaijan[a]	1 700 (subsidy)	267 (opportunity cost of export USD 226 + 18% VAT)	none	120	All natural gas produced domestically. Opportunity cost of export to the European market.
Belarus	-593 (no subsidy)	209 (import cost USD 174.4 + 20% VAT)	for households, eliminated from 1 January 2016	238	All natural gas imported from Russia. Cross-subsidies to households through above-market tariff for commercial users.
Georgia	-64 (no subsidy)	191 (import cost USD 162 + 18% VAT)	VAT exemption for Thermal power plants	236	Natural gas imported from Azerbaijan and Russia. Cross-subsidies to Thermal power plants and households through above-market tariff for commercial users.
Moldova	-22 (no subsidy)	307 (import cost USD 256 + 20% VAT)	reduced VAT rate for households (8% instead of 20%)	386	All natural gas imported from Russia. Differentiated tariff for different categories of users.
Ukraine	3 137 (subsidy)	332 (import cost USD 277 + 20% VAT)	none	195-201	Some natural gas produced domestically, the rest imported. Cost of natural gas import according to Naftogaz. Range due to a possible data discrepancy on the tariff for industry.

Notes: All estimates for 2015, except for Azerbaijan, for which the year is 2014.

a. The cost of insurance, freight, transportation and distribution to end users were not available for all countries, and thus are excluded from the reference prices in this table. Therefore, the obtained price-gap estimates of subsidies to natural gas consumers are on the low side. More detail is available in price-gap tables of the individual country chapters, but some of the country chapters also have simplified calculations net of VAT, which is accounted for in this summary table.

Source: Authors' summary of the information from individual country chapters in this report.

Among the region's fossil-fuel subsidies that are more opaque and remained unquantified are various tax breaks for fossil-fuel producers, including within Production Sharing Agreements and Host Government Agreements that govern taxation of large international projects of natural gas and oil extraction and pipeline transportation in Azerbaijan and Georgia.

Government support to energy efficiency and renewable energy sources

The EaP countries' governments provide also support to energy efficiency and renewables but on a much smaller scale than subsidies to fossil fuels. Only Belarus and Ukraine provide sizeable support to energy efficiency and renewable energy, in the range of USD 285 and USD 364 mln, respectively, in 2014. This includes national energy-efficiency programmes and feed-in tariffs for renewables. For renewable energy, the insignificant value of government support is partly explained by the so far limited uptake in biomass, wind and solar. Hydropower, including small hydropower, remains the main renewable energy source in the Caucasus, where it is viewed mainly as a low-cost option that can cross-subsidise thermal power plants rather than be subsidised itself. Table 1.5 provides an overview of the quantified and unquantified subsidies to energy efficiency and renewable energy in the region, with more details available in the country chapters.

Table 1.5. **Energy-efficiency and renewable energy subsidies in the EaP countries, USD million**

	2011	2012	2013	2014	2015	Major subsidy schemes
Armenia		No quantified subsidies				Purchase guarantees and feed-in tariff for renewables
Azerbaijan		No quantified subsidies				VAT and customs duty exemption for energy-efficiency and renewable-energy projects, differentiated tariff for hydro and wind
Belarus	259	364	358	285	n.c.	National Programme of Energy Efficiency, feed-in tariff and tax breaks for renewables
Georgia		No quantified subsidies				Feed-in tariffs and tax breaks for hydropower
Moldova	n.c.	n.c.	0.14	0.8	0.39	Feed-in tariff for renewables
Ukraine	n.c.	441	802	364	294	State Targeted Programme on Energy Efficiency, feed-in tariff for renewables, zero excise tax rate for bioethanol. Other tax breaks for renewables were discontinued in 2015

Note: **n.c.**: not calculated.

Source: Authors' presentation based on the summary tables in the country chapters.

Against this background, the implementation of energy-efficiency and renewable-energy projects in the region depends to a large extent on international co-operation, in particular loans from multilateral development banks. The World Bank, the European Bank for Reconstruction and Development, KfW, and the Asian Development Bank remain critical players in this area, with examples of funded projects listed in the individual country chapters.

Political economy and energy subsidy reform in the EaP countries

The reform of subsidies to fossil-fuel production can be described as a low-hanging, but prickly, fruit with respect to promoting energy efficiency and reducing emissions from fuel combustion (Gerasimchuk et al. 2017). Low-hanging, because ending fossil-fuel subsidies can save significant amounts of both public money and bring immediate climate benefits through the switch to price-driven energy-saving and renewable-energy development.

Yet it is also prickly because of its political economy sensitivities, full of difficulties, complexities, challenges and barriers. And this is valid for both non-OECD and OECD countrires. One of the key challenges is a high sensitivity in terms of impacts of energy-subsidy reform on socially vulnerable groups. For example, over many years, various strategic documents in Belarus and Ukraine included plans to reform energy subsidies, but the governments have been postponing these politically sensitive decisions for a long time due to the fears of political implications. For certain years, electricity, gas and heat tariffs for households were not revised to reflect inflation, increasing international prices and production costs of utility suppliers.

However, subsidies do not reduce the cost of energy, they just move it onto the population in a different way – a way that may suit political circumstances in the short term, but not in the long run. Someone still pays – but through taxes, foregone expenditure, borrowing from the international market, or lack of investment into energy infrastructure and quality of service. Inefficiency of subsidies actually increases the cost burden on society.

There is only one way to truly reduce energy prices: by focusing on the fundamentals of supply and demand, and removing market distortion.

Moreover, as demonstrated by the research of the OECD, World Bank, IEA, IMF, GSI and other organisations, more often than not energy subsidies fail to deliver against their stated policy objectives such as poverty alleviation and improving industrial competitiveness. Instead, they can accrue to unintended beneficiaries. The same holds true for production subsidies that can increase the inefficiencies of energy companies, including state-owned ones (Victor, 2009).

This study identifies and quantifies subsidies that skew the "playing field" in favour of fossil fuels, thus presenting barriers to energy efficiency and the development of renewables. This diagnosis signals the need for reforms that would eliminate the existing distortions.

By itself, the baseline information collected for this report is not sufficient to provide detailed policy recommendations to individual EaP countries. It should also be noted that the EaP countries are in the constant process of designing and implementing energy pricing reform even though they are not always framed and discussed as the reforms of energy subsidies. Meanwhile, there is also a wealth of international knowledge on the issue of energy subsidies and some lessons learned from other countries can be valuable for the EaP region as well.

The conclusions presented below draw on the outcomes of the stakeholder consultations in each of the EaP countries as well as on best international practices and extensive work of the IISD's Global Subsidies Initiative (Beaton, C. et al., 2013) and the OECD.

Benefits from energy subsidy reform

Several countries have reformed their fossil-fuel subsidies in 2014-15, seizing the opportunity of low energy prices on the international market (IEA, 2016b). There is thus a growing body of evidence testifying to the benefits of fossil-fuel subsidy reform.

First, elimination of fossil-fuel subsidies creates fiscal space for governments to use these resources for more targeted support to the vulnerable groups as well as other causes, from repayment of public debt to improving healthcare or supporting energy-efficiency measures. Ukraine provides an example of how subsidies can be turned into energy-efficiency investments (Box 1.2).

Box 1.2. Turning subsidies into energy-efficiency investments in Ukraine

Ukraine's Ministry of Regional Development, Construction, Housing and Communal Services, supported by Germany and the European Union, is carrying out an Energy Efficiency Reform focusing on the residential building sector. This reform is multifaceted, but focuses on turning inefficient subsidies into energy-efficiency investments. This also helps tackle the immense investment needs in the sector. Savings from reduced energy-related social subsidies after energy-efficiency investments are implemented creates a revenue stream, which is consolidated through the newly established Energy Efficiency Fund. Parliament recently adopted the Law on the Energy Efficiency Fund (2017). The EU and Germany have already committed to contribute to the Fund's activities to kick off initial subsidy savings, while the International Finance Corporation has agreed to set-up a Multi-Donor Technical Fund to manage donor funds. Ukraine has recognised that its energy independence depends on significant energy-efficiency improvements.

Source: Summary based on Duhr (2017).

Second, a review of studies on the economic impact of reforming subsidies to the consumption of fossil fuels suggests that phasing these out leads to increases in global real income or GDP, especially for net energy importers (Burniaux and Chateau, 2014; Whitley. and van der Burg, 2016). These gains are the result of more efficient allocation of resources saved from subsidy reform.

Third, there are also likely to be health and environmental benefits accruing from reforming fossil-fuel subsidies. Analysis conducted by the IEA, using its data on fossil-fuel consumption subsidies in developing countries, estimated that a phase-out of these subsidies between 2011 and 2020 would lead to lower emissions of air pollutants such as SO_2, NO_x and particulate matter, which are harmful to public health and the environment (IEA/OPEC/OECD/World Bank, 2010). Recent research by the GSI based on modelling in 20 countries found that the removal of fossil-fuel subsidies between now and 2020 could lead to average national emission reductions of approximately 11%. This research also found that if 30% of the savings from subsidy removal are redirected to renewable energy and energy efficiency, the national average emission reduction estimates increase to 18% (Merrill, L. et al., 2015).

Need for transparency over energy subsidies in the EaP countries

In the EaP region, stakeholders in the energy policy and expert circles are well aware of the cost-recovery issues in the energy system and existing cross-subsidies. However, defining these policies as subsidies is uncommon in the region and cross-subsidies often remain "invisible" for society at large.

This study presents the first consistent record of energy subsidies in the EaP region and analyses, to the extent possible, cross-subsidisation where it exists (Belarus, Georgia, Ukraine). This information can be used by both policy makers and the general public.

In this context and with the aim of improving transparency across different energy subsidies, the EaP governments could consider the following possible measures:

- Review and improve the definition of subsidy in national legislation and budgetary documents. A clear definition in line with internationally-recognised practices is the building block for further adequate analysis.
- Regularly estimate tax expenditure that result from various tax breaks and tax advantages provided to individual groups and industries and prepare tax expenditure reports which will inform the legislature and society on fiscal losses from such policies. OECD countries prepare such reports on an annual basis and these reports are available in the public domain.
- Regularly analyse the evolution of subsidies in the sector and maintain a detailed database which can be particularly useful in the decision-making process on energy subsidy reforms.

Elements of preparing for energy subsidy reform and impact on energy affordability

In reviewing international experience with energy-subsidy reform one message stands out above all others: countries should be prepared. This may seem obvious. But all too often countries implement reform because of a sudden crisis or an international requirement, and find themselves missing internal co-ordination and research and public support that would allow for effective and decisive change. Preparation is essential.

As summarised in the title of one dedicated study by the World Bank – "Balancing Act" (World Bank, 2013) – the issue of reforming energy subsidies in the EaP countries is a delicate task of creating enabling conditions for a sustainable energy system while providing targeted support to those who might be negatively affected by the reform.

Governments should prepare for energy subsidy reform holistically. Energy subsidies are usually a long term, structural, problem – and they need structural solutions. Many countries formulate effective plans to rationalise one particular subsidy, but may neglect the broader problem. Why do energy subsidies exist and how they could be addressed at the root cause? The GSI suggests that a holistic approach to energy subsidy reform includes three tracks (Figure 1.4):

- getting the prices right
- building support for reform
- managing the impacts of reform.

Recommendations on the pace and structure of the required changes in energy pricing and taxation, communication strategies and designing policies on mitigating possible negative impacts of the reform all depend on individual country contexts. Meanwhile, energy subsidy reform always requires research, consultations and efforts across many agencies within the government and groups of stakeholders. This is particularly true in terms of anticipating and managing the reform's impact that can be both direct and indirect.

Figure 1.4. **A holistic approach to energy subsidy reform**

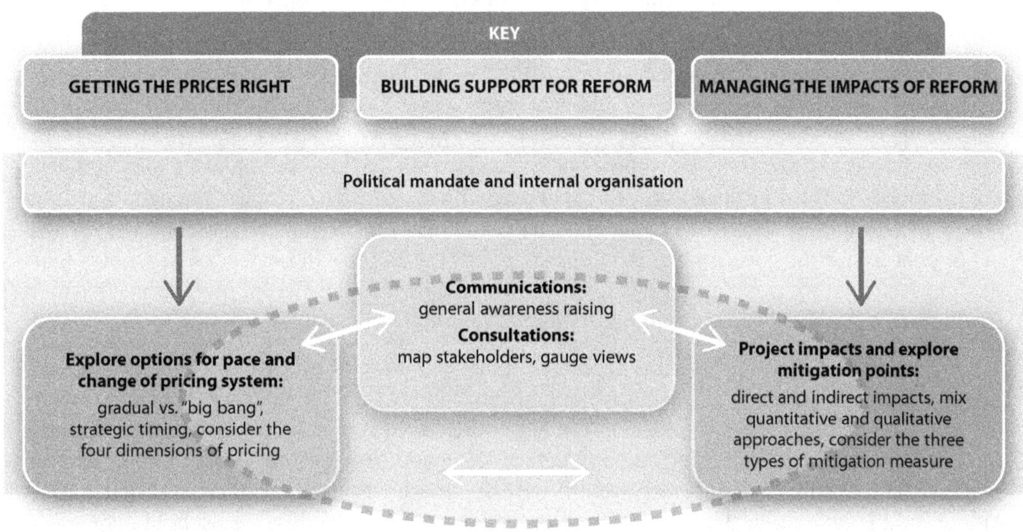

Source: Adapted from Beaton, C. et al. (2013).

Energy affordability

Energy affordability is a particular policy concern for decision makers when considering energy subsidy reforms. Although there is no universally accepted definition of energy affordability, nor is there one singe indicator to measure it, some internationally recognised practices exist that help to measure energy affordability and energy poverty (e.g. the "10% rule" and the "Relative Poverty Line" indicator). Raising energy prices can make good economic and environmental sense but should not lead to increased affordability challenges when overall policy reform is considered. Using part of the additional revenue generated from higher taxes, for example, can help avoid increased energy affordability risk and even reduce it if sufficient revenue is allocated to support vulnerable consumers (OECD, 2018, forthcoming).

Working with the government of Moldova on analysing the fiscal, social and environmental impacts from the possible reform of two major energy subsidy schemes, identified as part of this current study, the OECD has sought to support Moldovan authorities in their efforts to advance policy reforms with regard to energy subsidies. The analysis shows who will lose and who will gain from the reform, what will be the impact of the reform on the public budget but also on households' disposable income, what social measures could be put in place to protect vulnerable groups that would be affected by the reform. This work also shows how such analysis can be approached (issues, data) and practically conducted in co-operation with different parts of the government and other stakeholders in the country (Box 1.3).

Box 1.3. **Energy subsidy reform and energy affordability in Moldova**

As a follow-up to the inventory of energy subsidies in Moldova, and as requested by the Moldovan government, the OECD has conducted analysis of the potential impact of reforming selected fossil-fuel subsidies on energy affordability for vulnerable households in Moldova. The study has also reviewed the impact of reform on the public budget and on potential GHG emission reductions.

The analysis models the impact of reforming the two largest government support schemes for domestic users, the reduced VAT rate on natural gas consumption and the VAT exemption on electricity and heat consumption. The standard VAT rate in Moldova is 20%. The VAT imposed on gas consumed by households is 8%, and no VAT is imposed on electricity and heat consumption. Reform of these subsidies will mean increasing VAT rates to the standard 20% rate, which will raise the price of gas, electricity and heat for Moldovan households. This is a major concern for the government. Appropriate policy measures will be needed to support low-income sectors of the population. The OECD study analyses five different protection measures (scenarios), estimating their varying costs for the national budget.

The results of the analysis show that raising the VAT rate for electricity consumption will be the easiest to roll out. This will have only a small impact on household electricity use and income. On the other hand, increasing the VAT rate for heat consumption will significantly raise costs for households. As indicated in Figure 1.5, low-income groups (with income ranging from MLD 0-1 000 per capita per month) will be hard hit by such an increase. If the VAT rate on heat is increased, the share of the heat consumption bill only in household disposable income will be above 20% for these income groups. The government will thus need to design some kind of compensation arrangement to support vulnerable sectors of the population.

The chief reason why these consumers will suffer from the VAT reform is because many people in these income groups (43%) live in Chisinau and Balti, Moldova's two main cities, the only cities in the country linked to the centralised district heating system. Different compensation scenarios, analysed in the study, result in different costs for both consumers and for the government.

Box 1.3. **Energy subsidy reform and energy affordability in Moldova** *(continued)*

Figure 1.5. **Impact of various scenarios for increasing VAT on heat consumption, expressed as a percentage of household income in Moldova**

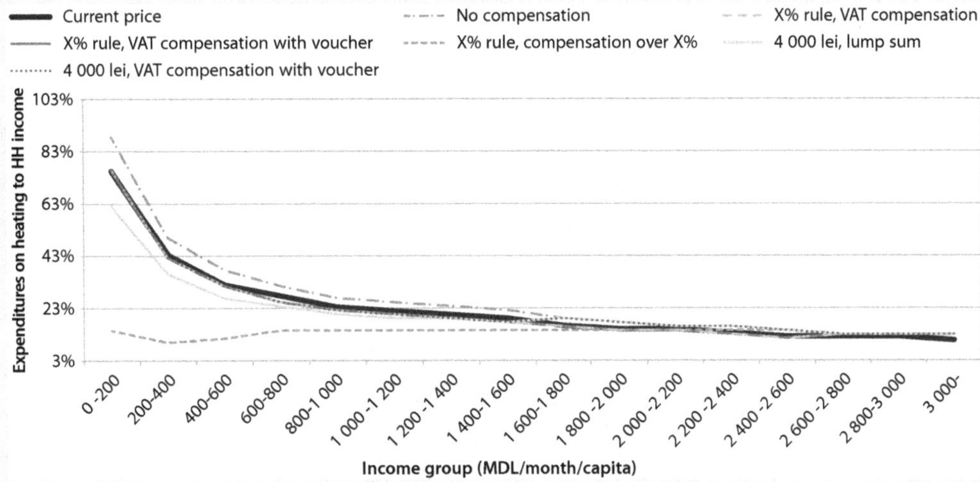

Source: OECD (2018), forthcoming.

Managing impacts of energy subsidy reforms also necessitates complementary policies that span macroeconomic, social, industrial, energy, transport, banking and environmental solutions. Figure 1.6 provides a summary of examples of such policies that can be considered as part of the reform plan.

Figure 1.6. **Complementary policies for managing impacts of energy subsidy reform**

Industry/business
- Support to restructure sectors e.g. retraining programmes
- Measures to improve energy efficiency
- Investments in infrastructure

Social
- Cash transfers: (un)conditional
- Social safety nets, pensions, health insurance
- Increase (minimum) wages
- Pro-poor expenditure

Energy
- Investment in renewable or alternative energies, rural electrification, etc.
- Energy conservation, energy security, energy efficiency policies

Macro-economic
- Policies to manage inflation
- Strengthen market forces and encourage competition

Banking
- Can help roll out cash transfers
- Credit facilities, e.g. for small and medium-sized enterprises and micro-credit

Transport
- Expanding public transport systems
- Alternatives for freight (rail or inland waterways)
- Transitional support for taxi drivers

Source: Adapted from Beaton, C. et al. (2013).

While the reform of energy subsidies is both complex and politically sensitive, it is truly at the heart of sustainable development and the shift to low-carbon economy. The EaP countries have already accumulated a wealth of experience reforming their energy subsidies that can help them move further along this challenging, but unavoidable path.

Energy subsidy reforms do not happen in a void. The macroeconomic situation as well as existing policy frameworks (energy pricing policy, taxation policy, climate-related policies) will directly impact the pace and amplitude of the reform. In many countries, including in the EaP region, energy subsidy reforms are part and parcel of general energy sector reforms. The rest of this chapter discusses how the economic and policy environment condition the pace and breadth of energy subsidy reforms in the EaP region.

Macroeconomic situation in the EaP countries

The six countries of the EaP region differ in the size of their population and economy, as well as the level of economic development. Ukraine is by far the largest of the six economies, followed by Azerbaijan and Belarus, whose GDP is roughly equivalent, and then Georgia, Armenia and Moldova (Table 1.6). The total population of the EaP countries was around 75 mln people in 2015.

Table 1.6. **Key economic indicators of the EaP countries in 2015**

	Population, million	GDP growth rate	GDP, billion current USD
Armenia	3.0	3.0%	10.5
Azerbaijan	9.7	1.1%	53.0
Belarus	9.5	-3.9%	54.6
Georgia	3.7	2.8%	14.0
Moldova	3.6	-0.5%	6.6
Ukraine	45.2	-9.9%	90.6

Source: World Bank (2017).

To enable cross-country comparisons, this chapter relies on the World Bank Open Data and other sources of international statistics. It should also be pointed out that exchange rates of the national currencies in the six countries have been volatile over the period 1991-2017. In particular, because national currencies of most countries in the region depreciated against the USD in 2015, their GDP shrank in dollar terms even when the economy grew in real terms.

Despite many differences, the six countries enjoy several common strengths, including a highly educated workforce and the continued opening of their economies to trade and investment opportunities. Armenia, Georgia, Moldova and Ukraine are WTO members, while Azerbaijan and Belarus are in the process of negotiating their accession. As for energy trade and investment, as of March 2017, all six EaP countries have signed the EU-led Energy Charter Treaty and later ratified it, with the exception of Belarus, which applied the Treaty provisionally (IEC, n.d.). Armenia and Belarus are also members of the Eurasian Economic Union (EAEU) and its Customs Union (see Box 1.4), which provides for further integration of the countries' energy systems with other EAEU members.

Box 1.4. Eurasian Economic Union and its implications for energy markets in Armenia and Belarus

The Eurasian Economic Union (EAEU) was created in 2014, after a number of economic integration agreements among countries of the former Soviet Union, in particular the Common Economic Space among the Russian Federation, Belarus and Kazakhstan (EAEU, 2014). The Treaty on the EAEU is the founding document of the organisation, which, as of February 2017, included Armenia, Belarus, Kazakhstan, the Kyrgyz Republic and the Russian Federation. Those five countries were also members of the Customs Union and the Free Trade Zone. Vietnam is also a member, and several other countries that were not part of the former Soviet Union are negotiating accession to it.

Among the EAEU members, Kazakhstan and the Russian Federation are net exporters of energy, while Armenia, Belarus and the Kyrgyz Republic are net importers. The Treaty on the EAEU proclaims the creation of common markets of electric power, natural gas, oil and petroleum products, co-operative development of infrastructure, and co-ordinated tariff policies. The Treaty also establishes common access to the services of state natural monopolies in the spheres of electric power (distribution and administration), as well as natural gas, oil and petroleum products (transport and transit). The common market is to be based on energy balance forecasts. A key priority for the EAEU is satisfying internal demand for electric power and energy in the member countries. Under the Treaty, the common market of electric power will begin to operate by 1 June 2019. Common markets of gas, oil and petroleum products are projected to begin operation from 1 January 2025.

Under the Treaty on the EAEU, tariffs for state monopolies' services are determined and regulated by national authorities, taking into account government subsidies and other forms of support. Energy prices in the common energy market should not exceed those in domestic markets of the EAEU member states. Unhindered access to services of the natural gas transportation system is granted only for the natural gas originating from the territory of the EAEU members.

Electricity market

At present, each EAEU member has its own government-owned exporter-importer of electric power. In the mid-term, member states intend to harmonise the market with the Russian model (which was selected because the Russian Federation has a capacity market, system services and an adequate level of safety). Technically, it should not be difficult to create a common market, since the electrical power systems of the Soviet era are operated on the same frequency, 50Hz, and are synchronised, with the exception of Armenia, which is expected to join the synchronised regime in the near future. The establishment of a common market for electric power will undoubtedly influence contract prices in the EAEU member states, since electric power in the Russian Federation is generally cheaper than in other member states.

The market for oil, natural gas and petroleum products

Trade in natural gas, oil and petroleum products among the EAEU member states is now regulated by bilateral intergovernmental agreements. The Russian Federation's Gazprom is a monopolistic supplier of natural gas to Armenia and Belarus. When a common energy market is created within the EAEU, Gazprom is likely to lose its monopoly in Armenia and Belarus, since they will have the opportunity to buy natural gas from Kazakhstan.

Significantly, within the EAEU Customs Union, oil, natural gas and petroleum products are not subject to export and import taxes, which ensures lower prices for imports from the Russian Federation and Kazakhstan for Armenia, Belarus and the Kyrgyz Republic compared with those of other countries. These rules are valid only for interior consumption of these energy commodities within the EAEU. Volumes of interior consumption are determined based

Box 1.4. **Eurasian Economic Union and its implications for energy markets in Armenia and Belarus** *(continued)*

on supply balances signed annually at an intergovernmental level. Re-export of raw materials exempted from export tax is prohibited. After the establishment of the common market for oil and petroleum products, EAEU member states will have to give up their regulation of internal prices for petroleum products (which remain in effect in Belarus and Kazakhstan) and unify export taxes for oil and petroleum products outside the EAEU (or even cancel them).

However, the export tax unification process has proved difficult. The Russian Federation does not levy export tax on oil and petroleum products supplied to Belarus, but Belarus levies an export tax when selling refined petroleum products made from Russian raw materials to countries outside the EAEU. The Russian Federation thus insisted on the harmonisation of Belarus' export taxes on energy with its own. Until 2014, these taxes were at least partially paid by Belarus to the budget of the Russian Federation. In 2014, this practice was discontinued when the Russian Federation partially reallocated the fiscal burden from the export tax on petroleum products to the domestic tax on oil extraction. At present, the Russian Federation considers the cost of export taxes levied by Belarus on petroleum products a subsidy from its budget to that of Belarus (revenue foregone by the Russian Federation but collected by Belarus). This annual subsidy can be estimated to be at least USD 2.1 bln, based on an oil price of USD 45 per barrel (Manenok, 2017). Given that the Russian Federation plans to further reduce export taxes on energy and increase taxes on extraction, the export tax unification process will remain a sensitive issue for Belarus.

Source: Summary prepared by Oleksiy Shapovalov.

The EaP countries shared a common macroeconomic pattern: a sharp decrease in GDP in the years after the disintegration of the Soviet Union in 1991, followed by restructuring and modernisation of their economies and restoration of economic growth in late 1990s and 2000s. Overall, from 1991 to 2015, the six EaP economies have all grown in real terms (World Bank, 2017) and developed a large services sector that contributes to over half of the value added in each of the countries (Figure 1.7). Meanwhile, the six countries' economic performance is sensitive to fluctuations in international markets (especially in the case of Azerbaijan, the only exporter of energy commodities in the region) and regional linkages.

Figure 1.7. **Structure of the economy, % of GDP in 2015**

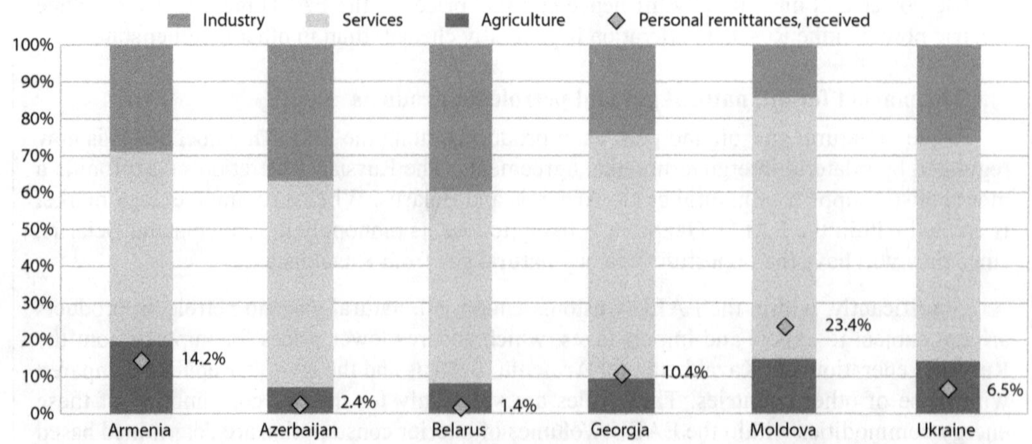

Source: World Bank (2017), http://data.worldbank.org.

The Russian Federation and the European Union are the two key trading partners and sources of remittances for the EaP countries. As a result of the global financial and economic meltdown that started in 2008, the economic recession in the Russian Federation and Ukraine triggered by the drop in global commodity prices, and the conflict over Crimea and in Eastern Ukraine, the economic performance of the region suffered (see individual country chapters for more detail). Armenia, Moldova and Ukraine had more years of negative GDP performance, and as of 2015, had lower GDP per capita than Azerbaijan, Belarus and Georgia (Figure 1.8 and individual country chapters). All EaP countries experience fiscal pressures: central budget deficits ranged from 0.5% in Azerbaijan to 4.8% in Armenia in 2015, while Belarus was the only country with a budgetary surplus (1.4%) (Eurostat, 2016).

Figure 1.8. **GDP per capita, purchasing power parity (current international USD)**

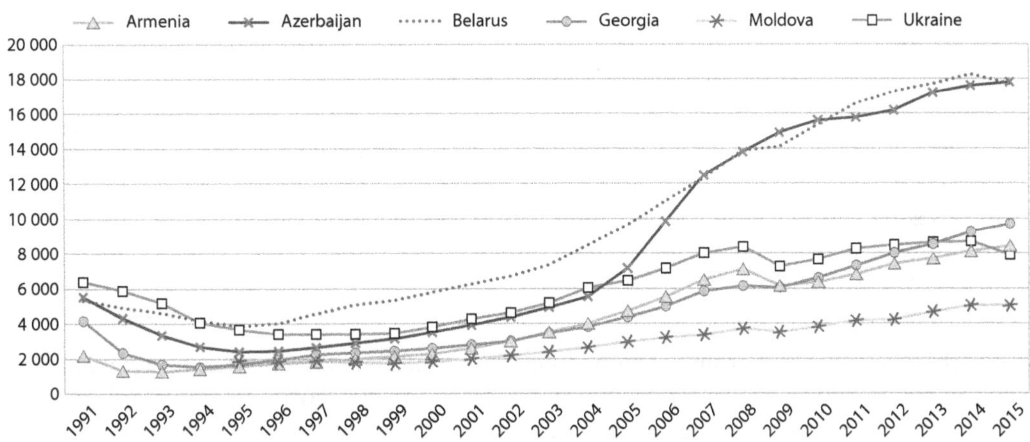

Source: World Bank (2017), http://data.worldbank.org.

The impact of these external factors has been amplified by the remaining structural weaknesses in many EaP countries. These include the large informal sector of the economies, the significant role of remittances in national income in Armenia, Georgia and Moldova, the 2015 crisis in the Moldovan financial sector, and the increased dependence of Ukraine on international financial institutions. Enhancing macroeconomic stability, supporting further growth and improvement of living standards is a key priority for all EaP countries. The EaP countries continue to make efforts to modernise and diversify their economies, to reform their socio-economic policies and to conform to best policy practices and global standards.

The energy sector and its main reforms

In the political and economic transition from central planning to a market orientation, the energy systems of the EaP countries have undergone several waves of reforms and restructuring. These changes, still in progress in the region, are subject to several key drivers.

First, after independence, the EaP countries needed to match the new political reality with the inter-linkages and interdependence in the energy and other sectors they had inherited. In the Soviet era, all 15 states functioned as complementary parts of the same centrally planned economy. Armenia in particular was left in a challenging situation, with its power sector largely dependent on imported fuels, but installed electricity generation capacity exceeding the country's needs and thus partly idle.

Second, with the exception of Azerbaijan, the EaP countries are net energy importers (Figure 1.9). The Russian Federation, Azerbaijan and to a certain extent, the Central Asian states are key energy suppliers in the region. Increasingly, the EaP countries are set to leverage their strategic position between the energy-exporting Russian Federation and Central Asia on the one hand, and the European Union as a major market for natural gas and oil, on the other.

Box 1.5. **Energy mix in the EaP countries**

In terms of the fuel mix, the structure of energy production and consumption in the EaP countries changed much less in the period after independence. The region's energy sector remains heavily dominated by fossil fuels. With the exception of Ukraine, the region has seen an increase of the share of natural gas in the total primary energy supply. For Azerbaijan, this can be explained by increased own production of natural gas, while for Belarus, Armenia, Moldova and to a certain extent Georgia, the main driver has been affordable import of natural gas, mainly from the Russian Federation. Individual country chapters provide more detail on the structure of energy demand and supply in the region.

Renewable energy plays an extremely limited role in the region, with the exception of significant hydropower generation in Georgia. Belarus, Ukraine and Moldova also produce biomass and biofuels for energy use. Armenia and Ukraine have nuclear power generation, while Belarus is in the process of completing its first nuclear power plant.

Source: Authors' summary.

Third, the transition from a planned economy and barter to market-based decisions has coincided with a lack of revenue and capital for infrastructure maintenance and modernisation. The depreciated assets built in Soviet times are still the backbone of the energy infrastructure in the EaP countries. As a result, the region's economies are highly energy-intensive. Figure 1.10 shows that per unit of energy consumed, each of the EaP countries produced more dollars of GDP in 2014 than in 1990, but that energy productivity gains have varied, from relatively incremental improvements in Ukraine to more qualitative changes in Belarus, Georgia and especially Armenia, which has recently reconfigured its use of energy.

The need for new management structures and sources of finance in the EaP countries continues to evolve. After the breakup of the Soviet Union, each of the EaP countries set up dedicated ministries in charge of energy policies and vertically integrated national energy companies.

Ownership

Subsequently, the countries' paths diverged. In Azerbaijan and Belarus, energy assets remain under government ownership. Private, including foreign, investment has been permitted only in new energy assets, in particular, large offshore oil and gas fields in Azerbaijan and new power plants in Belarus.

In Armenia, Georgia, Moldova and Ukraine, vertically integrated energy assets have been at least partially unbundled, commercialised and privatised. This process coincided with another change in ownership. State-owned enterprises from the Russian Federation, Kazakhstan and Azerbaijan have entered joint ventures with host governments and taken control of a number of key supply, transmission and distribution assets in the region,

Figure 1.9. **Total primary energy supply of EaP countries in 2014, million tonnes of oil equivalent**

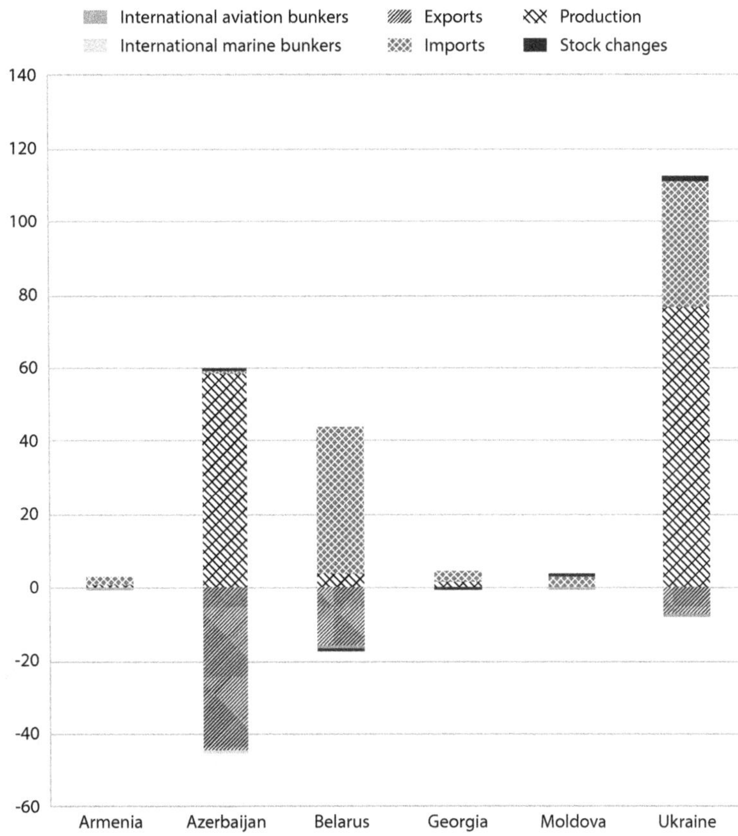

Source: IEA Energy Balances Statistics (n.d), www.iea.org/statistics/topics/energybalances/.

Figure 1.10. **Energy productivity in EaP countries, GDP per unit of energy use, constant 2011 PPP USD per kg of oil equivalent**

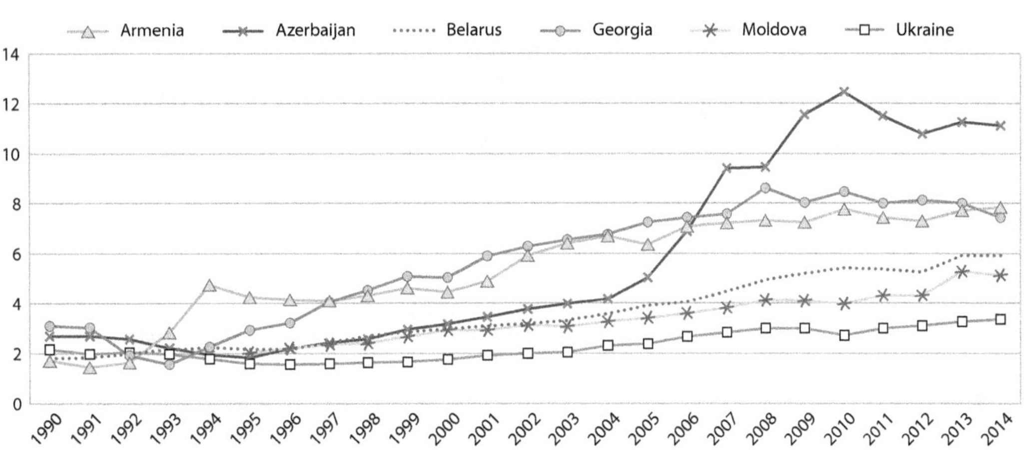

Source: World Bank (2017), http://data.worldbank.org.

either as a way to settle debts for energy supplies, or in the course of privatisation. In the electricity sector, as of early 2017, the Russian Federation's InterRAO owned generation assets in Georgia and Moldova. Azerbaijan's state-owned company SOCAR and Kazakhstan's KazMunaiGas both played a significant role in the natural gas sector in Georgia. Gazprom's subsidiaries were active in both natural gas and electricity generation in Armenia, and Gazprom was a key player in the natural gas sector of both Moldova and Belarus, in particular controlling the transit gas pipeline to the EU. In Azerbaijan, the new export transit pipelines for oil and natural gas were built by a consortium of foreign investors, with SOCAR having a minority stake. The only EaP government that retained full ownership of its natural gas infrastructure was Ukraine. This has become a source of many disputes with the Russian Federation over repayment of Ukraine's debts, natural gas prices and political tensions.

The Russian Federation and other energy-exporting countries gradually moved to international market prices, leaving the EaP countries increasingly dependent on mobilising finance through reforms of energy pricing and energy taxation policies.

Energy pricing policies

The term most commonly used to describe energy pricing in the EaP region is "tariff regulation" ("тарифное регулирование"). This term is self-explanatory: energy prices are still mostly regulated in the EaP countries because it remains critical for the EaP countries' policies to protect vulnerable social households, support industrial competitiveness and restrain inflation. Energy price liberalisation remains socially and politically sensitive. Table 1.7 provides an overview of the key characteristics of energy pricing policies by country. These are closely linked with taxation and subsidisation policies discussed later in this chapter.

Table 1.7. **Key characteristics of energy pricing policies in the EaP countries**

<table>
<tr><th></th><th>Armenia</th><th>Azerbaijan</th><th>Belarus</th><th>Georgia</th><th>Moldova</th><th>Ukraine</th></tr>
<tr><td>Price-setting authority</td><td>Public Services Regulatory Commission</td><td>Tariff Council</td><td>Council of Ministers, as prepared by the Ministry of Economy</td><td>Georgian National Energy and Water Supply Regulatory Commission</td><td>National Energy Regulatory Agency</td><td>National Commission for State Regulation of Energy and Public Utilities</td></tr>
<tr><td>Natural gas</td><td rowspan="2">Regulated prices</td><td rowspan="5">Regulated prices</td><td rowspan="3">Regulated prices, cross-subsidies</td><td rowspan="2">Mostly regulated prices, elements of both cross-subsidies and deregulation</td><td rowspan="3">Regulated prices</td><td>Regulated for households, deregulated for industry</td></tr>
<tr><td>Electricity</td><td>Regulated prices, cross-subsidies</td></tr>
<tr><td>Heat</td><td>n.a.</td><td>n.a.</td><td>Regulated prices</td></tr>
<tr><td>Liquid petroleum products</td><td rowspan="2">Deregulated prices</td><td rowspan="2">Regulated prices</td><td rowspan="2" colspan="3">Deregulated prices</td></tr>
<tr><td>Coal and other solid fuels</td></tr>
</table>

Note: **n.a.**: not applicable.

Source: Authors' presentation based on the summary tables in the country chapters.

Except for Belarus, where energy prices are subject to the decision of the Council of Ministers after preparation by the Ministry of Economy, all EaP countries have set up dedicated bodies for energy tariff-setting. The degree to which these new institutions have become independent regulators has varied across countries and periods between the waves of reforms. Interference from governments and state-owned energy companies in tariff-setting has been quite common, and the recovery of costs in the energy sector continues to be lower than it could be.

The natural gas, heat and electricity sectors remain subject to price regulation in all EaP countries, for consumers as well as often for producers. Tariffs are normally differentiated by different groups of consumers and producers. Formally, price-setting methodologies for most energy types are publicly available and at least in theory are based on the so-called "cost-plus" methodology. However, even where "cost-plus" methodologies cover operational costs, the cost recovery is often not sufficient to recover long-term costs, such as financing of replacement capacity and expansion to satisfy possible increase in demand.

The most deregulated segment is the market of liquid petroleum products. Figure 1.11 presents a comparison of pump prices for gasoline and diesel in the EaP countries, according to a *Deutsche Gesellschaft für Internationale Zusammenarbeit* (GIZ) survey conducted in mid-November 2014. The differences in prices across countries are explained by four factors: *i)* exemption from Russian Federation's export tax under EAEU for Belarus (see Box 1.5); *ii)* continued price regulation in Azerbaijan and Belarus; *iii)* differences in fuel taxation across the EaP countries; and *iv)* differences in refining and transportation costs.

Figure 1.11. **Pump prices for gasoline and diesel in EaP countries in mid-November 2014, USD**

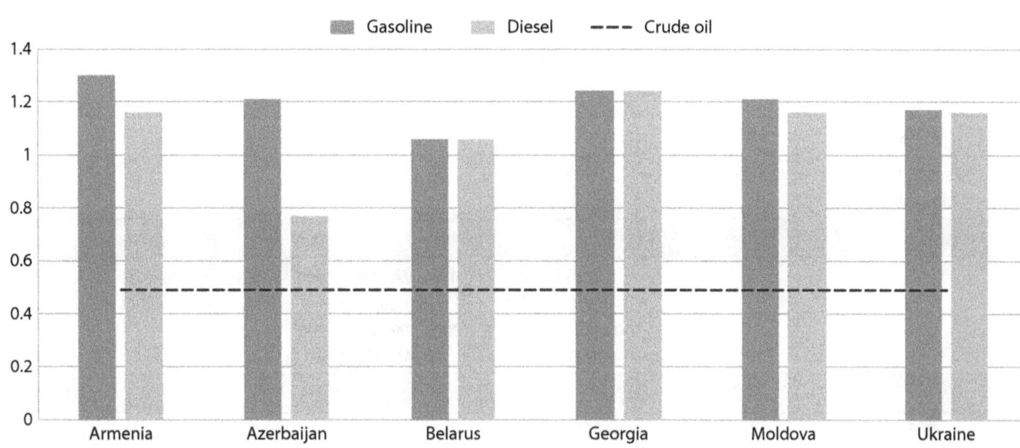

Source: GIZ (2015).

Pricing policies, including pricing methodologies, tariff structures and regulatory procedures, continue to evolve in the EaP region. During the preparation of the report, several such changes have occurred, and individual country chapters indicate as of which date the provided information is valid. It is certain that pricing policies will continue to be dynamic in the EaP countries in the next decade.

Main taxation policies in the energy sector

In the past two decades, the EaP countries have made efforts to rationalise their initially heavily regulated fiscal systems in order to reduce administrative barriers, simplify taxation and thus increase the collection of tax revenue. The baseline taxation in all EaP countries includes VAT, corporate profit tax, individual income tax, property tax, land tax and a single tax for small businesses – all codified at the national level and approved by the parliaments as law. Most countries also charge additional local taxes, a road tax on vehicles and fees for environmental pollution. None of the EaP countries has a carbon tax except Ukraine where the tax rate is extremely low.

In the extractive sector, the three countries that have scalable production of fossil fuels – Azerbaijan, Belarus and Ukraine – charge a mining tax on their production, which is differentiated by type of deposit. Azerbaijan and Georgia also have special taxation regimes for large-scale energy projects implemented by foreign investors such as oil and gas extraction and pipelines, under the so-called Production Sharing Agreements (PSAs) and Host Government Agreements (HGAs).

Table 1.8. **VAT and excise tax rates on energy consumption in the EaP countries as of early 2017**

	Armenia	Azerbaijan	Belarus	Georgia	Moldova	Ukraine
Gasoline						
VAT rate	20%	18%	20%	18%	20%	20%
Excise rate	Not differentiated by grade	Differentiated by grade	Differentiated by grade	Not differentiated by grade	Not differentiated by grade	Differentiated by grade
Diesel						
VAT rate	0%	18%	20%	18%	20%	20%
Excise rate	Not differentiated by grade	Differentiated by grade	Differentiated by grade	Not differentiated by grade	Not differentiated by grade	Differentiated by grade
CNG						
VAT rate	20%	18%	20%	18%	20%	20%
Excise rate	Starting from May 2016	No	Yes	Yes	No	Yes
Natural gas						
VAT rate	20%	18%	20% for all users (0% for households before January 2016)	18%, VAT exemption for natural gas consumed by thermal power stations	8% for households only, 20% for other users	20%
Electricity						
VAT rate	20%	18%	20% for all users (0% for households before January 2016)	18%	0% for households, 20% for other users	20%
Heat						
VAT rate	20%	18%	20% for all users (0% for households before January 2016)	18%	0% for households, 20% for other users	20%

Source: Based on information provided in individual country chapters.

The import and export of energy products is subject to customs duties. In addition, consumption of gasoline and diesel in all EaP countries, as well as compressed natural gas (CNG) in Armenia, Belarus, Georgia and Ukraine, is also subject to excise tax, as summarised in Table 1.8. As practised internationally, the rates of excise taxes are determined by the government and relatively frequently revised to reflect the energy price fluctuations in the international market and to raise enough funds for the national budgets. Azerbaijan, Belarus and Ukraine differentiate excise tax rates depending on the grade of gasoline and diesel, while Armenia, Georgia and Moldova have a single excise tax rate for gasoline and a single excise tax rate for diesel. Natural gas, electricity and heat are not subject to excise taxes in the EaP countries.

VAT and excise taxes form part of the end price for energy goods, and thus exist within the wider context of energy price regulation in the EaP countries (see previous section). Exemption from taxes (for example, VAT exemption for diesel in Armenia) and adjustments in excise tax rates are among the toolkit of the EaP governments to reduce consumer energy prices. Tax breaks are also used to promote investment in the energy sector in the region, and to a certain extent, energy efficiency and renewable energy. All these tax breaks are a type of subsidy and are discussed in more detail in the individual country studies.

Climate policy targets

All EaP countries participate in global efforts to mitigate climate change and adapt to it. Following the breakup of the Soviet Union, decline in industrial activities and shifts in the structure of the economy, the EaP region experienced deep cuts in greenhouse gas (GHG) emissions compared with the 1990 level (a benchmark frequently used in the processes supported by the United Nations Framework Convention on Climate Change, or UNFCCC). At present (latest data for 2013, for CO_2 emissions from all sources), annual CO_2 emissions per capita in most EaP countries are lower than the EU average (6.7 tonnes): 6 tonnes in Ukraine, 3.8 tonnes in Azerbaijan, 2 tonnes in Georgia, 1.8 tonnes in Armenia and 1.4 tonnes in Moldova. In Belarus, they are the same as the EU average – 6.7 tonnes per capita (World Bank, 2017). Figure 1.12 provides more detail on the dynamics of CO_2 emissions per capita in the region, focusing on emissions from fuel combustion only and using IEA data (IEA Energy Balances Statistics, n.d.). These data demonstrate that CO_2 emissions in the energy sector of the EaP countries remained stable over the period 2004-14. However, without a further transformational change, improving living standards in the region may result in an increase in energy consumption and emissions.

In the lead-up to the UNFCCC conference in Paris in 2015, like other countries, all EaP countries submitted their Intended Nationally Determined Contributions (INDCs) with emission reduction targets (Table 1.9). Most countries committed to emission targets that are lower than their emissions in 1990, but higher than their current level of emissions, thus saving "space for economic growth" within the concept of "shared, but differentiated responsibility".

Meanwhile, the EaP countries have a significant energy efficiency potential, and thus room for emission reduction. Energy savings can be achieved across the board, particularly in such sectors as in district heating, electricity generation and networks, and industry and buildings (IEA, 2015).

Renewable energy development is also an important direction for climate change mitigation policies in the region. In particular, the Caucasus republics have a significant potential for small hydropower plants, while Ukraine and Belarus can produce low-cost biomass and biofuels. The region can also further tap its wind and solar potential.

Figure 1.12. **CO_2 emission per capita in the EaP countries, tonne of CO_2**

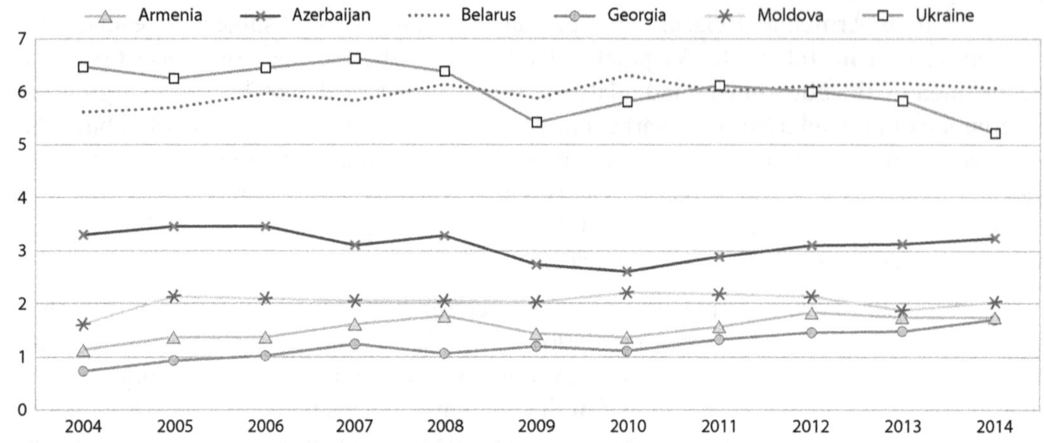

Note: Emissions from fuel combustion only.

Source: IEA Energy Balances Statistics (n.d.).

The legislative base for energy efficiency and renewable energy in the region has been developing, thanks in part to the process of harmonisation of national standards and practices with the EU benchmarks. However, energy-efficiency improvements require significant investment – and these to a large extent depend on energy policies in the EaP countries. In particular, energy price regulations (consumer subsidies) are a hurdle for investors in the electricity and heat sector. At present they have some difficulty recovering their costs, including operational costs in some EaP countries, and long-term marginal costs, including the cost of capital, in most of the region (see discussion in individual country chapters on how sales prices compare with cost-recovery benchmarks).

Table 1.9. **Climate commitments of the EaP countries in the lead-up to UNFCCC Paris Agreement in 2015**

	Emissions, million tonnes of CO_2 eq., excluding LULUCF[a]		Commitments within Intended Nationally Determined Contributions	
	1990	2030	Unconditional	Conditional on a global agreement addressing technical co-operation and access to low-cost financial resources
Armenia[b]	-	-	Capping emissions at annual average of 5.4 tonnes per capita over 2015-50 (in 2010, Armenia's emissions stood at 2.14 tonnes per capita)	-
Azerbaijan	73.3	47.6	At least 35% below 1990 level	-
Belarus	139.2	100.2	At least 28% below 1990 level	-
Georgia	48.0	32.7	At least 15% below a business-as-usual scenario	At least 25% below a business-as-usual scenario
Moldova	43.4	15.6	At least 64%-67% below 1990 level	At least 78% below 1990 level
Ukraine	944.4	566.6	At least 40% below 1990 level	-

Notes: a. Land use, land-use change and forestry.

b. Armenia did not report its emissions in 1990 and intended emissions in 2030 in its INDC.

Source: UNFCCC (2015), http://www4.unfccc.int/submissions/INDC/Submission%20Pages/submissions.aspx.

References

APEC (2009), *APEC Summit. Leaders' Declaration: Sustaining Growth, Connecting the Region*, Asia-Pacific Economic Co-operation, Singapore. www.apec.org/Meeting-Papers/Leaders-Declarations/2009/2009_aelm.aspx.

Beaton, C. et al. (2013), *A Guidebook to Fossil-Fuel Subsidy Reform for Policy-Makers in Southeast Asia*, International Institute for Sustainable Development – Global Subsidies Initiative, Geneva. www.iisd.org/gsi/fossil-fuel-subsidies/guidebook.

Burniaux, J. M. and J. Chateau (2014), "Greenhouse Gases Mitigation Potential and Economic Efficiency of Phasing-Out Fossil Fuel Subsidies", *International Economics*, No. 140, pp. 71-88.

EAEU (2014), *The Treaty on the Eurasian Economic Union*, Eurasian Economic Union. www.un.org/en/ga/sixth/70/docs/treaty_on_eeu.pdf.

Eurostat (2016), *European Neighbourhood Policy: East – Economic Statistics*, Eurostat, Luxembourg. http://ec.europa.eu/eurostat/statistics-explained/index.php/European_Neighbourhood_Policy_-_East_-_economic_statistics.

FFFSR (2015), *Fossil Fuel Subsidies Reform Communiqué, 2015*, Friends of Fossil Fuel Subsidies Reform. http://fffsr.org/communique.

Gerasimchuk, I. (2014), *A Crash Course on Subsidy Definition by Dante, Shakespeare and Russian Folklore,* International Institute for Sustainable Development-Global Subsidies Initiative, Geneva. www.iisd.org/gsi/news/crash-course-subsidy-definition-dante-shakespeare-and-russian-folklore.

Gerasimchuk, I. (2012), *Fossil Fuels at What Cost? Government Support for Upstream Oil and Gas Developments in Russia*, International Institute for Sustainable Development and World Wide Fund Russia, Geneva, Moscow. www.iisd.org/gsi/sites/default/files/ffs_awc_russia_eng.pdf.

Gerasimchuk, I. et al. (2017), *Zombie Energy: Climate Benefits of Ending Subsidies to Fossil Fuel Production*, International Institute for Sustainable Development and Global Subsidies Initiative, Geneva and London. www.iisd.org/library/zombie-energy-climate-benefits-ending-subsidies-fossil-fuel-production.

Gerasimchuk, I. et al. (2012), *State of Play on Biofuel Subsidies: Are Policies Ready to Shift?*, International Institute for Sustainable Development and Global Subsidies Initiative, Geneva. www.iisd.org/gsi/sites/default/files/bf_stateplay_2012.pdf.

GIZ (2015), *International Fuel Prices 2014, Data Preview, Deutsche Gesellschaft für Internationale Zusammenarbeit*, Eschborn, Germany. https://www.giz.de/expertise/downloads/giz-2015-en-ifp2014.pdf.

G20 (2009), *Pittsburgh Summit: Leaders' Statement, G-20.* www.g20.utoronto.ca/2009/2009communique0925.html.

IEA (2016a), *Energy Subsidies Database 2012-2014*, International Energy Agency, Paris. www.worldenergyoutlook.org/resources/energysubsidies/.

IEA (2016b), *World Energy Outlook 2016*, International Energy Agency, Paris.

IEA (2015), *Eastern Europe, Caucasus and Central Asia: Energy Policies beyond IEA Countries*, OECD Publishing/International Energy Agency, Paris. https://www.iea.org/publications/freepublications/publication/IDR_EasternEuropeCaucasus_2015.pdf.

IEA (2006), *Carrots and Sticks: Taxing and Subsidising Energy*, International Energy Agency, Paris. https://www.iea.org/publications/freepublications/publication/carrots-and-sticks-taxing-and-subsidising-energy.html.

IEA (n.d.), *Energy Balances Statistics,* International Energy Agency, Paris. www.iea.org/statistics/topics/energybalances/.

IEA/OPEC/OECD/World Bank (2010), *Analysis of the Scope of Energy Subsidies and Suggestions for the G-20 Initiative, Joint Report*, International Energy Agency, Organisation of the Petroleum Exporting Countries, Organisation for Economc Co-operation and Development, World Bank. www.oecd.org/env/45575666.pdf.

IEC (n.d.), *The Energy Charter Treaty*, International Energy Charter, Brussels. www.energycharter.org/process/energy-charter-treaty-1994/energy-charter-treaty/.

IMF (2015), *How Large are Global Energy Subsidies*?, International Monetary Fund, Washington, DC. www.imf.org/external/pubs/cat/longres.aspx?sk=42940.0.

IMF (2013), *Energy Subsidy Reform: Lessons and Implications*, International Monetary Fund, Washington, DC. https://www.imf.org/external/np/pp/eng/2013/012813.pdf.

Jones, D. and R. Steenblik (2010), *Subsidy Estimation: A Survey of Current Practice*, International Institute for Sustainable Development, Geneva. www.iisd.org/publications/pub.aspx?id=1293.

Koplow, D. (2009), *Measuring Energy Subsidies Using the Price-Gap Approach: What Does It Leave Out?*, International Institute for Sustainable Development, Geneva. www.iisd.org/pdf/2009/bali_2_copenhagen_ff_subsidies_pricegap.pdf.

Lang, K. (2010), *Defining Fossil-Fuel Subsidies for the G-20: Which Approach is Best?*, International Institute for Sustainable Development and Global Subsidies Initiative, Geneva. www.iisd.org/gsi/sites/default/files/pb5_defining.pdf.

Manenok, T. (2017), *«Черный» сценарий для белорусской нефтянки: отменит ли Россия экспортные пошлины на нефть и нефтепродукты?,* Belrynok. ("'Black' Scenario for Belarussian Oil Producers: Will Russia Cancel Export Duties on Oil and Oil Products?"), Belrynok, TUT.BY, 5 January. https://news.tut.by/economics/526403.html.

Merrill, L. et al. (2015), *Tackling Fossil Fuel Subsidies and Climate Change: Levelling the Energy Playing Field*, International Institute for Sustainable Development and Global Subsidies Initiative, Geneva. http://norden.diva-portal.org/smash/get/diva2:860647/FULLTEXT02.pdf.

OECD (2018, forthcoming), *Assessing Energy Affordability and Environmental Impacts of Reforming Major Energy Subsidy Schemes in the Republic of Moldova*, OECD Publishing, Paris, forthcoming.

OECD (2015a), *Inventory of Support Measures for Fossil Fuels*, OECD Publishing, Paris.

OECD (2015b), *Taxing Energy Use 2015: OECD and Selected Partner Economies*, OECD Publishing, Paris.

OECD (2013a), *Analysing Energy Subsidies in the Countries of Eastern Europe, Caucasus and Central Asia,* OECD Publishing, Paris. https://www.oecd.org/env/outreach/EHS%20report_20%20August%202013_ENG.pdf.

OECD (2013b), *Inventory of Estimated Budgetary Support and Tax Expenditures Relating to Fossil Fuels*, OECD Publishing, Paris. www.oecd.org/site/tadffss/publication.

OECD (2010a), *Measuring Support for Energy, Version 1.0,* OECD Publishing, Paris. https://www.oecd.org/env/45339216.pdf.

OECD (2010b), *OECD's Producer Support Estimate and Related Indicators of Agricultural Support: Concepts, Calculations, Interpretation and Use (The PSE Manual)*, Trade and Agriculture Directorate, OECD Publishing, Paris.

Duhr, S. (2017), *Turning Subsidies into Energy Efficiency Investments*, presentation at the conference "Unlocking Private Finance for Greener, Low-Carbon Growth and Energy Efficiency in the Eastern Partnership and Central Asia", Brussels, 29-30 June, OECD Publishing, Paris.

The Economist (2015), "Pump Aligning", 17 January, London. www.economist.com/news/finance-and-economics/21639589-few-countries-are-taking-advantage-lower-oil-prices-cut-subsidies-pump.

UNFCCC (2015), *Intended Nationally Determined Contributions of the EaP Countries*, United Nations Framework Convention on Climate Change Secretariat, Bonn. http://www4.unfccc.int/submissions/INDC/Submission%20Pages/submissions.aspx.

UN SDKP (2015), *UN Sustainable Development Goals – SDG 12: Ensure Sustainable Consumption and Production Patterns*, United Nations Sustainable Development Knowledge Platform, New York. https://sustainabledevelopment.un.org/sdg12.

Victor, D. (2009), *The Politics of Fossil Fuel Subsidies*, International Institute for Sustainable Development and Global Subsidies Initiative, Geneva. https://www.iisd.org/gsi/sites/default/files/politics_ffs.pdf.

Whitley, S. and L. van der Burg (2016), *Fossil Fuel Subsidy Reform: From Rhetoric to Reality,* Overseas Development Institute, London. http://newclimateeconomy.report/2015/wp-content/uploads/sites/3/2016/04/Fossil-fuel-subsidy-reform_from-rhetoric-to-reality.pdf.

World Bank (2017), *World Bank Open Data*, World Bank, Washington, DC. http://data.worldbank.org.

World Bank (2013), *Balancing Act: Cutting Energy Subsidies while Protecting Affordability*, World Bank, Washington, DC. https://openknowledge.worldbank.org/bitstream/handle/10986/12296/9780821397893.pdf?sequence=7.

WTO (1996), *Agreement on Subsidies and Countervailing Measures*, World Trade Organization, Geneva. https://www.wto.org/english/docs_e/legal_e/24-scm_01_e.htm.

Chapter 2

Armenia's energy subsidies

This chapter identifies, documents and provides estimates of the various subsidies in Armenia that relate to the production or use of coal, oil and related petroleum products, natural gas, and electricity and heat generated on the basis of these fossil fuels. The chapter also briefly looks at the subsidies benefiting energy-efficiency measures and renewable energy sources. An overview of the country's energy sector is first given to place the measures listed into context. In addition, the chapter discusses pricing and tax policies in the energy sector in Armenia. The analysis summarises the context, the state of play, and the mechanics of the complex and evolving landscape of energy subsidies in the country.

Key findings

For a combination of geopolitical and economic reasons, Armenia had no choice but to reform its energy system and phase out the bulk of the subsidies inherited from the Soviet period. The bottom-up approach revealed only very limited subsidies, which do not appear to create significant distortions in consumer energy choices. The cumulative value of the six identified subsidies for fossil fuels in Armenia was USD 37 mln (AMD 17.7 bln) in 2015. This is low compared to other countries in the region, which reflects the progress of reform and is consistent with the findings of the price-gap approach. Armenia's staple fuel is natural gas coming mainly from the Russian Federation. The price-gap approach revealed no subsidy to it, since the price of gas purchased from Gazprom is considerably higher than in other countries of the region.

The low level of energy subsidisation may, to a certain extent, explain why energy subsidies are little discussed in Armenia. Instead, policy makers and stakeholders commonly refer to tariff reform. The consumer tariffs are determined on the basis of the cost-recovery principle. However, it has yet to be established whether generators are able to fully recover their costs after accounting for the change in fuel price, transmission and distribution losses. Another subject for study is whether gas import prices and low tariffs on increased consumption are discouraging consumers from adopting energy-saving practices.

The tax structure appears to be the most critical area for both Armenia's energy system and the discussion of government support and tariff reform. Exempting value-added tax (VAT) on diesel and excise tax for imported natural gas is intended to ensure that the cost of electricity based on natural gas is low, keeping down consumer tariffs.

To address the challenge, the Public Services Regulatory Commission, the independent regulator, will gradually need to increase consumer tariffs for electricity, to keep up with the rising cost of generation and generators' demand for capital investment. At the same time, Armenia already has some of the highest energy tariffs in the region, and for electricity and natural gas, residential tariffs are higher than industrial tariffs, given the increasing cost of distribution at lower voltages. In contrast to some other countries in the region, there is no cross-subsidisation between different types of consumers. Any further reform in the electricity sector will be both sensitive and difficult, and the latest attempt to raise consumer tariffs, in 2015, resulted in widespread social protests and the introduction of a new subsidy for low-income electricity consumers. With the downward revision of electricity prices for consumers in August 2016, the government discontinued the subsidy for low-income electricity consumers.

Three out of the six energy subsidies identified as a result of the bottom-up inventory fall into the category of targeted support for vulnerable consumers, an integral element of any energy subsidy reform. Although these measures can be classified as energy subsidies, their primary objective is social protection.

The three other subsidy schemes identified represent government revenue foregone by exempting diesel from VAT and exempting natural gas and compressed natural gas (CNG) from excise tax. However, diesel fuel is subject to a relatively high excise tax, and the excise tax exemption from CNG was phased out as of 1 May 2016. The government is planning to eliminate VAT exemption for diesel under the new tax code applicable in 2018. In the fuel sector, further rationalisation may thus involve reconsideration of the VAT exemption for diesel and of excise tax rates on all fuels.

Government support for renewables in Armenia appears to be limited. The feed-in tariff for small hydro plants is much lower than the residential tariff and producer tariffs for other electricity-generation technologies, including gas-fired thermal plants. For wind and biogas generation, the feed-in tariff is relatively high. However, the value of state support provided to these sectors is low, given the negligible role of wind and biogas in Armenia's electricity mix. The feed-in tariff was only introduced in 2015, because solar power had been generated only at autonomous units that will begin to connect to the grid in 2017.

At the same time, most programmes supporting energy efficiency and renewables have received financing from international institutions, such as the World Bank and International Financial Corporation (IFC), the European Bank for Reconstruction and Development (EBRD), Germany's KfW Bank, the Global Environmental Fund (GEF) and the European Union (EU). Continuation of these donor and IFI programmes is likely to remain critical for the further uptake of energy efficiency and renewable energy generation.

Armenia needs to provide an enabling environment for incentivising generation based on renewables on a large scale. Globally, the cost of renewables, especially of wind and solar, has fallen with technological innovation. However, integration and evacuation of such intermittent power remains a challenge. The government needs to create a policy framework that allows the sale of such power through market-based mechanisms as open access or permitting net metering, so that excess power can be sold to the grid at market rates. Armenia can further adopt demand-side measures such as energy-efficiency incentives to reduce energy consumption. For large-scale deployment of renewables and energy-efficiency measures, the availability of finance at low rates will be key. Government support in the form of state guarantees or firm power purchase agreements can help generators raise funds at the market.

Government savings from phasing out support for fossil fuels can be redirected to the development of clean energy alternatives and energy-efficiency measures. Further, any increase in the price of fuel or electricity for consumers can be mitigated by providing targeted support for low-income households. However, political acceptance of the electricity subsidy and pricing reforms will require educating the public about the new policy, coupled with an appropriate communication strategy. This will involve developing a national awareness-raising campaign and developing partnerships and alliances with nongovernmental actors in disseminating key facts on electricity subsidies and pricing reform.

Armenia is already well-known for having reduced its greenhouse gas (GHG) emissions to a quarter of what they were in 1990. As part of a wider reform of its energy sector, reform of fossil fuel subsidies has contributed to the decarbonisation of Armenia's economy. The context of these reforms in Armenia, especially in the energy crisis of the early 1990s, is unique. Heavy reliance on imported fuels and an old and poorly maintained transmission and distribution network put Armenia at risk of supply interruptions, price fluctuations and energy outages. The country has undergone not only energy policy changes, but a much harder, more fundamental transformation of its economy and public attitudes. Nevertheless, some technical aspects of Armenia's experience can serve as good practice for replication in the wider region of the EU Eastern Partnership countries and Central Asia.

Macroeconomic situation and energy sector overview

Armenia went through an economic transformation after gaining its independence in 1991. After the collapse of the Soviet Union, the country's GDP dropped by 53% in the three years from 1990 to 1993 (World Bank, 2015). A period of hyperinflation and unemployment resulted in outward migration and a sharp increase in poverty (IMF, 2001).

Armenia then introduced drastic economic reforms, including stronger monetary and fiscal policies, as well as structural and institutional reforms. As a result of the reforms and an influx of foreign investment, remittances and funding from donors, the economy began to recover (World Bank, 2014). GDP growth averaged 5.3% from 1994 to 1999, and accelerated to 11.2% in the period 2000-08. Small-scale agriculture, services, jewellery production and other market-oriented manufacturing replaced the heavy industry inherited from the Soviet era that disintegrated in the early years of independence (World Bank, 2014).

The global financial crisis caused Armenia's GDP to contract by 14.2% in 2009, but the country's economic growth has averaged 4.2% annually since 2010 (World Bank, 2015). In 2014, GDP growth slowed to 3.4%, and the economy was set to decelerate further in 2015 and 2016, given the persistent weakness of the Russian economy, combined with falling global prices for mining and metals products, which negatively affect Armenian exports (World Bank, 2014). Tables 2.1 and 2.2 provide the most recent key economic indicators from international and national sources.[1]

Table 2.1. **Macroeconomic indicators**

		International statistics		National statistics	
Indicator	Unit	Year	Value	Year	Value
Population	mln	2014	2.97	2015	3.01
GDP	USD bln	2014	10.27	2014	11.65
GDP per capita	USD	2014	3 159	2014	3 869
Energy production	mtoe	2013	0.81	2014	0.81
Net energy imports	mtoe	2013	2.21	2014	2.33
Total primary energy supply (TPES)	mtoe	2013	2.97	2014	3.04
TPES per capita	toe	2013	1.00	2014	1.01
Electricity consumption	TWh	2013	5.46	2014	5.35
Electricity consumption per capita	MWh/capita	2013	1.84	2014	1.78
CO_2 emissions[a]	Mt of CO_2	2013	5.42	2012	5.3
CO_2 per capita[a]	t of CO_2	2013	1.83	2012	1.76

Note: a. CO_2 emissions from fuel combustion only.

Source: Authors' compilation based on IEA (2015), World Bank (2015), Armstat (2015a), Ministry of Energy and Natural Resources of Armenia, or MENR (2015), UNDP and GEF (2015).

Table 2.2. **Average exchange rate**

	2012	2013	2014	2015
Average exchange rate, AMD per USD	401.74	409.54	415.77	477.85

Source: Central Bank of Armenia, as reported by Rate.Am (2015).

Energy supply

Armenia's total primary energy supply (TPES) plummeted after the collapse of the Soviet Union, when oil product supply dropped by 90% and the supply of natural gas was halved. Even after more than a decade of economic growth, the TPES in 2014 was still 61% below the 1990 level (Figure 2.1). Over the last 20 years, however, efforts have been made to revamp the Armenian energy sector. From 2002 to 2014, Armenia's TPES increased by 62%, driven primarily by a 128% increase in natural gas supply and a 20% increase in hydropower production (IEA, 2015; UNDP and GEF, 2015).

Figure 2.1. **Total primary energy supply, 1990-2014**

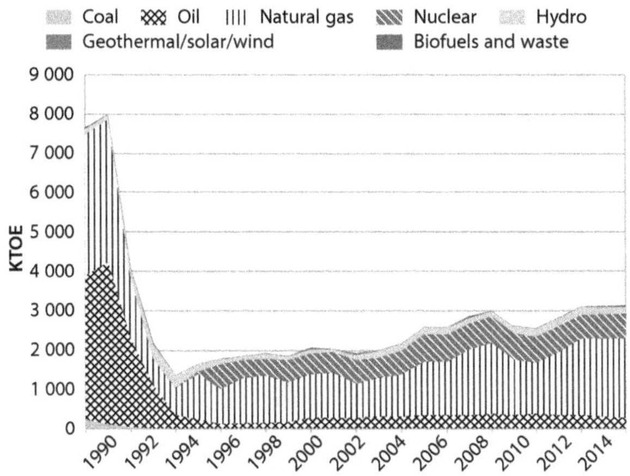

Figure 2.2. **Primary energy supply in 2014 by fuel**

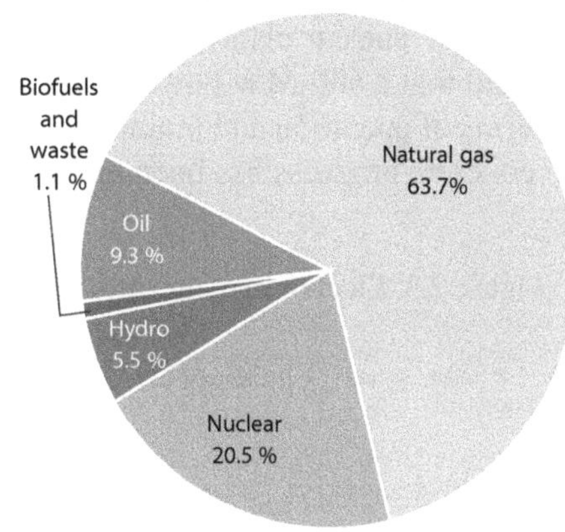

Source: Authors' compilation based on IEA (2015), MENR (2015).

As shown in Figure 2.2, Armenia's energy balance has become largely dependent on natural gas, which constituted 64% of TPES in 2014, up from only 46% in 2002. Oil and oil products accounted for 9.3% in 2014, while nuclear power and hydropower accounted for 20.5% and 5.5%, respectively. Manure and firewood are largely used as fuel in rural areas of Armenia and accounted for 1.1% of TPES in 2014. Remarkably, coal is totally absent from Armenia's energy mix. As there is no domestic extraction of fossil fuels, Armenia covers 75% of its total energy needs with imported oil and gas (IEA, 2015). In 2014, Armenia imported USD 814 mln worth of oil, gas and other mineral fuels, of which 75% was sourced from the Russian Federation, 12.5% from Iran (in an exchange of Iranian gas for Armenian electricity, see below), and the rest from other countries.

In 2014, electricity production remained 25% below the 1990 level, but from 2002 to 2014, it increased by 40%, primarily due to the increased supply of natural gas and the expansion of gas-fired generation capacity. Electricity generation totalled 7 750 GWh in 2014. In the electricity mix, hydropower accounted for roughly 26%, nuclear for 32% and gas-fired thermal power contributed 42% (see Figure 2.3 and Figure 2.4 for details).

Installed electricity generating capacity (operational capacity) in Armenia was 4 147 (3 206) megawatts in 2014: 2 476 (1 521) MW of gas-fired thermal power plants, 1 252 (1 252) MW of hydropower and 407 (407) MW of nuclear (IEA, 2015). The installed capacity of the electricity system exceeds the uppermost requirement for the electricity load. This provides the economic rationale for the swap arrangement with Iran under which Armenia supplies 3 kWh of electricity per cubic metre of Iranian gas.

Despite an estimated 4 300 MW of renewable energy capacity potential in Armenia, installed wind and biogas capacity (operational capacity) amounted to a modest 3.7 (3.7) MW, co-generated heat and power (CHP) – 14.1 (8) MW in 2014, respectively, while solar photovoltaic installations are negligible. In the coming years, the power system assets need to be replaced and upgraded, following the government's plan to retire its oldest thermal power plant (TPP) by 2017. The Armenian government also formally agreed in 2007 to decommission the Medsamor nuclear power plant (NPP), whose capacity is 407 MW, in 2016, but its technical lifespan was extended by 10 years due to insufficient replacement capacity. The Russian Federation will provide Armenia a USD 270 mln loan and a USD 30 mln grant to extend the service life of the plant until 2026. The funds will be provided for 15 years, with a five-year grace period and an interest rate of 3% per annum (ARKA News Agency, 2015). The Armenian government initially planned to build a new 1 000 MW nuclear plant as a replacement in 2026. After in-depth surveys, however, it was decided that a 600 MW power unit would be a better choice, since it will be more flexible in terms of operation and maintenance. Financing of the new NPP remains a challenge, and no concrete progress has been made to date (Financial Portal ArmInfo, 2016).

Figure 2.3. **Electricity generation by source, 1990-2014, GWh**

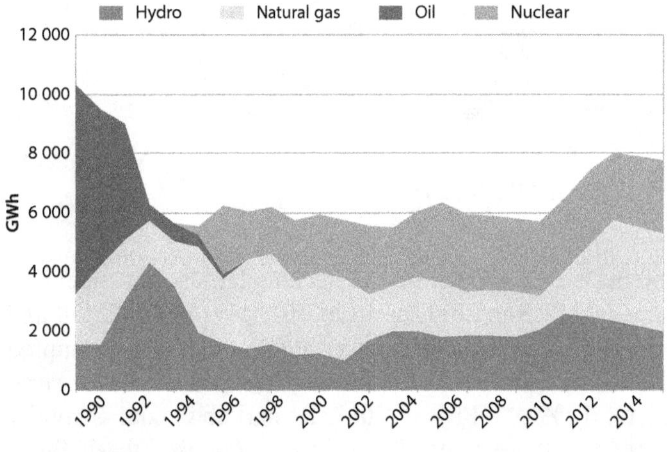

Figure 2.4. **Electricity generation in 2014, % by source**

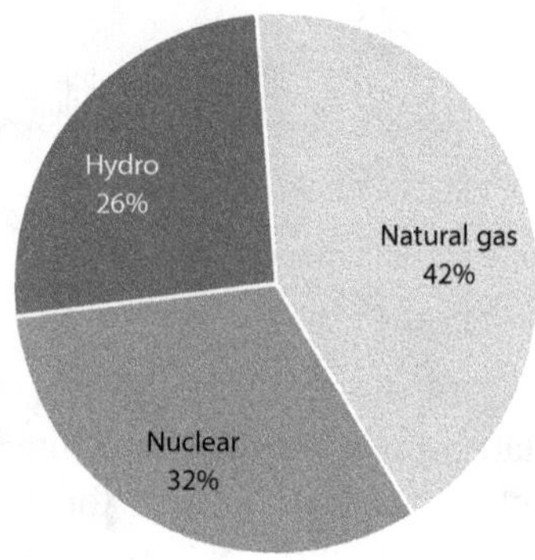

Source: Authors' compilation based on IEA (2015), MENR (2015).

Recent years have seen an unprecedented expansion of the natural gas distribution system. In 2015, the gasification rate stood at 95% in Armenia. Given the constant increases in electricity prices, households have switched to natural gas for heating and cooking where possible (Sargsyan et al., 2006).

Gasification has also been adopted in the transport sector, where compressed natural gas (CNG) accounted for 70% of fuels used in 2014. CNG, 2.5 times cheaper than gasoline, is promoted as a cleaner fuel and as the key fuel for public transport development.

After the collapse of the Soviet Union and the energy crisis of the early 1990s, the district heating system in Armenia virtually ceased to exist. The concept of autonomous heating, in which a small gas-fired boiler supplies heat to one or to several buildings, has not proved popular. Wall-hung natural gas boilers are now considered to be the most convenient and modern mode of apartment heating in Armenia.

Energy demand

Armenia's total final energy consumption (TFEC) is dominated by the residential sector. Its share of TFEC was 36.5% in 2014, followed by transport (29%), industry (18.5%) and the commercial and public sectors (16%).

Natural gas is used across all end-use sectors and as feedstock for electricity generation, accounting for about 62% of TFEC in 2014. About 22% of TFEC is electricity to supply households, businesses and industry, while oil, representing 16% of TFEC, is used in transport, industry and businesses (MENR, 2015).

Energy sector structure, ownership and governance

The Ministry of Energy and Natural Resources (MENR) formulates Armenia's energy policy and has primary responsibility for the energy sector. Regulatory implementation is the responsibility of the Public Services Regulatory Commission of Armenia (PSRC), established in 1997 by presidential decree. PSRC is an autonomous regulatory agency; government entities may not interfere with its decisions. It is a multi-member body responsible for electricity, natural gas, water and telecommunications (EBRD, n.d.). Figure 2.5 schematically represents the main players in both the electricity and natural gas sectors.

Figure 2.5. **Structure of the electricity and gas sectors in Armenia**

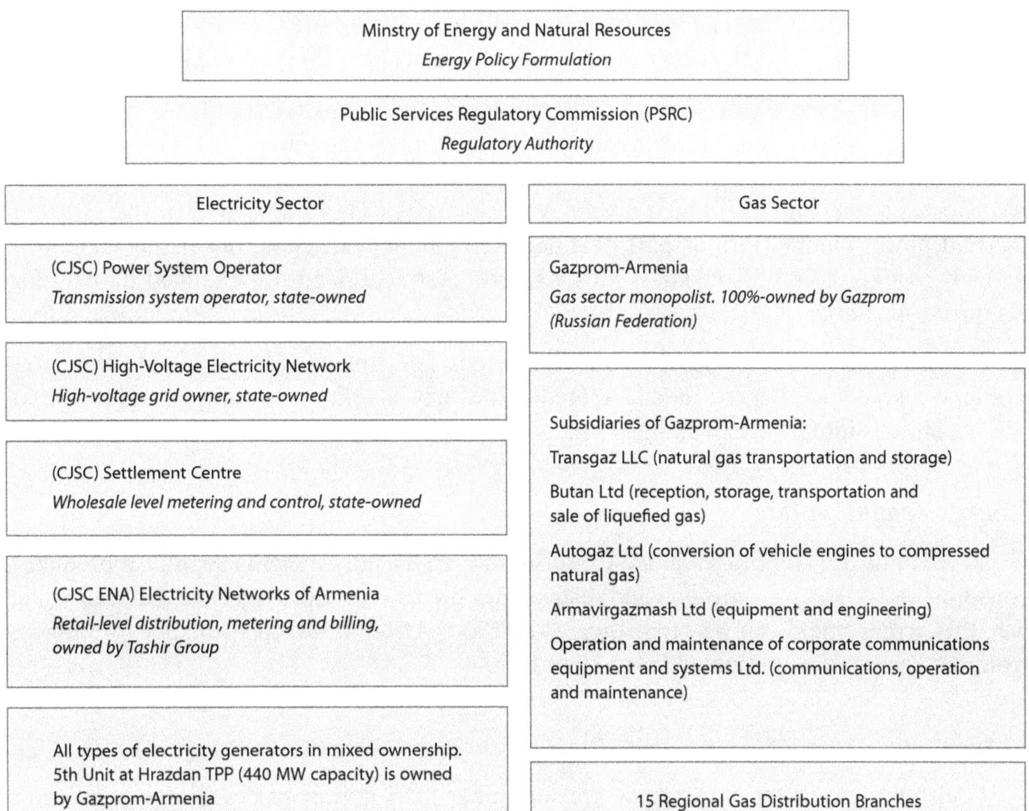

Source: Authors' compilation based on IEA (2015), Gazprom Armenia (2015).

The power sector is legally and financially unbundled, but is regulated under a "single-buyer model" guided by the principle of cost-reflective tariffs.

Generation has been partially privatised. As of March 2016, only the Yerevan TPP and Metsamor NPP remained in state ownership. The introduction of cost-reflective tariffs (see Annex 2.A3 on Armenia for details on the methodology) in the electricity sector has led to ample investments in capacity and networks, which has improved reliability considerably (IEA, 2015). In addition to large-scale generation (natural gas, large hydro and nuclear), small-scale electricity generation (predominantly hydro) has received significant political and regulatory attention in recent years, as part of Armenia's efforts to diversify its power mix. Small-scale plants enjoy simplified project approval procedures (MENR, 2015).

The distribution company ENA (Electric Networks of Armenia) has not only been privatised, but changed owners over the years. It was first owned by a British company, Midland Resources Holding Ltd, registered offshore, which sold it to the Russian state-owned company INTER RAO in 2005 (PanARMENIAN, 2005; Aravot, 2015). More recently, INTER RAO sold 100% of its ENA shares to a private Russian-registered company, the Tashir Group, owned by an Armenian businessman.

ENA purchases electricity directly from generating companies and sells it to customers, and therefore has three separate contracts with High Voltage Grids CJSC, Settlement Center CJSC and Power System Operator CJSC (see Figure 2.5). Transmission remains in state ownership: the state-owned High Voltage Grids CJSC is paid for electricity transmission according to the tariffs adopted by the PSRC.

However, this exclusive right, previously granted to ENA for five years, recently expired. Under PSRC Decision 20A of 10 February 2016, ENA needs to enable other holders of trading rights to access the distribution network if this is technically feasible.

The natural gas sector remains an integrated and regulated utility, which is now fully owned by the Russian Federation's state-owned gas monopoly Gazprom. The Armenian government used its remaining shares in the gas sector, namely in the company ArmRosGazprom and Combined Cycle Power Plant (CCGT) unit No. 5 at the Hrazdan thermal power plant (TPP), as part of a debt settlement with Gazprom in January 2014. After becoming a 100% subsidiary of Gazprom, ArmRosGazprom changed its name to Gazprom-Armenia.

No unbundling or opening of the natural gas market is planned (IEA, 2015). Diesel and gasoline markets are not regulated. Armenia does not have its own refineries. Five or six private entities import diesel and gasoline to Armenia.

Energy pricing policy

The Public Services Regulatory Commission (PSRC) of Armenia regulates producer, consumer as well as transmission and distribution prices for natural gas and electricity. For gas, this arrangement is a way to mitigate risk from Armenia's heavy reliance on imports from the Russian Federation and also from Iran.

Natural gas

Consumer prices for natural gas are set higher than import prices. Large consumers pay less than smaller ones, reflecting Armenia's commitment to abandon subsidies of natural gas consumption (GoA, 2006).[2] Further research is needed to evaluate how much consumers still benefit from the relatively low price of gas imported from the Russian Federation and to what extent the producer and consumer price differential is adequate. Low prices of gas imports and low tariffs for increased consumption may be acting as a disincentive for consumers to adopt energy-saving practices.

Armenia's import of natural gas from the Russian Federation is now channelled through the sale of gas from Gazprom to its subsidiary, formerly called ArmRosGazprom. The company changed its name to Gazprom-Armenia after the Armenian government, as noted above, transferred its remaining 20% stake to Gazprom, as part of a debt settlement, in January 2014. As of 1 April 2013, under the "Procedure for establishing the prices of natural gas for delivery to Armenia", an agreement between the two governments, the Russian Federation undertook not to charge a 30% customs duty on the export of natural gas to Armenia. The import price was cut from USD 270 to USD 189 per 1 000 m^3, and further reduced to USD 165 per 1 000 m^3 in September 2015 (IEA, 2015). Gas prices were further reduced to USD 150 per 1 000 m^3 in April 2016 (PanARMENIANet, 2016). However, the existence and the extent of the potential "supranational" subsidy scheme needs to be assessed in the context of the opportunity cost to Gazprom. The subsequent analysis discusses how to select the benchmarks used in calculating the price-gap-based estimate for gas subsidies in Armenia.

Increases in electricity prices (see next section) have facilitated the expansion of the natural gas network, and, where possible, users have switched to gas for heating and cooking (Sargsyan et al., 2006). Natural gas is relatively affordable, but the government provides support for low-income families and certain social groups, such as Armenian border communities, for the use of gas.

Compressed natural gas[3] is an important transport fuel in Armenia, but further research is needed to shed light on price levels and price formation mechanisms.

Electricity

Armenia's electricity sector is a well-known example of a drastic tariff reform after the collapse of the Soviet Union and the energy crisis of the early 1990s. In late 1996, the government of Armenia (with international donor assistance) took measures to impress upon customers the link between service quality and payment of bills. Electricity tariffs for industrial, commercial and household customers were set at equal levels, beginning a process of tariff rebalancing and removal of cross-subsidies. Armenia embarked on a path towards privatisation of the electricity sector in 1997, selling several small hydropower generation assets. The biggest source of economic losses was the distribution company, the entity that oversaw the final point of service delivery and payment. Resolute efforts to privatise the distribution company began in 1998. An independent regulator, the Public Services Regulatory Commission (previously known as the Armenian Energy Regulatory Commission, AERC) was set up. The Law on the Regulatory Body for Public Services later expanded its authority to other sectors, including water and sewage, and telecommunications. With extensive support from international donors, the government of Armenia began tackling the sources of the electricity sector's two most significant problems: commercial losses and nonpayment.

Reinstallation of meters[4] to reduce losses and improve collection efficiency, and basing electricity tariff on the cost-reflective tariff principle, has brought efficiency gains, as users have invested in more energy-efficient technologies. However, to cushion the new increases in electricity prices, in August 2015, the tariffs for vulnerable groups were set at a below-market level, and the government of Armenia started compensating ENA for the losses via direct budget transfers (see more below and in Table 2.A1.1 on Armenia).

At present, consumer prices are higher or lower for end-consumer groups with lower or higher voltage connections, respectively. Household consumers pay the highest price. This price structure reflects the increasing cost of distribution at lower voltages (due to losses). Thus, there are no cross-subsidies from industrial to household consumers in Armenia, unlike in several other countries of the EU Eastern Partnership (EaP) and Central Asia.

Prices for electricity producers are set individually. The thermal power generators obtain the highest prices[5] (+/- 40 AMD/kWh, in 2014). Large hydro and nuclear have the lowest tariffs (+/- 10 AMD/kWh) and small hydro tariffs lie in the mid-range (+/- 22 AMD/kWh). Price dynamics are not consistent across producers. For instance, the producer tariff of International Energy Corporation (IEC Hydro) increased by 21% from 2014 to 2015, while the tariff for the Vorotan hydropower plant (HPP) was reduced by 4% over the same period. The Yerevan combined-cycle gas turbine plant (CCGT) saw its tariff increase by 77% from 2013 to 2015, while the tariff for Hrazdan TPP was increased by only 23% over the same period. ENA purchases electricity from each producer at its individual tariff and averages out the costs. Figure 2.6 illustrates the variations in producer tariffs for different plants (for numerical values, see Annex 2.A2). This way, the bundling of the low-cost hydro power and the high-cost thermal power allows the suppression of the average electricity price for generation and consequently for consumers.

Figure 2.6. **Average annual tariff by electricity producers in Armenia, 2011-15, AMD/kWh**

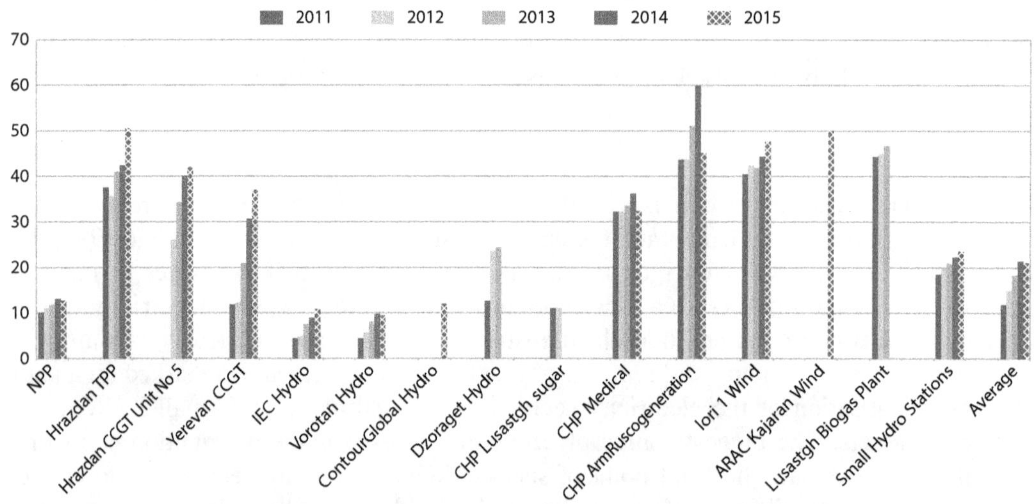

Source: Authors' compilation based on PSRC.

This arrangement also enables cross-subsidies for wind and biomass power plants as well as to ArmRosCogeneration, Armenia's only and partially functioning co-generated heat and power (CHP) plant supplying heat to household consumers.[6] For instance, in 2014, average producer electricity tariff for ArmRosCogeneration was AMD 60.1/kWh, while the maximum consumer tariff was AMD 41.85/kWh (since 1 August 2014, for 0.38 kV voltage-fed consumers, including households, daytime tariff).

Further assessment of transmission and distribution costs is needed to evaluate whether consumer prices are sufficient to cover the cost of production at Armenia's high-cost facilities or if they receive a portion of low-cost producers' margin. Given the very low producer tariff for large hydropower plants in Armenia, it is possible that the producer tariff is structured in a way that uses the potential natural resource rent in the hydropower sector to minimise the average price for consumers. Such analysis, however, is beyond the scope of this report.

Petroleum products

Gasoline and diesel prices in Armenia are not regulated. However, the State Commission for the Protection of Economic Competition monitors gasoline and diesel prices to ensure there is no cartel pricing or excessive profits in any market segment. According to the *Deutsche Gesellschaft für Internationale Zusammenarbeit* or GIZ (2015), Armenia's gasoline and diesel prices at the pump were USD 1.25 and 1.15 per litre respectively in mid-November 2014. This was above the "green" benchmark (US price levels), placing the country in the category where fuel prices are taxed rather than subsidised (see next section for a discussion of energy taxation). At the same time, petroleum products are not the main engine fuel in Armenia. As explained above, compressed natural gas (CNG) accounted for 70% of the fuel used in road transport in 2014.

Table 2.3. **Price policies for different energy carriers in Armenia**

Energy carrier	Pricing policy	Price categories	Price levels
Natural gas	Regulated "cost plus" pricing for natural gas. Further research is required on the pricing of compressed natural gas.	Import (producer) prices determined by a bilateral agreement with the Russian Federation. Differentiated pricing between consumption <10 000 m³/month (including households) and consumption ≥10 000 m³/month (mainly heavy industry).	Import price of USD 189 per 1 000 m³ from 2013 to 2015. In December 2015, this was revised to USD 165 per 1 000 m³ and in April 2016, cut to USD 150 per 1 000 m³. Household and consumers <10 000 m³/month: price fixed at AMD 156 000 per 1 000 m³ including VAT since 2013 (USD 326.5 at the yearly average exchange rate for 2015). From 1 January 2017, prices revised to AMD 139 000 per 1 000 m³. Consumers with consumption ≥1 000 m³/month: (large consumers) prices have been fixed at USD 276.98 per 1 000 m³ including VAT since 2013 (AMD 0.13 mln at the yearly average exchange rate for 2015). As of 1 January 2017, prices were revised to USD 242.1 per 1 000 m³ and USD 212 per 1 000 m³ for canned food, beverages, dairy products.
Electricity	Regulated "cost-plus" pricing.	Producer prices consist of power and capacity components, each differentiated by producer. Feed-in tariff system for renewable energy (excluding large hydro). Consumer prices differentiated by day and night, consumer groups differentiated by power supply voltage and households.	Average 2015 producer prices ranged from AMD 9.4 to AMD 50.48 per kWh, including VAT. Consumer prices as of 1 August 2016 ranged from AMD 30.7 (night tariff, 110 kV voltage) to AMD 46.2 (day tariffs, 0.38 kV voltage) per kWh, including VAT. Starting on 1 February 2017, consumer prices (day tariffs, 0.38 kV voltage) were further revised and set at AMD 44.98 per kWh.
Liquid petroleum products	Not regulated	Not regulated.	Not regulated. Pump prices of USD 1.15 and1.25 per litre for diesel and gasoline, respectively, in November 2014 (GIZ, 2015).

Source: Authors' compilation based on IEA (2015), MENR (2015), PSRC (2015a).

Taxation policy

The fiscal system of Armenia relies on seven principal taxes: the value added tax (VAT), profit tax, income tax, property tax, land tax, excise and the so-called simplified tax for small businesses. The VAT is fixed at 20% for all products (taxable turnover of goods and services), including energy, with the exception of imported diesel (see below).

Table 2.4 outlines the main elements of taxation in the energy sector, broken down by activity. The country's limited resource endowment provides a fair explanation for the absence of taxes aimed at rent capture (e.g. royalties or special profit tax). For large hydro, the only sector where significant rents can be expected, rent accumulation by producers is limited by low tariffs.

Table 2.4. **Taxation of energy in Armenia**

Subject to taxation	Baseline tax system: VAT, profit tax, property tax, land tax, simplified tax	Excise tax
Gazprom-Armenia as gas importer and consumers of gas	Applicable as appropriate	Exempt from excise tax on imported natural gas
Firms filling in vehicles with CNG	Applicable as appropriate	Excise tax will be levied from May 2016 at the rate of AMD 8 330 per 1 000 m^3
Importers and consumers of hydrocarbon products	All fuels subject to VAT at 20%, with the exception of diesel	2016 excise rates are: • for gasoline: AMD 25 000 per tonne[a] • for diesel: 10%, but not less than AMD 35 000 per 1 tonne • for liquefied petroleum gas (LPG): AMD 1 000 per 1 tonne

Note: a. If the sum of the excise tax set for 1 tonne of gasoline and the VAT calculated according to the legislation is less than AMD 120 000, the excise tax will be added to the amount, so that the sum of the excise tax and the VAT for 1 tonne of petrol equals AMD 120 000.

Source: Authors' compilation based on Ministry of Finance (MoF) Tax Law (1997) and MoF Excise Tax (2000).

Gasoline, petroleum products and petroleum gases are the most heavily taxed fuels and are subject to both VAT and excise tax.

The only fuel exempt from VAT is diesel. At the same time, diesel fuel is subject to an excise tax at the rate of 10%, but not less than AMD 35 000 per 1 tonne. Diesel fuel is widely used in agriculture and some industries, including by small and medium-sized enterprises (SMEs). But exemption of diesel from VAT may distort energy consumers' choices and confer a potential subsidy, or foregone government revenue, according to the OECD methodology (OECD, 2013). The National Assembly is planning to eliminate the VAT exemption for diesel as a fuel under the new Tax Code effective from 2018, however, in order to mitigate the impact of increased diesel price for agriculture, excise tax will be reduced from the current AMD 35 000 per 1 tonne to AMD 13 000 per tonne.

While, as noted above, the VAT rate is flat for all products (set at 20%), excise tax rates vary by fuel (see Table 2.4). Two fuels are exempt from excise tax: natural gas, the staple feedstock of Armenia's electricity sector, and compressed natural gas (CNG). As of May 2016, excise tax will also be levied on CNG, an important transport fuel in Armenia. To this end, the legislation on excise tax was amended in October 2015. Excise tax on CNG will be paid by firms that serve vehicles by filling engines with CNG, at a rate of AMD 8 330 per 1 000 m^3.

The exemption of imported natural gas from the excise tax and the differentiated excise rate on other fuels may influence consumer choices. It is necessary to further analyse market structure and price formation to assess whether excise rate-setting can create distortions in the market and whether these rates sufficiently reflect environmental and other externalities.

Greenhouse gas emissions and climate policy

Armenia's energy-related emissions of carbon dioxide totalled 5.3 Mt in 2012, a quarter of the country's emissions in 1990. This dramatic decrease can be attributed to reduced energy consumption and changes in the energy mix (see the sections on energy supply and demand above) after the collapse of the Soviet Union, and policy reforms, including increases in energy tariffs. The power generation sector accounts for 31% of energy-related CO_2 emissions, followed by transport (23%), households (20%), manufacturing (12%), agriculture (8%) and commercial and other services (6%).

Armenia ratified the Kyoto Protocol in 2002 as a non-Annex I Party and thus did not have quantitative commitments for GHG emissions reduction while the Protocol was in force. Armenia nevertheless supports the objective of the UN Framework Convention on Climate Change (UNFCCC). Activities to slow GHG emissions are in line with the country's economic, energy and environmental objectives.

In recent years, Armenia has adopted a number of laws and regulations and drawn up national and sectoral programmes to encourage sustainable and low-carbon development. The framework documents in this domain include the Intended Nationally Determined Contributions of the Republic of Armenia under the UNFCCC (INDC, adopted in 2015), the National Energy Security Concept (adopted in 2013), the Investment Plan for the Scaling-up of Renewable Energy Programme (SREP, adopted in 2014), Energy Security Action Plan (adopted in 2014) and Armenia Least Cost Energy Development Plan (2015).

The key legal acts include:

- Law "On Atmospheric Air Protection" (1994, amended in 2008 and 2011)
- Law "On Energy" (2001, amended in 2014, new amendments have been included in the agenda of the National Assembly)
- Law "On Energy Efficiency and Renewable Energy" (2004, amended in 2011, proposals for new amendments are included in the agenda of the National Assembly)
- Law "On Waste" (2004)
- Forest Code of Republic of Armenia (2005).

Armenia plans further measures to mitigate climate change. Foremost of these is the construction of a new nuclear power plant (600 MW in 2026). Other key mitigation actions that are in effect, planned or are ongoing (see Annex 2.A4 for more information) include:

- Improving energy efficiency of Municipal Heat Supply (implemented, UNDP-GEF "Improving Energy Efficiency of Municipal Heating and Hot Water Supply" Project, Global Environmental Fund, or GEF grant, World Bank grant, local budgets)
- Energy Efficiency Project (World Bank, R2E2 Fund, GEF grant for matching government of Armenia resources and on-lending through revolving fund R2E2)
- Improving energy efficiency in buildings (Ministry of Nature Protection, Ministry of Urban Development, UNDP, UNDP-GEF "Improving energy efficiency in buildings" Project, GEF grant)
- Green Urban lighting (UNDP-GEF Green Urban Lighting Project, GEF grant, government of Armenia, local authorities)
- Yerevan Street Lighting Project (EBRD, Ministry of Nature Protection, Yerevan Municipality, EBRD's sovereign loan)

- Green for Growth Fund (loan agreement to strengthen Republic of Armenia bank lending capacity to support energy efficiency projects at the level of small and medium enterprises)
- The European Commission's Project "Supporting participation of Eastern Partnership and Central Asian Cities in the Covenant of Mayors".

National definition and discussion of energy subsidies

Armenia's legislation does not provide any extensive national definition of subsidies. A rudimentary interpretation of Decree No. 1937-N (GoA, 2003), however, provides the following example of how subsidies have been codified in the national legislation:

> "Compensation of the damage (or part of it) suffered by the company due to the price for production, export, import, works and services being lower than the minimum profitable price as a result of state assignment and/or price determination… A subsidy shall not be issued for the purchase of capital assets or increase in equity, and as an increment on company revenue generated by its current activities."

Addressing agriculture support in the context of the World Trade Organization (WTO) membership, Decree No. 2310-N (GoA, 2005) defines a subsidy as a "free budget transfer to economic actors", and refers to mechanisms used in other countries, such as fixed producer prices, price support through import quotas and tolls, land processing support and support for the acquisition of means for production.

With the caveat that the information available at present is incomplete, it appears that, in practice, regulatory activities in Armenia use the notion of subsidy only with respect to its simplest form: direct transfers (Figure 2.7). At the same time, in the energy sector, the notions of "state support" and "state aid" are not used with any more clarity.

Figure 2.7. **What does Armenia include in the national definition of subsidy?**

Covered by the national definitions of both "subsidy" and "state support"

Covered only by the national definition of "state support"

Not included in the national definition of either "subsidy" or "state support"

Direct budget transfers	Tax expenditures	Induced transfers	Transfer of risk to government	References
				Decree No. 1937-N, 2003; Decree No. 2310-N, 2005

The government of Armenia has not published its own estimates of fossil-fuel subsidies. There are two relevant studies focusing on Armenia: *Implementing Energy Subsidy Reforms: Evidence from Developing Countries*, by the World Bank (Vagliasindi, 2013), and a review of public expenditures by the World Bank (2014b).

The INOGATE Report, *A Review of Energy Tariffs in INOGATE Partner Countries* (June 2015), also hypothesises about a potential implicit subsidy provided to gas for the electricity swap with Iran, but the findings needs to be investigated and confirmed (investigation into this cross-border subsidy is beyond the scope of this study).

Table 2.5 summarises the main findings of the previous research and the knowledge frontier by subsidy type. These serve as a point of departure for subsequent analysis.

Table 2.5. **Subsidy overview**

Energy subsidy	Key findings
Direct budget transfer of funds and liabilities	• Included in national subsidy definitions (except liabilities) • Vulnerable groups pay lower tariffs and utilities receive compensation for providing energy to them at a loss; the list of eligible households is approved by the government, which keeps a record of these allocations on a monthly basis
Tax expenditures (tax revenue foregone)	• Not included in national subsidy definition • No tax expenditure published by the government of Armenia • Diesel fuel is exempt from VAT, and natural gas is exempt from the excise tax • The government of Armenia decided to phase out exemption of CNG from excise tax as of 1 May 2016
Induced transfers (income or price support provided to producers or consumers through various regulations)	• Not included in the national subsidy definition • No price-gap estimates available from IEA or other international sources
Transfer of risk to government	• Not included in the national subsidy definition • No significant discussion of the issue

Government support for fossil fuels

Energy subsidies are limited compared with some peer countries in the EaP and Central Asia region. Armenia does not pursue a pro-subsidy policy, in relation to either consumption or production. However, a combination of the bottom-up approach to subsidy identification and price-gap analysis has revealed several fossil-fuel subsidies.

Price-gap estimates of consumer subsidies

The International Energy Agency (IEA) provides price-gap estimates of subsidies to end consumers of fossil fuels and electricity in most countries, but no such estimates exist for Armenia. The main reason is that there are no such subsidies in Armenia, as confirmed by the calculations in this study. However, for the sake of consistency, we provide a brief discussion of the possible application of the price-gap approach to natural gas pricing in Armenia. This approach follows exactly the same logic as in the analysis of the other EaP countries.

Price gap = Reference price – Net tariff

Subsidy = Price gap × Units consumed

For Armenia, as a net importer, the reference price is the price of gas imports (Table 2.6). The weighted average domestic price of gas in Armenia is higher than this reference price (hence the negative values), which means that there is no subsidy for domestic consumption of gas.

However, the question of gas taxation and its adequacy is beyond the reach of the price-gap approach and is better answered by the bottom-up inventory of subsidies discussed below.

Table 2.6. **Price-gap estimates of consumer subsidies in the gas sector of Armenia in 2015 (nominal 2015 million USD)**

Consumer groups	Share	Net tariff per 1 000 m³	Gross tariff per 1 000 m³	bcm	Purchase cost per 1 000 m³	Price gap per 1 000 m³	Subsidy USD
Residential	37%	272	326	0.927129	165	-107	-99
Industry and transport	63%	231	277	1.594481	165	-66	-105
Total				**2.52161**			**0**
Weighted average			**295**			**-81**	

Source: Authors' estimates based on World Bank (2015), PSRC (2015), Rate.Am (2015).

Bottom-up inventory of government support for fossil fuels

Tables 2.7a and 2.7b list the six subsidies to fossil fuels identified in Armenia, while Annex 2.A1 provides more detailed descriptions of each of the schemes. Table 2.8 explains the methodology used for the quantification of each of the subsidies.

Table 2.7a. **Estimates of major fossil-fuel subsidies in Armenia, AMD million**

Subsidy	Type of subsidy	2011	2012	2013	2014	2015
Compensation to households for electricity price increases	Consumer subsidy, direct budget transfer	n.a.	n.a.	n.a.	n.a.	3 450[a]
Compensation of the natural gas fee to low-income families	Consumer subsidy, direct budget transfer	544	516	1 053	646	n.a.
Social support for border communities	Consumer subsidy, direct budget transfer	n.a.	n.a.	n.a.	n.a.	928
Exemption of diesel fuel from VAT	Consumer subsidy, government revenue foregone	8 932	10 919	10 585	10 932	7 613
Exemption of imported natural gas from excise tax[b]	Consumer subsidy, government revenue foregone	1 448	1 719	1 653	1 716	1 660
Exemption of compressed natural gas from excise tax [b]	Consumer subsidy, government revenue foregone	3 018	3 482	3 790	4 013	4 037
Total for quantified fossil-fuel subsidies		**13 943**	**16 636**	**17 081**	**17 306**	**17 688**

Notes: a. Estimates are for the months of August to December 2015.

b. Potential for double-counting exists here, because excise tax can only be levied once, and cannot be levied both on imported gas and the portion of imported gas used as CNG in vehicles. However, excise tax rates vary, depending on products and their uses. The excise tax benchmark rate for imported natural gas in these calculations is much lower than the rate that will apply to CNG in Armenia from 1 May 2016. OECD bottom-up inventories normally recognise the possibility of double-counting and do not seek to eliminate it.

Source: Authors' compilations and calculations based on data provided by the MENR and Armstat (2011, 2012, 2013, 2014, 2015b).

Table 2.7b. **Estimates of major fossil-fuel subsidies in Armenia, USD million**

Subsidy	Type of subsidy	2011	2012	2013	2014	2015
Compensation to households for electricity price increases	Consumer subsidy, direct budget transfer	n.a.	n.a.	n.a.	n.a.	7.22[a]
Compensation of the natural gas fee to low-income families	Consumer subsidy, direct budget transfer	1.46	1.28	2.57	1.55	n.a.
Social support for border communities	Consumer subsidy, direct budget transfer	n.a.	n.a.	n.a.	n.a.	1.94
Exemption of diesel fuel from VAT	Consumer subsidy, government revenue foregone	23.98	27.18	25.85	26.29	15.93
Exemption of imported natural gas from excise tax [b]	Consumer subsidy, government revenue foregone	3.89	4.28	4.04	4.13	3.47
Exemption of compressed natural gas from excise tax[b]	Consumer subsidy, government revenue foregone	8.10	8.67	9.25	9.65	8.45
Total for quantified fossil-fuel subsidies		**37**	**41**	**42**	**42**	**37**

Notes: a. Estimates are for the months of August to December 2015.

b. Potential for double-counting exists here, because excise tax can only be levied once, and cannot be levied both on imported gas and the portion of imported gas used as CNG in vehicles. However, excise tax rates vary, depending on products and their uses. The excise tax benchmark rate for imported natural gas in these calculations is much lower than the rate that will apply to CNG in Armenia from 1 May 2016. OECD bottom-up inventories normally recognise the possibility of double-counting and do not seek to eliminate it.

Source: Authors' compilations and calculations based on data provided by the MENR and Armstat (2011, 2012, 2013, 2014, 2015b).

Table 2.8. **Approaches used to quantify fossil-fuel subsidies in Armenia**

Subsidy scheme	Quantification method
Compensation to households for electricity price increases	Subsidy estimate taken at face value from government sources (Ministry of Energy and Natural Resources of the Republic of Armenia)
Compensation of the natural gas fee to low-income families	Subsidy estimate taken at face value from government sources (Ministry of Energy and Natural Resources of the Republic of Armenia)
Social support for border communities	Subsidy estimate taken at face value from government sources (Ministry of Territorial Administration and Emergency Situations)
Exemption of diesel fuel from VAT	Authors' calculations: application of the standard VAT rate (20%) to the value of imported diesel
Exemption of imported natural gas from excise tax[a]	Authors' calculations: application of the relevant excise rate (AMD 1 000 per tonne, gas conversion rate used is 0.7kg per m^3) to the value of imported natural gas
Exemption of compressed natural gas from excise tax[a]	Authors' calculations: retrospective application of the rate effective from 1 May 2016 (AMD 8 330 per 1 000 m^3) to the volumes of CNG consumed in previous years

Note: a. Potential for double-counting exists here, because excise tax can only be levied once, and cannot be levied both on imported gas and the portion of imported gas used as CNG in vehicles. However, excise tax rates vary, depending on products and their uses. The excise tax benchmark rate for imported natural gas in these calculations is much lower than the rate that will apply to CNG in Armenia from 1 May 2016. OECD bottom-up inventories normally recognise the possibility of double-counting and do not seek to eliminate it.

Source: Authors' summary.

Very broadly, the subsidies belong to two categories: support for vulnerable groups in the form of direct budget transfers (but provided to the utilities selling at a loss rather than to consumers themselves), and government revenue foregone from under-taxing fuels. The beneficiaries of all these subsidies are consumers.

The government of Armenia implements three subsidy schemes to support vulnerable groups: compensation for electricity price increases (since August 2015, to households consuming 250 kWh of electricity per month and to small businesses consuming up to 500 kWh per month), partial compensation of natural gas fees to low-income households, and support for border communities.

In all cases, the subsidy is targeted to the subscribers listed and approved by the responsible government agencies. More than one-fifth of Armenia's population lives below the poverty line, according to official data (IMF, 2011). Unofficial estimates range far higher. Increases in prices for electricity and natural gas for households, along with the expected chain effect in raising the costs of food and essential durable goods, risk increasing dissatisfaction with the government. Even though subsidies support consumption of energy, it can be argued that these three support schemes are primarily welfare policies, rather than measures promoting energy use.

In 2015, the government compensated households for the electricity price increase through direct budget transfers. It has discontinued such subsidies with the downward revision of electricity tariff from August 2016, on account of the declining imported gas prices, which, in turn, reduced the impact on consumers.

The government forgoes revenue by under-taxing certain fossil fuels: an exemption for imported diesel (from VAT with the flat rate of 20% for all products), and for imported natural gas as well as for compressed natural gas (from excise tax applicable at different rates to other fuels).

Armenia's exemption of diesel from VAT is by far its largest fossil-fuel subsidy, at roughly USD 25 mln per year in the period observed. Diesel is the main fuel used in rural areas, and the exemption is viewed as a way of supporting rural development. Exemption of diesel from VAT is, however, partly compensated for by the higher excise tax imposed on diesel. However, under the new Tax Code applicable in 2018, elimination of the VAT exemption for diesel is under discussion. To mitigate the impact of the increased price of diesel for agriculture, the excise tax will be reduced from AMD 35 000 per tonne to AMD 13 000. Moreover, the VAT exemption does not appear to have created significant distortions in the transport fuel markets, given the dominance of CNG engines in the vehicle fleet.

Natural gas is used both as a feedstock in electricity, cooking and heating and as a transport fuel (as CNG). The excise tax exemption thus benefits all these uses. Armenia has already started to reform this fuel subsidy by introducing the tax on the most "lucrative" use of natural gas – as CNG, in vehicles. As of 1 May 2016, CNG will be subject to excise tax at the rate of AMD 8 330 per 1 000 m^3.

No producer subsidies or other forms of consumer subsidies have been identified in Armenia. At the same time, export-import arrangements with the Russian Federation and Iran, as well as preferential loans from multilateral development banks, may have broader implications for the end-price of fuels in Armenia and require further research, which is beyond the scope of this report.

The other export-import arrangement worth noting is with the Russian Federation. Both Armenia and the Russian Federation are members of the Eurasian Economic Union and the Customs Union. For this reason, the Russian Federation does not impose export duties on fuel sold to Armenia and Belarus. Nevertheless, natural gas tariffs for consumers in Armenia, though lower than in European countries, are considerably higher than in the neighboring countries. Gazprom-Armenia is also the largest taxpayer in Armenia.

The sales price to Armenia (on the border) is to a certain extent an internal issue for Gazprom, which exports gas from the Russian Federation to its 100%-owned subsidiary, Gazprom-Armenia. However, the Ministry of Energy regulates the price. In addition, the recent drop in the gas price on the border has had no impact on end consumers, so this may be considered an investment in own business rather than a subsidy.

The Armenian energy sector has traditionally benefited from the support of multilateral development banks. On 19 February 2016, for instance, the government announced that it would receive a USD 30 mln loan from the World Bank on preferential terms. The money will be provided to the state-owned Metsamor NPP and Yerevan TPP power-generating stations, so that they can repay short-term loans extended by Armenian commercial banks. The former minister of energy announced that the low-interest loan (at a rate of 1.5%) would be repaid over 30 years. Part of the financing gap in the system (AMD 22.4 bln or USD 45.2 mln), which had accrued as a result of ENA's nonpayment to Metsamor NPP and Yerevan TPP, was included in the new electricity tariffs endorsed on 1 August 2015 and is paid each month. The amount was expected to be fully paid to Metsamor NPP and Yerevan TPP by 31 July 2016 (Harutyunyan, 2016).

Government support for energy efficiency

This study did not identify any measures to increase energy efficiency in Armenia that could be classified as subsidies. However, several programmes to promote energy efficiency in Armenia have been supported by international donors, including the World Bank and the International Finance Corporation, Germany's KfW, the Global Environmental Facility, the European Bank for Reconstruction and Development and the Asian Development Bank. Several such programmes are being implemented or planned (see Annex 2.A4).

Government support for renewable energy

Armenia provides both purchase guarantees and feed-in tariffs for power generated by small HPPs, wind turbines, solar energy mini producers (PV) and biogas plants.

The Energy Law mandates that in the first 15 years of operation, 100% of electricity produced by new renewable energy systems must be purchased at tariff levels set by the PSRC. The Amendment to the Energy Law adopted in 2014, extending the Power Purchasing Agreement from renewable sources from 15 to 20 years, was intended to encourage renewable energy generation. This creates regulatory incentives for the development of wind, solar, geothermal and biomass technologies, with on-lending provided by local commercial banks in programmes supported by the World Bank, EBRD, UNDP/GEF and KfW.

However, tariffs for hydropower plants are much lower than residential tariffs and producer tariffs for thermal plants. The lower cost of hydropower generation helps reduce the average cost of electricity. In contrast, feed-in tariffs for wind and biogas are relatively high, and it can be argued that the feed-in tariff provides a subsidy in the form of an induced transfer to these two types of renewable energy sources (see Annex 2.A2). However, the role of wind and biogas in Armenia's total energy mix so far is limited.

The feed-in tariff for solar energy was introduced only in 2015. Solar energy producers are mainly autonomous (up to 150 kW) and generate energy mostly for their own needs. When these producers generate more electricity than they consume, they will sell this excess capacity to the grid and be paid a tariff of 50% of the rates PSRC sets for other consumer groups.

Annex 2.A1

Fossil-fuel subsidies in Armenia

Table 2.A1.1. **Compensation for electricity price increases**

Subsidy category	Consumer subsidy, direct budget transfer to Electric Networks of Armenia (ENA), since 1 August 2015
Stimulated activity	Consumption of electricity by low-income households that consume less than 250 kWh of electricity a month and small businesses consuming up to 500 kWh per month
Subsidy name	**Reimbursement of the cost of electricity supplied to households that consume less than 250 kWh of electricity per month and small businesses consuming up to 500 kWh per month**
Jurisdiction	National
Legislation/endorsing organisation	Ministry of Energy and Natural Resources of the Republic of Armenia
Policy objective(s) of subsidy	Partial compensation for electricity price increases for low-income households
End recipient(s) of subsidy	Households (604 000 out of 766 889 customers, or about 79%) that, on average, use 250 kWh of electricity, and small businesses consuming up to 500 kWh per month
Time period	From 1 August 2015 for one year (preliminary decision)
Background	The single electricity distribution company in Armenia, Electric Networks of Armenia (ENA), formally requested that the Public Services Regulatory Commission (PSRC) raise the price of electricity by 40% (AMD 17.08 including VAT for households). This prompted large-scale protests that blocked the main thoroughfare in the capital, Yerevan. The PSRC decided instead to raise the electricity tariff for households by AMD 6.93 per kilowatt hour (16.5%), taking effect on 1 August 2015. To compensate ENA for its losses selling electricity to poor households at this regulated tariff, the government provides budgetary transfers to the company on a monthly basis. The allocation comes from the state budget with the approval of the Ministry of Energy and Natural Resources, which calculates the monthly compensation amounts based on cost estimates from ENA. The cost of this scheme will be covered by the funds received from the privatisation of Vorotan Cascade Hydropower Plants.
Amount of subsidy conferred	August 2015: AMD 1 008.10 mln (USD 2.10 mln) September 2015: AMD 923.80 mln (USD 1.92 mln) October 2015: AMD 558.00 mln (USD 1.18 mln) November 2015: AMD 509.4 mln (USD 0.94 mln) December 2015: AMD 451.1 mln (USD 0.93 mln) Total (August-December 2015): AMD 3 450.4 mln (USD 7.07 mln)
Information sources	Data provided by the Ministry of Energy and Natural Resources of the Republic of Armenia

Table 2.A1.2. **Compensation for natural gas supplied to low-income families**

Subsidy category	Consumer subsidy, direct budget transfer to Gazprom-Armenia (formerly CJSC ArmRosGazprom)
Stimulated activity	Consumption of natural gas by low-income households
Subsidy name	**Partial compensation of the fees for natural gas supplied to low-income families**
Jurisdiction	National
Legislation/endorsing organisation	Government of the Republic of Armenia Decision 15 September 2011No. 1327-A About partial compensation of the natural gas fee supplied to low-income families and subject to payment to ArmRosGazProm CJSC (since 2015, the company has been renamed Gazprom-Armenia) RA Government decision: 29 December 2011, No. 1888-A RA Government decision: 31 March 2011, No. 335-N RA Government decision: 22 March 2012, No. 331-A RA Government decision: 14 June 2012, No. 743-A RA Government decision: 20 September 2012, No. 1186-A RA Government decision: 27 December 2012, No. 1651-A RA Government decision: 7 March 2013, No. 213-A RA Government decision: 6 June 2013, No. 574-A RA Government decision: 17 April 2014, No. 425-A
Policy objective(s) of subsidy	Mitigation measure to protect low-income households
End recipient(s) of subsidy	The list of low-income families is approved by the government through the Ministry of Labour and Social Affairs
Time period	2011-present Specific periods and amounts of the compensation are mentioned in each government decision
Background	One-fifth of Armenia's population lives below the poverty line, according to official data (IMF, 2011). Unofficial estimates range far higher. Low-income families are charged a reduced gas tariff. The list of households eligible for the reduced tariff is approved by the government. In recent years, low-income families in Armenia paid only AMD 100 per cubic metre of natural gas, while the full tariff was set at AMD 132 in 2012 and 2013, and raised to AMD 156 (USD 0.38) per cubic metre in 2014. The government compensates Gazprom-Armenia for the difference between the cost of gas and regulated tariffs for low-income families via direct budgetary transfers to the company on a monthly basis, The allocation comes from the state budget under approval of the Ministry of Energy and Natural Resources, which calculates the monthly compensation amounts based on cost estimates from Gazprom-Armenia.
Amount of subsidy conferred	2011: AMD 543.5 mln (USD 1.5 mln) 2012: AMD 516.0 mln (USD 1.3 mln) 2013: AMD 1 053.0 mln (USD 2.6 mln) 2014: AMD 646.2 mln (USD 1.6 mln) 2015: n.a. Total (2011-15): AMD 2758.7 mln (USD 6.9 mln)
Information source	Data provided by the Ministry of Energy and Natural Resources of the Republic of Armenia

Table 2.A1.3. **Social support for RA border communities**

Subsidy category	Consumer subsidy, direct budget transfer
Stimulated activity	Consumption of electricity and natural gas in border communities
Subsidy name	**Social support for households in RA border communities**
Jurisdiction	National
Legislation/endorsing organisation	RA Law 203-N adopted on 1 December 2014 on Social Support for Border Communities (in force from 1 January 2015 to 1 January 2018)

Table 2.A1.3. **Social support for RA border communities** *(continued)*

Policy objective(s) of subsidy	Social assistance
End recipient(s) of subsidy	Consumers in border communities
Time period	From 1 January 2015 to 31 December 2017
Background	Armenians in border communities are subject to military conflict on the border. The government's aim is to protect them from increases in electricity and natural gas prices. The Armenian government compensates subscribers resident on the border for at least 50% of electricity and natural gas fees. This helps reduce poverty in rural areas. The list of border community subscribers is approved by the Ministry of Labour and Social Affairs and the Ministry of Territorial Administration and Development.
Amount of subsidy conferred	2015: AMD 928 mln (USD 1.94 mln)
Information sources	Data provided by the Ministry of Territorial Administration and Development

Table 2.A1.4. **Exemption of diesel fuel from VAT**

Subsidy category	Consumer subsidy, government revenue foregone
Stimulated activity	Consumption of diesel in agriculture and other activities
Subsidy name	**Exemption of diesel fuel from VAT**
Jurisdiction	Reduced prices for households, agriculture, etc.
Legislation/endorsing organisation	Law on Value-Added Tax (LA-118 of 14 May 1997, amended 26 December 1997; LA-177 of 28 December 1998; LA-276 of 26 December 2000; LA-126 of 14 December 2001; LA-288 of 11 December 2002; LA-478-N of 27 November 2006; LA-189-N of 21 August 2008; LA-146-N of 26 December 2008; LA-246-N of 8 December 2010; LA-192-N of 22 December 2010; LA-208-N of 15 April 2011; LA-126-N of 6 December 2011; LA-334-Ն of 19 December 2012; LA-240-N of 12 November 2013; LA-111-N of 21 June 2014; LA-129-N of 7 May 2015; RA-41-N, etc.) Article 15. Import or sale of diesel fuel is exempt from VAT
Policy objective(s) of subsidy	Promotion of economic and food security, development of rural areas and agriculture
End recipient(s) of subsidy	All users of diesel
Time period	No specific period is mentioned in the law
Background	Imported diesel is exempted from VAT. For all other products, the VAT rate is a flat 20%. The value of the subsidy can be calculated by applying the 20% rate to the value of diesel imported in Armenia each year. Diesel is the main fuel used in agriculture, and this tax break is designed to alleviate poverty in rural areas and promote food security.
Amount of subsidy conferred	2011: AMD 8 932.4 mln (USD 23.98 mln) 2012: AMD 10 918.8 mln (USD 27.18 mln) 2013: AMD 10 585.1 mln (USD 25.85 mln) 2014: AMD 10 931.7 mln (USD 26.29 mln) 2015: AMD 7 612.6 mln (USD 15.93 mln) Total (2011-15): AMD 48 980.6 mln (USD 119.23 mln)
Information sources	Armstat (2015b), Data on Foreign Trade of the Republic of Armenia for 2015. www.armstat.am/file/article/f._t-2015-10-nish-5.pdf Armstat (2014). Data on Foreign Trade of the Republic of Armenia for 2014. www.armstat.am/file/article/ft_8nish_2015_5.pdf Armstat (2013). Data on Foreign Trade of the Republic of Armenia for 2013. www.armstat.am/file/article/ft_8nish_2014_5.pdf Armstat (2012). Data on Foreign Trade of the Republic of Armenia for 2012. www.armstat.am/file/article/ft_8nish_2013_5.pdf Armstat (2011). Data on Foreign Trade of the Republic of Armenia for 2011. www.armstat.am/file/article/ft_8nish_12_5.pdf

Table 2.A1.5. **Exemption of imported natural gas from excise tax**

Subsidy category	Consumer subsidy, government revenue foregone
Stimulated activity	Consumption of imported natural gas through reduced prices for households, energy generation, industry, transport and other activities
Subsidy name	**Exemption of imported natural gas from excise tax**
Jurisdiction	National
Legislation/endorsing organisation	Law on Excise Tax (LA-79 of 7 July 2000, amended 14 December 2001; LA-280, 25 December 2003; LA-64-N, 26 December 2008; LA-28-N, 7 October 2010; LA-126-N, 19 December 2012; LA-250-N, 22 May 2014; LA-24-N, 29 October 2015; LA-116-N, etc.) Article 5. Excise Tax Rates 1. The following excise tax rates shall be established: Product codes by ATG AA: 2 711 (excluding 2 711 11 and 2 711 21), name of the product group: oil gases and other gas-like hydrocarbons (except for natural gas), Taxable base unit: 1 tonne; rate of excise tax (AMD): 1 000
Policy objective(s) of subsidy	Reduction of end-price of natural gas for households, electricity generation, industry, transport and other consumers
End recipient(s) of subsidy	Practically all consumer groups
Time period	From Soviet times to present. The 2000 Law on Excise Tax does not set any time limitations on the exemption.
Background	Natural gas is used across all end-use sectors and as feedstock for electricity generation, accounting for about 62% of Armenia's total final energy consumption in 2014. All natural gas is imported. Given the constant increases in electricity prices, many households have also switched to natural gas for heating and cooking. Recent years have seen an unprecedented expansion of natural gas distribution networks, and the gasification rate reached 95% in 2015. The value of the subsidy can be calculated by applying the benchmark rate to the volume of natural gas imported to Armenia each year. The benchmark rate is set at AMD 1 000 per tonne. The volume of imported natural gas is normally reported in cubic metres, and the conversion is based on the average density of natural gas at 0.7 kg per cubic metre.
Amount of subsidy conferred	2011: AMD 1 448.37 mln (USD 3.89 mln) 2012: AMD 1 718.85 mln (USD 4.28 mln) 2013: AMD 1 652.74 mln (USD 4.04 mln) 2014: AMD 1 715.63 mln (USD 4.13 mln) 2015: AMD 1 660.26 mln (USD 3.47 mln) Total (2011-15): AMD 8 195.85 mln (USD 19.80 mln)
Information sources	PSRC (2015c), Report on key indicators of the gas sector in 2015. www.psrc.am/images/docs/reports/gas/2015/4-er/gaz-xoranard-tari.pdf PSRC (2014), Report on key indicators of the gas sector in 2014. www.psrc.am/images/docs/reports/gas/21401.pdf PSRC (2013), Report on key indicators of the gas sector in 2013. www.psrc.am/docs/reports/gas/Himnakan_bnutagir_4_2013.pdf PSRC (2012), Report on key indicators of the gas sector in 2012. www.psrc.am/docs/reports/gas/Himnakan_bnudagir_4_2012.pdf PSRC (2011), Report on key indicators of the gas sector in 2011. www.psrc.am/docs/reports/gas/Himnakan_bnudagir_4_2011.pdf

Table 2.A1.6. **Exemption of compressed natural gas from excise tax**

Subsidy Category	Consumer subsidy, government revenue foregone
Stimulated Activity	Use of compressed natural gas (CNG) in vehicles
Subsidy name	**Exemption of compressed natural gas from excise tax**
Jurisdiction	National
Legislation/endorsing organisation	Law on Excise Tax (LA-79 of 7 July 2000, amended 14 December 2001; LA-280, 25 December 2003; LA-64-N, 26 December 2008; LA-28-N, 7 October 2010; LA-126-N, 19 December 2012; LA-250-N, 22 May 2014; LA-24-N, 29 October 2015; LA-116-N). The latter amended Article 5 of the law – Excise Tax Rates with the following (excise tax rates shall be established): Product codes by ATG AA: 2711 21; name of the product group: Compressed Natural Gas; taxable base unit: 1 000 m³; rate of excise tax (AMD): 8 330. Excise tax shall be paid by CNG filling activity-implementing legal and physical persons (including branches and representatives of foreign legal entities registered in the RA)
Policy objective(s) of subsidy	Use of CNG in vehicles as a cleaner and cheaper fuel, making possible lower public transport fees and road transport development
End recipient(s) of subsidy	Users of vehicles converted to CNG, especially public transport, that is, the majority of Armenia's population
Time period	From introduction of the Excise Tax Law in 2000 (possibly earlier) to 1 May 2016
Background	Recent years have seen an unprecedented expansion of the natural gas distribution system, including an expanded network of CNG filling stations. CNG is the dominant transport fuel in Armenia, accounting for 70% of all fuels used in transport in 2014. CNG is 2.5 times cheaper than gasoline. CNG is also promoted as a cleaner fuel and the main fuel used in public transport. The volumes of CNG consumed in Armenia's transport sector are regularly reported. The value of the subsidy was calculated by applying to them, retrospectively, the rate that will be applicable from 1 May 2016 (AMD 8 330 per 1 000 m³).
Amount of subsidy conferred	2011: AMD 3 018.46 mln (USD 8.10 mln) 2012: AMD 3 481.94 mln (USD 8.67 mln) 2013: AMD 3 789.82 mln (USD 9.25 mln) 2014: AMD 4 012.56 mln (USD 9.65 mln) 2015: AMD 4 036.72 mln (USD 8.45 mln) Total (2011-15): AMD 18 339.49 mln (USD 44.12 mln)
Information sources	PSRC (2015c), Report on key indicators of the gas sector in 2015. www.psrc.am/images/docs/reports/gas/2015/4-er/gaz-xoranard-tari.pdf PSRC (2014), Report on key indicators of the gas sector in 2014. www.psrc.am/images/docs/reports/gas/21401.pdf PSRC (2013), Report on key indicators of the gas sector in 2013. www.psrc.am/docs/reports/gas/Himnakan_bnutagir_4_2013.pdf PSRC (2012), Report on key indicators of the gas sector in 2012. www.psrc.am/docs/reports/gas/Himnakan_bnudagir_4_2012.pdf PSRC (2011), Report on key indicators of the gas sector in 2011. www.psrc.am/docs/reports/gas/Himnakan_bnudagir_4_2011.pdf

Annex 2.A2

Government support for renewable energy

Table 2.A2.1. **Producer tariffs for renewables in comparison with those for conventional power sources**

Feed-in tariffs for power producers in Armenia for the period 1 July 2015-1 July 2016 were adopted under PSRC Decision No. 157 N of 29 May 2015.

	Feed-in tariffs for renewables in Armenia for 2011-15 (AMD, VAT included)					
Year	Average residential electricity tariff	Small hydropower plants (constructed on natural water flows)	Small hydropower plants (constructed on irrigation systems)	Small hydropower plants (constructed on potable water aqueducts)	Wind power plants	Power plants that use biomass as primary energy
2011	26.667	23.14	15.42	10.28	40.51	44.31
2012	26.667	23.46	15.64	10.43	42.41	44.94
2013	34.667	24.34	16.23	10.82	41.95	46.63
2014	38.517	25.27	16.85	11.23	44.41	48.41
1 July 2015	38.517	25.41	16.93	11.29	45.61	48.65
1 July 2016	45.45	28.36	18.90	12.60	50.91	50.91
1 July 2017	41.647	28.504	18.998	12.667	51.174	51.174 (including for solar power plants)

Source: PSRC (2015b).

Tariffs for power producers in Armenia are adopted individually by PSRC respective Decisions.

Table 2.A2.2. **Average tariffs for conventional power sources in Armenia for 2011-15 (AMD, VAT included)**

Year	NPP	TPP	Large hydro	CHP
2011	10.07	25.33	4.75	34.69
2012	10.99	26.09	6.01	38.24
2013	11.81	31.70	8.63	42.11
2014	13.03	37.65	9.50	46.72
2015	12.76	42.13	10.88	37.74
2016 (January-March)	12.17	44.48	16.30	42.90

Source: PSRC (2015b).

Annex 2.A3

National methodology underlying tariffs for electricity and natural gas

The Public Services Regulatory Commission (PSRC) of Armenia establishes the procedure for setting and reviewing tariffs. The PSRC has a clear methodology for setting tariffs for all companies in the sector. It does not, however, have a clear methodology for determining how much revenue should accrue from each customer class or for determining the end-user tariff structure and rates within each class that will achieve the class revenue.

- **Principles of setting regulated tariffs.** According to the Energy Law, the PSRC can either set the specific monetary value of the tariff or establish a clear formula for calculating the tariff based on parameters defined in the Energy Law. The basic principles of setting tariffs for electric and thermal energy and natural gas, as well as sizes of payments for rendered services, are as follows:
  - Providing for compensation of justified operation and maintenance costs as well as the depreciation allocations of the fixed assets and nonmaterial assets essential for the conduct of the Licensed Operation in compliance with the License provisions.
  - Providing an opportunity for reasonable profit.
  - Inclusion of justified loan service costs.
  - Establishment of differentiated tariffs for customers dependent on the consumption volume, requested capacity, season, time of use, connection terms, type of service.
  - Inclusion of justified and essential insurance costs.
  - Inclusion of justified costs related to compliance with environmental norms.
  - Inclusion of mothballing and preservation costs of the installations subject to mothballing, in conformance with the RoA Government Energy Development Programme.
  - Ensuring that the costs of the safekeeping of the utilised nuclear fuel be met and that the requisite allocations to the Nuclear Plant Decommissioning Fund be made.
  - Inclusion of justified technical and commercial losses.
  - Inclusion of other justified and necessary costs as provided by the legislation.
- **Setting and implementation of regulated tariffs**

- The Commission shall set the procedures for setting and reviewing tariffs, and the forms and list of documents (application package) to be submitted by the Licensees in that regard.
- The established tariffs shall become effective 30 days after the adoption of the Resolution. Tariffs shall be in effect for a minimum of 6 months, except in the event that a Licensee breaches the conditions of its License issued by the Commission. In those cases, the Commission may adjust the Licensee's tariffs prior to the expiration of the effective period, and those tariffs will remain effective until such time as the Licensee corrects its breach.
- The Commission can set a long-term tariff for the operation of the Licensee.
- The established tariff may be expressed as a definite number value, or as a clear formula based on certain calculation of parameters.
- Tariff review may take place upon the initiative of both the interested Licensee, as well as the Commission. The Commission shall review (reaffirm or adjust) the tariffs and make a decision within 90 days of the receipt of the Licensee's Application package for tariff review.
- Tariffs can be reviewed and renewed upon the initiative of the Commission according to the procedures set forth by the Commission, based on the results of the economic activity, investment programmes of the Licensee, as well as Licensee's compliance with the customer service quality requirements.
- A Licensee can sell electrical and thermal energy and natural gas or provide licenced services at a lower tariff than established by the Commission, provided that it does not or will not jeopardise the Licensed Operation and/or is not aimed at the acquisition of a monopoly status in the market and if such tariff decrease is carried out at the account of the Licensee's profit. In the event of such tariff decrease, when establishing a new tariff, the Commission shall disregard possible losses of the Licensee due to tariff decrease.
- The Commission shall approve the marginal (allowed) values (percentage wise or absolutely) of the required indicators (profitability, depreciation, own needs, losses, fuel specific consumption, etc.) for tariff calculation or shall approve tariff calculation methodologies.

Table 2.A3.1. **Methodology of price margin calculation in Armenia**

The price margin calculation is based on the principle of securing the revenue needed to Licensee, according needed revenue (**NR**), calculated using the following formula:

$$NR = CEP + OMC + D + T + BTD + AP \pm \sum \Delta M_i / 3$$

where

CEP	The cost of electricity purchased by the Licensee
OMC	Licensed activities necessary for the operation and maintenance costs
D	Licensed activities, including depreciation of fixed assets
T	Taxes defined by Armenian legislation (except profit tax and value added tax), fees, duties and other mandatory payments
BTD	The amount of bad/trustless debtors/debitors
AP	Allowable profit value of the assets involved in the Licensed activities
ΔM	The amount to be refunded in *i*-th year in accordance with Paragraphs 16 and 19-22 of this methodology
i	Number of years for which the amount of compensation shall be determined in accordance with Paragraphs 16 and 19-22 of this methodology, and may not exceed those mentioned in point 3.

The purchase price of electricity is determined by the following formula:

$$CEP = \frac{(DS + ON)/(1 - LN/100) + OS - EPD \times LTN/100}{1 - LTN/100} \times EAPP$$

where

DS	The amount of electric energy sales by Licensee in the domestic market (kWh)
ON	Licensee own needs and economic needs for the amount of electrical energy consumption (kWh)
LN	The allowable amount of the loss in distribution network (%), calculated via electric energy amount entering the distribution network
OS	Other electric energy sales by Licensee (kWh)
EPD	In the Producer-Distributor border (demarcation point) electric energy amount delivered by the Generator/producer to the Distributor (kWh)
LTN	The accepted rate of the losses of electric energy in the transmission network (%)
EAPP	The Licensee average purchase price of electric energy (AMD/kWh)

Annex 2.A4

Ongoing and planned donor investment in energy efficiency and renewable energy projects in Armenia

Several multilateral and bilateral donors are actively involved in promoting renewable energy in Armenia. The table below summarises donor contributions and their areas of involvement.

Year	Name of project	Donor/ implementing agency	Financial resources	Project objective
2010-14	Construction of small hydropower plant (HPP)	EBRD, IFC, WB and KfW	On-lending through Armenian commercial banks	Promotion of renewable energy, to help increase energy supply and develop private-sector involvement in cost-effective use of renewable energy sources for electricity production
2010-16	Armenia Sustainable Energy Finance Project	IFC, supported with funds from the Ministry of Finance of Austria	Loan USD 30 mln	Establishment of a sustainable market for investments in energy efficiency and renewable energy
2010-17	Caucasus Sustainable Energy Finance Facility (branded as Energocredit)	EBRD, EU, EBRD Special Shareholder Fund, Austrian Ministry of Finance	Loan from EBRD of USD 28 mln and grant from EU Neighborhood investment facility (NIF) and EBRD Shareholders' Special Fund	Provision of financing to local participating financial institutions for on-lending for energy efficiency and renewable energy in residential private sector investments
2011-14	Third National Communication	GEF-UNDP	Grant USD 480 000	Development of the National Communication of the Republic of Armenia on Climate Change and submission to the Conference of the Parties to the Convention
2011-14	UNDP-GEF Small Grants Programme	GEF-UNDP	Grant USD 303 000	Promotion of the demonstration, development and transfer of low-carbon technology at the community level
2011	Renewable Energy Road Map for Armenia	GEF-WB	Grant	Preparation of a Renewable Energy Roadmap for Armenia, identifying economically and financially viable potential targets of renewable energy in the short (2013), mid-term (2015), and long term (beyond 2020). It also outlines steps for achieving these targets
2011	Clean Energy and Water Programme for energy efficiency and renewable energy solutions in community energy and water use	USAID	Grant USD 76 000	Increase of energy efficiency in rural areas through introducing EE and RE solutions aimed at improving water supply, outdoor lighting and heating
2011	National Energy Balance	USAID-Tetra Tech	Grant USD 500 000	Support for developing the national energy balance according to IEA and Eurostat requirements for the years 2010-12. Project outcomes help improve National GHG Inventory and reporting on mitigation actions.

Year	Name of project	Donor/ implementing agency	Financial resources	Project objective
2012	Energy Efficiency Project	GEF-WB	Grant USD 1.82 mln	Reduction of GHG emissions by removing barriers to the implementation of energy efficiency investments in the public sector
2012	Develop an energy-efficiency lending product, helping households in Armenia reduce energy costs, consumption and CO_2 emissions	Green for Growth Fund	Loan USD 15.354 mln	On-lending via local banks to create credit lines for energy efficiency loans for households and businesses, to reduce energy consumption and increase energy efficiency
2012	Low-GHG-emission development/Armenia Least-Cost Energy Development Plan	USAID	Grant USD 400 000	Support in drafting a new Energy Strategy of Armenia based on Least Cost Generation Plan to increase the country's energy security
2012	Study on Improving Energy Efficiency in Residential Buildings	EBRD	Grant EUR 90 000	Review and analysis of the legal, regulatory, institutional, technical and operational framework of urban housing stock in Armenia for implementation of EE improvements
2013	Residential Energy Efficiency for Low-Income Households (REELIH) programme	USAID-Habitat	Grant USD 3.63 mln	Upgrading of residential energy efficiency for low-income households
2013	Green Urban Lighting	GEF-UNDP	Grant USD 1.6 mln	Promotion of energy saving and reduction of GHG emissions by increasing the energy efficiency of municipal lighting in the cities of Armenia through municipal investment programmes and national policies
2013	Irrigation System Enhancement Project	WB	Loan USD 33.1 mln	Reduction in energy consumption and improvement of irrigation conveyance efficiency in targeted irrigation schemes; improving availability and reliability of important sector data and information for decision makers and other stakeholders
2013	Black See Buildings Energy Efficiency Plan Project (BSBEEP)	EC	Grant USD 123 000	Support of cross-border partnership for economic and social development based on combined resources and creation of administrative capacity for the design and implementation of local development policies.
2014	Access to renewable and efficient energy in the municipalities of Vayk and Spitak	EC-Habitat	Grant EUR 1.7 mln	Support for the municipalities of Spitak and Vayq, developing and testing a replicable and efficient model(s) of energy savings through use of efficient measures and renewable sources in residential and public buildings, incorporated in their Community Development Plans/Sustainable Energy Action Plans, aligned with the Covenant of Mayors requirements
2014	Energy-Efficient Public Buildings and Housing in Armenia (NAMA)	UNDP	Grant USD 25 000	Promotion of energy saving in new construction and capital renovation of buildings supported by public funds and/or owned and managed by public institutions
2014	Investment Plan for the Scaling-up Renewable Energy Programme (SREP)	Strategic Climate Fund (SCF) within the framework of the Climate Investment Funds (CIF)	Grant and low-interest loan USD 40 mln	Identification of renewable energy technologies and projects that can best contribute to Armenia's energy, economic and environmental development goals and outlining the activities that must be carried out to realise the projects (photovoltaic, geothermal, heat pumps and solar water heaters)

Year	Name of project	Donor/ implementing agency	Financial resources	Project objective
2014-18	Social and Energy Efficiency Housing Finance Programme	AFD/EU/National Mortgage Company of Armenia	EUR 10 mln credit line and EUR 1.5 mln grant from EU NIF	Loans for on-lending to private households outside the center of Yerevan and in rural Armenia to finance energy-efficient investments in housing for low- and middle-income families. The programme helps reduce the main barrier to energy efficiency investments, the lack of access to affordable financing
2014-17	Technology Needs Assessment	GEF-UNEP	Grant USD 120 000	Assistance in country-driven technology assessment to identify environmentally sound technologies that can address climate change mitigation
2014	Akhurian River Water Resources Integrated Management Programme	KfW	Loan EUR 70 mln	Construction of Kaps reservoir and gravity system for irrigation of 1 248 hectares of land through pumping by gravity. Decommissioning eight pumping stations will save electricity
2014	Feasibility Study of Vedi Reservoir construction	AFD	Loan EUR 1.52 mln	Construction of Vedi reservoir to irrigate 4 000 hectares of land in Ararat Valley. Replacing 2 800 hectares of mechanical irrigation with gravity irrigation will reduce electricity consumption

Notes

1. In the interest of inter-country comparability, this section builds on data from international sources, such as the World Bank and the International Energy Agency. These data however have certain discrepancies with Armenia's own statistics, principally the data of the National Statistical Service of the Republic of Armenia (Armstat, 2015a). For all key indicators, the chapter attempts to provide references to both national and international statistics, including Armenia's National Greenhouse Gas Inventory Report (UNDP and GEF, 2015).

2. When Gazprom started raising its gas price in 2006, the Government of Armenia initially provided subsidies to gas consumers. From 2005 to 2008, Gazprom's average sales price to the countries of the EU Eastern Partnership (EaP) and Central Asia increased by USD 100/kcm, from USD 60 to USD 160/kcm (Gazprom Armenia, 2015). The increase followed a surge in European prices which, against the backdrop of potential capacity problems with gas supply to the EU, highlighted to Gazprom the cost of continuing the low price policy for customers in the EaP and Central Asia countries. Nonetheless, European prices continued to outpace the EaP and Central Asia average.

3. CNG comes from piped gas compressed locally in Armenia.

4. 100% of electricity consumers have meters installed. There is no connection to the grid without a meter. New customers have to pay for the installation of meters, but after one year, ENA repays the cost by monthly deductions from the electricity bill. The installed meters are considered to be in the ENA ownership.

5. Prices are calculated considering tariff rates for electricity supplied (AMD per kWh) and capacity (AMD per kW).

6. The co-generated heat and power plant has certain problems with organising the sale of thermal energy and therefore electricity production based on heat load. The plant attempts to subsidise heat by a higher electricity tariff. This is the only CHP with a district heating system connected to a number of apartment buildings (reportedly 39 buildings, 1 kindergarten, 1 office; the connection rate in the residential buildings is 43%, with the total number of connected subscribers amounting to only 474 apartments; other consumers in the same buildings use other heating options). Based on the above-mentioned PSRC Decision 20 "A" of 10 February 2016, ArmRosCogneration is making efforts to supply electricity directly to the aluminium foil producer ARMENAL, which, in its turn, is part of the Russian aluminium producer RUSAL. ArmRosCogeneration has made significant capital investments in its plant but the co-generation technology is still not viable, and it is difficult for the company to recover its investments.

References

Aravot (2015), "Today's Young People are our Only Hope", 27 June. www.aravot.am/2015/06/29/587928/.

ARKA News Agency (2015), "Armenian Nuclear Power Plant Reconnected to National Power Grid", 28 October. http://arka.am/en/news/technology/armenian_nuclear_power_plant_reconnected_to_national_power_grid_/.

Armstat (2015a), *Data on Macroeconomic and Demographic Indicators*, National Statistical Service of the Republic of Armenia. www.armstat.am/en/.

Armstat (2015b), *Data on Foreign Trade of the Republic of Armenia for 2015,* National Statistical Service of the Republic of Armenia. www.armstat.am/file/article/f._t-2015-10-nish-5.pdf.

Armstat (2014), *Data on Foreign Trade of the Republic of Armenia for 2014,* National Statistical Service of the Republic of Armenia. www.armstat.am/file/article/ft_8nish_2015_5.pdf.

Armstat (2013), *Data on Foreign Trade of the Republic of Armenia for 2013*, National Statistical Service of the Republic of Armenia. www.armstat.am/file/article/ft_8nish_2014_5.pdf.

Armstat (2012), *Data on Foreign Trade of the Republic of Armenia for 2012*, National Statistical Service of the Republic of Armenia. www.armstat.am/file/article/ft_8nish_2013_5.pdf.

Armstat (2011), *Data on Foreign Trade of the Republic of Armenia for 2011*, National Statistical Service of the Republic of Armenia. www.armstat.am/file/article/ft_8nish_12_5.pdf.

EBRD (n.d.), *Armenia Country Profile,* European Bank for Reconstruction and Development, Yerevan.

Financial Portal ArmInfo (2016), "Operations Launched in Armenia to Prolong Lifespan of Nuclear Power Plant", 21 January. www.finport.am/full_news.php?id=23635&lang=3.

Gazprom Armenia (2015), *Gazprom Armenia website.* http://armenia.gazprom.ru/organization/.

GIZ (2015), *International Fuel Prices 2014: Data Preview*, Deutsche Gesellschaft für Internationale Zusammenarbeit.

GoA (2015), *Protocol Decision No. 41 of 10 September 2015 on Approving the Intended Nationally Determined Contributions of the Republic of Armenia under the UN Framework Convention on Climate Change*, Government of the Republic of Armenia, Yerevan. http://www4.unfccc.int/ndcregistry/PublishedDocuments/Armenia%20First/INDC-Armenia.pdf.

GoA (2006), *Decree No. 449-N on State Property Alienation and Natural Gas Price Mitigation Measures*, Government of the Republic of Armenia, Yerevan.

GoA (2005), *Decree No. 2310-N on Concept of Agriculture Subsidizing Directions and Mechanisms*, Government of the Republic of Armenia, Yerevan.

GoA (2003), *Decree No. 1937-N on Approval of RA State Budget Subsidies and Grants Allocation Procedure for Legal Entities*, Government of the Republic of Armenia, Yerevan.

Harutyunyan, S. (2016), *World Bank Loan to Cover Armenian Energy Losses*. www.azatutyun.am/content/article/27560668.html.

IEA (2015), *Eastern Europe, Caucasus and Central Asia: Energy Policies Beyond IEA Countries*, OECD/International Energy Agency. https://www.iea.org/publications/freepublications/publication/IDR_EasternEuropeCaucasus_2015.pdf.

IMF (2011), *Republic of Armenia: Poverty Reduction Strategy Paper – Progress Report*, International Monetary Fund. https://www.imf.org/external/pubs/ft/scr/2011/cr11191.pdf.

IMF (2001), *The Economic Transition in Armenia*, International Monetary Fund. https://www.imf.org/external/np/speeches/2001/073101.htm.

INOGATE (2015), *A Review of Energy Tariffs in INOGATE Partner Countries: Armenia, Azerbaijan, Belarus, Georgia, Kazakhstan, Kyrgyzstan, Moldova, Tajikistan, Turkmenistan, Ukraine, Uzbekistan*, June 2015, Interstate Oil and Gas Transportation to Europe, Brussels, Kiev. www.inogate.org/documents/A_Review_of_Energy_Tariffs_in_INOGATE_Partner_Countries.pdf.

MENR (2015), *Draft Energy Balance Report*, Ministry of Energy and Natural Resources of Armenia, Yerevan.

MoF (2000), *Excise Tax Law of the Republic of Armenia*, Ministry of Finance of Armenia, Yerevan.

MoF (1997), *The Law of the RA on Taxes*, Ministry of Finance of Armenia, Yerevan.

OECD (2013), *Analysing Energy Subsidies in the Countries of Eastern Europe, Caucasus and Central Asia*, OECD Publishing, Paris. https://www.oecd.org/env/outreach/EHS%20report_20%20August%202013_ENG.pdf.

PanARMENIAN.net (2016), "Armenia Gas Tariff May Drop Starting from July 1", 21 May. www.panarmenian.net/eng/news/212820/.

PanARMENIAN.net (2005), "RAO 'UES of Russia' Plans to Supply Electricity from Armenia to Turkey and Iran", 23 February. www.panarmenian.net/m/arm/news/12198.

PSRC (2015a), *Electricity Tariffs*,Public Services Regulatory Commission of Armenia, Yerevan. www.psrc.am/am/sectors/electric/tariffs.

PSRC (2015b), *Feed-in Tariffs for Renewables and Average Tariffs for Conventional Power Sources in Armenia for 2011-2015*, Public Services Regulatory Commission of Armenia, Yerevan. www.psrc.am/.

PSRC (2015c), *Report on Key Indicators of the Gas Sector in 2015*, Public Services Regulatory Commission of Armenia, Yerevan. www.psrc.am/images/docs/reports/gas/2015/4-er/gaz-xoranard-tari.pdf.

PSRC (2014), *Report on Key Indicators of the Gas Sector in 2014*, Public Services Regulatory Commission of Armenia, Yerevan. www.psrc.am/images/docs/reports/gas/21401.pdf.

PSRC (2013), *Report on Key Indicators of the Gas Sector in 2013*, Public Services Regulatory Commission of Armenia, Yerevan. www.psrc.am/docs/reports/gas/Himnakan_bnutagir_4_2013.pdf.

PSRC (2012), *Report on Key Indicators of the Gas Sector in 2012*, Public Services Regulatory Commission of Armenia, Yerevan. www.psrc.am/docs/reports/gas/Himnakan_bnudagir_4_2012.pdf.

PSRC (2011), *Report on Key Indicators of the Gas Sector in 2011*, Public Services Regulatory Commission of Armenia, Yerevan. www.psrc.am/docs/reports/gas/Himnakan_bnudagir_4_2011.pdf.

Rate.Am (2015), *Armenian Dram Exchange Rates*, Rate.Am. http://rate.am/am/armenian-dram-exchange-rates/central-bank-armenia.

Sargsyan, G. et al. (2006), "From Crisis to Stability in the Armenian Power Sector: Lessons Learned from Armenia's Energy Reform Experience", World Bank Working Paper No. 74. http://siteresources.worldbank.org/INTARMENIA/Resources/Armenia-Energy-Crisis-to-Stability.pdf.

UNDP and GEF (2015), *Third National Communication on Climate Change,* United Nations Development Programme and Global Environmental Facility. http://unfccc.int/resource/docs/natc/armnc3.pdf.

Vagliasindi, M. (2013), *Implementing Energy Subsidy Reforms: Evidence from Developing Countries. Directions in Development;Energy and Mining*, World Bank, Washington, DC. https://openknowledge.worldbank.org/handle/10986/11965.

World Bank (2015), *World Bank World Development Indicators,*World Bank, Washington, DC. http://data.worldbank.org/country/armenia.

World Bank (2014), *Armenia Overview,* World Bank, Yerevan. www.worldbank.org/en/country/armenia/overview.

World Bank Group (2014), *Republic of Armenia Public Expenditure Review: Expanding the Fiscal Envelope, World Bank,* Washington, DC. https://openknowledge.worldbank.org/handle/10986/21063.

Chapter 3

Azerbaijan's energy subsidies

This chapter identifies, documents and provides estimates of the various subsidies in Azerbaijan that relate to the production or use of coal, oil and related petroleum products, natural gas, and electricity and heat generated on the basis of these fossil fuels. The chapter also briefly looks at the subsidies benefiting energy-efficiency measures and renewable energy sources. An overview of the country's energy sector is first given to place the measures listed into context. In addition, the chapter discusses pricing and tax policies in the energy sector in Azerbaijan. The analysis summarises the context, the state of play, and the mechanics of the complex and evolving landscape of energy subsidies in the country.

Key findings

Azerbaijan is the only net energy exporter among the EU Eastern Partnership countries, which largely determines the structure of its energy subsidies. This structure is more similar to that of the oil-producing countries of Central Asia and, to a lesser extent, to the Gulf countries. The main challenge in analysing energy subsidies in Azerbaijan is the lack of transparency and publicly available information on the level of support for consumption and production of fossil fuels in the country. Similarly, little relevant information is disclosed by state-owned energy companies that are both recipients of subsidies and vehicles for providing government support for energy consumers.

Given the fiscal pressures resulting from the global financial and economic slowdown and the drop in world oil and gas prices, there is an ongoing discussion on budget and fiscal policy optimisation in Azerbaijan. Azerbaijan's national strategy "Azerbaijan 2020: Look into the Future" (adopted in 2012) provides that, among the country's strategic objectives, "special attention will be paid to the establishment of fiscal discipline in the sphere of forming and using budget resources, correcting distribution of funds and increasing the efficiency of expenses. Quick assessments of various budget risks (foreign, financial, operational risks) will be carried out" (President of Azerbaijan, 2012).

Energy subsidy review should be an indispensable part of this process, given the importance of the energy sector to Azerbaijan's economy, as well as the scale and the multitude of forms of government support for fossil-fuel energy in Azerbaijan. At the same time, this review cannot be limited to budgetary expenditure and should include tax privileges for energy companies, as well as the root causes that ultimately necessitate budgetary transfers to AzerEnerji, AzeriGas and AzerIstilikTechizat. These causes include the regulated prices of natural gas, electricity, heat and petroleum products.

Azerbaijan reformed its electricity tariff and prices for petroleum products in 2007, which helped to curb growing energy demand and inefficiencies of energy use. However, the country did not adopt a block tariff for electricity and other forms of targeted support for vulnerable groups that could have helped to reduce the subsidy further, as illustrated by international best practice.

After the price reform of 2006, the energy tariff was revised again in the spring of 2016. Despite the increase, depreciation of the Azerbaijani manat means that the subsidy, in the form of regulated domestic prices and opportunity costs of importing energy, remains intact.

Various forms of support for fossil fuel energy production and consumption also work against Azerbaijan's adopted targets of diversifying its economy, improving energy efficiency and increasing the share of renewable energy to 20% of the total electricity generated by 2020.

At the same time, the leadership of Azerbaijan remains committed to better integration in international energy markets, attracting investment and improving the country's overall competitiveness. Increasing transparency and stakeholder dialogue on energy subsidies and tariff-setting would be an important step in bringing Azerbaijan closer to fulfilling these goals. Such stakeholder consultations will help identify those energy subsidies that are inefficient, as well as the ways to phase them out while protecting vulnerable groups through targeted support.

Macroeconomic situation and energy sector overview

As in most former Soviet Union states, the economy of Azerbaijan was badly hit by the breakup of the Soviet Union.[1] From 1989 to 1995, the economy shrank by 62.5% (World Bank, 2015d), but since then, and driven by a rapid rise in exports of oil and gas, its economy has grown dramatically. GDP increased by 344% between 2000 and 2014, reducing poverty levels from 50% in 2001 to 5.3% in 2013 (World Bank, 2015c).

Table 3.1. **Azerbaijan's macroeconomic indicators**

Key indicators	Year and unit	International statistics	National statistics
Population	*2014, mln*	9.30	9.48
GDP	*2014, USD bln*	74.15	75.19
GDP per capita	*2014, USD*	7 902	7 986
Energy production	*2014, mtoe*	58.78	61.13
Net imports	*2014, mtoe*	-44.54	-45.87
TPES	*2014, mtoe*	14.32	..
TPES per capita	*2014, toe*	1.50	..
Electricity consumption	*2014, TWh*	21.00	16.91
Electricity consumption per capita	*2014, MWh*	2.20	..
CO_2 emissions	*2014, Mt of CO_2*	30.79	30.2
CO_2 emissions per capita	*2012, t of CO_2*	3.23	..

Source: IEA (2016), World Bank (2015d), AzerStat (2015c).

Azerbaijan's petroleum sector accounted for more than 90% of total exports in 2014 (Comtrade, 2015) and 48.5% of GDP in 2010 (ECS, 2011). However, the country has made only limited progress in instituting market-based economic reforms. Economic inefficiencies are a drag on long-term growth, particularly in non-energy sectors. Stagnation in energy output since 2010 has resulted in a drop in oil revenue, leading to a significant reduction of public spending and slowdown of Azerbaijan's GDP growth. With the recent fall in global energy prices, it needs to diversify to strengthen its economic position (World Bank, 2015c).

Table 3.2. **Weighted average exchange rate**

	2012	2013	2014	2015	2016[a]
Weighted average exchange rate, AZN per USD	0.7856	0.7844	0.7844	1.0261	1.6

Note: a. The exchange rate for the last year was provided by the Statistical Committee of the Republic of Azerbaijan, 2016.

Source: Central Bank of Azerbaijan (2016b).

Energy supply

Azerbaijan has rich deposits of oil and natural gas, onshore and offshore. In the past decade, it has become a major energy producer (IEA, 2015a), with oil reserves estimated at 952 mln tonnes (Mt) in 2012, and natural gas reserves at 991 bln m³ (IEA, 2015b). Energy production rose by 183% in 1990-2014, driven by a 237% rise in crude oil production and a 101% increase in natural gas production (Figure 3.2).

Azerbaijan was a net importer of energy in the early 1990s, but by 2014, exported more than 75% of its domestic energy production, that is, 37.7 mln tonnes of oil equivalent (mtoe) of oil and oil products, and 6.8 mtoe of natural gas (IEA, 2016).

Almost all this post-Soviet oil and gas production came from international oil and gas company investments into offshore fields in the Caspian Sea, including the Azeri-Chirag-Gunashli (ACG) oilfield complex and a giant Shah Deniz gas field. The same international companies also invested in export infrastructure, which includes the Baku-Tbilisi-Ceyhan oil pipeline (BTC), which runs through Georgia to Turkey and the Mediterranean Sea, and the South Caucasus Pipeline, which transports gas from Azerbaijan to Georgia and then Erzurum in Turkey. The South Caucasus Pipeline is so far the only completed pipeline of the Southern Gas Corridor designed to supply Europe with Caspian gas, in particular gas from Shah Deniz 2 development (TAP-AG, 2015). The other two elements of the Southern Gas Corridor are the Trans-Anatolian pipeline and the Trans-Adriatic pipeline. As of early 2016, the Trans-Anatolian pipeline was under construction. An older and relatively low capacity Baku-Supsa oil pipeline cuts through Georgia and the Baku-Novorossiysk oil pipeline through the Russian Federation, both of which terminate at the Black Sea coast.

Figure 3.1. **Map of the existing and planned oil and gas pipelines from Baku**

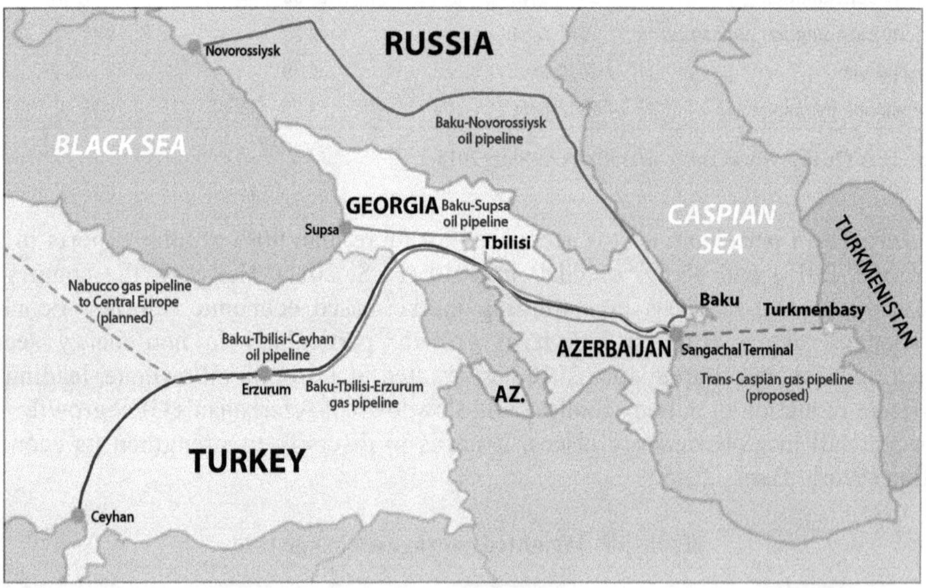

Source: Map created by Thomas Blomberg, © CC BY-SA 3.0.

Compared to 1990, total primary energy supply (TPES) in Azerbaijan in 2014 declined by 36.8%, primarily due to lower supply to the Azerbaijani industrial sector (IEA, 2016). Between 2000 and 2014, the country's TPES grew by 26.8%. Natural gas accounted for 67.4% and oil for 31.0% of TPES in 2014, while hydropower and biofuels and waste accounted for 0.8% and 1.1%, respectively.

Figure 3.2. **Total energy production, 1990-2014**

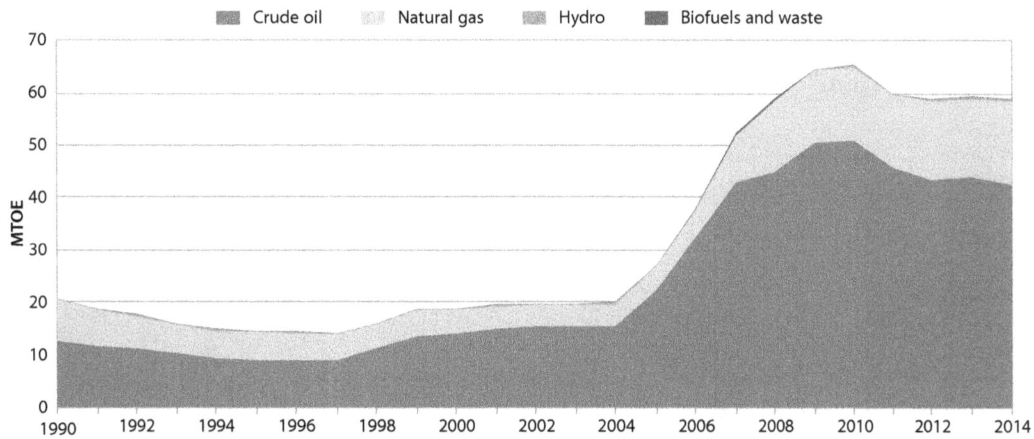

Source: Authors' presentation based on IEA (2016).

Figure 3.3. **Total primary energy supply, 1990-2014**

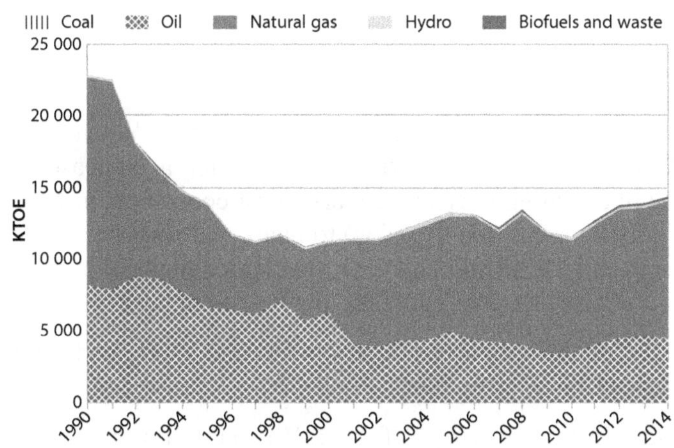

Source: Authors' presentation based on IEA (2016).

Figure 3.4. **Primary energy supply 2014 by fuel**

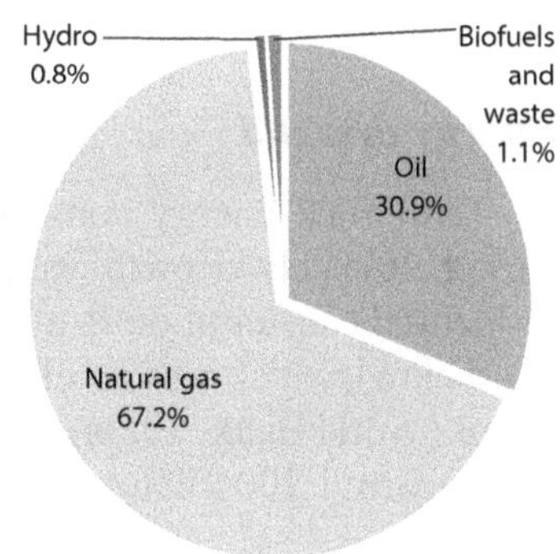

Azerbaijan is fully electrified and self-sufficient in electricity generation. The installed generating capacity of power stations was 7 232 megawatts (MW) in 2014; the share of thermal power stations in electricity generation is 83.4% (6 032 MW), the rest being almost exclusively hydropower stations' capacity (1 200 MW) (Huseynova, 2015). There is no nuclear power generation in Azerbaijan.

The country generated a total of 24.7 terawatt hours (TWh) of electricity in 2014, of which 94.5% came from natural gas, 5.3% from hydroelectricity and 0.2% from heavy oil (*mazut*) and diesel. Azerbaijan has seen notable investments in new gas-fired generation over the past decade, with capacity increasing by 1.5 gigawatts (GW) since 2005. Electricity generation has increased by 31.3% from 2000 to 2014, driven by a 525% increase in gas-fired generation (Figure 3.5). Like Armenia and Georgia, Azerbaijan has seen its electricity generation switch to gas as the key feedstock. Gas-fired generation has almost completely replaced heavy oil (*mazut*) and diesel in the country's electricity balance.

According to the state-owned electricity monopoly, JSC AzerEnerji, demand for electricity in Azerbaijan is expected to increase by almost 140% by 2025. The peak demand is also expected to double by the years 2022-23 (ECS, 2011).

Figure 3.5. **Electricity generation by source, 1990-2014**

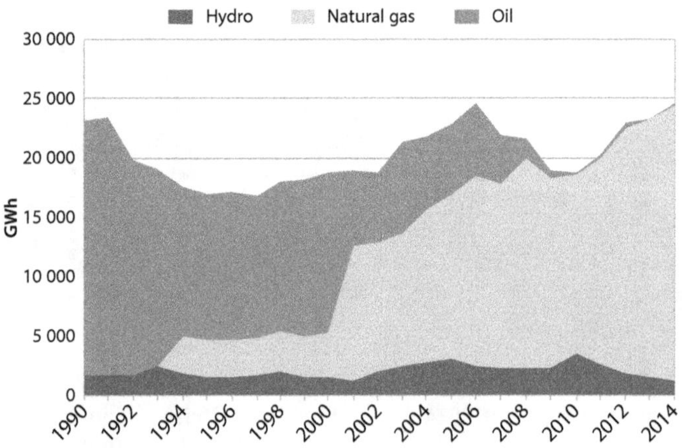

Figure 3.6. **Electricity generation by source, 2014**

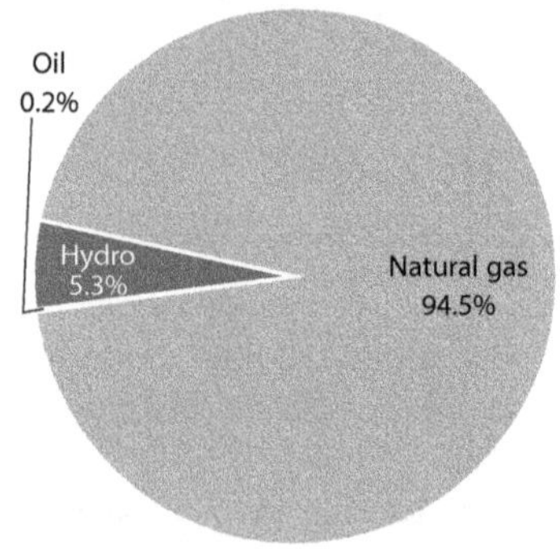

Source: Authors' presentation based on IEA (2016).

Energy demand

Total final energy consumption (TFEC) in Azerbaijan increased by 32% over the period 2000-14. Growth would probably have been stronger if not for a decrease in residential consumption as a result of a tripling in electricity prices for consumers in 2007 (see below), which was an effort (albeit on this one occasion) to phase out subsidies to the sector (World Bank, 2013a). Consequently, residential power consumption plunged by 58% from nearly 1 200 kilotonnes of oil equivalent (ktoe) in 2006 to 495 ktoe in 2010.

Since then, however, residential consumption has been on the rise again, and 2014 registered a 31% increase in residential TFEC over 2000.

According to the International Energy Agency (IEA, 2016), natural gas and oil accounted for more than 80% of TFEC, of which 43% is gas used for power generation and 40% oil used for transport. Diesel consumption decreased after price increases in 2006 and 2007, but consumption of gasoline kept growing, in spite of equivalent price increases in correlation with GDP and growth in the number of personal vehicles (World Bank, 2013b). Electricity makes up 17% of all energy consumption. District heating plays only a minor role in domestic consumption (IEA, 2015b).

Energy sector structure, ownership and governance

Azerbaijan's energy sector is dominated by the state-owned energy companies, and several international oil and gas companies also have large stakes in upstream oil and gas production (Figure 3.7).

Upstream exploration and production is primarily organised through production-sharing agreements (PSAs), in which the State-Owned Company of the Azerbaijan Republic (SOCAR) represents the government of Azerbaijan and also takes part in the contracting consortium, with international oil companies including British Petroleum (BP), Chevron, ExxonMobil, Statoil, Petronas, Total, LUKOIL and several others. As of early

2016, SOCAR's share in the production of the giant Azeri-Chirag-Gunashli oilfield was 11%, and its share of production in Azerbaijan's largest gas field, Shah Deniz, was 10%. In similar joint ownership arrangements with international companies, SOCAR has stakes in all oil- and gas-exporting pipelines (Baku-Tbilisi-Ceyhan, South Caucasus Pipeline, Baku-Supsa and Baku-Novorossiysk).

Figure 3.7. **Structure of the energy sector in Azerbaijan**

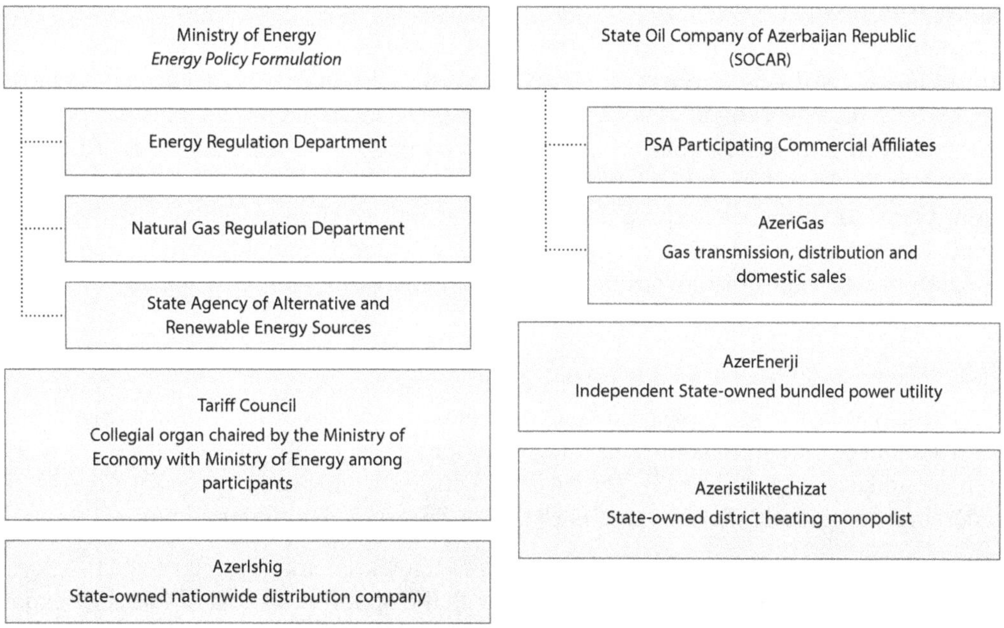

Source: Authors' presentation based on IEA (2015b), SOCAR (2015a), BP (2015a), AzerEnerji (2015), Tariff Council (2015).

Mid- and downstream, SOCAR is a government-instituted monopoly. It operates the two oil refineries in Baku inherited from the Soviet era (Heydar Aliyev Baku Refinery and Azerneftyagh Oil Refinery), with 400 000 barrels per day in processing capacity. In addition, SOCAR is a majority owner of PETKIM, a major petrochemical company based in Turkey, which has begun construction on a new refinery in the area of Izmir. SOCAR owns fuel-filling stations under the SOCAR brand in Azerbaijan, Georgia, Romania, Switzerland and Ukraine.

Gas transmission, distribution and sales are organised through SOCAR's subsidiary AzeriGas, which is reported to be financially, though not legally, unbundled from SOCAR as part of a 2002 reform to isolate the cost of suppressed prices.

The electricity market is a closed market, operated mainly by the state-owned company, AzerEnerji JSC. AzerEnerji operates the country's thermal and hydropower plants, with the exception of several small hydropower plants that have been privatised. Until February 2015, AzerEnerji operated as a bundled monopoly, managing electricity production, transmission, distribution and sales. However, on 10 February 2015, Bakielektrikshabaka Open Joint Stock Company, the regional distribution company established to supply electricity to the capital city of Baku (Huseynova, 2015), was renamed AzerIshig OJSC and made the nationwide distribution company for electricity (AzerIshig, 2015).

District heating is limited mainly to Baku and the surrounding areas, where heat is supplied by the state-owned monopoly, Azeristiliktechizat (ECS, 2011).

The Ministry of Energy is formally in charge of sector oversight and energy policy formulation and participates in the Tariff Council, which sets both producer and consumer prices.[2] The President and President's Office can reportedly recommend that the Tariff Council consider social concerns when setting tariffs, which on at least one occasion has led to the cancellation of tariff increases (Hasanli, 2015).

Energy pricing policy

Energy is subject to price regulation in Azerbaijan. Table 3.3 below presents the current tariffs for different types of energy. According to the Energy Charter Secretariat (ECS, 2011), the government included the transition to a "cost recovery plus 10% return" tariff policy as a mid-term goal in its State Programme for the Development of the Fuel and Energy Sector (2005-2015), which was adopted in 2005. However, the government's commitment to this goal may be in doubt. Even if the commitment to cost-recovery remains strong, there at least is reason to discuss whether it should be production cost or opportunity cost that is the government's point of departure in its tariff policy.

Natural gas

Natural gas tariffs are broken down into wholesale, retail and transmission, in addition to a discounted price for gas used in the generation of electricity, and for certain energy-intensive industries. Additionally, the tariff structure includes a category for natural gas processing. For households, the tariff is flat regardless of consumption volumes.

Azerbaijan is a gas-abundant country with a potential for significant gas exports. Domestic consumption is thus also associated with the opportunity cost of foregone export revenue. BP (2015b) reports a total gas production of 17 bln m^3 in 2014, of which 9 bln m^3 was consumed domestically and nearly 8 bln m^3 was exported. Just over 5 bln m^3 was sold to Spain, 0.2 to the Russian Federation, 0.3 bln m^3 to Iran and 1.9 bln m^3 to other post-Soviet countries, which may be assumed to represent Georgia, given that it is Azerbaijan's only post-Soviet offset market apart from the Russian Federation (SOCAR, 2015a). Since 2007, Azerbaijan has been exporting minimal quantities of gas to Turkey as well but with the construction of the Trans-Anatolian Gas pipeline Azerbaijan is expected to export 16 bln m^3 of gas through Turkey: 6 bln m^3 will be used by Turkey itself while 10 bln m^3 of gas will be transferred further to the European countries (Rzayeva, 2015). Depending on the source of data, these numbers may differ, but the order of magnitude remains the same.

The highest price of natural gas for retail consumers is USD 97 per 1 000 m^3, which is higher than SOCAR's reported production cost of USD 36 per 1 000 m^3 (SOCAR, 2015a), but significantly lower than the gas price in Azerbaijan's main export market, Turkey, where the import parity price was USD 343 per 1 000 m^3 in 2014 (IGU, 2015). Since 2014, the natural gas price has been on the decline, but Azerbaijan's domestic prices are still lower than another appropriate benchmark,[3] the European market's 12-month average for January-December 2015, which was USD 270 per 1 000 m^3 (World Bank, 2016a). More detailed discussion of benchmarking is provided in the section on price-gap subsidy estimation below.

AzeriGas is reported to receive not only government transfers, but both postponed tax payments and tax debt forgiveness to cover the gaps in its costs, including within distribution and retail (AzeCabMin, 2011). This points toward cost-recovery challenges resulting from Azerbaijan's domestic gas pricing policies.

Table 3.3. **Price policies for different energy carriers in Azerbaijan in early 2016**

Energy carrier	Pricing policy	Price categories	Price in AZN [a]	USD eq.
Natural gas [b]	Regulated	Processing	AZN 5.5 per 1 000 m^3	5.36
		Transmission per 100 km	AZN 2.0 per 1 000 m^3	1.95
		Wholesale to distributors	AZN 42.0 per 1 000 m^3	40.93
		Retail	AZN 100.0 per 1 000 m^3	97.45
		Chemical steel, aluminium and power industry	AZN 80.0 per 1 000 m^3	77.97
		Industry with monthly consumption under 10 bln m^3		
Electricity [b]	Regulated	AzerEnerji JSC production	AZN 0.041 per kWh	0.04
		Private production of small hydropower plants	AZN 0.025 per kWh	0.024
		Wind-power plants	AZN 0.045 per kWh	0.044
		Consumer price	AZN 0.07 per kWh	0.068
		Transmission tariff	AZN 0.02 per kWh	0.019
		Energy supply through 35 and 110 kW lines, stable daily freight demand, chemical and aluminium industry enterprises, with average monthly energy consumption not less than 5 mln KWh, for the production of steel melting based on mining	Daytime (8 a.m. to 10 p.m.) 1kVh AZN 0.042	0.041
			Night-time (10 p.m. to 8 a.m.) 1kVh AZN 0.02	0.019
Liquid petroleum products [b]	Regulated retail, wholesale and producer prices	95-octane consumer price	AZN 0.80 per litre (incl. VAT)	0.78
		95-octane producer price	AZN 0.35 per litre (incl. 64% excise tax)	0.34
		Diesel consumer price	AZN 0.60 per litre (incl. VAT)	0.58
		Diesel producer price	AZN 0.35 per litre (incl. 64% excise tax)	0.34
District heating	Regulated	Households	AZN 0.15 per m^2 per month (incl. VAT)	0.15
		Non-residential consumers	AZN 0.15 per m^2 per month (incl. VAT)	0.15
			AZN 30 per Gcal	29.23
Coal	Regulated	Wholesale price	AZN 39-76 per tonne	38-74
	Information for coke coal only	Producer price	AZN 28-54 per tonne	27-53
2015 AZN/USD average exchange rate			*1.0261*	

Notes: a. Prices in the table are exclusive of VAT and excise tax unless otherwise indicated.

b. In January 2017, Azerbaijan introduced differentiated prices for gas and electricity. Under the new tariffs, consumers will pay AZN 0.11 for electricity consumption above 300 KWh per month. An annual gas consumption of higher than 1 700 m^3 will cost the population AZN 200.00 per 1 000 m^3. Consumer prices for 95-octane petroleum also increased, and currently stand at AZN 1.15. The Tariff Council commented on this issue, confirming that imported 95- and 98-octane petroleum products are not regulated by the Council.

Source: Authors' summary based on Tariff Council (2016), Central Bank of Azerbaijan (2016a).

Electricity

Electricity prices in Azerbaijan are regulated, and the country is one of the very few in the EU Eastern Partnership and Central Asia region that has not adopted a block tariff in the retail sector. Over the course of nearly two decades, the tariff has been charged regardless of household consumption levels. The electricity prices have been adjusted only once over this prolonged period. Electricity tariffs were increased in 2007 from USD 0.024 to USD 0.075 (AZN 0.06) per kWh (ECS, 2011). This, together with improved metering and collection practices, increased sector revenue significantly (Fichtner Ltd, 2013). Though one-off, this tariff increase did succeed in controlling the strong demand growth among residential consumers. As explained above, after the passage of this measure, residential power consumption plunged by 58% from nearly 1 200 ktoe in 2006 to 495 ktoe in 2010. As of early 2016, electricity consumption was still below pre-reform levels of 2007.

The tariffs set in 2007 remained in place until late spring 2016, when the price for residential consumers increased to AZN 0.07 per kWh. Due to the depreciation of the Azerbaijani manat, the consumer electricity tariff is now lower in dollar terms than in 2007 (USD 0.068 per kWh). This raises the question whether consumer demand is likely to accelerate again. Using domestic fuel prices (see below), as of early 2016, the levelised cost of electricity production estimates ranged from USD 0.024 to 0.035 per kWh. This indicates that Azerbaijan's regulated electricity tariffs in early 2016 were still above cost-recovery levels. At the same time, payment collection issues persist (World Bank, 2013b) in addition to debt forgiveness granted to AzerEnerji (AzeCabMin, 2015; AzeCabMin, 2011; TREND.AZ, 2015; and TREND.AZ, 2013), which suggests there may be some difficulty in recovering costs.

District heating

District heating tariffs are regulated. For households, the tariff is charged by the living area. For non-residential consumers, the tariff is calculated by heated area or by gigacalorie consumed (Table 3.3). For non-residential consumers, this corresponds to USD 29.25 per Gcal.

It is difficult to assess whether the price level for domestic consumers is adequate. It should be noted that uncoupling the basis for tariff calculation from consumption does not encourage energy efficiency, a common issue in the former Soviet countries. This practice may be expected to lead to over-consumption.

Petroleum products

All petroleum products, including gasoline and diesel, are sold at regulated prices, which are differentiated by producer, wholesale and retail prices. In early 2016, retail prices corresponded to USD 0.78 and USD 0.58 per litre of gasoline and diesel, respectively. The *Deutsche Gesellschaft für Internationale Zusammenarbeit* (GIZ, 2014) reports similar price levels in 2012, which placed Azerbaijan above the red benchmark (corresponding to the world crude oil price equivalent) for gasoline and below it for diesel. In the GIZ classification, this pricing policy ranked Azerbaijan between countries with fuel subsidies and those with high fuel subsidies.

Until 2006, prices for petroleum products in Azerbaijan were significantly lower than in neighbouring countries, which led to fuel smuggling to Georgia and the Russian Federation. To address this problem and raise budget revenue, Azerbaijan raised prices for liquid petroleum products in 2006 and in 2007. In the second instance, this price reform coincided with a significant increase in regulated tariffs for electricity, water supply and public transport (World Bank, 2013b; Regnum, 2007).

Taxation policy

Azerbaijan's energy sector tax system is a combination of a baseline system and special regimes under host government agreements (HGAs) and production-sharing agreements (PSAs). In addition, tax relief can be granted to selected companies on an individual basis under the Law on Application of the Special Economic Regime for Export-Oriented Oil and Gas Operations, which took effect on 17 April 2009, and through investment promotion certificates introduced by Presidential Decree on 18 January 2016. Azerbaijan is considering setting up Special Economic Zones and has adopted relevant legislation. However, as of April 2016, none had yet been created (PWC, 2016).

National system

Azerbaijan's baseline taxes are Value Added Tax (VAT), profit tax, property tax, road tax, land tax, import tax and export tax (Table 3.4). According to the Tax Code, small businesses can pay a single tax under a simplified scheme (Parliament of Azerbaijan, 2000). There is also a withholding tax (WHT) on repatriation of profits by foreign companies. Upstream, within the national system, energy-extractive industries are subject to a mining tax (royalty), but in practice, the tax applies to a declining share of production from old fields, mostly onshore. The mining tax is deductible for the purposes of profit tax. The tax is applied to the wholesale price of oil at the rate of 26%, to natural gas at the rate of 20%, and to coal at the rate of 3% (Parliament of Azerbaijan, 2000).

Table 3.4. **Azerbaijan's national system of energy taxation**

Baseline tax system	**VAT, profit tax, property tax, road tax, land tax, import tax, export tax**		
Specific taxes	***Excise tax, mining tax (royalty)***		
Energy sector taxation	**Upstream**	**Midstream**	**Downstream**
Oil	Applicable as appropriate. The baseline rate of corporate profit tax is 20%	No specific tax	Excise tax
Natural gas	Mining tax (royalty): 26% for oil, 20% for gas, deductible from corporate income tax	No specific tax	No specific tax
Electricity	no specific tax	No specific tax	No specific tax
Liquid petroleum products	n.a.	n.a.	Excise tax
Coal	Mining tax (royalty): 3%	n.a.	Excise tax

Note: **n.a.**: not applicable.

Source: Authors' summary based on Ernst & Young (2015b), Deloitte (2015), BakerMcKenzie (2009), BP (1994).

An accelerated rate of depreciation applies for geological and exploration costs with respect to corporate income tax. This rate is 25%, the same as for means of transport and equipment and computers. This is higher than the standard rate of 20% for most other asset classes (Parliament of Azerbaijan, 2000).

The VAT rate is 18%, and all domestic energy sales are subject to VAT. In some cases, the Tariff Council specifies consumer tariffs, including VAT (Tariff Council, 2016).

Host government agreements

New export pipelines funded by consortia, including international investors, are regulated by host government agreements (HGAs). HGA participants are only subject to a profit tax of 27% and social fund contributions for local employees. The participants are exempt from all other taxes. Subcontractors involved in the construction and operation of new export pipelines are exempt from all taxes except social fund payments (Ernst & Young, 2015b). HGA conditions are grandfathered through amendments in tax policies.

Production-sharing agreements

Large offshore fields that started producing in the post-Soviet period are subject to production-sharing agreements (PSAs) and hence a special tax treatment. PSAs grant a separate tax regime for each agreement (project), which includes negotiated bonuses and acreage fees. PSA conditions are grandfathered through amendments in tax policies.

A comprehensive review of Azerbaijan's more than 30 PSAs is beyond the scope of this research. However, a review of the Azeri-Chirag-Gunashli PSA, the so-called "Contract of the Century" (BP, 1994) yields the following details. Crude oil is split between the participating international companies (contractors), on the one hand, and the government, represented by SOCAR, on the other. Revenue from the sales of crude oil is divided into two categories, and so is the oil itself: to cover costs ("cost oil") and to generate profit ("profit oil"). Operational expenditures are covered by sales from production first. Then, 50% of the remaining oil can be used to cover capital expenditures. The residual profit oil is then split between companies and the government, depending on the real rate of return (RROR) earned by participating companies, on the following basis: 70% (company share) for RROR up to 16.75%, 45% for RROR up to 22.75% and 20% for RROR over 22.75%.

Free gas[4] is not part of any PSA, and SOCAR retains the right to develop such resources. The participating companies may produce associated gas, which is relinquished free of charge to SOCAR. Apart from these provisions, the PSA contractors are obliged to pay 25% profit tax from their activities within the PSA, hire an increasing number of local workers and require employees to pay income tax to Azerbaijan on the part of their income related to activities in the country. For other PSAs, the profit tax rate ranges between 20% and 32% (Ernst & Young, 2015b).

Figure 3.8 illustrates the financial flows resulting from the Azeri-Chirag-Gunashli (ACG) PSA. In this illustration, the State Oil Fund of Azerbaijan (SOFAZ) and the State Social Fund fall outside the fiscal system, and payments to them are not taxed. They are nevertheless worth noting in terms of the overall picture of the government's revenue from PSAs. SOFAZ is Azerbaijan's equivalent of a sovereign wealth fund, where revenues from the implementation of PSAs are accumulated, managed and preserved as reserves for the future. As of the beginning of 2016, SOFAZ had accumulated funds of USD 35 bln, roughly equivalent to Azerbaijan's annual GDP at the devalued 2016 rate.

The budget of SOFAZ is approved separately from the national budget of Azerbaijan, and is not part of it. Still, every year, SOFAZ transfers significant funds to the national budget. For instance, SOFAZ's total 2016 budget was approved by the President of Azerbaijan in the amount of AZN 8.2 bln (USD 5.4 bln), 22% more than its expected revenue in a period of low world oil prices. SOFAZ's biggest expenditure item was the AZN 6 bln (USD 4 bln) transfer to the national budget.

In addition, SOFAZ funds various strategic development and social development projects, many of which are infrastructure investments. These include development of oil and gas infrastructure and Azerbaijan's participation in the construction of the Southern Gas Corridor, at AZN 1.8 bln (President of Azerbaijan, 2015a), the Fund's second biggest expenditure in 2016.

Table 3.5. **Oil and gas related expenditures by SOFAZ (in AZN million)**

2013	2014	2015	2016
372.6[a]	1 308.6 (548.7[b])	997 (693[a])	1 822.8 (2 355[b])

Note: a. Budget as executed.
b. Budget as approved.

Source: President of Azerbaijan (2015a).

Figure 3.8. **Financial flows under Azeri-Chirag-Gunashli PSA**

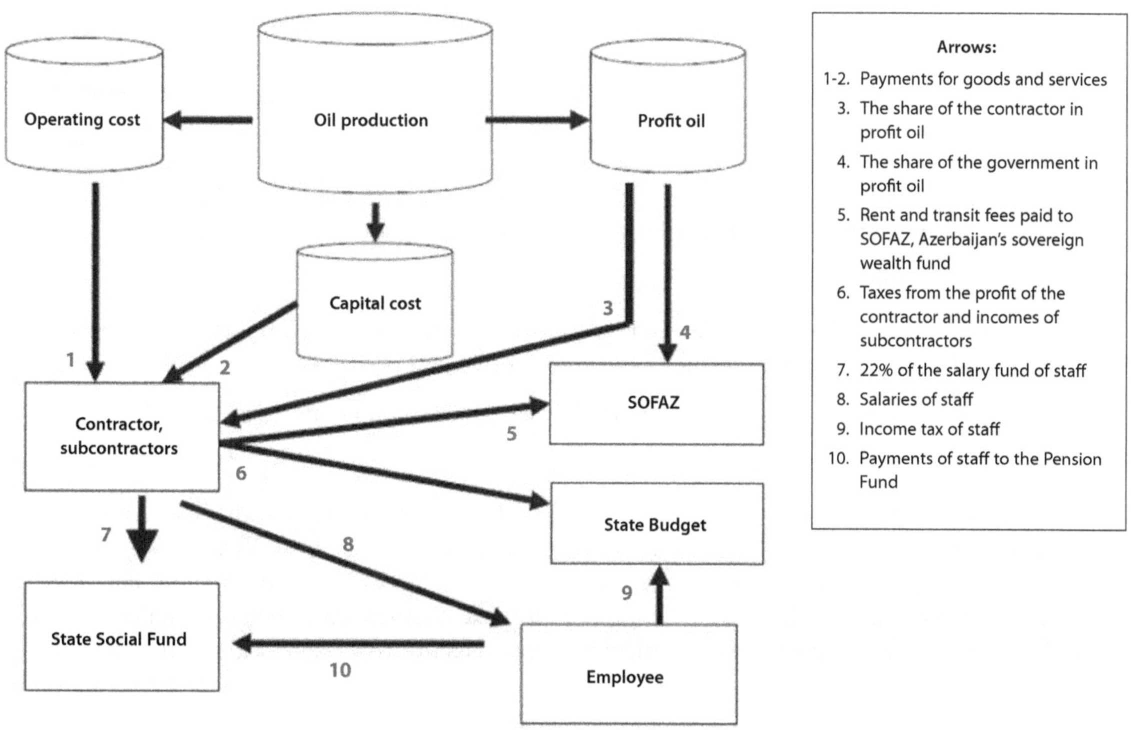

Source: Reproduced from Bagirov (2007).

Tax benefits granted on an individual basis

Tax relief can be granted to companies on an individual basis under two arrangements.

First, there is the "manual control" arrangement for selected companies, specifically in the upstream oil and gas sector. The basis for this is the Law on Application of Special Economic Regime for Export-Oriented Oil and Gas Operations, which came into force on 17 April 2009. This law applies to export-oriented oil and gas operations carried out by contractors and subcontractors. The law is valid for 15 years, but may be extended. To receive individual exemptions, companies should have a permanent taxable presence (normally, a permanent establishment with operations and employees) in Azerbaijan and obtain a special certificate, issued separately for each contract. The certificate is granted by the Ministry of Energy, generally for a period specified in the contractor's or subcontractor's contract. The holders of the certificate can benefit from the following tax privileges (PWC, 2016):

- local companies are permitted to choose between *i)* profit tax at a rate of 20% or *ii)* 5% withholding tax (WHT) on gross revenues
- foreign subcontractors are taxable only by a 5% WHT
- a 0% VAT rate on procured goods and services
- exemption from dividend WHT and taxation on the branch's net profits
- exemption from customs duties and taxes
- exemptions from property (real-estate and capital goods) tax and land (use) tax.

Second, the Presidential Decree of 18 January 2016 introduced additional investment promotion certificates that are not specific to the export-oriented oil and gas industry. Among the priorities of this policy is the attraction of investment in industrial parks, manufacturing plants and research (ABC.az, 2016). Based on the wording of the legislation, energy companies do not appear to be the intended beneficiaries of the scheme, but potentially, some of them, including those specialising in energy efficiency and renewable energy, may become eligible for such investment promotion certificates and associated tax benefits. The Ministry of Economy grants investment promotion certificates to the companies and individuals based on their business plans. The related tax benefits are in place for seven years from the date of the issue of the certificate and include the following:

- 50% of the profit is exempt from income tax
- 100% exemption from VAT and customs duties and taxes for import of equipment and devices approved by the relevant executive authority
- 100% exemption from property (real-estate and capital goods) tax
- 100% exemption from land (use) tax.

Although various analytical sources (e.g. OECD, 2003) discuss the existence of numerous environmental charges for air pollution and water discharges, as well as charges for solid waste, current research has not been able to identify any environmental charges or taxes in Azerbaijan. This may well imply that these charges have been eliminated. Nor did the PSA review uncover any technical prescriptions limiting gas-flaring or discharges of drill-cutting waste to the sea.

Greenhouse gas emissions and climate policy

Azerbaijan ratified the United Nations Framework Convention on Climate Change (UNFCCC) in 1995 and its Kyoto Protocol in 2000. As a non-Annex I country, however, Azerbaijan did not undertake quantitative obligations to reduce greenhouse gas (GHG) emissions. The energy sector contributed more than 80% of total emissions in 2005 (Aliyev, 2013).

According to British Petroleum (BP, 2015b), CO_2 emissions related to energy production and consumption totalled nearly 35 mln tonnes in 2005, then dipped to below 26 mln tonnes in 2010, rising again to 32 mln tonnes in 2014. Some doubt has been cast on the accuracy of the dataset from British Petroleum (BP, 2015b). In particular, Aliyev (2015) reports a total of nearly 50 mln tonnes of CO_2 equivalent in 2010, of which the energy industry accounted for 37 tonnes.

Azerbaijan has established a Climate Change and Ozone Centre in charge of assessing climate change impacts and developing mitigation strategies. The Centre is part of the Hydrometeorological Department of the Ministry of Ecology and Natural Resources (AzMinEco, 2015b).

Azerbaijan is reported to take a pro-active role in mitigating climate change through domestic policies (Aliyev, 2013 and 2015). It also participates in international climate change negotiations (Gallagher, 2014). The Ministry of Ecology lists among its climate-related achievements mainly projects implemented by donor organisations. The last self-assessment report dates from 2005 (AzMinEco, 2015a).

In preparing for the UNFCCC conference of the parties in Paris, Azerbaijan submitted its Intended Nationally Determined Contribution (INDC) in September 2015 (INDC of Azerbaijan, 2015). Under this INDC, Azerbaijan aims to reduce its GHG emissions from all sources by 35% by 2030, to 47.665 megatonnes of CO_2 equivalent excluding land use, land-use change and forestry (LULUCF), compared with the base year of 1990, when the total was 73.331 megatonnes of CO_2 equivalent (excluding LULUCF). This suggests that there is room for Azerbaijan to increase its emissions from the present level.

In 2004, to limit GHG emissions and increase energy efficiency, Azerbaijan adopted the State Programme on the Use of Alternative and Renewable Energy Sources (Government of Azerbaijan, 2004). The programme ran from 2005 to 2013. To facilitate implementation of the State Programme, a State Agency on Renewable and Alternative Energy Sources (AREA, sometimes also abbreviated as SAARES or ABEMDA) was established, in 2009. The Agency was initially founded under the Ministry of Energy and charged both with promoting alternative energy and implementing relevant investment projects. Since then, it has undergone several legal transformations. Most recently, on 24 November 2016, it was transformed into a "public legal entity" under the Ministry of Energy (President of Azerbaijan, 2016). There are reports (Malikov, n.d.) that AREA was in charge of the development of the National Strategy on the Use of Alternative and Renewable Energy Sources for the period 2012-20, but it has not been possible to determine the current status of this effort.

Azerbaijan's mid-term National Strategy, "Azerbaijan in 2020: Look into the Future," mentions energy efficiency and renewable-energy development among the country's priorities (President of Azerbaijan, 2012). In particular, Azerbaijan targets:

- an increase of the share of renewable energy in electricity generation to 20% by 2020 (in 2011 its share was 10%, including 9.8% from hydropower plants (HPPs), and 0.2% from other renewable energy (RE) sources) (Malikov, n.d.)
- an increase of the share of renewable energy in all energy consumption to 9.7% by 2020 (in 2011, it was 2.3%) (Malikov, n.d.).

At the same time, the Strategic Road Map for the Development of Utilities in Azerbaijan (electricity and thermal energy, water and gas supply), approved by Presidential Decree of 6 December 2016, envisages the construction of 420 MW renewable power plants, including 350 MW wind, 50 MW solar and 20 MW bioenergy power plants.

One of the key documents on energy efficiency in Azerbaijan is the State Programme for the Development of the Fuel and Energy Sector (2005-2015). This included measures to improve the use of hydrocarbon energy resources, as well as steps intended to reduce energy losses, prevent theft and reduce the inefficient use of energy, in order to help cover the demand for electricity and natural gas (Huseynova, 2015).

In addition, Azerbaijan ratified the Energy Charter Treaty and the Protocol on Energy Efficiency and Related Environmental Aspects. Since 2000, investments in generation and transmission and the conversion of some power plants from heavy oil (mazut) to natural gas have also improved power plant efficiency and reduced emissions and other adverse environmental impacts (Huseynova, 2015).

National definition and discussion of energy subsidies

As in the chapters on other countries of the EU's Eastern Partnership, the following discussion of energy subsidies in Azerbaijan relies on the subsidy definition from the Agreement on Subsidies and Countervailing Measures signed by 162 member countries of the World Trade Organization (WTO). According to this definition, the different forms of subsidies include:

- direct transfers of funds (e.g. grants, loans and equity infusion), potential direct transfers of funds or liabilities (e.g. loan guarantees)
- government revenue foregone or not collected (e.g. fiscal incentives such as preferential tax rates, tax exemptions and tax credits)
- government-provided goods or services other than general infrastructure at below-market rates (e.g. charges set at below-market rates for oil and gas transport through the country's territory), or purchases of goods at above-market rates
- income or price support, for instance, through regulation of prices, markets and other industry-specific activities.

However, Azerbaijan is not a member of the World Trade Organization, and the WTO definition of subsidies thus has little significance for its national legislation and discussions.

At the same time, especially given the fiscal pressures resulting from the global financial and economic slowdown and the drop in world oil and gas prices, an ongoing discussion on budget and fiscal policy optimisation is being conducted in Azerbaijan. The National Strategy "Azerbaijan 2020: Look into the Future" (adopted in 2012) provides that among the country's strategic objectives, "special attention will be paid to the establishment of fiscal discipline in the sphere of forming and using budget resources, correcting distribution of funds and increasing the efficiency of spending. Quick assessments of various budget risks (foreign, financial, operational risks) will be carried out" (President of Azerbaijan, 2012).

As in most other countries, the national legislation of Azerbaijan, including documents related to the budgetary process, clearly uses the notion of "subsidies" to define direct budgetary transfers (President of Azerbaijan, 2015b, IMF, 2015), the first group of subsidies under the WTO definition. In particular, there is an ongoing discussion of agricultural subsidies in Azerbaijan, which are funded directly out of the state budget (Kerimhanova, 2015; FAO REU, 2012).

Tax exemptions are also being discussed. For example, in late 2015, when the Tax Code of Azerbaijan was amended, a discussion took place in the *Milli Majlis* (Azerbaijan's Parliament) on whether tax exemptions for export-oriented oil and gas companies, in particular the VAT exemption for imported equipment, were still justified, given the increasing budgetary pressures in view of the low world price of oil (TREND.AZ, 20 October 2015). However, these tax benefits remained in place, and such government agencies as the Ministry of Energy and the Ministry of Economy predominantly view them as necessary incentives rather than harmful subsidies.

In practice, it is possible to assume that direct transfers are acknowledged in Azerbaijan as subsidies; and tax expenditure is discussed as a form of government support as well (Figure 3.9).

Figure 3.9. **What does Azerbaijan include in the national definition of government support?**

Dark shading	Covered by the national definitions of both "subsidy" and "state support"
Light shading	Covered only by the national definition of "state support"
No shading	Not included in the national definition of either "subsidy" or "state support"

Direct budget transfers	Tax expenditures	Induced transfers	Transfer of risk to government	Reference
Covered by both "subsidy" and "state support" (dark shading)	Covered by both "subsidy" and "state support" (dark shading)	Not included (no shading)	Not included (no shading)	President of Azerbaijan (2015b)

At the same time, as in other EaP countries, consumer subsidies have been historically discussed in Azerbaijan under the banner of energy tariff reform, and the memories of the tripling of electricity prices and prices of petroleum products in 2006-07 were still very vivid in early 2016.

Transfer of risk to the government as a form of subsidy is a category likely to be less familiar to stakeholders. Risk and the cost of non-payments have been and are still transferred to the government, although metering and collection practices have improved in recent years.

Azerbaijan does not publish its own subsidy estimates or tax expenditure budgets. The availability of information was thus a major challenge in preparing this section.

There is some fragmentary analysis of Azerbaijan's energy subsidies from the World Bank and the IEA. The World Bank did a case study on Azerbaijan's consumer subsidy reform in 2006-07 (World Bank, 2013b) and analysed consumer prices for energy in the regional study *Balancing Act,* on "Cutting Energy Subsidies while Protecting Affordability" (World Bank, 2013a). Both publications from the World Bank generally qualify Azerbaijan's consumer subsidy reform of 2006-07 as an overall success story of managing energy demand.

The dataset supporting the IEA's *World Energy Outlook 2015* (2015d) contains an estimate of Azerbaijan's fossil-fuel consumer subsidies based on a price-gap approach, totalling USD 1.5 bln (Table 3.6). The considerable drop in the value of subsidies in 2014 compared with 2013 is due to the drastic decline in the world energy prices that IEA uses as a benchmark in its calculations. The USD 1.5 bln worth of consumer subsidies amounted to 2% of Azerbaijan's GDP in 2014. The IEA estimates are used for triangulation of the authors' findings, described below.

Table 3.6. **IEA estimates of fossil-fuel consumer subsidies in Azerbaijan based on the price gap approach, USD billion**

Subsidised fossil fuel	2012	2013	2014
Oil	0.9	1.1	0.3
Electricity	0.6	0.7	0.5
Gas	0.9	1.0	0.7
Coal	-	-	-
Total	2.4	2.8	1.5

Source: Reproduced from IEA (2015d).

The authors' research has relied on tariff data from the Azerbaijani Tariff Council for an understanding of domestic price formation, reporting by British Petroleum on its Caspian operations for information on the Azerbaijani PSA regime and international legal and accounting firms for information on energy taxation. In addition, media reports and industry presentations for general information on the Azerbaijani energy sector were used. Throughout, the sources used are explicitly referenced.

Table 3.7 summarises the key findings on the legislative basis of different subsidy schemes and data availability by subsidy categories used by the OECD (OECD, 2013). These serve as a departure point for the rest of the chapter.

Table 3.7. **Subsidy overview**

Energy subsidy	Key findings
Direct transfer of funds and liabilities	• Discussed in Azerbaijan as subsidies (except liabilities) • Transfers from the national budget to AzerEnerji and AzeriGas have been significant • Transfers from SOFAZ for the construction of Southern Gas Corridor have been identified in 2016
Tax expenditures (tax revenue foregone)	• Tax revenue can be foregone in order to secure investment under three types of tax regime: *i)* national; *ii)* PSAs and HGAs; and *iii)* individual preferences under government certificates • Tax expenditures are recognised as a form of government support, but discussed as "investment incentives" rather than subsidies • Tax postponements and forgiveness to AzerEnerji and AzeriGas (documented in 2014 and 2015)
Induced transfers (income or price support provided to producers or consumers through various regulations)	• Discussed in Azerbaijan within tariff-setting practices and tariff reform • A partial reform of consumer subsidies in 2006-07 is documented by the World Bank as an overall successful case • Consumer prices are suppressed for gas, electricity, petroleum products and district heating compared with free-market pricing • IEA estimates fossil-fuel consumer subsidies in Azerbaijan at USD 1.5 bln in 2014
Transfer of risk to government	• Not recognised or discussed as a subsidy • Risk and cost of non-payments have been and are still transferred to the government, although metering and collection practices have improved in recent years

Government support for fossil fuels

To quantify fossil-fuel subsidies in Azerbaijan, the authors have used a combination of the bottom-up approach to subsidy identification and price-gap analysis. For price-gap calculations, the authors follow exactly the same logic as the IEA price-gap methodology used in the analysis of the other EaP countries in this report:

Price gap = Reference price – Net tariff

Subsidy = Price gap × Units consumed

Price-gap estimates of consumer subsidies

Azerbaijan is a net exporter of natural gas and oil. In contrast with all other countries of the EU Eastern Partnership, the reference price for Azerbaijan is the opportunity cost of export for external markets, and not the import parity price (which is used for Armenia, Belarus, Georgia, Moldova and Ukraine). In other words, for natural gas and oil in Azerbaijan, the reference price is the export parity price understood as the price of a product at the nearest international hub, adjusted for transport costs. All calculations are net of VAT.

At the same time, it is quite common for oil- and gas-producing countries to argue that a justifiable reference price is not an export parity price, but production costs. Furthermore, for electricity, the levelised cost of generation is the only appropriate reference price benchmark for both net exporters and net importers of energy. Energy production costs are thus also provided in the analysis below.

Table 3.8 summarises the price-gap estimates from the calculations, which is the main quantitative estimate of fossil-fuel subsidies in Azerbaijan from this study. Azerbaijan's subsidies for both natural gas and electricity consumption are estimated at USD 1.7 bln in 2014, or 2.3% of the 2014 GDP.

Table 3.8. **Price-gap estimates of fossil-fuel subsidies in Azerbaijan in 2014**

Fuel	Price-gap subsidy estimate
(+) Natural gas	USD 1.7 bln
(-) Double-counting of support for electricity through suppressed gas prices for generators	*USD 0.9 bln*
(+) Electricity	USD 0.9 bln
(+) Petroleum products	n.c.
(+) Coal	n.c. and likely small
Total	**USD 1.7 bln**

Notes: **n.c.**: not calculated. Price-gap estimates are based on authors' calculations

Natural gas

Table 3.9 presents a price-gap analysis for natural gas in Azerbaijan. Consumption volumes have been taken from the country's official 2014 Energy Balance (AzerStat, 2015d).

SOCAR reports natural gas production costs at USD 36 per 1 000 m^3 in 2014 (SOCAR, 2015a). Gas prices (tariffs) range from USD 78 to 97 per 1 000 m^3 (see also Table 3.3 above). The average weighted by consumption volume is USD 87 per 1 000 m^3. Thus, current sales prices substantially exceed domestic production costs.

However, Azerbaijan's domestic gas tariff is substantially below not only the levels in neighbouring Armenia and Georgia but also Azerbaijan's closest export opportunity, Turkey. If Azerbaijan were to export volumes that are currently consumed domestically, the country would generate additional revenue. This additional revenue constitutes the opportunity cost of selling fuel domestically at below current international prices. In 2014, the average wholesale gas price in Turkey was USD 343 per 1 000 m^3 (IGU, 2015). Since 2014, gas prices have been decreasing, and for the lack of more recent price data from the Turkish market, the opportunity sales price has been set at the European 12-month average from January to December 2015 – that is, USD 270 per 1 000 m^3, according to the latest data from World Bank (2016a), less estimated transport costs. Overall, the European market price appears to be a justifiable benchmark, given Azerbaijan's current plans to increase its natural gas exports to Europe through the Southern Gas Corridor.

Precise estimates of potential gas transport costs from Azerbaijan to Europe and appropriate netback pricing (that is, export market price less transport costs) would require substantial and diligent research. For purposes of illustration, these can be approximated using, first, the designed length of the proposed Southern Gas Corridor project (3 500 km)

(TAP-AG, 2015) as a conservative estimate of the distance to European markets and, second, the average third-party transport tariff for the Russian Unified System of Gas Supply (USGS), which is USD 1.25 per 1 000 m³ per 100 km (Yafimava, 2015).[5]

Table 3.9. **Price gap subsidy estimates for natural gas by consumer group, 2014**

Prices and costs	Unit	Electricity generators	Priority industrial consumers	Other end consumers
Sales price	USD per 1 000 m³	78	78	97
AzeriGas production costs	USD per 1 000 m³	36	36	36
Opportunity cost for AzeriGas if selling at international market prices (or reference price)	USD per 1 000 m³		226	
Volume consumed	Billion m³	6.3	0.3	5.6
Price gap	USD per 1 000 m³	148	148	129
Total subsidy based on the opportunity cost method	USD bln	0.9	0.05	0.7
Total for end consumption of gas (exclusive of support for electricity generators)	USD bln		0.77	
Total for all groups of consumers	USD bln		1.7	

Source: Authors' calculations based on Tariff Council (2015), Gazprom (2015), SOCAR (2015a), AzerStat (2015d), World Bank (2016a), World Bank (2016b), Sigra Group Analysis.

Combined, these two estimates yield a transport cost of nearly USD 44 per 1 000 m³ (1.25 × 35). This means that the differential (price gap) between the highest gas price in Azerbaijan (USD 97) and the European 12-month average price adjusted for transport costs (270–44 = 226) is USD 129 per 1 000 m³ (226–97), which is the opportunity cost for gas producers in Azerbaijan and a potential subsidy to domestic consumption. According to the price-gap analysis in Table 3.8, Azerbaijan is losing approximately USD 1.7 bln per year compared with its opportunity sales option.

Considering modest electricity prices, under-pricing of natural gas for electricity generators may be considered an electricity consumption subsidy rather than a gas-consumption subsidy. If one excludes the support for electricity generators (USD 0.9 bln) from the total (USD 1.7 bln), the subsidy to end consumption of gas in 2014 was USD 0.8 bln. This is approximately the same as the IEA estimate for the natural gas subsidy, which was USD 1 bln in 2013 and USD 0.7 bln in 2014.

Petroleum products

It has not been possible to ascertain production (refining) costs for petroleum products in Azerbaijan. The calculation of netback costs, including transport costs to export markets, is also a challenge. Nonetheless, Figures 3.10 and 3.11 offer comparison with adjacent markets, using pump prices in mid-November 2014 as reported by GIZ (GIZ, 2015). The pump prices and the values in Figures 3.10 and 3.11 are inclusive of VAT and excise taxes – which are different depending on the country, hence the rationale for benchmarking is limited. The consumer price gap for gasoline is insignificant for all countries except Turkey (which generally has quite high gasoline prices by international standards), while for diesel, Georgia, Armenia and Turkey all have significantly higher prices. However, in the absence of a sound methodological foundation, it is premature to provide quantitative estimates of a potential subsidy.

Figure 3.10. **Diesel prices in USD/litre in mid November 2014**

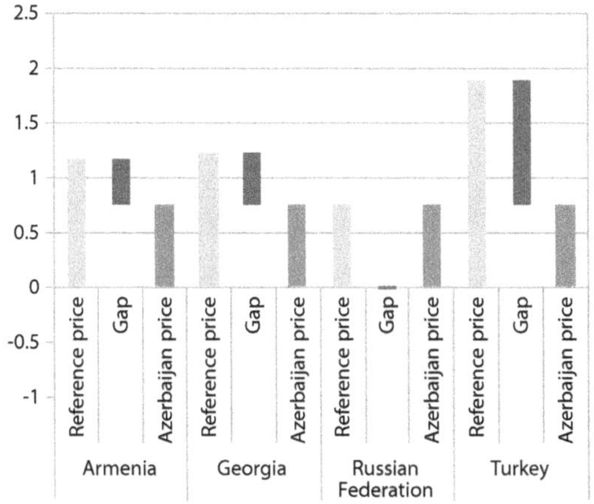

Figure 3.11. **Gasoline prices, USD/litre in mid November 2014**

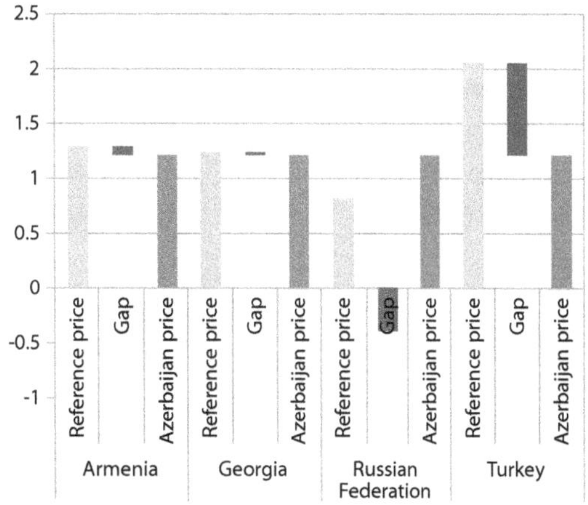

Source: Authors' presentation based on GIZ (2015).

Through the course of 2015 and early 2016, the Azerbaijani manat depreciated significantly, while regulated prices of petroleum products in local currency remained constant. Thus, the more relevant domestic pump prices are USD 0.78 and USD 0.58 per litre for gasoline and diesel, respectively, versus the USD 1.21 and USD 0.77 prices applied in Figures 3.10 and 3.11. It is probable that this depreciation has increased the price gap. However, in the absence of updated data for other markets, only a comparison of the situation as of mid-November 2014 is possible.

At the same time, as indicated above, the IEA estimates consumption subsidies for petroleum products in Azerbaijan at USD 0.3 bln in 2014 and USD 1.1 bln in 2013.

Electricity and heat

Unlike natural gas, electricity is not traded across borders to a significant degree. Accordingly, the price gap must employ production cost as the price gap's reference price. The levelised cost of electricity (LCOE) is a common method for comparing the production cost of electricity across sources. In particular, the LCOE takes account of varying capital intensity, operation and maintenance costs, as well as fuel costs. Among other things, the LCOE approach answers the question of what sources of electric generation may be economically justified at a given sales price for electricity. This section provides LCOE estimates for Azerbaijan, which, compared with prevailing sales prices, allow for a price-gap analysis for electric power, however rudimentary.

Fichtner Ltd (2013) provides a levelised cost estimate for combined-cycle gas turbine (CCGT) power production in Azerbaijan at USD 0.024 per kWh and offers USD 0.053 per kWh as an "international levelised cost estimate". Current producer tariffs (USD 0.040 per kWh) exceed the domestic cost estimates, but not the international benchmark (Table 3.3).

Fuel cost assumptions are not clear from Fichtner Ltd (2013). Table 3.10 therefore presents a parallel simple levelised cost (sLCOE) calculation using the methodology suggested by OpenEI (2016) and the same assumptions as Fichtner Ltd (2013) when possible. The two estimates of domestic levelised cost correspond to a one US cent difference per kWh (0.024 and 0.035 USD/kWh). However, the respective international benchmark estimates differ significantly; this is probably due to the difference in the opportunity fuel price.

Table 3.10. **Levelised cost of power production for CCGT plants in Azerbaijan**

	Unit	Fichtner	Own calculations (Sigra Group)
Fichtner and Sigra Group			
Specific investment	USD per kW	975	975
Operation and management	% of CAPEX	n.a.	0%
Fuel cost (local)	USD per MWh	5	n.a.
Fuel cost (international)	USD per MWh	5	n.a.
Efficiency	%	58%	n.a.
Size	MW	450	n.a.
Full operating hours	Hours per year	6 000	6 000
Useful life	Years	25	25
Discount rate	%	10%	10%
Own calculations (Sigra Group)			
Capacity factor	%	n.a.	68.5%
Domestic fuel cost	USD per 1 000 m^3	n.a.	78
Domestic fuel cost	USD/mmbtu (1 mln British Thermal Units)	n.a.	2.210
Conversion factor	1 000 m^3/mbtu	n.a.	0.028
Opportunity fuel cost	USD per 1 000 m^3		270
Opportunity fuel cost	USD/mmbtu		7.65
Heat rate	btu/kWh	n.a.	7 667
Capital recovery factor			0.110
Levelised costs			
sLCOE Domestic gas price	USD/kWh	n.a.	0.035
sLCOE Opportunity gas price	USD/kWh	n.a.	0.077
Levelised unit cost local gas price	USD/kWh	0.024	n.a.
Levelised unit cost international gas price	USD/kWh	0.053	n.a.
Current prices			
AzerEnerji JSC production	USD/kWh		0.040
Consumer price	USD/kWh		0.058
Exchange rate	*AZN/USD USD 2015 average*	n.a.	*1.0261*

Note: **n.a.**: not applicable.

Source: Authors' summary based on Fichtner Ltd (2013), OpenEI (2016), EIA (2015b) and Sigra Group analysis.

In sum, neither approach indicates electricity consumption subsidies in Azerbaijan if we use domestic fuel prices. Introducing the opportunity cost of gas reveals a potential subsidy, depending on the opportunity cost applied. The parallel calculation method offered above can also be used to identify at what domestic gas price levelised costs would be equal to the current producer tariff. The sLCOE equals USD 0.040 per kWh at a gas price of USD 102 per 1 000 m^3. Accordingly, any opportunity gas price above USD 102 per 1 000 m^3, which would be a highly conservative opportunity gas price estimate, would justify higher current electricity prices than the current producer tariff.

Given the lack of operation and maintenance estimates by Fichtner Ltd (2013), the authors' own parallel calculation is subject to the same omission. Accordingly, levelised cost estimates should in fact be higher. Given the limited 5-cent differential between the estimated domestic levelised cost (USD 0.035 per kWh) and the tariff for AzerEnerji generation (USD 0.040 per kWh), it is also possible that introducing operation and maintenance cost would raise the levelised cost estimate above current tariffs, resulting in a subsidy from the point of view of purchase cost as well.

Applying a price gap between the domestic wholesale price of USD 0.04 per kWh and the internationalised levelised cost of USD 0.077 per kWh to Azerbaijan's 24.8 TWh production in 2014 (AzerStat, 2015g), yields a total estimate of a consumer subsidy for electricity of USD 0.9 bln in 2014, which includes the support through the under-pricing of gas for electricity generators. This is higher than the IEA price-gap estimate, which puts electricity consumption subsidies in Azerbaijan at USD 0.5 bln in 2014 and USD 0.7 bln in 2013.

Estimating electricity consumer subsidies is further complicated by two additional challenges. The first is the potential under-collection of payments from households (World Bank, 2013b). Not much data is available on this subject in the public domain, but AzerEnerji does receive direct budget transfers to address this problem (see below in the section on the bottom-up inventory, as well as Table 3.A1.1).

The second challenge is co-generation of heat and power. Virtually no information is available on heat generation costs. District heating also does not cover Azerbaijan in its entirety: it is provided mainly in the capital city of Baku and its surroundings. However, throughout the EaP and Central Asia region, district heating is heavily subsidised and often cross-subsidised through electricity tariffs. It is justifiable to assume that the same situation may exist in Azerbaijan.

Bottom-up inventory of government support for fossil fuels

The paucity of data available has limited the scope for a verifiable bottom-up inventory of fossil-fuel subsidy schemes in Azerbaijan. This report has relied on media reports, whose ambiguity may be a source of misinterpretation. Only a limited number of schemes have been identified, and quantitative estimates can only be considered indicative.

Table 3.11 summarises the findings, while Annex 3.A1 provides more detailed information on each of the schemes. In terms of direct transfers, AzerEnerji, AzeriGas and the district heat provider AzerIstilikTechizat appear to be recipients of funds from the national budget. The amounts of transfers are reported at face value from media reports, where available.

Table 3.11. **Oil-related expenditure of SOFAZ in AZN million**

Projects	2013	2014	2015	2016
Construction of Star oil-processing complex	372.6	223.54		127
Transfers to Southern Gas Corridor projects	-	49.831	692.85	241.9
Construction of Oil and Gas Processing and Petrochemical Complex	-	363.34 (0[a])	-	-
Financing of government share in oil and gas pipelines	-	51	-	-
Total	**372.6[a]**	**1 308.6 (548.7[b])**	**997 (693[a])**	**1 822.8 (2 355[b])**

Notes: a. Budget as executed.

b. Budget as approved.

Source: President of Azerbaijan (2015a).

Though technically off-budget, SOFAZ, Azerbaijan's sovereign wealth fund, also provides direct transfers to the oil and gas sector. As discussed earlier, in the 2016 SOFAZ budget (Table 3.5), Azerbaijan's participation in the construction of the Southern Gas Corridor was funded at the level of AZN 1.8 bln (President of Azerbaijan, 2015a). Table 3.11 provides information on specific types of oil-related investments supported by SOFAZ in the period 2013-16.

There are two additional types of budget transfers for special categories of energy consumers. First, Azerbaijan provides support for internally displaced persons for electricity consumption. This subsidy is administered as an allowance of 150 kilowatt-hours per person per month, and funded by the State Refugee Committee (World Bank, 2013b).

Second, farmers receive an allowance for petroleum products that is transferred to individual plastic cards issued by Kapital Bank. In 2015, the value of this annual subsidy was AZN 40 (USD 39) per hectare of farmed land. This subsidy dates back to 2007, when the prices of regulated diesel and other petroleum products were raised and it was decided to compensate farmers for this price increase (Kerimhanova, 2015).

It is less clear what measures should be included in the bottom-up inventory for the category of tax expenditure, since, as explained above, Azerbaijan has several tax regimes for upstream oil and gas operations. There is a national tax regime and then special tax provisions under PSAs and HGAs. However, outside special arrangements with international consortia within PSAs and HGAs, it seems logical to list at least the tax breaks under the Law on Application of Special Economic Regime for Export-Oriented Oil and Gas Operations, which came into force on 17 April 2009. There is insufficient information on the scale of the operations subsidised under this law, which made their quantitative assessment impossible, and no estimates from government sources are available in the public domain.

Induced transfers to energy consumers through regulated prices have been discussed above using the price-gap method. No official bottom-up estimates of this support are available.

Government support for energy efficiency and renewable energy

In April 2014, the government of Azerbaijan passed Resolutions No. 112 and 113, which exempt the import of equipment and technology used in energy efficiency and alternative and renewable energy from customs duties and VAT (Huseynova, 2015). Since there are exactly the same exemptions for the import of equipment and technology for the oil and gas sector, the 2014 Resolutions eliminate the negative distortion that previously existed with respect to energy efficiency and development of renewable energy.

The Tariff Council has the authority to provide preferential tariffs for producers of electricity from renewable energy sources; however, this authority has so far been exercised only to a limited extent. As indicated in Table 3.3 in the Price Policy section of this chapter, the electricity producer tariff is differentiated. Since 2008, the producer tariff for AzerEnerji's thermal power plants has been AZN 0.041 per kWh (USD 0.040), whereas for small private hydropower plants, it was lower, at AZN 0.025 per kWh (USD 0.024). The tariff for wind power plants was slightly higher than the thermal power plant benchmark, and was set at AZN 0.045 per kWh (USD 0.044). All these producer tariffs are lower than the price paid by consumers, which is AZN 0.06 per kWh (USD 0.058).

Table 3.12. **Bottom-up inventory of fossil-fuel subsidies in Azerbaijan**

Subsidy	Subsidy mechanism (e.g. tax waiver or price support)	Activity	Estimated annual amount, AZN mln 2012	2013	2014	2015 plan (as of April)	Source/method of calculation
Direct budget transfers (including spending on fossil-fuel-related infrastructure)							
Budget support for AzerEnerji	Compensation for losses	Electricity generation	141.7	72	37.7	n.a.	Qafqazinfo.az (10 September 2013), "Corruption Facts at AzerEnerji Revealed by Hackers". www.qafqazinfo.az/iqtisadiyyat-4/hakerlerin-azerenerji-de-uze-cixardigi-korrupsiya-49750 ABC.az (n.d.), "Fitch: AzerEnerji Expects Power Rates to Stay Unchanged in 2014-17". http://abc.az/eng/interview/200.html
Budget support for AzeriGas	Compensation for expenditures	Supply of natural gas	n.a.	n.a.	n.a.	n.a.	Azertag (29 December 2005), "AzeriGas did not Receive Subsidies". http://azertag.az/xeber/AZARIQAZA_SUBSIDIYA_AYRILMIR-332895
Budget support for AzerIstilikTechizat	Compensation for expenditures	District heating	n.a.	n.a.	n.a.	n.a.	APA.az (27 November 2015), AzeriGas: "AzerIstilikTechizat Owes us 43 mln Manats Debt". http://m.apa.az/az/news/406296
Direct funding of energy projects from SOFAZ	Financing of investment	Various, including construction of upstream infrastructure					In the 2016 SOFAZ budget, Azerbaijan's participation in the construction of the Southern Gas Corridor is funded directly by SOFAZ at the level of AZN 1.8 bln (USD 1.1 bln) (President of Azerbaijan, 2015a).
Support for internally displaced persons	Direct transfer from the State Refugee Committee	Electricity consumption by a vulnerable group	n.a.	n.a.	n.a.	n.a.	The State Refugee Committee provides allowance for electricity consumption by internally displaced persons in the communities of Barmek and Bayva (World Bank, 2013b).
Support for farmers	Direct transfer via plastic cards	Diesel and other petroleum product consumption by farmers	n.a.	n.a.	n.a.	n.a.	AZN 40 per hectare of farmed land per year (Kerimhanova, 2015)
Subtotal direct budget transfers			141.7	72	37.7	43	

Table 3.12. **Bottom-up inventory of fossil-fuel subsidies in Azerbaijan** *(continued)*

Subsidy	Subsidy mechanism (e.g. **tax waiver or price support**)	Activity	Estimated annual amount, AZN mln				Source/method of calculation
			2012	*2013*	*2014*	*2015 plan (as of April)*	
Tax expenditure							
Tax breaks under the Law on Application of Special Economic Regime for Export-Oriented Oil and Gas Operations • Local companies are permitted to choose between: *i)* a profit tax at a rate of 20%; or *ii)* a 5% WHT on gross revenue • Foreign sub-contractors are taxable only at a 5% WHT • A 0% VAT rate on procured goods and services • Exemption from a dividend WHT and taxation on branch's net profits • Exemption from customs duties and taxes • Exemptions from property tax (real-estate and capital goods) tax and land (use) tax	Government revenue foregone	Upstream oil and gas activities	n.a.	n.a.	n.a.	n.a.	Law on Application of Special Economic Regime for Export-Oriented Oil and Gas Operations, which took effect 17 April 2009 (PWC, 2016). Information on the scale of the operations subsidised under this law is limited, making their quantitative assessment impossible.
Induced transfers (income or price support)							
Gasoline (Premium, AI-95)	Regulated prices	Gasoline consumption	n.a.	n.a.	n.a.	n.a.	Tariff Council (n.d.), "Tariffs for Oil Products".www.tariffcouncil.gov.az/?/az/content/72/
Gasoline (AI-92)	Regulated prices		n.a.	n.a.	n.a.	n.a.	Tariff Council (n.d.), "Tariffs for Oil Products". www.tariffcouncil.gov.az/?/az/content/72/
Diesel	Regulated prices	Diesel consumption	n.a.	n.a.	n.a.	n.a.	Tariff Council (n.d.), "Tariffs for Oil Products".www.tariffcouncil.gov.az/?/az/content/72/
Heavy oil (*mazut*) and kerosene	Regulated prices	Heavy oil (*mazut*) and kerosene consumption	n.a.	n.a.	n.a.	n.a.	Tariff Council (n.d.), "Tariffs for Oil Products". *i)* www.tariffcouncil.gov.az/?/az/content/72/; *ii)* Milli.az NewsPortal (28 November 2011), "Tariff Council Increased Price for Some of the Communal Services". http://news.milli.az/economy/82557.html
Natural gas	Regulated prices	Natural gas consumption, including for electricity generation	n.a.	n.a.	n.a.	n.a.	(1) Tariff Council (n.d.), "Tariffs for Natural Gas Wholesale and Retail Prices"; SOCAR (2014), "Financial Report by SOCAR for 2014". www.socar.az/socar/assets/documents/az/socar-annual-reports/illik-hesabat2014az.pdf
Electricity	Regulated prices	Electricity consumption	n.a.	n.a.	n.a.	n.a.	Tariff Council (n.d.), "Tariffs for Electricity". www.tariffcouncil.gov.az/?/az/content/70/

Note: **n.a.**: not available.

Source: Authors' summary.

Annex 3.A1

Fossil-fuel subsidies

Table 3.A1.1. **Budget transfers to AzerEnerji**

Subsidy category	Grants and other direct payments
Stimulated activity	Operations of AzerEnerji are supported by the compensation of its losses
Subsidy name	**Budget transfers to AzerEnerji**
Jurisdiction	National
Legislation/endorsing organisation	• Presidential decrees • Decisions adopted by the Cabinet of Ministers
Policy objective(s) of subsidy	Addressing social concerns about electricity consumption
End recipient(s) of subsidy	AzerEnerji
Time period	From 1991 until the present, i.e. since independence from the Soviet Union
Background	AzerEnerji is state-owned and the largest electric power producer in the country. Since the collapse of the Soviet Union, several reforms have been conducted to ensure effective budget support for the electricity sector. The mass installation of electric bill counters (electric meters) has reduced the use of electricity as residents have become more aware of their electricity consumption. This goal was to increase efficiency and reduce spending in this sector. However, as a result of nonpayment for its services, AzerEnerji accumulates debts and cannot always respect its tax payment obligations to the state budget. AzerEnerji's financial losses are covered (subsidised) by the state budget.
Amount of subsidy conferred	2012: AZN 141.7 mln (USD 180.37 mln) 2013: AZN 72 mln (USD 91.77 mln) 2014: AZN 37.7 mln (USD 48.06 mln)
Information sources	**Official documents:** • AzeCabMin (2010), On the Regulation of Debts of Major Energy Consumers Dealing with Wholesale Natural Gas and Petroleum Products, 9 August 2010, Cabinet of Ministers of the Republic of Azerbaijan, Baku. http://cabmin.gov.az/?/az/pressreliz/view/351/ • Ministry of Justice (2009), The Abolishment of Natural Gas Prices for the General Population, 29 December 2009, Ministry of Justice of the Republic of Azerbaijan, Baku. www.e-qanun.az/framework/18961 **Media Reports:** • Axar.az News Portal (9 December 2013), "Why Is AzerEnerji in Debt Again?", Axar.az News Portal, Baku. http://axar.az/news/3703 • Mediaforum News (29 December 2009), "President Pardons the Debts for Natural Gas Usage for the General Population", Mediaforum News, Baku. • Musavat Newspaper (19 August 2010), "The Energy Debts of the Population Should be Abolished", Musavat Newspaper, Baku. http://musavat.com/news/iqtisadiyyat/ehalinin-de-enerji-borclari-silinmelidir_83123.html?welcome=1 • Qafqazinfo.Az (21 January 2014), "The Millions are Allocated, but They Are Indebted Again", Qafqazinfo, Baku. www.qafqazinfo.az/musahibe-17/milyonlar-xerclenir-yene-borclari-var-68027 • Rafiqoglu, A. (17 August 2010), "Accumulated Energy Debts Abolished", ANSPress, Baku. • Report Information Agency (27 April 2015), "'Azersu' and 'Azerenerji' Are Indebted to Government", Report Information Agency, Baku. http://report.az/i-nfrastruktur/azersu-ve-azerenerji-nin-vergi-borcu-yaranib/

Table 3.A1.2. **Budget transfers to AzeriGas**

Subsidy category	Grants and other direct payments
Stimulated activity	Operations of AzeriGas are supported by compensation of its losses
Subsidy name	**Budget transfers to AzeriGas**
Jurisdiction	National
Legislation/endorsing organisation	• Presidential decrees • Decisions adopted by the Cabinet of Ministers
Policy objective(s) of subsidy	Addressing social concerns with respect to natural gas, heat and electricity consumption
End recipient(s) of subsidy	AzeriGas
Time period	From 1991 until the present, i.e. since independence from the Soviet Union
Background	AzeriGas is the state-owned natural gas monopoly. Since the collapse of the Soviet Union, there have been several reforms to ensure effective budget support for Azerbaijan's gas sector. As a result of the mass installation of gas bill counters (gas meters), the use of gas in the country has decreased as residents have become more aware of their consumption. This was done with the aim of increasing the efficiency and spending in this sector. However, as a result of nonpayment for its services, AzeriGas accumulates debts and cannot always respect its tax payment obligations to the state budget. AzeriGas financial losses are covered (subsidised) by the state budget.
Amount of subsidy conferred	Not available in public sources
Information sources	**Official documents:** • AzeCabMin (2010), On the Regulation of Debts of Major Energy Consumers Dealing with Wholesale Natural Gas and Petroleum Products, 9 August 2010, Cabinet of Ministers of the Republic of Azerbaijan, Baku. http://cabmin.gov.az/?/az/pressreliz/view/351/ • Ministry of Justice (2009), The Abolishment of Natural Gas Prices for the General Population, 29 December 2009, Ministry of Justice of the Republic of Azerbaijan, Baku. www.e-qanun.az/framework/18961 **Media reports:** • Axar.az News Portal (9 December 2013), "Why Is AzerEnerji in Debt Again?", Axar.az News Portal, Baku. http://axar.az/news/3703 • Mediaforum News (29 December 2009), "President Pardoned the Debts for Natural Gas Usage for the General Population", Mediaforum News, Baku. • Musavat Newspaper (19 August 2010), The Energy Debts of the Population Should Be Abolished, Musavat Newspaper, Baku. http://musavat.com/news/iqtisadiyyat/ehalinin-de-enerji-borclari-silinmelidir_83123.html?welcome=1 • Qafqazinfo.Az (21 January 2014), "The Millions Are Allocated, but They Are Indebted Again", Qafqazinfo, Baku. www.qafqazinfo.az/musahibe-17/milyonlar-xerclenir-yene-borclari-var-68027 • Rafiqoglu, A. (17 August 2010), Accumulated Energy Debts Abolished, ANSPress, Baku. • Report Information Agency (27 April 2015), "'Azersu' and 'Azerenerji' Are Indebted to Government", Report Information Agency, Baku. http://report.az/i-nfrastruktur/azersu-ve-azerenerji-nin-vergi-borcu-yaranib/

Table 3.A1.3. **Budget transfers to AzerIstilikTechizat**

Subsidy category	Grants and other direct payments
Stimulated activity	Operations of AzerilstilikTechizat are supported by compensation of its losses
Subsidy name	**Budget transfers to AzerIstilikTechizat**
Jurisdiction	National
Legislation/endorsing organisation	• Presidential decrees • Decisions adopted by the Cabinet of Ministers
Policy objective(s) of subsidy	Addressing social concerns with respect to heat consumption
End recipient(s) of subsidy	AzerIstilikTechizat
Time period	From 1991 until the present, i.e. since independence from the Soviet Union
Background	AzerIstilikTechizat is the state-owned district-heating company, providing heating during the winter months for a very small part of the population. The share of this subsidy in the overall energy subsidy landscape is insignificant. However, according to media reports, the debts generated by AzerIstilikTechizat to AzeriGas have generated problems for the functioning of both companies.
Amount of subsidy conferred	In 2015, this subsidy was planned at the level of AZN 43 mln. Not available for previous years. Equivalent value in USD: 40.76 mln (at 1.0261 USD/AZN)
Information sources	**Media reports:** • Ali, U. R. (18 November 2015), "Why Providing Heat to Apartments in Baku Was Stopped – Reasons", Oxu.az, Baku. http://ru.oxu.az/society/102636 • Salaeva, A. (29 November 2015), "The Date for Restarting the Supply of Heat to Apartments of Baku Announced", 1News.az, Baku. www.1news.az/society/20151119040452735.html • Salaeva, A. (20 November 2015), "The Number of Heat Boiler Houses in Baku Announced", 1News.az, Baku. www.1news.az/society/20151120021718602.html

Table 3.A1.4. **Regulated prices for natural gas**

Subsidy category	Induced transfers
Stimulated activity	Natural gas consumption, including in electricity and heat generation
Subsidy same	**Regulated price for natural gas**
Jurisdiction	Tariff (Price) Council of the Azerbaijan Republic
Legislation/endorsing organisation	Decisions adopted by the Tariff (Price) Council of the Azerbaijan Republic (formed by representatives of the Ministries of Economy and Industry, Finance, Taxes, Justice, Energy, Transport, Communication and Information Technologies, Agriculture, Health, Education, Labour and Social Defence of the People, Committees of Customs Control and State City Building and Architecture)
Policy objective(s) of subsidy	Addressing social concerns about consumption of natural gas, electricity and heat, as well as providing natural gas to several energy-intensive industries
End recipient(s) of subsidy	Consumers of natural gas
Time period	From 1991 until the present, i.e. since independence from the Soviet Union
Background	The structure of the Tariff (Price) Council of the Republic of Azerbaijan was approved by Decree No. 341 of the President of the Republic of Azerbaijan, dated 26 December 2005. To account for the social concerns of the population since independence, natural gas prices have been regulated by the Cabinet of Ministers. Since 2005, price regulation has been a responsibility of the Tariff (Price) Council. The chemical, steel, aluminium and power industry, and other industries with a monthly consumption of under 10 bln m^3 of gas benefit from reduced tariffs.
Amount of subsidy conferred	Not publicly available
Information sources	Tariff Council (2015a), Tariff Council – About, Tariff Council of the Republic of Azerbaijan, Baku. www.tariffcouncil.gov.az/?/en/content/44/ Tariff Council (n.d.), Tariffs for Natural Gas Wholesale and Retail Prices, Tariff Council of the Republic of Azerbaijan, Baku. www.tariffcouncil.gov.az/?/az/content/66/ State Customs Committee (2002), On the Founding of the Tariff Committee, State Customs Committee of the Republic of Azerbaijan, Baku. http://customs.gov.az/az/nkq17.html

Table 3.A1.5. **Regulated prices for electricity**

Subsidy category	Induced transfer
Stimulated activity	Electricity consumption
Subsidy name	**Regulated price for electricity**
Jurisdiction	Tariff (Price) Council of the Azerbaijan Republic
Legislation or endorsing organisation	Decisions adopted by the Tariff (Price) Council of the Azerbaijan Republic (formed by representatives of the Ministries of Economy and Industry, Finance, Taxes, Justice, Energy, Transport, Communication and Information Technologies, Agriculture, Health, Education, Labour and Social Defence of the People, Committees of Customs Control, and State City Building and Architecture)
Policy objective(s) of subsidy	Addressing social concerns about consumption of electricity
End recipient(s) of subsidy	Consumers of electricity
Time period	From 1991 until the present, i.e. since independence from the Soviet Union
Background	The structure of the Tariff (Price) Council of the Republic of Azerbaijan was approved by Decree No. 341 of the President of the Republic of Azerbaijan, dated 26 December 2005. To account for the social concerns of the population since independence, electricity prices have been regulated by the Cabinet of Ministers. Since 2005, price regulation has been a responsibility of the Tariff Council. In nearly two decades, electricity prices were adjusted only once. Electricity tariffs were increased in 2007 from USD 0.024 to 0.075 (AZN 0.06) per kWh (ECS, 2011) which, coupled with improved metering and collection practices, increased the sector's revenue significantly (Fichtner Ltd, 2013). Although this was a one-off measure, this tariff increase did succeed in controlling strong demand among residential consumers. Residential power consumption plunged by 58% from nearly 1 200 ktoe in 2006 to 495 ktoe in 2010. As of early 2016, electricity consumption was still below pre-reform levels of 2007. The tariffs set in 2007 remained in place until late spring 2016, when the price for residential consumers increased to 0.07 manat/kWh. Due to the depreciation of the Azerbaijani manat, the consumer electricity tariff is now lower in dollar terms than in 2007 (USD 0.068/kWh at the 2015 average AZN/USD exchange rate of 1.0261).
Amount of subsidy conferred	Not publicly available
Information sources	Tariff Council (2015a), Tariff Council – About, Tariff Council of the Republic of Azerbaijan, Baku. www.tariffcouncil.gov.az/?/en/content/44/ Tariff Council (n.d.), Tariffs for Natural Gas Wholesale and Retail Prices, Tariff Council of the Republic of Azerbaijan, Baku. www.tariffcouncil.gov.az/?/az/content/66/ State Customs Committee (2002), On the Founding of the Tariff Committee, State Customs Committee of the Republic of Azerbaijan, Baku. http://customs.gov.az/az/nkq17.html

Notes

1. In the interest of inter-country comparability, this section builds on data from international sources such as the World Bank and the International Energy Agency. These data, however, have certain discrepancies with the State Statistical Committee of the Republic of Azerbaijan (AzerStat). In some instances, national sources provide more recent data. Therefore, for all key indicators, the chapter seeks to provide references to both national and international statistics.

2. Given the dominant role of SOCAR and AzerEnerji in the country's energy sector, one might question to what degree the division of roles between policy, regulation and business are distinct between the Ministry, Tariff Council and national energy companies. Further research is needed into the distinction between state companies and government bodies in shaping and influencing energy policy and decisions.

3. Azerbaijan expects to significantly increase its natural gas exports to Europe through the construction of the Southern Gas Corridor.

4. Free gas in this context refers to "free", as opposed to associated, petroleum gas. This is natural gas that can be produced separately from oil.

5. Needless to say, this approximation is rough. The USGS transport tariff is used, given the lack of better estimates of current transport costs. Assuming that the USGS is fully depreciated, this estimate has been accepted as closer to the actual transport cost through existing networks than estimating a levelised cost for the Southern Energy Corridor, which will be a new project. The distance estimate is conservative because it only includes landing in Italy, and not the distance to the end-point or the detour of existing networks from the Balkans through Eastern Europe.

References

ABC.az (5 March 2016), "Investment Promotion Certificate Operates in Azerbaijan since March", http://abc.az/eng/news/94682.html.

ABC.az (n.d), "Fitch: AzerEnerji Expects Power Rates to Stay Unchanged in 2014-17". http://abc.az/eng/interview/200.html.

Ali, U.R. (18 November 2015), "Why Providing Heat to Apartments in Baku was Stopped – Reasons", Oxu.az, Baku. http://ru.oxu.az/society/102636.

Aliyev, I. (2015), *Azerbaijan: 2015 Paris Agreement and Intended Nationally Determined Contributions (INDCs) to be Submitted to United Nations Framework Convention on Climate Change (UNFCCC) in 2015.*

Aliyev, I. (2013), *Clima East: Support for Climate Change Mitigation and Adaptation in Russia and ENP East Countries, EU Climate Policy Roadshow Azerbaijan National Workshop.*

APA.az (27 November 2015), "AzeriGas: AzerIstilikTechizat Owes us 43 Million Manat Debt", APA.az, Baku. http://m.apa.az/az/news/406296.

Axar.az News Portal (9 December 2013), "Why is AzerEnerji in Debt Again?", Axar.az News Portal, Baku. http://axar.az/news/3703.

Azadlig Newspaper (23 January 2012), "The Mystery of Premium Gasoline in SOCAR Stations", *Azadlig Newspaper*, Baku. www.azadliq.info/12720.html.

AzeCabMin (2015), *Act on Estimates of Major State Taxpayers' Income and Expense, 9 June 2015,* Cabinet of Ministers of the Republic of Azerbaijan, Baku.

AzeCabMin (2011), *Decision No. 133 of 10 August 2011: A Number of State-Owned Enterprises on Debt Settlement,* Cabinet of Ministers of the Republic of Azerbaijan, Baku.

AzeCabMin (2010), *On the Regulation of Debts of Major Energy Consumers Dealing with Wholesale Natural Gas and Petroleum Products, 9 August 2010,* Cabinet of Ministers of the Republic of Azerbaijan, Baku. http://cabmin.gov.az/?/az/pressreliz/view/351/.

AzerEnerji (2015), *AzerEnerji – About Us,* AzerEnerji, Baku. www.azerenerji.gov.az/index.php.

AzerIshig (2015), *Azərbaycan Elektrik Şəbəkəsi haqqında ümumi məlumat* (General Information on Azerbaijan's Electricity Network), *AzerIshig, Baku.* www.azerishiq.az/index.php?lang=en&menu=about&id=9.

AzerStat (2015a), *Average for Prices and Tariffs for Consumer Products and Services to the Population,* State Statistical Committee of the Republic of Azerbaijan, Baku.

AzerStat (2015b), *Electricity Production and its Share,* State Statistical Committee of the Republic of Azerbaijan, Baku. www.stat.gov.az/source/balance_fuel/az/001_2.xls.

AzerStat (2015c), *Energy,* State Statistical Committee of the Republic of Azerbaijan, Baku. www.stat.gov.az/source/balance_fuel/az/005_5.xls.

AzerStat (2015d), *Energy Balance in 2014,* State Statistical Committee of the Republic of Azerbaijan, Baku. www.stat.gov.az/source/balance_fuel/.

AzerStat (2015e), *Main Indicators for the Industry,* State Statistical Committee of the Republic of Azerbaijan, Baku. www.stat.gov.az/source/industry/az/001.xls.

AzerStat (2015f), *Population of Azerbaijan,* State Statistical Committee of the Republic of Azerbaijan, Baku. www.stat.gov.az/source/demoqraphy/ap/az/1_1.xls.

AzerStat (2015g), *Power Generation 1913-2014,* State Statistical Committee of the Republic of Azerbaijan, Baku. www.stat.gov.az/source/balance_fuel/az/005_4.xls.

AzerStat (2015h), *The Production of Electricity,* State Statistical Committee of the Republic of Azerbaijan, Baku. www.stat.gov.az/source/balance_fuel/az/005_4.xls.

AzerStat (2015i), *The Production of Energy Products,* State Statistical Committee of the Republic of Azerbaijan, Baku. www.stat.gov.az/source/balance_fuel/az/002_11-13.xls.

Azertag (29 December 2005). "AzeriGas did not Receive Subsidies", *Azertag*, Baku. http://azertag.az/xeber/AZARIQAZA_SUBSIDIYA_AYRILMIR-332895.

AzMinEco (2016), *Investment Promotion Certificate*, Ministry of Economy of the Republic of Azerbaijan, Baku.

AzMinEco (2015a), *National Capacity Self Assessment for Global Environment Management in Azerbaijan,* Ministry of Ecology and Natural Resources of the Republic of Azerbaijan, Baku.

AzMinEco (2015b), *Overview of Climate Change and Ozone Center of the National Hydrometeorological Department of the Ministry of Ecology and Natural Resources of Azerbaijan Republic,* Ministry of Ecology and Natural Resources of the Republic of Azerbaijan, Baku.

Bagirov, S. (2007), *Azerbaijan's Oil Revenues: Ways of Reducing the Risk of Ineffective Use.* www.policy.hu/bagirov/ResearchPaper.pdf.

BakerMcKenzie (2009), *Getting the Deal Through – Oil Regulation – Azerbaijan,* BakerMcKenzie.

Beaton, C. et al. (2013), *A Guidebook to Fossil-Fuel Subsidy Reform for Policy-Makers in Southeast Asia,* IISD-GSI, Geneva. https://www.iisd.org/gsi/sites/default/files/ffs_guidebook.pdf.

BP (2015a), *BP Azerbaijan PSA Legal Documentation,* British Petroleum, Baku. www.bp.com/en_az/caspian/aboutus/legalagreements.html.

BP (2015b), *Statistical Review of World Energy,* British Petroleum, London. www.bp.com/en/global/corporate/energy-economics/statistical-review-of-world-energy.html.

BP (1994), *Agreement on the Joint Development and Production Sharing for the Azeri and Chirag Fields and the Deep Water Portion of the Gunashli Field in the Azerbaijan Sector of the Caspian Sea,* British Petroleum. www.bp.com/content/dam/bp-country/en_az/pdf/legalagreements/PSAs/ACG_PSA.pdf.

Central Bank of Azerbaijan (2016a), *AZN Rates – Search by Period,* Central Bank of the Republic of Azerbaijan, Baku. http://en.cbar.az/other/azn-rates?act=betweenForm&from[day]=1&from[month]=1&from[year]=2015&to[day]=31&to[month]=12&to[year]=2015&rateID=usd.

Central Bank of Azerbaijan (2016b), *November Bulletin*, Central Bank of the Republic of Azerbaijan, Baku.

Comtrade (2015), *UN Comtrade Trade Database,* United Nations Commodity Trade Statistics Database. http://comtrade.un.org/data/.

Deloitte (2015), *Tax Highlights 2015 Azerbaijan,* Deloitte, Baku.

ECS (2013), *In-Depth Review of Energy Efficiency Policy of Azerbaijan,* Energy Charter Secretariat, Brussels.

ECS (2011), *Azerbaijan Follow-Up In-Depth Review of the Investment Climate and Market Structure in the Energy Sector,* Energy Charter Secretariat, Brussels.

EIA (2015a), *Annual Energy Outlook 2015,* US Energy Information Administration, Washington, DC. www.eia.gov/forecasts/aeo/pdf/0383(2015).pdf.

EIA (2015b), *Average Tested Heat Rates by Prime Mover and Energy Source, 2007-2013.* US Energy Information Administration,Washington, DC. www.eia.gov/electricity/annual/html/epa_08_02.html.

EIA (2015c), *Natural Gas: US Industrial Prices,* US Energy Information Administration, Washington, DC. www.eia.gov/dnav/ng/hist/n3035us3m.htm.

Ernst & Young (2015a), *Global Oil & Gas Tax Guide,* Ernst & Young. www.ey.com/Publication/vwLUAssets/EY-2015-Global-oil-and-gas-tax-guide/$FILE/EY-2015-Global-oil-and-gas-tax-guide.pdf.

Ernst & Young (2015b), *Guide to Doing Business in Azerbaijan,* Ernst & Young, Baku. www.ey.com/Publication/vwLUAssets/EY-business-guide-azerbaijan-2015/$FILE/EY-business-guide-azerbaijan-2015.pdf.

FAO REU (2012), *Assessment of the Agriculture and Rural Development Sectors in the Eastern Partnership Countries – The Republic of Azerbaijan*, Food and Agriculture Organization of the United Nations Regional Office for Europe and Central Asia, Budapest.

Fichtner Ltd (2013), *Update of the Power Sector Master Plan of Azerbaijan 2013-2025,* Fichtner Ltd. www.inogate.org/documents/3_FICHT-11527706-v2-Final_Report_Azerbaijan.pdf.

Gallagher, L. (2014), *Azerbaijan and Georgia: Taking the Silent Lead on Climate Action,* Climate Home, 12 June. www.climatechangenews.com/2014/06/12/azerbaijan-and-georgia-are-taking-the-silent-lead-on-climate-action/.

Gazprom (2015), *Gazprom in Numbers – Databook,* Gazprom, Moscow.

GIZ (2015), *International Fuel Prices 2014 – Data Preview, Deutsche Gesellschaft für Internationale Zusammenarbeit*, Berlin.

GIZ (2014), *International Fuel Prices 2012/2013 Eighth Edition, Deutsche Gesellschaft für Internationale Zusammenarbeit*, Berlin.

Government of Azerbaijan (2004), *The State Program on the Use of Alternative and Renewable Energy Sources in Azerbaijan Republic,* Government of the Republic of Azerbaijan, Baku.

GSI (2014), *Comparison of Fossil-Fuel Subsidy and Support Estimates,* Global Subsidies Initiative, Geneva. www.iisd.org/gsi/sites/default/files/ffs_methods_estimationcomparison.pdf.

Hasanli, A. (2015), "Ilham Aliyev Cancels Decision on Increasing Fuel Prices", Trend News Agency, Baku, 14 January. http://en.trend.az/azerbaijan/politics/2353077.html.

Huseynova, H. (2015), *Alternative and Renewable Energy Outlook for Azerbaijan 2014 – Policy Paper,* Konrad Adenauer Stiftung, Berlin. www.kas.de/wf/doc/kas_40177-1522-35-30.pdf?150123132359.

IEA (2016), *World Energy Balances*, OECD Publishing/International Energy Agency, Paris.

IEA (2015a), *Country Report Azerbaijan,* International Energy Agency, Paris. www.iea.org/statistics/statisticssearch/report/?country=AZERBAIJAN&product=balances&year=20124.

IEA (2015b), *Eastern Europe, Caucasus and Central Asia: Energy Policies Beyond IEA Countries,* OECD/International Energy Agency, Paris. https://www.iea.org/publications/freepublications/publication/IDR_EasternEuropeCaucasus_2015.pdf.

IEA (2015c), *Fossil-Fuel Subsidies: Methodology and Assumptions.* International Energy Agency, Paris. www.worldenergyoutlook.org/resources/energysubsidies/methodology/.

IEA (2015d), *World Energy Outlook 2015 Fossil Fuel Subsidies Database,* International Energy Agency, Paris. www.worldenergyoutlook.org/media/weowebsite/2015/Subsidies20122014.xlsx.

IGU (2015), *Wholesale Gas Price Survey – 2015 Edition,* International Gas Union, Des Plaines, Illinois.

IMF (2015), *Counting the Cost of Energy Subsidies,* International Monetary Fund, Washington, DC. www.imf.org/external/pubs/ft/survey/so/2015/NEW070215A.htm?utm_source=twitterfeed&utm_medium=twitter.

IMF (2013), *Energy Subsidy Reform: Lessons and Implications,* International Monetary Fund, Washington, DC.

INDC of Azerbaijan (2015), *Intended Nationally Determined Contribution of the Republic of Azerbaijan.* http://www4.unfccc.int/submissions/INDC/Published%20Documents/Azerbaijan/1/INDC%20Azerbaijan.pdf.

Kerimhanova, T. (2015), *Стоит ли уменьшать объем субсидий в Азербайджане?, Biznesinfo* ("Is it Worth Reducing the Volume of Subsidies in Azerbaijan?"), 25 May 2015.

Lund, D. (2002), "Rent Taxation When Cost Monitoring Is Imperfect", *Resource and Energy Economics*, Vol. 24/3, pp. 211-228.

Malikov, J. (n.d.), *Renewable Energy Strategy of the Republic of Azerbaijan.*

Mediaforum News (2009), "President Pardoned the Debts for Natural Gas Usage for the General Population", Mediaforum News, Baku, 29 December.

Milli.az NewsPortal (2013), "The Prices for Gasoline and Diesel Increased", Milli.az NewsPortal, Baku, 3 December. http://news.milli.az/economy/230415.html.

Milli.az NewsPortal (28 November 2011), "*Tariff Council Increased Price for Some of the Communal Services*", Milli.az NewsPortal, Baku. http://news.milli.az/economy/82557.html.

Ministry of Finance (2015a), *Home Page,* Ministry of Finance of the Republic of Azerbaijan, Baku, www.maliyye.gov.az/en.

Ministry of Finance (2015b), *Presentation of the State and Summary Budgets for the Republic of Azerbaijan in 2016,* Ministry of Finance of the Republic of Azerbaijan, Baku.

Ministry of Justice (2009), *The Abolishment of Natural Gas Prices for the General Population, 29 December 2009,* Ministry of Justice of the Republic of Azerbaijan, Baku. www.e-qanun.az/framework/18961.

Musavat Newspaper (19 August 2010), "The Energy Debts of the Population Should Be Abolished", Musavat Newspaper, Baku. http://musavat.com/news/iqtisadiyyat/ehalinin-de-enerji-borclari-silinmelidir_83123.html?welcome=1.

OECD (2013), *Analysing Energy Subsidies in the Countries of Eastern Europe, Caucasus and Central Asia.* OECD Publishing, Paris. https://www.oecd.org/env/outreach/EHS%20report_20%20August%202013_ENG.pdf.

OECD (2003), *The Use of Economic Instruments for Pollution Control and Natural Resource Management in Eastern Europe, Caucasus and Central Asia*, CCNM/ENV/EAP(2003)5, OECD Publishing, Paris.

OpenEI (2016), *Transparent Cost Database.* http://en.openei.org/apps/TCDB/levelized_cost_calculations.html.

Orujova, N. (10 March 2014), "Alternative Ways of Energy Supply in Azerbaijan", AzerNews, Baku. www.azernews.az/business/64969.html.

Parliament of Azerbaijan (2000), *The Tax Code of the Republic of Azerbaijan, Approved by Law No. 905-IG of the Republic of Azerbaijan of 11 July 2000, with Revisions and Amendments,* Parliament of the Republic of Azerbaijan, Baku.

Pirani, S. (2016), "Azerbaijan's Gas Supply Squeeze and the Consequences for the Southern Corridor", *OIES Paper: NG 110*, The Oxford Institute for Energy Studies, University of Oxford, Oxford. https://www.oxfordenergy.org/wpcms/wp-content/uploads/2016/07/Azerbaijans-gas-supply-squeeze-and-the-consequences-for-the-Southern-Corridor-NG-110.pdf.

President of Azerbaijan (2016), *Presidential Decree on Some Changes for the Improvement of State Management*, President of the Republic of Azerbaijan, Baku. www.president.az/articles/21806.

President of Azerbaijan (2015a), *Presidential Decree on the Budget of the State Oil Fund of the Republic of Azerbaijan in 2016,* President of the Republic of Azerbaijan, Baku. http://ru.president.az/articles/17386.

President of Azerbaijan (2015b), *The Law of the Republic of Azerbaijan on the State Budget of the Republic of Azerbaijan for 2015,* President of the Republic of Azerbaijan, Baku. www.maliyye.gov.az/sites/default/files/Budget_law_2015.pdf.

President of Azerbaijan (2013a), *Presidential Decree No. 550 of 5 December 2013 on Some Issues of Regulation of Tariffs (Prices) for Housing and Communal Services,* President of the Republic of Azerbaijan, Baku. www.pravo.by/main.aspx?guid=3871&p0=P31300550&p1=1.

President of Azerbaijan (2012), *Azerbaijan 2020: Look into the Future,* President of the Republic of Azerbaijan, Baku.

PWC (2016), *Azerbaijan – Corporate Tax Credits and Incentives,* PricewaterhouseCoopers, Baku.

Qafqazinfo.Az (2014), "The Millions are Allocated, but They are Indebted Again", *Qafqazinfo*, Baku, 21 January. www.qafqazinfo.az/musahibe-17/milyonlar-xerclenir-yene-borclari-var-68027.

Qafqazinfo.Az (2013), "Corruption Facts at AzerEnerji Revealed by Hackers", Qafqazinfo.az, Baku, 10 September. www.qafqazinfo.az/iqtisadiyyat-4/hakerlerin-azerenerji-de-uze-cixardigi-korrupsiya-49750.

Rafiqoglu, A. (2010), "Accumulated Energy Debts Abolished", ANSPress, Baku, 17 August.

Regnum (2007), *Повышение цен в Азербайджане, или шок без терапии: Азербайджан за неделю, 16 January 2007* ("Price Increase in Azerbaijan, or a Shock without Therapy", *Azerbaijan in a Week*, 16 January 2007), Regnum, Baku.

Report Information Agency (2015), "AzerSu and AzerEnerji are Indebted to Government", Report Information Agency, Baku, 27 April. http://report.az/i-nfrastruktur/azersu-ve-azerenerji-nin-vergi-borcu-yaranib/.

Rzayeva, G. (2015), *The Outlook for Azerbaijani Gas Supplies to Europe: Challenges and Perspectives,* Oxford Energy Institute, Oxford.

Salaeva, A. (2015), "The Date for Restarting the Supply of Heat to Apartments of Baku Announced", 1News.az, Baku, 29 November. www.1news.az/society/20151119040452735.html.

Salaeva, A. (2015), "The Number of Heat Boiler Houses in Baku Announced", 1News.az, Baku, 20 November. www.1news.az/society/20151120021718602.html.

SOCAR (2015a), *2014 Annual Report of the State Oil Company of the Republic of Azerbaijan,* State Oil Company of the Azerbaijan Republic, Baku. www.socar.az/socar/assets/documents/en/socar-annual-reports/annual_report2014.pdf.

SOCAR (2015b), *SOCAR Website – Organization*, State Oil Company of the Azerbaijan Republic, Baku. www.socar.az/socar/en/company/organization/azerigas-production-union.

SOCAR (2014), *Financial Report by SOCAR for 2014,* State Oil Company of the Azerbaijan Republic, Baku. www.socar.az/socar/assets/documents/az/socar-annual-reports/illik-hesabat2014az.pdf.

Sputnik News Agency (2016), "Do Gasoline Stations Cheat Us?", Sputnik News Agency, 11 January. http://sputnik.az/life/20160111/403308069.html.

State Customs Committee (2002), *On the Founding of the Tariff Committee,* State Customs Committee of the Republic of Azerbaijan, Baku. http://customs.gov.az/az/nkq17.html.

TAP-AG (2015), *TAP-AG – Southern Energy Corridor,* Trans Adriatic Pipeline. www.tap-ag.com/the-pipeline/the-big-picture/southern-gas-corridor.

Tariff Council (2016), *Tariff Council – Tariffs,* Tariff Council of the Republic of Azerbaijan, Baku. www.tariffcouncil.gov.az/?/en/content/95/.

Tariff Council (2015), *Tariff Council – About,* Tariff Council of the Republic of Azerbaijan, Baku. www.tariffcouncil.gov.az/?/en/content/44/.

Tariff Council (2007), "The Tariff Council Held a Meeting on 6th January 2007", Tariff Council of the Republic of Azerbaijan, Baku. www.tariffcouncil.gov.az/?/az/pressreliz/view/8/.

TREND.AZ (2015), *В Азербайджане предлагается сократить налоговые льготы для нефтегазовой сферы* ("Azerbaijan Proposes to Reduce Tax Expenditure in the Oil and Gas Field") TREND.AZ, Baku, 20 October.

TREND.AZ (3 August 2015), "AzerEnerji was Given a Delay of 5 Years due to Debt", TREND.AZ, Baku. http://az.trend.az/business/energy/2421795.html.

TREND.AZ (24 July 2013), "A Decision on Allocating USD 73 Million for Farmers in Azerbaijan was Adopted for 2013", TREND.AZ, Baku. http://az.trend.az/business/economy/2173887.html.

World Bank (2016a), *Pink Sheet January 2016,* World Bank, Washington, DC. www.worldbank.org/en/research/commodity-markets.

World Bank (2016b), *Pump Prices, Gasoline and Diesel,* World Bank, Washington, DC. http://data.worldbank.org/indicator/EP.PMP.DESL.CD, http://data.worldbank.org/indicator/EP.PMP.SGAS.CD.

World Bank (2015a), *Commodity Markets Monthly Data,* World Bank, Washington, DC. www.worldbank.org/en/research/commodity-markets.

World Bank (2015b), *Ease of Doing Business Index,* World Bank, Washington, DC. www.doingbusiness.org/rankings.

World Bank (2015c), *World Bank Country Overview – Azerbaijan,* World Bank, Washington, DC. www.worldbank.org/en/country/azerbaijan/overview.

World Bank (2015d), *World Bank World Development Indicators,* World Bank, Washington, DC. https://data.worldbank.org/data-catalog/world-development-indicators.

World Bank (2013a), *Balancing Act: Cutting Energy Subsidies While Protecting Affordability,* World Bank, Washington, DC. https://openknowledge.worldbank.org/bitstream/handle/10986/12296/9780821397893.pdf?sequence=7.

World Bank (2013b), *Implementing Energy Subsidy Reforms: Evidence from Developing Countries,* World Bank, Washington, DC. http://documents.worldbank.org/curated/en/566201468177234043/pdf/735180PUB0EPI00200pub0date010031012.pdf.

Yafimava, K. (2015), *Evolution of Gas Pipeline Regulation in Russia: Third Party Access, Capacity Allocation and Transportation Tariffs,* Oxford Energy Institute, Oxford. https://www.oxfordenergy.org/wpcms/wp-content/uploads/2015/03/NG-95.pdf.

Chapter 4

Belarus' energy subsidies

This chapter identifies, documents and provides estimates of the various subsidies in Belarus that relate to the production or use of coal, oil and related petroleum products, natural gas, and electricity and heat generated on the basis of these fossil fuels. The chapter also briefly looks at the subsidies benefiting energy-efficiency measures and renewable energy sources. An overview of the country's energy sector is first given to place the measures listed into context. In addition, the chapter discusses pricing and tax policies in the energy sector in Belarus. The analysis summarises the context, the state of play, and the mechanics of the complex and evolving landscape of energy subsidies in the country.

Key findings

After the breakup of the Soviet Union, Belarus inherited a large industrial sector that has been used as a vehicle for cross-subsidisation of energy tariffs for households. As a result, over the last 25 years, it has developed a complex system of energy subsidies that lacks transparency. In addition to cross-subsidisation through industrial tariffs, energy subsidies to households are also partially covered from local and, ultimately, the national budget. The total amount of quantified fossil-fuel subsidies was USD 1.6 bln in 2014 (2.1% of GDP). The bulk of subsidies comes in the form of regulated residential tariffs for heat (the largest subsidy, estimated at USD 0.8 bln, in 2014), electricity and natural gas. Renewables received about USD 5 mln worth of support in 2014 through a feed-in tariff, with biogas being the main beneficiary. The slow progress to cost-reflective tariffs is working against the efforts to encourage energy efficiency and renewable energy innovations.

Strategic documents of Belarus' government have long and repeatedly stated the need to reform energy subsidies. However, progress has been slow, due to social concerns. The global economic crisis of 2009, followed by an increase in Belarus' external debt and other economic difficulties, exacerbated the need for reform. First steps towards reforming energy subsidies were taken in 2011, and differentiation by consumption volume in electricity and gas tariffs was introduced in 2013. Despite these measures, the value of energy subsidies rose considerably from 2010 to 2014, thanks to an increase in the price of imported gas from the Russian Federation, as well as the dramatic depreciation of the Belarusian ruble. This situation prompted the government to take further steps in the direction of the energy subsidy reform. To raise more revenue for the budget, the government phased out the value added tax (VAT) exemption for utility services provided to households, starting in January 2016.

Based on national statistical data (Belstat, 2016), it is possible to sketch what energy subsidy reform means for Belarusians in practical terms. If energy subsidies to households are fully eliminated, utility tariffs for residential consumers will have to increase by 2.5 times the rate at the beginning of 2016. At current prices and exchange rates, this means that an annual utility bill per person will need to increase from USD 60 to USD 150, or from USD 180 to USD 450 for a family of three people. On average, throughout the year, this family's monthly bill will be USD 38. An average monthly salary in Belarus in February 2016 was around USD 330 before payments for mandatory social insurance and personal income tax, according to Belstat estimates. The utility bill is lower in summer and higher in winter. Therefore, as a result of energy subsidy reform during the peak heating season, utility costs for an average three-person family will reach USD 57.7, of which USD 43 will cover heating costs, USD 7.3 electricity and USD 7.4 use of natural gas.

Considering the existing socio-economic challenges Belarus faces, energy subsidy reform needs to be implemented in a step-wise manner and include well-planned social protection measures. Better targeting of subsidies to low-income households appears to be one of the most relevant aspects of energy subsidy reforms. Ideally, targeted means-tested social protection schemes need to be rolled out ahead of tariff increases.

The following analysis shows that phasing out subsidies for gas and electricity will be less challenging and could be implemented by 2020. Reaching full cost-recovery in the heating sector may be more sensitive and will require time. Meanwhile, cutting heat consumption by introducing energy efficiency measures in the residential sector could ease the process. In turn, savings from energy subsidy reform can be reallocated toward better targeted support for vulnerable groups, as well as special funds to support energy efficiency measures.

Macroeconomic situation and energy sector overview

Like other economies in the EU's Eastern Partnership region, the Republic of Belarus went through a profound economic crisis after the breakup of the Soviet Union. The GDP contracted by as much as 11.7% in 1994. The economy resumed its growth in 1996, driven by a combination of factors such as favourable terms of export, mainly to the Russian Federation and the EU, and an increase in labour productivity. The GDP remained steady and reached 11.4% in both 1997 and 2004 (World Bank, 2015b). However, the recent global economic crisis negatively affected export demand and capital borrowing terms, which led to an economic slowdown in 2009-14. The government introduced a stringent monetary and fiscal policy in 2011-12, which helped to stabilise the macroeconomic situation (World Bank, 2014). However, in 2015, Belarus' GDP shrank by 3.9%, mainly as a result of economic difficulties in the Russian Federation, Belarus' main trade partner. Table 4.1 provides key macroeconomic indicators for Belarus based on both international and national statistics.

Table 4.1. **Macroeconomic indicators**

	International statistics		National statistics	
Population	*2013, mln*	9.47	*December 2015, mln*	9.498
GDP	*2014 USD bln*	76.14	*2015 BYR bln*	869 702
GDP/capita	*2014 USD*	8 040	*2015 BYR*	91 646
GDP growth	*2014 yoy %*	1.6%	2015	-3.9%
Energy production	*mtoe*	4.12		
Net energy imports	*mtoe*	26.60		
Total primary energy supply (TPES	*mtoe*	30.50	2015	25.725
TPES/capita	*toe*	3.22		
Electricity consumption	*TWh*	34.99	2015	36.7
Electricity consumption per capita	*MWh/capita*	3.7	2015	3.86
CO_2 emissions	*Mt of CO_2*	71.12		
CO_2/capita	*t of CO_2*	7.51		
Total GHG emissions			Mt of $CO_{2eq.}$ excl. LULUCF 2012	89.2

Source: Authors' compilation based on IEA (2015a, Belstat (2015, Belstat (2016, Ministry of Natural Resources and Environmental Protection (2014.

On 1 July 2016, Belarus devalued its currency by a factor of 10 000. The exchange rate on this date was BYR 2.0053 per USD.

Table 4.2. **Weighted average exchange rate**

	2010	2011	2012	2013	2014	2015
Weighted average exchange rate USD/BYR	2 994	5 606	8 370	8 971	10 260	16 254

Source: National Bank of Belarus (2015).

Energy supply

After the collapse of the Soviet Union and the resulting economic depression, total primary energy supply (TPES) of Belarus dropped from 45.5 mln tonnes of oil equivalent (mtoe) in 1990 to 24.7 mtoe in 1995 (see Figure 4.1). Since then, the energy supply has gradually risen, ranging between 26.1 and 29.8 mtoe in 2009-13. In 2013, TPES was 40% below the 1990 level. As shown in Figure 4.4, natural gas and oil account for the largest shares of the country's energy mix, at 63.9% and 27.2%, respectively, and these shares remained relatively constant over the last decade (IEA, 2015b).

Figure 4.1. **Total primary energy supply, 1990-2013**

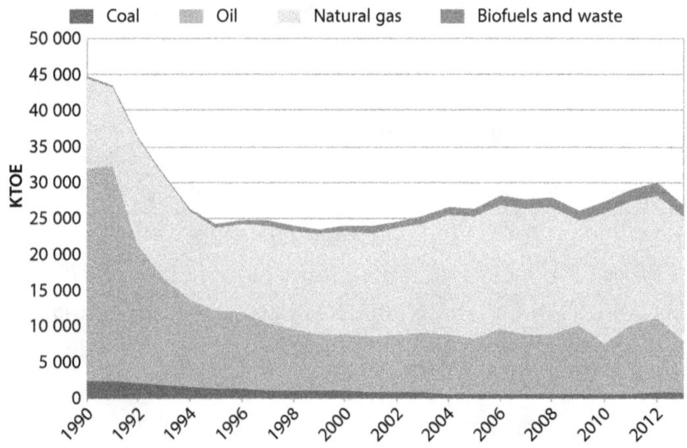

Source: Authors' compilation based on IEA (2015a).

Figure 4.2. **Primary energy supply by fuel in 2013**

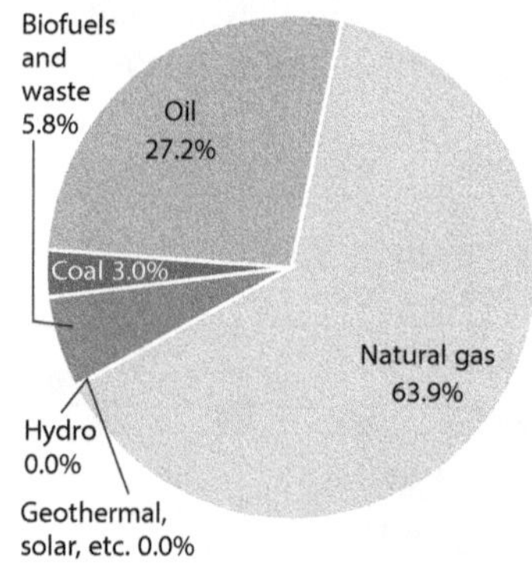

Source: Authors' compilation based on IEA (2015a).

The share of biofuels and waste in TPES grew to 5.8% in 2013, as the government of Belarus introduced incentives for biomass use in heat generation. Other energy sources play a marginal role in the TPES. Total installed capacity (TIC) of electricity production in Belarus was at 8 362 MW as of January 2012. Large combined heat and power (CHP) plants constitute 41.9% of TIC, large thermal power plants (TPPs) contribute 53%, while small thermal and wind power plants account for the remainder. TIC has increased by 1 420 MW since the 1990s and is projected to grow further, to 11 900 MW by 2020 (Energy Charter Secretariat, 2013).

Electricity production was at 31.5 terawatt hours (TWh) in 2013, 20% lower than in 1990 but 26% higher than in 2001. Figure 4.3 illustrates that the fuel structure of electricity generation has changed dramatically since 1990, when oil and gas had approximately equal shares of 50% each. Oil use in electricity production dropped to just 2.6%, and reliance on imported gas has expanded to 98% in 2013. However, the gas expansion trend was briefly interrupted in 2009, when electricity generation from gas dropped to 81.7%, while oil use increased to 17.9% due to the global economic depression and gas supply shortages from the Russian Federation. Hydropower and biofuels use has expanded since the 1990s, but their shares are still marginal in total electricity production (IEA, 2015b).

Figure 4.3. **Electricity generation by source, GWh**

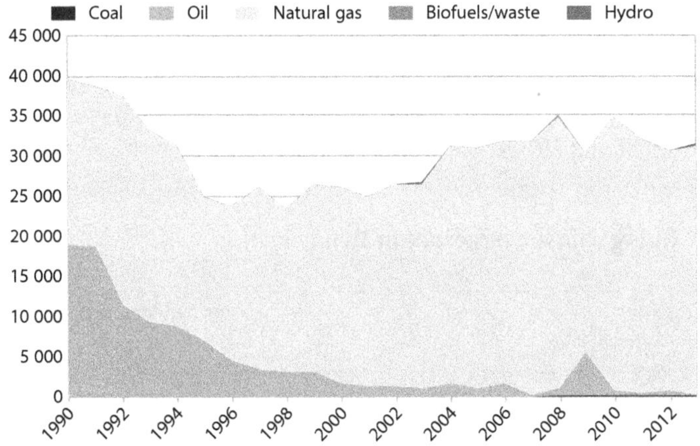

Source: Authors' compilation based on IEA (2015a).

Figure 4.4. **Electricity generation, GWh by source in 2013**

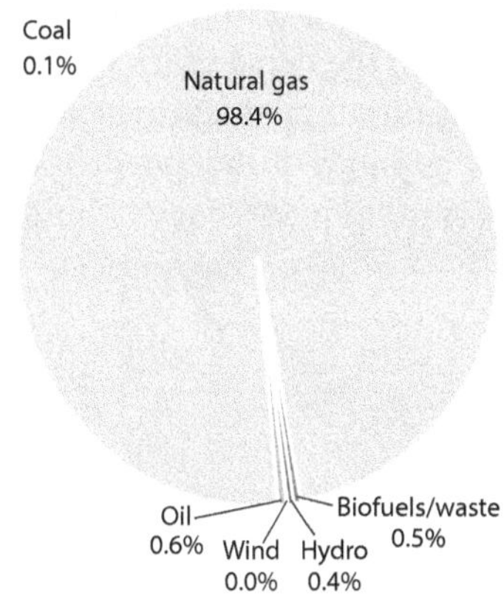

Source: Authors' compilation based on IEA (2015a).

Belarus is a net energy importer. Domestic production covers only about 15% of internal demand. In 2013, about 39.5 mtoe of energy resources were imported, predominantly from the Russian Federation. Crude oil and natural gas constituted the bulk of energy imports, at 53.9% and 42.6%, respectively (IEA, 2015a).

The main measure for increasing energy supply through 2020 will be the inauguration of the first unit of the nuclear power plant in 2018 and its second unit in 2020. Their total capacity will be 2 388 MWt, further exploitation is planned to integrate them more effectively into the national energy system. Electricity output is anticipated to be 7.1 bln kWh in 2020, increasing the share of nuclear energy in total electricity generation to 17.8%. This will make possible a partial replacement of natural gas by nuclear energy in Belarus' energy mix.

Belarus has a well-developed export-oriented refining and petrochemical industry. In 2013, it exported 13.9 mtoe of oil products to neighbouring countries (mainly Ukraine) and a number of EU countries, such as the Baltic states, the Netherlands, the United Kingdom, Italy and elsewhere (IEA, 2015b).

Energy demand

Belarus' significant economic growth since the mid-1990s has not had a considerable impact on energy demand, due to the change in the structure of the economy. Energy demand has fluctuated roughly at the same level since 1996. Total final consumption (TFC) of energy resources was at 19.9 mtoe in 2013. The residential sector was the main consumer (5.2 mtoe in 2013), followed by industry (4.6 mtoe) and transport (4.4 mtoe). Energy use in transport has been the fastest area of growth in demand (IEA, 2015a).

Energy sector structure, ownership and governance

Belarus' energy sector is dominated by state-owned companies that operate under the supervision of the Ministry of Energy, as shown schematically in Figure 4.5.

State Production Association (SPA) of Power Industry BelEnergo is a vertically integrated company that owns and operates the electricity and heat sector in Belarus. It has six subsidiaries that serve as regional distribution system operators (IEA, 2015b). About 50% of the demand for heat is covered by BelEnergo and the rest is served by local district heating companies owned by municipalities or industrial enterprises. In recent years, the number of independent electricity providers has risen, as foreign investors have been permitted to own newly built power plants (Energy Charter Secretariat, 2013).

Figure 4.5. **Energy sector structure of Belarus**

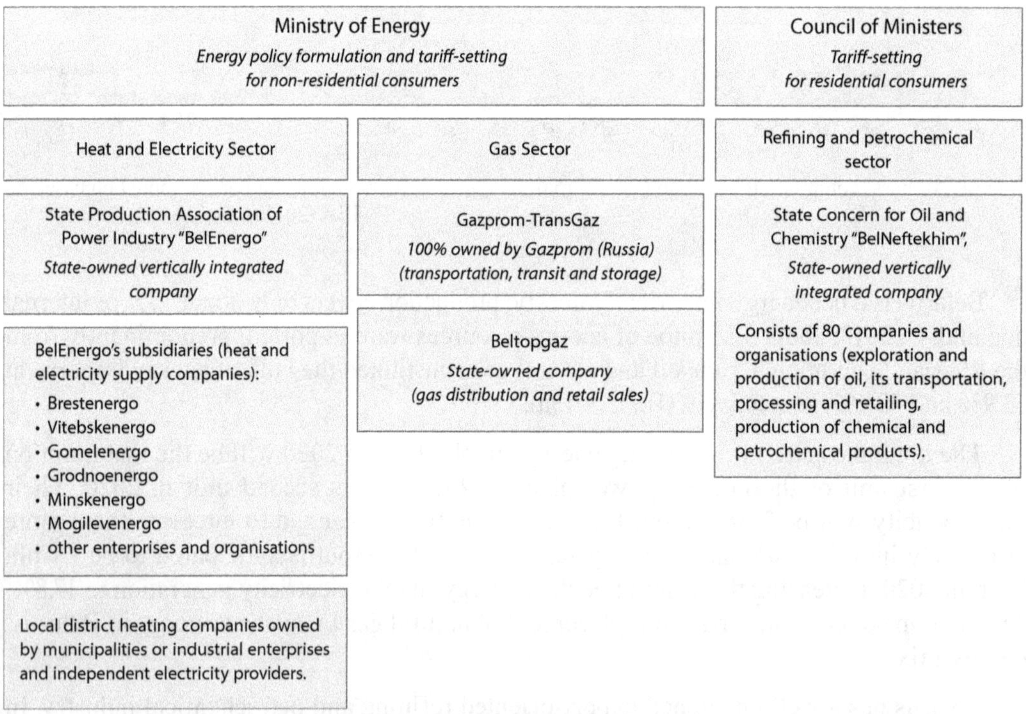

Source: Authors' compilation based on IEA (2015b), Energy Charter Secretariat (2013).

The natural gas market essentially includes two companies. Gazprom-Transgaz (100% owned by the Russian monopolist Gazprom) provides transport services and operates transit and storage systems. Beltopgaz, a fully state-owned company, controls gas distribution and retail market of hard fuels and liquefied petroleum gas (LPG). Beltopgaz has seven subsidiaries (regional distribution companies) that supply gas to end users in all sectors (IEA, 2015b).

The State Concern for Oil and Chemistry Belneftekhim, a state monopoly in the petrochemical sector, reports directly to the Council of Ministers of the Republic of Belarus. It consists of 80 companies and organisations engaged in a full cycle of oil extraction, transport and processing, as well as producing a range of petrochemical products (IEA, 2015b).

There is no independent regulator in Belarus. Regulation of the energy sector and tariff setting is largely performed by the Ministry of Economy, which is responsible for setting electricity and heat tariffs for industrial and for non-residential consumers. Tariffs for households are established by the Council of Ministers, while regional executive committees regulate heat tariffs for consumers who are not covered by the Council of Ministers (IEA, 2015b).

Energy pricing policy

From 1992 to the present, energy pricing in Belarus has been based on a complex system of cross-subsidisation. The legal basis of this policy is laid down in Law No. 255-3 on Pricing of 10 May 1999 and Presidential Decree No. 72, On Certain Issues of Tariff Regulation, of 25 February 2011. To ensure a balance between the interests of consumers and energy supply companies, the Council of Ministers approved Resolution No. 222 on 17 March 2014. This resolution lays out the key procedures of tariff setting for natural gas and LPG, as well as for electricity and heat. The Resolution regulates the establishment of the so-called "base prices" (tariffs), which reflect all production and transport costs, including expenditures on repair services, depreciation of funds, salaries and social contributions, taxes and insurance, as well as normative profits. Under the Resolution, investment needs are covered through the reflection in the tariffs of such components as costs of depreciation and loans, and normative profits. In addition, transfers from the budget and national non-budgetary funds can also be made to cover investment needs.

Beltopgaz provides the Ministry of Economy with cost estimates for the supply of natural gas and LPG. BelEnergo prepares them for electricity and heat. Taking these cost estimates into consideration, the Ministry of Economy sets a "base price" for each energy type. However, tariffs for certain groups of end consumers are established below "base prices". In such cases, the revenue shortfall is compensated for through cross-subsidisation from higher tariffs for other consumer groups (Council of Ministers, Resolution No. 222, 2014). Table 4.3 provides an overview of current tariffs for households and non-residential consumers.

According to the Ministry of Energy of Belarus, "base prices" for energy, which are set at the level of full recovery of economically justified costs, do not adequately reflect the "cost-plus" reference (cost recovery plus standard profits). Since this report uses "base prices" as the benchmark for subsidy calculations, the obtained results are rather conservative, and in reality the level of subsidisation is even higher.

Table 4.3a presents the key features of energy pricing for both households and commercial users. Table 4.3b provides the dynamics of tariffs for households only from 2015 to 2016.

Natural gas

The price of imported gas is agreed upon between the Russian gas monopoly Gazprom and the Ministry of Energy of Belarus. Gas prices for end consumers are regulated by the state according to the procedures described above. Gas tariffs for households are cross-subsidised at the expense of industrial consumers. However, certain industrial sectors are also subsidised through lower tariffs. For example, glass manufacturing and producers of fertilisers benefited from reduced gas tariffs, which were 11% lower than those for other sectors in 2015 (Ministry of Energy, 2015b). All industrial consumers and the majority of households have gas meters installed (Energy Charter Secretariat, 2013).

Electricity

Electricity tariffs are highly differentiated depending on the consumer group, particularly industrial consumers with a capacity higher than 750 kVA and more (dual-rate tariff), industrial consumers with a connected capacity up to 750 kVA (flat-rate tariff), electrified public transport, public institutions, street lighting systems, etc. Electricity and heat tariffs for non-residential consumers are pegged to the USD exchange rate (Energy Charter Secretariat, 2013). Electricity tariffs for households (also called "residential consumers") are differentiated by peak and off-peak time periods and by electricity use. In particular, households with electric stoves for cooking have a lower electricity tariff than those with gas stoves for cooking (see Tables 4.3a and 4.3b).

Among the so-called non-residential consumers (also referred to as "legal entities" or "organisations"), public health institutions, social service institutions, religious and some other organisations benefit from tariffs subsidised at the same level as households.

In certain cases, feed-in tariffs are provided to strategic investors into new electricity capacity, in which case they are approved by individual presidential decrees (IEA, 2015b).

Heating

Heat tariffs are differentiated by consumer groups (households, public-funded organisations, industrial enterprises, etc.) and regions (see Tables 4.3a and 4.3b). According to the World Bank (2014a) study, in 2012, households paid only a fraction of heat production costs, ranging from 10% to 21% (17.2% on average. The percentage depends on a number of factors, including the size of district heating system and its condition, fuel used and efficiency of production).

Figure 4.6. **Cross-subsidisation in the heating sector of Belarus**

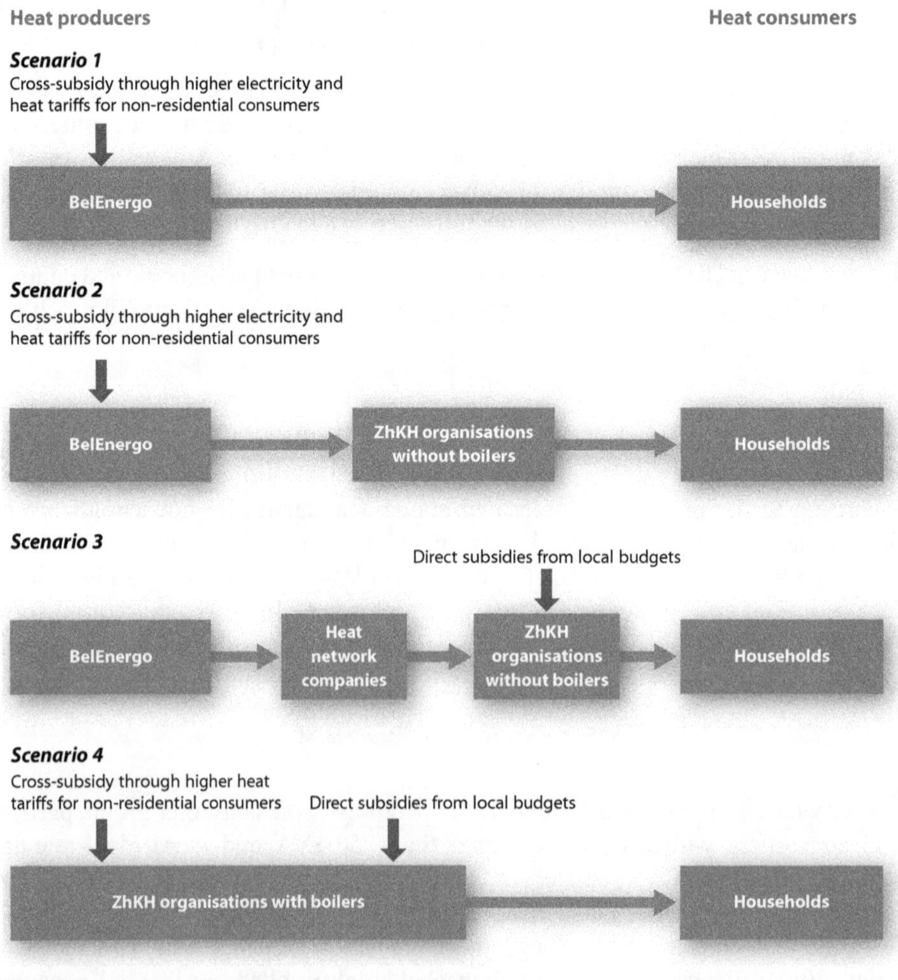

Source: Authors' compilation.

There are several ways to compensate heat producers in Belarus for losses resulting from selling heat to households at prices set below cost-recovery levels. Figure 4.6 illustrates these complex schemes under four scenarios of heat supply chains.

Three of these scenarios involve BelEnergo. BelEnergo, or more exactly the units it owns that co-generate heat and electricity, does not receive direct budgetary transfers. Under Scenario 1, where BelEnergo-owned units supply heat directly to households, they cover their revenue shortfall through a double cross-subsidy: through higher tariffs for non-residential consumers of heat, on the one hand, and through higher tariffs for non-residential consumers of electricity, on the other.

Scenario 2 is exactly the same in terms of the double cross-subsidy through higher heat and electricity tariffs for non-residential consumers. The only difference is that BelEnergo first supplies heat to housing and communal service organisations (commonly referred to as ZhKH, based on the Russian abbreviation) which then supply it to households. ZhKH organisations pay exactly the same preferential tariff as households.

Under Scenario 3, BelEnergo supplies heat to its subsidiary heat network companies, the tariff for which is cost-reflective. ZhKH organisations purchase heat from heat network organisations and apply for direct transfers from local budgets to compensate for the difference between heat cost and regulated tariffs for households.

Scenario 4 is valid for ZhKH organisations that generate their own heat in boiler houses instead of purchasing it. Boiler houses generate heat only (no electricity) and can recover only 10% of production costs through household tariffs. ZhKH organisations compensate for their losses from heat generation first by charging higher heat tariffs on non-residential consumers, and second by applying for direct subsidies from local budgets.

Petroleum products

Prices for petroleum products are regulated by the Belarusian State Concern for Oil and Chemistry BelNeftekhim (other than oil products sold by the CJSC Belarusian Oil Company) under the Regulation "On procedure for the establishment of wholesale or retail prices of petroleum products produced and (or) sold on the territory of the Republic of Belarus" (Belneftekhim Order No. 79, 2013). BelNeftekhim approves marginal wholesale and retail prices of oil products (see Table 4.3a). According to the *Deutsche Gesellschaft für Internationale Zusammenarbeit* (GIZ, 2015), Belarus' gasoline and diesel prices at the pump were both at USD 1.06 per litre in mid-November 2014. This was above the "green" benchmark (US price levels), placing the country in the category where fuel prices are taxed rather than subsidised (see next section for the discussion of energy taxation). However, due to a major change in the BYR exchange rate in 2014 and 2015, prices for these transport fuels are considerably lower when expressed in USD.

Table 4.3a. **Price policies**

Energy carrier	Pricing policy	Price categories	Price levels in 2015[a]
Natural gas	"Cost-plus" methodology, with cross-subsidisation among different consumer groups embedded in the tariff	For households, the gas tariff depends on the period of the year (lower during the heating season), the availability of meters and use of individual gas boilers. For legal entities, the gas tariff varies by economic sector (lowest for chemical and glass producers) and consumption volume.	Prices for households and organisations paying the same tariff as households (as of July 2015): BYR 2 281.8/m^3 (BYR 623.3/m^3 during the heating season) (Ministry of Energy, 2015c); For legal entities (as of July 2015, without VAT): BYR 1 971-4 108/m^3 (Ministry of Energy, 2015b).

Table 4.3a. **Price policies** *(continued)*

Energy carrier	Pricing policy	Price categories	Price levels in 2015[a]
Electricity	"Cost-plus" methodology, with cross-subsidisation among different consumer groups embedded in the tariff	For households, the electricity tariff varies depending on the minimum and maximum load periods and purpose of use (electric stoves, hot water and heat supply). For legal entities, the electricity tariff varies by consumer group and capacity.	For households and organisations paying the same tariff as households: BYR 567.5-1 907.6/kWh (Ministry of Energy, 2015d). Selected prices for legal entities (without VAT): industrial consumers: BYR 1 580.2/kWh if the capacity is up to 750 kVA; BYR 139 207.3 monthly fee + BYR 1 237.2/kWh if capacity is higher than 750 kVA; agricultural producers: BYR 1 203.1/kWh; street lighting: BYR 1 652.2/kWh; public transport: BYR 1 293.6/kWh certain public institutions: BYR 1 652.2/kWh (Ministry of Energy, 2015a).
Heat	"Cost-plus" methodology, with cross-subsidisation among different consumer groups embedded in the tariff	For industrial and other consumers, tariffs are highly differentiated depending on consumer category and the regional heat supply company.	For households and organisations paying the same tariff as households: thermal energy for heating and hot water supply – BYR 96 424/Gcal (Ministry of Energy, 2015d). For industrial and other consumers from 1 January 2015 (without VAT) BYR 523 558 to BYR 696 651/ Gcal (Ministry of Energy, 2015c).
Liquid petroleum products	Regulated, methodology is not publicly available	Differentiated depending on fuel quality	From 13 January 2015, petrol: BYR 10 000-14 000/ litre, diesel BYR 12 300-13 800/litre (Belneftekhim, 2015).
LPG	Regulated, cross-subsidised via gas tariffs for certain consumers	Differentiated depending on season and use.	LPG BYR 6 084/m³ (BYR 9 658.7/m³ during the peak heating season) (Ministry of Energy, 2015c).
Solid fuels, fuel briquettes and fuel wood, a category that mainly covers peat briquettes	Regulated by regional authorities, cross-subsidised	Differs by region.	Differs by region.

Note: a. Before 1 January 2016, households were exempt from VAT on natural gas, heat and electricity.

Source: Authors' compilation based on IEA (2015b), Energy Charter Secretariat (2013), Ministry of Energy (2015a), Ministry of Energy (2015b), Ministry of Energy (2015c) and Belneftekhim (2015).

Table 4.3b. **Increase in energy prices for households from 1 July 2015 to 1 July 2016, as a result of elimination of the VAT exemption for the consumption of natural gas, heat and electricity on 1 January 2016**

Energy type	Price category	Price as of 1 July 2015	Price as of 1 July 2016	Price as of 1 July 2016 in USD
Electricity/kWh	With gas stoves and consumption up to 300 kWh per month	BYR 953.8	BYR 1 188	USD 0.06
	With electric stoves and consumption up to 400 kWh per month	BYR 810.7	BYR 1 009	USD 0.05
	With consumption over the monthly limits	BYR 1 467.5	BYR 1 900	USD 0.09
Natural gas/cubic metre	During the heating season, up to 3 000 m³ per year	BYR 623.3	BYR 776	USD 0.04
	During the summer, up to 3 000 m³ per year	BYR 2 281.8	BYR 2 842	USD 0.14
	With consumption over the annual limits	BYR 2 588	BYR 3 738	USD 0.19

Table 4.3b. **Increase in energy prices for households from 1 July 2015 to 1 July 2016, as a result of elimination of the VAT exemption for the consumption of natural gas, heat and electricity on 1 January 2016** *(continued)*

Energy type	Price category	Price as of 1 July 2015	Price as of 1 July 2016	Price as of 1 July 2016 in USD
Heat/Gcal	Subsidised price	BYR 96 424	BYR 133 417	USD 6.65
	"Base price"	BYR 466 120	BYR 854 710	USD 42.62
LPG/cubic metre	During the peak heating season	BYR 9 568.7	BYR 12 030	USD 0.60
	In summer time	BYR 6 084	BYR 7 578	USD 0.38
Petroleum products/litre	Gasoline AI-92	BYR 11 100	BYR 11 100	USD 0.55
	Gasoline АИ-95	BYR 11 900	BYR 11 900	USD 0.59
	Diesel	BYR 12 300	BYR 12 300	USD 0.61
	Compressed natural gas (CNG)	BYR 6 200	BYR 6 000	USD 0.30
Fuel wood/solid cubic metre	Subsidised price for Minsk, not more than 4.9 m³ of dense fuel wood per year	BYR 40 500	BYR 40 500	USD 2.02
Fuel (peat) briquettes/tonne	For Minsk, not more than 2.5 tonnes per year	BYR 126 700	BYR 126 700	USD 6.32

Source: Council of Ministers Resolution No. 480 (2016b).

Taxation policy

The taxation system in Belarus is centralised, and virtually all taxes go into the national budget. The key baseline taxes, applicable to virtually all economic activities, are VAT (20%), profit tax, property tax and land tax. Small and medium-sized enterprises (SMEs) pay a single tax under a simplified scheme. Excise tax is levied on sales of several groups of products, including liquefied petroleum gas (LPG), compressed natural gas (CNG), petroleum products and biodiesel. Environmental tax is levied on polluting activities, while extraction tax is levied on production of oil (the amounts of oil extracted in Belarus are very small, and there is no commercial gas production), peat and brown coal. There are also other taxes, duties and charges, including, for instance, contributions to innovation funds. Table 4.4 provides further details.

Table 4.4. **Taxation of energy in Belarus**

Activity subject to taxation	Baseline tax system: VAT, profit tax, property tax, land tax, environmental tax, etc.	Extraction tax	Excise tax
Companies extracting and refining oil and gas	Applicable as appropriate	Extraction tax is applied to oil	n.a.
Companies extracting coal and peat	Applicable as appropriate	Extraction tax is applied to peat and brown coal	n.a.
Consumers of liquid petroleum products and LPG	Applicable as appropriate	n.a.	The excise tax is applied to LPG and compressed gas and differentiated for petroleum products
Companies generating electricity	Applicable as appropriate	n.a.	n.a.
Consumers of electricity	Applicable as appropriate	n.a.	n.a.

Note: **n.a.**: not applicable.

Source: Authors' compilation based on the Tax Code (National Assembly, 2002).

The Tax Code of the Republic of Belarus (National Assembly, 2002) provides for a number of tax benefits for renewable energy producers. In particular, imported renewable energy equipment is exempt from VAT. Further, land areas under renewable energy sites are exempt from land tax. In addition, a lowering coefficient is applied to the environmental tax rate with respect to emissions from the combustion of renewable energy sources (biomass, biogas, wood, etc.) for the production of electricity or thermal energy and with respect to wastewater discharge by thermal power stations using renewable energy sources.

Greenhouse gas emissions and climate policy

According to the National GHG Emissions Inventory (Ministry of Natural Resources and Environmental Protection, 2014), GHG emissions were at 89.2 Mt of CO_2-equivalent (without land use, land-use change and forestry, or LULUCF) in 2012. This is 35.8% lower than in 1990. The low level of emissions is explained by a significant decline in energy-intensive industrial activities, implementation of energy efficiency policies as well as a shift in the structure of the fuel mix towards natural gas. The energy sector accounts for the largest share of emissions (61.9%), followed by agriculture (26.2%). The sectors of waste treatment and industrial processes account for 7% and 4.8% of the total emissions, respectively.

The Republic of Belarus is an Annex I party to the Kyoto Protocol of the UN Framework Convention on Climate Change (UNFCCC). For the second period of the Kyoto Protocol, Belarus made a number of voluntary commitments to reduce the energy intensity of its GDP by 29%-32% by 2015 compared to the 2010 levels, and to reduce its GHG emissions by 8% by 2020 compared to 1990 (Ministry of Natural Resources and Environmental Protection, 2015b). Under its Intended Nationally Determined Contribution (INDC), Belarus has committed not to exceed 75% of its 1990 GHG emissions levels by 2030 (Ministry of Natural Resources and Environmental Protection, 2015a). Additional reductions in GHG emissions are planned of 25 mln-30 mln tonnes of CO_2 (or by 20%-22% compared with the baseline). These commitments will rely on the switch to best available technologies and draw only on national efforts in Belarus, without conditional financial assistance from abroad.

National definition and discussion of energy subsidies

Like other countries in the EU's Eastern Partnership region, national legislation of the Republic of Belarus contains only a narrow definition of subsidies (see Figure 4.7). In particular, the Budget Code (National Assembly, 2008) states that:

> "a subsidy is a budget transfer provided to an organisation or an individual, including individual entrepreneurs, on the condition of participation in financing (co-financing) with the objective of producing or selling of goods and services, or partial reimbursement of targeted expenditures."

The Budget Code also defines state support as "budget transfers to particular categories of legal entities and individual entrepreneurs in accordance with legislative norms" and specifies that support of the fuel and energy complex is funded from the national budget.

Furthermore, the Tax Code of the Republic of Belarus defines tax benefits, which are considered to be a form of state support, as "privileges provided to particular categories of taxpayers envisioned in this Code or other tax legislation and also international agreements of the Republic of Belarus in comparison with other taxpayers, including an opportunity not to pay a tax, charge (duty) or pay them at a lower rate".

Figure 4.7. **What does Belarus include in the national definition of a subsidy?**

	Covered by the national definitions of both "subsidy" and "state support"		Covered only by the national definition of "state support"		Not included in the national definition of either "subsidy" or "state support"

Direct budget transfers	Tax expenditures	Induced transfers	Transfer of risk to government	References
				Budget Code (National Assembly, 2008) defines "subsidies", while Tax Code, Article 43 (National Assembly, 2002), also includes "tax expenditures" in state support. Induced transfers are largely discussed as "cross-subsidies" between industrial consumers and households with respect to heat, electricity and natural gas tariffs.

At the same time, cross-subsidisation embedded in gas, heat and electricity tariffs has been discussed in detail in Belarus for a long time. These measures are classified as induced transfers according to classification of the support measures of the OECD.

The IEA has never included Belarus in its price-gap estimates of consumer subsidies, but several previous studies on the subject have been conducted. According to an assessment by the German Economic Team (GET, 2007), quasi-fiscal activities in the electricity, gas and heating sector amounted to 3.7% to 4.7% of GDP in 2006. A review of public expenditure by the World Bank (2011) quantified the fiscal cost of under-priced energy supplies to the residential sector at USD 0.84 bln, or 1.7% of Belarus' GDP in 2009. Additionally, 130 industrial consumers were effectively subsidised at 0.3% of GDP due to preferential electricity, heat and gas tariffs, and 106 non-residential consumers were allowed to defer payment of arrears for energy services.

Another study by the World Bank has focused on social aspects of heat tariff setting and its possible reform (World Bank, 2014b). The study finds that compared with previous years' estimates, the fiscal and quasi-fiscal cost of under-priced heat increased to USD 1 bln in 2012. According to the study, if accompanied by more targeted subsidies to vulnerable groups, the heat tariff reform will promote social justice, since well-off households currently benefit from heat subsidies more than low-income families (see Figure 4.8). Furthermore, the study advocated that elimination of electricity and heat cross-subsidies in Belarus will

Figure 4.8. **Distribution of heat subsidies in Belarus in 2012, share of population**

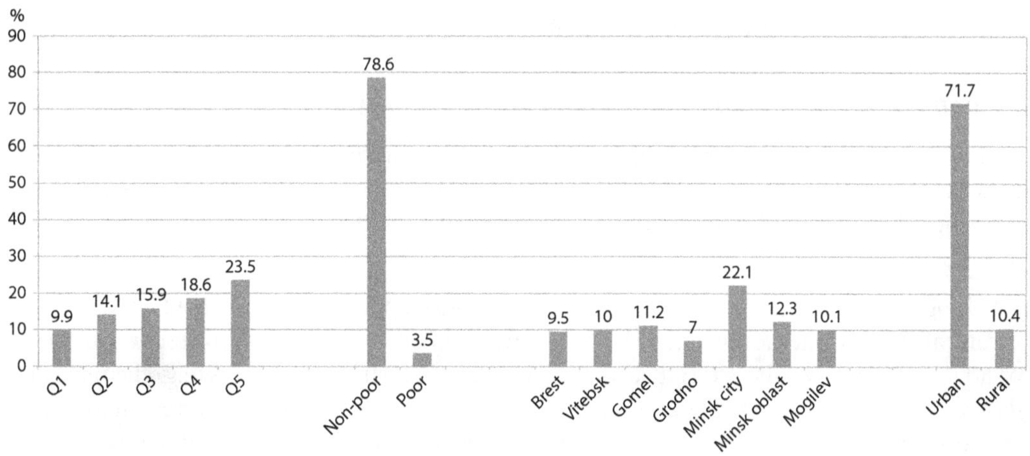

Source: World Bank (2014b).

promote industrial competitiveness, and the tariff for industrial consumers can be lowered in this case, because there will no longer be a need for the industrial tariff to include a surcharge for cross-subsidisation of residential tariffs.

Table 4.5 summarises the key findings on the legislative basis of different subsidy schemes, previous estimates of their value, and data sources.

Table 4.5. **Subsidy overview**

Energy subsidy	Key findings
Direct transfer of funds and liabilities	• Covered in the national definition of a subsidy • Envisioned in the Budget Code (National Assembly, 2008), execution of budget reported by the Ministry of Finance (2015) • Partly covered by the World Bank (2011) study
Tax expenditures (tax revenue foregone)	• Tax Code (National Assembly, 2002) has provisions for tax benefits for producers and consumers of energy
Induced transfers (income or price support provided to producers or consumers through various regulations)	• Under-pricing of electricity and heat tariffs for households; a complex system of cross-subsidisation; feed-in tariffs for preferential industrial consumers provided on an *ad hoc* basis; feed-in tariffs for renewable energy projects • Partly covered in GET (2007) and World Bank (2011, 2014a) studies
Transfer of risk to government	• Provisions for state guarantees and state loans are envisioned in the Budget Code (National Assembly, 2008).

Government support for fossil fuels

Unlike the analyses of Armenia, Georgia, Moldova and Ukraine, the lack of reporting on the value of direct budgetary transfers and tax expenditure in the energy sector has precluded a full-scale application of an inventory approach to energy subsidies in Belarus. However, tariff breakdowns and data on energy consumption by consumer groups and fuel types have proved to be more readily available. This report therefore first applies a price-gap approach to gas consumption in general and then to consumption of different types of energy by households, by far the most subsidised consumer category in Belarus.

In the instances where the study has relied on the price-gap approach for Belarus, it follows exactly the same logic as the IEA price gap methodology and the analysis of the other EaP countries in this report:

Price gap = Reference price – Net tariff

Subsidy = Price gap × Units consumed

Economy-wide price-gap estimates of consumer subsidies

For Belarus, as a net energy importer, the reference price is the price of the gas imports from the Russian Federation (Table 4.6). According to the IEA methodology, the reference price should include VAT, which was not levied on consumption of natural gas by households until 1 January 2016.

Using the import price as a benchmark, the price-gap approach reveals about USD 172 mln of natural gas subsidies for households. As discussed in other chapters of this report, subsidies for households are even larger. Households and certain industrial consumers (e.g. chemical and glass manufacturing) are being cross-subsidised through gas tariffs set at levels higher than cost-recovery for commercial consumers. In other words, the preferential natural gas tariff for households has been subsidised by the USD 765 mln surcharge on industrial consumers and legal entities.

Table 4.6. **Price-gap estimates of subsidies for gas consumers in Belarus in 2015 (nominal 2015 bln USD)**

	Unit	Households	Industry and legal entities
Import cost benchmark	USD per 1 000 m³	174.4 (import price) + VAT 20% = 209.3	
Consumption volume	bcm	1.8	18.4
Current tariff	USD per 1 000 m³	113.8	209.1 + VAT 20% = 250.9
Price gap per consumer category = Reference price minus consumer category tariff	USD per 1 000 m³	95.5	(-41.6)
Subsidy per consumer category	USD mln	172	(-765)
Weighted average domestic price	USD per 1 000 m³	238.4	
Price gap overall = Reference price minus weighted average domestic price	USD per 1 000 m³	(-29.1)	

Source: Authors' estimates based on World Bank (2015a), Belstat (2015), Ministry of Energy (2015b), Ministry of Energy (2015c).

It should be noted that the results obtained are only indicative, and do not reflect the full picture, due to a complicated system of cross-subsidisation. The analysis below seeks to complement these estimates by focusing on specific energy types and consumer groups.

Subsidy estimates by energy types and consumer groups

Induced transfers are the main form of fossil-fuel subsidies in Belarus. These are granted in the form of regulated tariffs for electricity, natural gas, heat, LPG and solid fuels. Certain cases of direct transfers either to consumers or producers were also identified, but detailed information on budget planning and execution is not available. Tax benefits were provided both to producers and consumers of energy. The authors' estimates of the value of energy subsidies in Belarus are listed below, totalling USD 1 039 mln in 2010 and USD 1 562 mln in 2014. These estimates fall within the same range as previous studies indicate (GET, 2007; World Bank, 2011; World Bank, 2014b).

When estimating induced transfers to residential consumers of heat, electricity and gas through a price-gap approach, the authors based their calculations on the difference between the weighted average tariff and official "base prices" (effectively levelised cost-recovery rates) set in accordance with Council of Ministers Resolution No. 222 (2014). This is the first time this benchmark has been used in a public study of subsidies in Belarus, leading to a new estimate. The World Bank study (2014b) that also relied on a price-gap approach was completed before Resolution No. 222 was adopted in 2014. The World Bank experts used the industrial tariff as a benchmark set above cost-recovery rates, and thus arrived at a higher estimate, in particular USD 1 bln in residential heat subsidies in 2012, compared with USD 0.5 bln in the findings below.

Tables 4.7 and 4.8 offer estimates of major energy subsidies, and detailed discussion of various measures.

Table 4.7. **Estimates of fossil-fuel subsidies in Belarus, BYR billion**

Subsidy	Type of subsidy	2010	2011	2012	2013	2014
Regulated heat tariff for households	Consumer subsidy, induced transfer	1 018	1 316	4 204	5 364	8 387
Regulated electricity tariff for households	Consumer subsidy, induced transfer	970	3 018	5 595	4 967	3 044
Regulated natural gas tariff for households	Consumer subsidy, induced transfer	617	1 303	2 685	2 190	2 872
Regulated prices for liquefied petroleum gas (LPG)	Consumer subsidy, induced transfer	n.c.	n.c.	n.c.	n.c.	n.c.
Regulated price for solid fuels (mainly peat briquettes)	Consumer subsidy, induced transfer	n.c.	n.c.	n.c.	n.c.	n.c.
VAT exemption on gas, electricity and heat provided to households (phased out in 2016)	Consumer subsidy, tax revenue foregone	507	626	1 007	1 335	2 038
Lowering coefficients applied to the environmental tax for thermal power plants providing electricity and heat to households	Consumer subsidy, tax revenue foregone	.	.	.	.	.
Funding of construction (reconstruction) of energy infrastructure in residential areas	Consumer subsidy, direct funding	.	.	.	.	1 151
National Programme for Development of Belarus' Energy System for the Period to 2016	Consumer subsidy, direct funding	n.a.	...	.	.	.
Total for quantified fossil-fuel subsidies		**3 111**	**6 264**	**13 491**	**13 856**	**17 493**

Note: **n.c.**: not calculated.

Source: Authors' estimates based on Belstat (2015), Council of Ministers (2016c) and Ministry of Finance (2015).

Table 4.8. **Estimates of fossil-fuel subsidies in Belarus, USD million**

Subsidy	Type of subsidy	2010	2011	2012	2013	2014
Regulated heat tariff for households	Consumer subsidy, induced transfer	340	235	502	598	817
Regulated electricity tariff for households	Consumer subsidy, induced transfer	324	538	526	394	154
Regulated natural gas tariff for households	Consumer subsidy, induced transfer	206	232	321	244	280
Regulated prices for LPG	Consumer subsidy, induced transfer	n.c.	n.c	n.c.	n.c.	n.c.
Regulated price for solid fuels (mainly peat briquettes)	Consumer subsidy, induced transfer	n.c.	n.c.	n.c.	n.c.	n.c.
VAT exemption with respect to gas, electricity and heat provided to households (phased out in 2016)	Consumer subsidy, tax revenue foregone	169	112	120	149	199
Lowering coefficients applied to the environmental tax for thermal power plants providing electricity and heat to households	Consumer subsidy, tax revenue foregone	.	.	.	.	.
Funding of construction (reconstruction) of energy infrastructure in residential areas	Consumer subsidy, direct funding	.	.	.	.	112
National Programme for Development of Belarus' Energy System for the Period to 2016	Consumer subsidy, direct funding	n.a.	.	.	.	.
Total for quantified fossil-fuel subsidies		**1 039**	**1 117**	**1 469**	**1 384**	**1 562**

Note: **n.c.**: not calculated; **n.a.**: not applicable.

Source: Authors' estimates based on Belstat (2015), Council of Ministers (2016c) and Ministry of Finance (2015c).

Table 4.9 provides further detail on the methodological approaches used for the quantification of subsidies. In particular, all quantified induced transfers are based on the gap between the official "base prices" set in accordance with Resolution No. 222 (2014) and weighted average tariffs for households approved by the Ministry of Economy and published by the Council of Ministers (2016c). Then, the difference between subsidised tariffs and the benchmark is multiplied by households' consumption volumes reported in (Belstat, 2015). The "base prices" have been selected as the most credible benchmark for the calculations, since they are already used as such by the national government and all key stakeholders in Belarus.

Table 4.9. **Methodological approaches used for the quantification of key energy subsidies in Belarus**

Subsidy scheme	Quantification method
Regulated heat tariff for households	Authors' calculations: heat tariffs for households are compared against the "base prices" provided in (Council of Ministers, 2016c) and multiplied by the amount of heat supplied to households according to Energy balance (Belstat, 2015)
Regulated natural gas tariff for households	Authors' calculations: gas tariffs for households are compared against the "base prices" reported in (Council of Ministers, 2016c) and multiplied by households' consumption volumes specified in the Energy balance (Belstat, 2015). Weighted average tariffs are calculated based on the volumes of gas supplied to different categories of households specified in declarations of gas supply companies (2013-14)
Regulated electricity tariff for households	Authors' calculations: electricity tariffs for households are compared against the "base prices" reported in (Council of Ministers, 2016c) and multiplied by households' consumption volumes specified in the Energy balance (Belstat, 2015). Weighted average tariffs are calculated based on the volumes of electricity supplied to different categories of households specified in declarations of electricity supply companies (2013-14)
VAT exemption on gas, electricity and heat provided to households	Authors' calculations: application of the standard VAT rate (20%) to the value of energy type consumed by households. Calculations are based on the data provided in (Belstat, 2015) and current tariffs (Council of Ministers, 2016c)
Funding of construction (reconstruction) of energy infrastructure in residential areas	Subsidy estimate is taken at face value from government sources (Ministry of Finance, 2015)

Source: Authors' summary.

As described above, household tariffs for electricity, natural gas and heat are cross-subsidised by setting tariffs for certain industrial consumers above the levelised cost-recovery level (according to the so-called "cost-plus" methodology).

The "cost-plus" tariff for gas (but not for heat or electricity that are fuelled by gas anyway) includes payments of about 10% to a special government fund that accumulates resources to provide subsidies to certain preferential legal entities, for instance, the glass industry and publicly funded social institutions. The special fund is managed by the Council of Ministers at the national level. There is no publicly available information on the structure of revenue and expenditures of this special fund.

Heat for households is additionally cross-subsidised both by higher tariffs on electricity for certain consumers and by direct transfers from local budgets. Local authorities can apply for compensation for these subsidies to the national budget, in line with Presidential Decree No. 550 (2013). Budget outlays on compensation to utility providers are planned according to the procedures defined in Ministry of Finance Resolution No. 67/21/70 (2014). However, information on the exact amount of allocated funds is not available. Hence, subsidies to households in the form of regulated tariffs are quantified using the price-gap methodology, as explained in Table 4.9. This approach also helps to avoid double counting.

In addition, Beltopgaz also provides fuel briquettes (made of locally extracted peat, of not more than 2.5 tonnes for a household per year) and LPG to households at subsidised prices. The losses incurred from selling fuel briquettes at subsidised prices are compensated for out of local government budgets through local fuel marketing organisations. Fuel wood is supplied by the same local marketing organisations at subsidised prices for not more than 4.9 m^3 of dense fuel wood per year, with losses also offset from local government budgets. Official data are not available on the total amount of support due to such measures.

Tables 4.7 and 4.8 show that the subsidies in the heating sector have increased more than twice in USD terms from 2010 to 2014. This results from the increase of imported gas prices (translated into higher "base prices"), while tariffs for households were increased only marginally. Thus, the gap between the benchmark ("base price") and tariffs for households widened. The amount of subsidies in the electricity sector dropped by about 46% in 2014, compared to 2013, largely due to the differentiation of tariffs by consumption volumes introduced in 2013 with the approval of Council of Ministers Resolution No. 52 (2013b).

Information is limited on direct budget transfers provided either to producers or consumers. In this category, it was possible to quantify only one subsidy. The Ministry of Finance (2015) reports that budget transfers of BYR 1 151 bln (USD 112 mln) were provided for construction and reconstruction of infrastructure (electricity and gas networks) in residential areas in 2014. The subsidised infrastructure belongs to the energy and gas supply companies reporting to the Ministry of Energy (Ministry of Finance, 2015).

According to the National Programme for Development of Belarus' Energy System for the Period to 2016, about BYR 8 250.5 bln (USD 899.4 mln) was to be disbursed from the national budget to cover partial reimbursement of interest on investment loans, repayment of loans attracted for the construction of the housing sector's utility infrastructure and capital investments for the period from 2011 to 2015 (Council of Ministers Resolution No. 194, 2012). The specific amount of funding for every measure is planned annually in the national budget. However, detailed budget documentation, and information on the actual allocation of funds, is not available, and these numbers are thus not included in the estimate of total subsidies.

Each year, the Council of Ministers approves a resolution providing for measures to support agricultural producers in preparation for field work, getting fodder and harvesting (see for example Council of Ministers Resolution No. 1 037, 2015a). Provision of preferential loans for purchase of required agricultural inputs, including diesel and gasoline, is among state support measures for agricultural producers. The banks are then compensated from national and local budgets, but the amount of transfers to the banks is not made public. This support is not specific to fossil fuels, since it also applies, for instance, to fertilisers.

Only two cases of tax exemptions have been found. The first is the VAT exemption for gas, electricity and heat provided to households. Revenue foregone on this account has increased from BYR 507 bln in 2010 to BYR 2 038 bln in 2014, although in USD terms, the increase is not as dramatic (a 17.8% increase, from USD 169 mln to USD 199 mln, see Table 4.8 and Table 4.A1.4). This measure was phased out in 2016, in an example of fossil-fuel subsidy reform in Belarus.

The second case of tax revenue foregone includes a relief on environmental tax (lowering coefficients applied) for thermal power plants that provide electricity and heat for households. Again, the data here are not sufficient to quantify this subsidy.

Means-tested, targeted support for low-income households is provided in the form of a monetary social allowance for various needs. These include utility payments either on a one-time or a monthly basis, in line with procedures defined in Presidential Decree No. 550 (2013) and Presidential Decree No. 41 (2012). However, there is no publicly available information on the value of such benefits and the share of utility payments in the total amount. As of the beginning of 2016, the government was considering changes in the existing social support system (Belta, 2016). Presidential Decree No. 78 of 23 February 2016 declared that 1 October 2016 would be the date for the introduction of a nonmonetary subsidy for partial compensation of utility payments. As of April 2016, the form of the nonmonetary subsidy had not yet been selected. The Decree also identifies the reallocation of saved budgetary transfers to utilities as a source of funding for targeted support that will cover the cost of utilities to low-income households.

By the end of 2016, the government plans to introduce a non-cash subsidy for a partial settlement of energy and housing services in cases where payments for them exceed 20% of the monthly-average aggregate income for urban households, or 15% of the same for rural households (Belta, 2016). This non-cash subsidy will be granted as a result of both applications from vulnerable households and identification of them based on the government-processed data on their income and expenses.

At the same time, plans to reform subsidies in the utility sector of Belarus have to be treated with caution. The government of Belarus has long planned to gradually phase out subsidies and increase district heating and electricity tariffs for households to cost-recovery levels, as reflected in the National Programme of Energy System Development by 2016 (Council of Ministers Resolution No. 194, 2012). In particular, it was planned to establish fully cost-reflective electricity tariffs by 2015. Cost-recovery of heat generation was planned to be increased to 30% by 2015. During the first phase of tariff reform (2012-14) some reduction of cross-subsidies in the gas and electricity sectors was achieved, and electricity, heat and gas tariffs were revised annually, based on the nominal growth of the average salary, 5.8% in 2014 (IEA, 2015b). However, as of the beginning of 2016, the ambitious targets for increasing cost-recovery rates had not been achieved, due to social concerns. The National Programme of Energy System Development is subject to reconsideration and redesign.

Government support for energy efficiency

In 2011, the Council of Ministers of the Republic of Belarus approved the National Programme on Energy Saving for the period from 2011 to 2015 (Council of Ministers Resolution No. 1 882, 2011). This set ambitious targets of reducing the energy intensity of GDP by 29%-32% by 2015 compared with 2010, and increasing the share of local energy resources in the fuel balance to 28% by 2015. A wide range of measures was planned to achieve these goals. The total required funding from all sources was estimated at USD 8.6 bln, of which 38% was identified as companies' own resources. National and local budgets were to contribute 27% and 15%, respectively and loans and other resources to account for the remaining 20%.

However, according to the Department of Energy Efficiency (n.d.), the total amount of funds provided from the national and regional budgets for energy-saving measures amounted to USD 1 439 mln, only 40% of which was initially planned for the duration of the Programme. The 2011-15 Programme's energy efficiency targets have not been reached, either. According to the new National Programme on Energy Saving for the period from 2016 to 2020, adopted by Resolution No. 248 of the Council of Ministers of 28 March 2016, in 2011-14, the energy intensity of Belarus' GDP fell by 8.3% (the GDP grew by 9.8%, but energy consumption virtually remained the same). The official data for 2015, the last year of the previous programme, are not yet available. No significant change was noted in either GDP or energy consumption in 2015 compared with 2014. The figure of 8.3% is a considerable reduction in energy intensity over 2011-14, but it is more than three times lower than the target set in 2011.

According to the government programme "Energy Saving" for 2016-20, which was adopted in March 2016 (Council of Ministers, 2016a), the energy intensity of GDP will be reduced by at least 2% by 2021, compared with 2015. The share of domestically sourced primary energy in total energy consumption is anticipated to reach at least 16% (mainly thanks to the inauguration of the nuclear power plant), including 6% from renewable energy sources. The funding for implementation of these energy-saving measures, based on Belarus' social and economic development parameters of Belarus, is envisaged at BYR 11 064 mln (USD 5 625 mln).

Table 4.10 provides more detail on the allocation of funds throughout the years. The allocated government support targeted implementation of energy efficiency measures in the organisations of social infrastructure and publicly funded institutions, as well as some other organisations.

Table 4.10. **Actual budget spending under the National Programme of Energy Saving 2011-15, USD million**

Sources of funding	2011	2012	2013	2014	2015	Total over 2011-15	Planned 2011-15
National budget	109	172	125	50	38	439	2 339
Local budgets	150	192	234	230	134	939	1 299
Total	**259**	**364**	**358**	**280**	**172**	**1 439**	**3 638**

Source: Department of Energy Efficiency (n.d.), Council of Ministers Resolution No. 1 882 (2011).

Government support for renewable energy

The legislative basis for stimulating feed-in tariffs for renewables was established by Law No. 204-3 (National Assembly, 2010) "On renewable energy sources" and Ministry of Economy Resolution No. 100 (2011) "On tariffs for electricity produced from renewable energy sources". Tariffs for electricity produced from renewable energy sources are established based on the electricity tariff for industry (installed capacity up to 750 kVA) and multiplied by a special increasing co-efficient varying based on the type of renewable energy and lifetime of the installation in question (first ten years and afterwards). According to Article 18 of Law No. 204-3 (National Assembly, 2010), renewable energy producers enjoy a guaranteed connection to the electricity grid. Even though the underlying legislation came into force in 2011, Belarus' production of renewable energy remained insignificant until 2014, when generation plants reached their planned capacity. In 2015, feed-in tariffs for renewables were further differentiated by type of energy, capacity and lifetime (Council of Ministers Resolution No. 45, 2015c).

Tables 4.11 and 4.12 quantify support for renewable energy through the feed-in tariffs by energy type. Calculation of the value of support is based on the volume of electricity purchases (USD 22.1 mln in 2014) provided by BelEnergo (n.d.) and increasing feed-in coefficients defined in Ministry of Economy Resolution No. 100 (2011) (see Table 4.A2.1 and Table 4.A2.2 for more details).

Renewable energy producers also benefit from tax breaks, but data limitations preclude quantitative assessments of such support measures. For example, the Tax Code (National Assembly, 2002, 2009) exempts renewable energy installations, add-ons and spare parts from VAT, according to p. 1.16 of Article 96. Land tax is also applied to plots of land under renewable energy installations (Paragraph 1.16 of Article 96). In addition, a lowering coefficient is applied to the environmental tax levied upon TPPs using biogas and biomass as feedstock (Paragraph 3.5. of Article 207).

To improve the unified government policy in the area of renewable energy development, two documents were enacted in 2015: the Presidential Decree of 18 May 2015, No. 209, "On the Use of Renewable Energy Sources" and Resolution of the Council of Ministers of 6 August 2015, No. 662, "On Determining and Allocating Quotas for Setting of the Renewable Energy Units" (2015b). These documents outline the procedure for setting, modernising and reconstructing of the existing units as well as determining and allocating quotas.

A national inter-agency commission was established to determine and allocate quotas for setting the renewable energy units. These quotas do not apply to units set up by organisations and individuals to cover their own energy needs and to the cases of investment contracts concluded and registered in due order before the Presidential Decree came into force.

The inter-agency commission established the 2016-18 quotas for total generation from renewables in the amount of 215 MWt, and the following breakdown by renewable energy types: biogas 32 MWt; wind 50 MWt; solar 15 MWt; hydropower 82 MWt; biomass 36 MWt. It also approved a list of organisations and individual entrepreneurs entitled to set renewable energy generation units within the allocated quotas.

Outside the quotas, under the investment contracts concluded prior to the Presidential Decree, construction is under way for renewable energy capacity up to 464.3 MWt, including: solar 291.6 MWt; wind 151.7 MWt; biogas 11.1 MWt; and biomass 9.9 MWt.

Table 4.11. **Estimates of government support for renewable energy in Belarus, BYR billion**

Subsidy	Type of subsidy	2010	2011	2012	2013	2014
Feed-in tariff for solar energy (coefficient 2.7)	Producer subsidy, induced transfer	n.a.	.	.	.	8.9
Feed-in tariff for wind energy (coefficient 1.3)	Producer subsidy, induced transfer	n.a.	.	.	.	6.6
Feed-in tariff for hydro (coefficient 1.1)	Producer subsidy, induced transfer	n.a.	.	.	.	3.1
Feed-in tariff for biogas (coefficient 1.3)	Producer subsidy, induced transfer	n.a.	.	.	.	33.8
Feed-in tariff for biomass and other (coefficient 1.3)	Producer subsidy, induced transfer	n.a.	.	.	.	0.9
Total for quantified RE subsidies		**n.a.**	**.**	**.**	**.**	**53.2**

Note: **n.a.**: not applicable.

Source: Authors' estimates based on BelEnergo (n.d.) and Ministry of Economy, Resolution No. 100 (2011).

Table 4.12. **Estimates of government support for renewable energy in Belarus, USD million**

Subsidy	Type of subsidy	2010	2011	2012	2013	2014
Feed-in tariff for solar energy (coefficient 2.7)	Producer subsidy, induced transfer	n.a.	.	.	.	0.865
Feed-in tariff for wind energy (coefficient 1.3)	Producer subsidy, induced transfer	n.a.	.	.	.	0.641
Feed-in tariff for hydro (coefficient 1.1)	Producer subsidy, induced transfer	n.a.	.	.	.	0.301
Feed-in tariff for biogas (coefficient 1.3)	Producer subsidy, induced transfer	n.a.	.	.	.	3.298
Feed-in tariff for biomass and other (coefficient 1.3)	Producer subsidy, induced transfer	n.a.	.	.	.	0.084
Total for quantified RE subsidies		n.a.	.	.	.	**5.189**

Note: **n.a.**: not applicable.

Source: Authors' estimates based on BelEnergo (n.d.) and Ministry of Economy Resolution No. 100 (2011).

It is anticipated over 2016-20 that deployment of new renewable energy units will continue, in compliance with these regulations and the annual allocation of quotas for the next three years. The extent of the deployment will be consistent with the task of increasing the share of primary energy supply from renewable energy sources in the total energy consumption by 1% (from 5% in 2015 to 6% in 2020).

Annex 4.A1

Fossil-fuel subsidies

Table 4.A1.1. **Regulated heat tariff for households**

Subsidy category	Income or price support → Market price support and regulation → Regulated prices set at below-market rates
Stimulated activity	Consumption of thermal energy
Subsidy name	**Regulated heat tariff for households**
Jurisdiction	National
Legislation or endorsing organisation	Presidential Decree No. 550 "On some issues of regulation of tariffs (prices) for housing and communal services" of 5 December 2013 (Paragraph 1.4.) Resolution of the Ministry of Finance of the Republic of Belarus No. 67/21/70 "On the approval of the procedure for funding of organisations providing utlities services to households" of 27 October 2014 Resolution of the Council of Ministers No. 1 116 "On the establishment of tariffs for households on gas, heat and electricity and approval of costs per unit of provided utilities" of 30 December 2013 (with amendments)
Policy objective(s) of subsidy	To keep heat tariffs for households low
End recipient(s) of subsidy	Households
Time period	From 1995 to present. There are plans to reduce the subsidy, but no specific timeline.
Background	Under point 1.4 of Presidential Decree No. 550 (2013), the heat tariff for households is established by the Council of Ministers of the Republic of Belarus. Households pay for heat consumed to housing and communal organisations (widely referred to as ZhKH organisations, based on the Russian abbreviation) while the ZhKHs buy thermal energy from energy supply companies at tariffs differentiated depending on the region where the heat is generated. Two main channels of subsidies maintain low heat tariffs for households, as illustrated in Figure 4.6: cross-subsidies through higher electricity and heat tariffs for industry, on the one hand, and budgetary transfers on the other. No estimates of budgetary transfers related to residential heat subsidy have been publicly reported. Under this process, the compensation money changes hands several times. Under Ministry of Finance Resolution No. 67/21/70 (2014), budget expenditures to cover the costs of housing and communal organisations (including heat supply) are planned by financial year. ZhKH organisations submit their calculations of the difference in tariffs to local executive committees and request coverage of the gap by a transfer from the local budget. In their turn, local budgets receive direct transfers (referred to as "subventions" in Russian, a special term used only for the transfer of funds between the national and local budgets in the case of Belarus) from the national budget to compensate their expenditure on residential heat subsidies. Given that data on the amount of budget transfers and cross-subsidisation are not available, induced transfers to households in the form of regulated heat tariffs are estimated indirectly, using a price-gap approach. In particular, current tariffs are compared against "base prices" (tariffs), which the government uses as a benchmark covering all production costs, and multiplied by the amount of heat consumed by households. Calculations are made based on the data on residential heat tariffs and "base prices" provided in Council of Ministers Resolution (2016c) and the amount of heat supplied to households according to the energy balance published in Belstat (2015).
Amount of subsidy conferred	2010: BYR 1 018 bln (USD 340 mln) 2011: BYR 1 316 bln (USD 235 mln) 2012: BYR 4 204 bln (USD 502 mln) 2013: BYR 5 364 bln (USD 598 mln) 2014: BYR 8 387 bln (USD 817 mln)

Table 4.A1.1. **Regulated heat tariff for households** *(continued)*

Calculations of the value of regulated heat tariff for households (calculations may slightly vary due to rounding)					
Indicator	**2010**	**2011**	**2012**	**2013**	**2014**
Heat supplied to households, thousand gigacalories (Gcal)	23 439	22 257	23 374	23 413	22 301
Heat supplied to organisations (for information only, not used in calculation)	49 036	46 703	48 063	46 069	44 592
Tariff for households, BYR per Gcal	43 458	49 333	60 140	70 898	90 058
"Base price", BYR per gigacalorie (cost recovery rate used as a benchmark for calculations)	86 894	108 468	240 000	300 000	466 119
Tariff for households, USD per Gcal	14.52	8.80	7.19	7.90	8.78
"Base price", USD per Gcal (cost-recovery rate used as a benchmark for calculations)	29.03	19.35	28.67	33.44	45.43
Price gap, USD per Gcal	14.51	10.55	21.49	25.54	36.65
Tariff for organisations (for information), USD per Gcal	43.70	44.03	30.33	28.30	43.85
Price-gap estimate of the payments by organisations (for information), 1 000 USD	719 667	1 152 804	79 717	-236 815	-70 616
Value of heat subsidy to households, 1 000 USD	340 075	234 785	502 293	597 883	817 387
Information sources	Presidential Decree No. 550 (2013), Ministry of Finance Resolution No. 67/21/70 (2014), Resolution No. 1 116 (2013a), Belstat (2015), Council of Ministers (2016c)				

Table 4.A1.2. **Regulated gas tariff for households**

Subsidy category	Income or price support → Market price support and regulation → Regulated prices set at below-market rates
Stimulated activity	Consumption of gas
Subsidy name	**Regulated gas tariff for households**
Jurisdiction	National
Legislation/endorsing organisation	Resolution of the Council of Ministers No. 52 "On some issues regarding the reduction of costs of providing utilities services" of 23 January 2013 Resolution of the Council of Ministers No. 1 116 "On the establishment of tariffs for households on gas, heat and electricity and approval of costs per unit of provided utilities" of 30 December 2013 (with amendments)
Policy objective(s) of subsidy	To keep gas tariffs for households low
End recipient(s) of subsidy	Households
Time period	From 1995 to the present
Background	Cross-subsidisation of household gas consumption is arranged at the expense of industrial consumers. Tariffs for households are established according to procedures defined in Presidential Decree No. 550 (2013) and Resolution No. 222 (2014). As of 1 March 2013, a three-level differentiation of tariffs for households was instituted, depending on their consumption volume (Council of Ministers Resolution No. 52, 2013b). Induced transfers to households are estimated based on gas tariffs for households compared against "base prices" (Council of Ministers Resolution, 2016c) and multiplied by the consumption volumes specified in the Energy balance (Belstat, 2015). Weighted average tariffs are calculated based on the volumes of gas supplied to different categories of households specified in gas supply company declarations (2013-14).
Amount of subsidy conferred	2010: BYR 617 bln (USD 206 mln) 2011: BYR 1 303 bln (USD 232 mln) 2012: BYR 2 685 bln (USD 321 mln) 2013: BYR 2 190 bln (USD 244 mln) 2014: BYR 2 872 bln (USD 280 mln)

Table 4.A1.2. **Regulated gas tariff for households** *(continued)*

Calculations of the value of regulated gas tariff for households (calculations may slightly vary due to rounding)					
Indicator	**2010**	**2011**	**2012**	**2013**	**2014**
Natural gas supplied to households, million m^3	1 749	1 694	1 898	1 877	1 839
Natural gas supplied to organisations, million m^3 (for information only, not used in calculations)	20 113	19 005	18 504	18 709	18 588
Household tariff in summer, BYR per m^3	462.0	786.5	1 447.6	1 500.0	2 281.8
Household tariffs in winter, BYR per m^3	219.1	373.0	686.5	711.3	623.3
Weighed average household tariff, USD per m^3	0.101	0.092	0.113	0.109	0.116
Tariff for organisations, BYR per m^3 (for information only, not used in calculations)	719.00	1 410	2 593.18	2 359	3 021
"Base price", USD per gigacalorie (cost-recovery rate used as a benchmark for calculations)	0.219	0.229	0.282	0.239	0.268
Price gap, USD per m^3	0.118	0.137	0.169	0.130	0.152
Tariff for organisations (for information only), USD per m^3	0.240	0.251	0.310	0.263	0.294
Price-gap estimate of the payments by organisations (for information), USD 1 000	434.74	430.08	515.98	442.68	492.54
Value of gas subsidy to households, USD 1 000	206	232	321	244	280
Information sources	Council of Ministers Resolution No. 52 (2013b), Council of Ministers Resolution No. 1 116 (2013a), Belstat (2015), Council of Ministers (2016c), Declarations of gas supply companies, 2013-14				

Table 4.A1.3. **Regulated electricity tariff for households**

Subsidy category	Income or price support → Market price support and regulation → Regulated prices set at below-market rates
Stimulated activity	Consumption of electricity
Subsidy name	Regulated electricity tariff for households
Jurisdiction	National
Legislation/endorsing organisation	Resolution of the Council of Ministers No. 52 "On some issues regarding the reduction of costs of providing utilities services" of 23 January 2013 Resolution of the Council of Ministers No. 1 116 "On the establishment of tariffs for households on gas, heat and electricity and approval of costs per unit of provided utilities" of 30 December 2013 (with amendments)
Policy objective(s) of subsidy	To keep electricity tariffs for households low
End recipient(s) of Subsidy	Households
Time period	From 1995 to the present
Background	Cross-subsidisation of household electricity consumption is provided by above cost-recovery tariffs for industrial consumers. Tariffs for households are established in line with procedures defined in Presidential Decree No. 550 (2013) and Council of Ministers Resolution No. 222 (2014). Starting from 1 March 2013, there was a three-level differentiation of tariffs for households depending on their consumption volumes (Council of Ministers Resolution No. 52, 2013b). Induced transfers to households are estimated based on electricity tariffs for households compared against "base prices" (Council of Ministers Resolution, 2016c) and multiplied by consumption volumes specified in the Energy balance (Belstat, 2015). Weighted average tariffs are calculated based on the volume of electricity supplied to different categories of households specified in declarations of electricity supply companies (2013-14).
Amount of subsidy conferred	2010: BYR 970 bln (USD 324 mln) 2011: BYR 3 018 bln (USD 538 mln) 2012: BYR 5 595 bln (USD 526 mln) 2013: BYR 4 967 bln (USD 394 mln) 2014: BYR 3 044 bln (USD 154 mln)

Table 4.A1.3. **Regulated electricity tariff for households** *(continued)*

Calculations of the value of regulated electricity tariff for households (calculations may slightly vary due to rounding)					
Indicator	**2010**	**2011**	**2012**	**2013**	**2014**
Electricity supply to households, million kWh	5 889	6 109	6 330	6 386	6 397
Electricity supply to organisations, million kWh (for information only, not used in calculations)	31 701	31 679	32 065	31 479	31 657
Tariff for households with electric cooking stoves, BYR per kWh	125.3	164.6	250.6	445.0	810.7
Tariff for households without electric cooking stoves, BYR per kWh	173.0	193.8	295.0	504.0	953.8
Weighted average tariff for households, USD per kWh	0.056	0.034	0.035	0.055	0.091
Industrial tariff, BYR per kWh (for information only, not used in calculations)	357.80	737.00	1 263.67	1 372.78	1 522.02
Industrial tariff, USD per kWh (for information only, not used in calculations)	0.120	0.131	0.127	0.1260	0.1243
"Base price", USD per kWh (cost-recovery rate used as a benchmark for calculations)	0.111	0.122	0.118	0.117	0.115
Price gap, USD per kWh	0.055	0.088	0.083	0.062	0.024
Tariff for organisations (for information), USD per kWh	0.120	0.131	0.127	0.1260	0.1243
Price-gap estimate of the payments by organisations (for information), USD 1 000	269.0	295.7	288.4	281.7	279.4
Value of electricity subsidy to households, USD 1 000	324	538	526	394	154
Information sources	Council of Ministers Resolution No. 52 (2013b), Council of Ministers Resolution No. 1 116 (2013a), Belstat (2015), Council of Ministers Resolution (2016c), Declarations of electricity supply companies, 2013-14				

Table 4.A1.4. **VAT exemption on utility tariffs for households**

Subsidy category	Government revenue foregone → Tax breaks and special taxes → Tax expenditures
Stimulated activity	Consumption of utilities
Subsidy name	**VAT exemption with respect to utility tariffs for households**
Jurisdiction	National
Legislation/endorsing organisation	Article 93 of Tax Code (2002, 2009)
Policy objective(s) of subsidy	To keep utility tariffs for households low
End recipient(s) of subsidy	Households
Time period	Starting from 1995 to 2015. Phased out starting 1 January 2016.
Background	According to Article 93 of the Tax Code (2002, 2009), the costs of energy resources supplied to households are not included in the VAT tax base. That meant that effectively, tariffs for households were kept at 20% below what they would have been without the VAT exemption. This tax exemption was phased out and the 20% VAT was included in utility tariffs starting on 1 January 2016. For the preceding year, the revenue foregone due to this measure is estimated based on applying the 20% rate to current tariffs (Council of Ministers Resolution, 2016c) and the amount of energy consumed by households (Belstat, 2015).
Amount of subsidy conferred	2010: BYR 507 bln (USD 169 mln) 2011: BYR 626 bln (USD 112 mln) 2012: BYR 1 007 bln (USD 120 mln) 2013: BYR 1 335 bln (USD 149 mln) 2014: BYR 2 038 bln (USD 199 mln)
Information sources	Tax Code (National Assembly, 2002, 2009), Belstat (2015), Council of Ministers Resolution (2016c)

Table 4.A1.5. **Funding of construction (reconstruction) of energy infrastructure in residential areas**

Subsidy category	Direct and indirect transfer of funds and liabilities → Direct spending → Earmarks
Stimulated activity	Consumption of utilities
Subsidy name	**Funding of construction (reconstruction) of energy infrastructure in residential areas**
Jurisdiction	National
Legislation/endorsing organisation	Law of the Republic of Belarus No. 304-3 "On the approval of the report on the execution of the state budget in 2014" Resolution of the Council of Ministers No. 194 "On the approval of the state programme for the development of the Belarusian energy system for the period by 2016" of 29 February 2012
Policy objective(s) of subsidy	To reduce housing construction costs
End recipient(s) of subsidy	Households
Time period	From 1995 to the present
Background	Direct budget transfers are granted for financing of the construction (reconstruction) of engineering infrastructure, in particular gas and electricity networks, in residential areas, for energy and gas supply companies that report to the Ministry of Energy. The amount of funds is publicly reported only for 2014. The amount is reported at face value based on the national budget execution report (Ministry of Finance, 2015).
Amount of subsidy conferred	2014: BYR 1 151 bln (USD 112 mln)
Information sources	Ministry of Finance (2015), Resolution No. 194 (2012)

Annex 4.A2

Subsidies for energy efficiency and renewable energy

Table 4.A2.1. **Funding of energy-efficiency projects**

Subsidy category	Direct and indirect transfer of funds and liabilities → Direct spending → Earmarks
Stimulated activity	Implementation of energy-efficiency projects
Subsidy name	**Funding of energy efficiency projects**
Jurisdiction	National
Legislation/endorsing organisation	Resolution of the Council of Ministers No. 1 882 "On the approval of the National Programme of Energy Saving for the Period from 2011 to 2015" of 24 December 2010
Policy objective(s) of subsidy	To support energy-saving measures
End recipient(s) of subsidy	Organisations of social infrastructure and other publicly funded institutions
Time period	2011-15 (duration of the state programme)
Background	The National Programme of Energy Saving for the Period from 2011 to 2015 (Council of Ministers Resolution No. 1 882, 2011) provides for budget funding for energy-saving projects implemented by organisations of social infrastructure and other publicly funded institutions. The total budget outlay planned was USD 2 339 mln from the national and USD 1 299 mln from the regional budgets respectively (in total, USD 3 638 mln). For five years, about USD 1 439 mln was allocated from the national and regional budgets to support energy-efficiency projects, according the Department of Energy Efficiency (n.d.). These allocations are reported at face value.
Amount of subsidy conferred	2011: BYR 1 452 bln (USD 259 mln) 2012: BYR 3 047 bln (USD 364 mln) 2013: BYR 3 212 bln (USD 358 mln) 2014: BYR 2 873 bln (USD 280 mln) 2015: BYR 2 796 bln (USD 172 mln)
Information sources	Resolution No. 1 882 (2011), Department of Energy Efficiency (n.d.)

Table 4.A2.2. **Feed-in tariff for renewable energy producers**

Subsidy category	Income or price support → Market price support and regulation → Feed-in tariff for renewable energy producers
Stimulated activity	Production of renewable energy
Subsidy name	**Feed-in tariff for renewable energy producers**
Jurisdiction	National
Legislation/endorsing organisation	Law of the Republic of Belarus No. 204-3 "On renewable energy sources" of 27 December 2010 Resolution of the Ministry of Economy of the Republic of Belarus No. 100 "On tariffs for electricity produced from renewable energy sources" of 30 June 2011
Policy objective(s) of subsidy	To promote the development of the renewable energy sector
End recipient(s) of subsidy	Renewable energy producers
Time period	From 2011 to the present
Background	Under Law No. 204-3 (National Assembly, 2010), energy supply organisations (BelEnergo and its subsidiaries) must purchase electricity from renewable energy producers at increased tariffs, based on the electricity tariff for industry (installed capacity up to 750 kVA) and multiplied by special increasing coefficients defined in Ministry of Economy Resolution No. 100 (2011). Estimation of the value of induced transfer provided through feed-in tariff to renewable energy producers is based on the volume of electricity purchases provided by BelEnergo (2014) and the increasing feed-in coefficients are laid out in Ministry of Economy Resolution No. 100 (2011).
Amount of subsidy conferred	2014: BYR 53.2 bln (USD 5.2 mln)
Information sources	Law No. 204-3 (National Assembly, 2010), Ministry of Economy Resolution No. 100 (2011), BelEnergo (2014)

References

BelEnergo (n.d.), *Volume of Electricity Purchases*, unpublished.

Belneftekhim (2015), *Retail Prices for Oil Products Distributed at Gas Stations,* Belarusian State Concern for Oil and Chemistry, Minsk. www.belneftekhim.by/docs/01072015_03.xlsx.

Belneftekhim (2013), *Order No. 79 on the Procedure of Establishment of Wholesale or Retail Prices of Petroleum Products Produced and (or) Sold on the Territory of the Republic of Belarus as of 28 February 2013*, Chairman of the Belarusian State Concern for Oil and Chemistry, Minsk.

Belstat (2016), *Macroeconomic Statistics,* National Statistical Committee of the Republic of Belarus, Minsk. www.belstat.gov.by/ofitsialnaya-statistika/makroekonomika-i-okruzhayushchaya-sreda/natsionalnye-scheta/godovye-dannye_11/proizvodstvo-valovogo-vnutrennego-produkta/.

Belstat (2015), *Energy Balance of the Republic of Belarus 2009-2014,* National Statistical Committee of the Republic of Belarus, Minsk.

Belta (2016), "*Non-Cash Subsidies for Housing and Communal Services will Be Introduced in Belarus from 1 May 2016*", Belta. www.belta.by/society/view/beznalichnye-subsidii-dlja-oplaty-zhku-pojavjatsja-v-belarusi-s-1-maja-179349-2016/.

Council of Ministers (2016a), *Resolution No. 248 on the Approval of the National Programme on Energy Saving for the Period from 2016 to 2020 of 28 March 2016*, Council of Ministers of the Republic of Belarus, Minsk.

Council of Ministers (2016b), *Resolution No. 480 of 21 June 2016*, Council of Ministers of the Republic of Belarus, Minsk. www.tarify.by.

Council of Ministers (2016c), *Tariffs for Heat and Electricity,* Council of Ministers of the Republic of Belarus, Minsk. www.tarify.by/.

Council of Ministers (2015a), *Resolution No. 1 037 on the Measures for the Preparation of Agricultural Enterprises to the Field Work, Establishment of a Strong Feed Base and Preparation for the Harvest in 2016*, Council of Ministers of the Republic of Belarus, Minsk.

Council of Ministers (2015b), *Resolution No. 662 on Determining and Allocating Quotas for Setting of the Renewable Energy Units of 6 August 2015*, Council of Ministers of the Republic of Belarus, Minsk.

Council of Ministers (2015c), *Resolution No. 45 on Tariffs for Electricity Produced from Renewable Energy Sources by Individual Entrepreneurs and Legal Persons who Are not Members of the SPA BelEnergo,* Council of Ministers of the Republic of Belarus, Minsk.

Council of Ministers (2014), *Resolution No. 222 on the Formation of Prices (Tariffs) on Natural and Liquefied Gas, Electricity and Heat of 17 March 2014,* Council of Ministers of the Republic of Belarus, Minsk.

Council of Ministers (2013a), *Resolution No. 1 116 on the Establishment of Tariffs for Households on Gas, Heat and Electricity and Approval of Costs per Unit of Provided Utilities of 30 December 2013,* Council of Ministers of the Republic of Belarus, Minsk.

Council of Ministers (2013b), *Resolution No. 52 on Some Issues Regarding Reduction of Costs for Providing Utilities Services of 23 January 2013*, Council of Ministers of the Republic of Belarus, Minsk.

Council of Ministers (2012), *Resolution No. 194 on the Approval of the National Programme for Development of the Belarusian Energy System for the Period by 2016 of 29 February 2012,* Council of Ministers of the Republic of Belarus, Minsk.

Council of Ministers (2011), *Resolution No. 1 882 on the Approval of the National Programme on Energy Saving for the Period from 2011 to 2015*, Council of Ministers of the Republic of Belarus, Minsk.

Department of Energy Efficiency (n.d.), *Budget Funding of Energy Saving Programme,* Department of Energy Efficiency, Minsk.

Electricity Supply Companies (2015), *Declarations of Electricity Supply Companies 2013-2014, Volume and Revenue of Electricity Supplied to Households,* unpublished.

Energy Charter Secretariat (2013), *In-depth Review of Energy Efficiency Policy of the Republic of Belarus,* Energy Charter Secretariat, Brussels.

GET (2007), *Quasi-Fiscal Activity in the Energy Sector in Belarus,* German Economic Team in Belarus.

GIZ (2015), *International Fuel Prices 2014, Data Preview, Deutsche Gesellschaft für Internationale Zusammenarbeit*, Eschborn, Germany. https://www.giz.de/expertise/downloads/giz-2015-en-ifp2014.pdf.

IEA (2015a), *Belarus: Indicators for 2012,* International Energy Agency, Paris. www.iea.org/statistics/statisticssearch/report/?country=Belarus&product=indicators&year=2012.

IEA (2015b), *Eastern Europe, Caucasus and Central Asia: Energy Policies Beyond IEA Countries*, OECD/International Energy Agency. https://www.iea.org/publications/freepublications/publication/IDR_EasternEuropeCaucasus_2015.pdf.

Ministry of Economy (2011), *Resolution No. 100 on Tariffs for Electricity Produced from Renewable Energy Sources,* Ministry of Economy of the Republic of Belarus, Minsk.

Ministry of Energy (2015a), *Electricity Tariffs for Legal Entities from 1 January 2015,* Ministry of Energy of the Republic of Belarus, Minsk. http://minenergo.gov.by/dfiles/000710_41120__jur_litsa_prajs.pdf.

Ministry of Energy (2015b), *Natural Gas Prices for Legal Entities and Individual Entrepreneurs,* Ministry of Energy of the Republic of Belarus, Minsk. http://minenergo.gov.by/dfiles/000710_46490__jur_litsa.pdf.

Ministry of Energy (2015c), *Prices for Natural Gas and LPG for the Population,* Ministry of Energy of the Republic of Belarus, Minsk. http://minenergo.gov.by/dfiles/000710_719603__gaz_naselenie.pdf.

Ministry of Energy (2015d), *Tariffs for Electricity and Heat for the Population,* Ministry of Energy of the Republic of Belarus, Minsk. http://minenergo.gov.by/dfiles/000710_853448__naselenie.pdf.

Ministry of Energy (2015e), *Tariffs for Thermal Energy for Industrial and Other Consumers from 1 January 2015,* Ministry of Energy of the Republic of Belarus, Minsk. http://minenergo.gov.by/ru/tariff.

Ministry of Finance (2015), *Reports on Budget Execution,* Ministry of Finance of the Republic of Belarus, Minsk. www.minfin.gov.by/ru/budget_execution/legislative_acts/e59779ce8f468cea.html.

Ministry of Finance (2014), *Resolution No. 67/21/70 on the Approval of the Procedure for Funding of Organisations Providing Utility Services to Households of 27 October 2014,* Ministry of Finance of the Republic of Belarus, Minsk.

Ministry of Natural Resources and Environmental Protection (2015a), *Intended Nationally Determined Contribution of the Republic of Belarus,* Ministry of Natural Resources and Environmental Protection of the Republic of Belarus, Minsk.

Ministry of Natural Resources and Environmental Protection (2015b), *Sixth National Communication of the Republic of Belarus to UNFCCC*, Ministry of Natural Resources and Environmental Protection of the Republic of Belarus, Minsk.

Ministry of Natural Resources and Environmental Protection (2014), *National Inventory of GHG Emissions of the Republic of Belarus, 1990-2012*, Ministry of Natural Resources and Environmental Protection of the Republic of Belarus, Minsk.

National Assembly of the Republic of Belarus (2010), *Law No. 204-3 on Renewable Energy Sources of 27 December 2010*, House of Representatives of the National Assembly of the Republic of Belarus, Minsk.

National Assembly of the Republic of Belarus (2008), *Budget Code of the Republic of Belarus No. 412-3, of 16 July 2008 (with Amendments)*, National Assembly of the Republic of Belarus, Minsk.

National Assembly of the Republic of Belarus (2002), *Tax Code of the Republic of BelarusNo. 166-3, of 19 December 2002 (with Amendments of 2009) and No. 71-3, of 29 December 2009*, National Assembly of the Republic of Belarus, Minsk.

National Assembly of the Republic of Belarus (1999), *Law No. 255-3 on Pricing, of 10 May 1999,* National Assembly of the Republic of Belarus, Minsk.

National Bank of Belarus (2015), *Weighted Average Exchange Rate of the Belarusian Ruble against Foreign Currencies on the Foreign Exchange Market,* National Bank of the Republic of Belarus, Minsk. www.nbrb.by/statistics/ForexMarket/AvrExRate/.

President of the Republic of Belarus (2016), *Presidential Decree No. 78 on Measures to Increase Efficiency of the Socio-Economic Complex of the Republic of Belarus, of 23 February 2016*, President of the Republic of Belarus, Minsk. http://president.gov.by/ru/official_documents_ru/view/ukaz-78-ot-23-fevralja-2016-g-13157.

President of the Republic of Belarus (2015), *Presidential Decree No. 209 on the Use of Renewable Energy Sources, of 18 May 2016*, President of the Republic of Belarus, Minsk.

President of the Republic of Belarus (2013), *Presidential Decree No. 550 on Some Issues of Regulation of Tariffs (Prices) for Housing and Communal Services, of 5 December 2013,* President of the Republic of Belarus. Minsk. www.pravo.by/main.aspx?guid=3871&p0=P31300550&p1=1.

President of the Republic of Belarus (2012), *Presidential Decree No. 41 on the State Targeted Social Support,* President of the Republic of Belarus, Minsk.

President of the Republic of Belarus (2011), *Presidential Decree No. 72 on Certain Issues of Tariff Regulation, of 25 February 2011*, President of the Republic of Belarus, Minsk.

World Bank (2015a), *Commodity Markets Monthly Data,* World Bank, Washington, DC. www.worldbank.org/en/research/commodity-markets.

World Bank (2015b), *World Development Indicators,* World Bank, Washington, DC. http://databank.worldbank.org/data/reports.aspx?source=2&country=BLR&series=&period=.

World Bank (2014a), *Belarus Overview,* World Bank, Minsk. www.worldbank.org/en/country/belarus/overview.

World Bank (2014b), *Heat Tariff Reform and Social Impact Mitigation: Recommendations for a Sustainable District Heating in Belarus,* World Bank, Washington, DC.

World Bank (2011), *Belarus Public Expenditure Review: Fiscal Reforms for a Sustainable Economic Recover, Volume 1, World Bank, Washington, DC.* http://documents.worldbank.org/curated/en/383241468206688585/pdf/635660ESW0whit0C00REV0ENG0LQ0111011.pdf.

Chapter 5

Georgia's energy subsidies

This chapter identifies, documents and provides estimates of the various subsidies in Georgia that relate to the production or use of coal, oil and related petroleum products, natural gas, and electricity and heat generated on the basis of these fossil fuels. The chapter also briefly looks at the subsidies benefiting energy-efficiency measures and renewable energy sources. An overview of the country's energy sector is first given to place the measures listed into context. In addition, the chapter discusses pricing and tax policies in the energy sector in Georgia. The analysis summarises the context, the state of play, and the mechanics of the complex and evolving landscape of energy subsidies in the country.

Key findings

Georgia does not actively pursue pro-subsidy policies on energy consumption and production. However, a number of measures in the natural gas and electricity sectors fall under the definition of subsidies in the broad sense understood by the World Trade Organization. Some of the energy subsidies identified are more commonly discussed in Georgia under the label of tariff reform and investment incentives.

As a net importer of energy and a country whose GDP is highly energy-intensive, Georgia is vulnerable to fluctuations in the international price of natural gas and petroleum products. The energy subsidies singled out in this report all aim to reduce this vulnerability by protecting socially vulnerable groups from electricity and natural gas tariff increases, on the one hand, and ensuring security of supply and investment in domestic hydropower generation, on the other.

Petroleum products and coal markets in Georgia are liberalised and consumers receive no subsidies. In the upstream segment, however, exemptions from value-added tax (VAT), import tax, property tax and excise for certain oil and gas related activities specified in the Law on Oil and Gas exist. Many apply to international companies operating in Georgia, in particular international oil and gas pipeline operators and users.

The electricity sector has been unbundled, and Georgia has continued its reforms of regulation and governance. In the consumption segment, the electricity tariff is differentiated by consumer type and consumption volume. Subsidising electricity consumers is formally prohibited by Georgia's Law on Electricity and Natural Gas (1999). However, this prohibition is not implemented in practice, even in the narrow sense of energy subsidies (for instance, the Tbilisi municipality provides direct budget transfers under electricity voucher schemes for households). In addition, VAT exemptions, winter restrictions on export of hydropower, and cross-subsidies are embedded in the electricity tariff, further protecting households from tariff increases, which remains a priority for the government.

In the electricity generation segment, subsidies are provided to certain types of producers in the form of regulated purchase (feed-in) tariffs. The government is determined to attract investment in the upgrading and extension of energy generation and infrastructure, including for better integration with neighbouring markets and possible electricity exports to Turkey, Azerbaijan and the Russian Federation. To attract investors, the government establishes tariffs for new electricity plants at a higher level than for the existing ones. For instance, the Khudoni hydropower plant is set to receive an estimated annual subsidy of USD 75 mln in the form of a preferential tariff, once it becomes operational after 2020. Electricity lines and land used as water reservoirs by electricity plants are also exempt from property tax.

In the natural gas sector, consumption is significantly subsidised, for the needs of both electricity generation and distribution for heating and cooking. Some of the natural gas is received partly as an in-kind payment and partly as cheap gas for transit through export pipelines from Azerbaijan to Turkey and from the Russian Federation to Armenia through Georgia's territory. Part of the gas is imported at mostly undisclosed prices. Natural gas subsidies come in the form of regulated tariffs, VAT exemption and direct budget transfers. Natural gas subsidies that have been quantified under this review amounted to USD 228 mln, or 1.4% of Georgia's GDP, in 2014. By far the most significant scheme (USD 208 mln in 2014) that can formally qualify as a fossil-fuel subsidy is the provision of natural gas below market value to thermal power plants (TPPs) and to the distribution companies that serve households. This subsidised gas is called "social gas", which indicates its purpose. It is primarily intended to protect households from paying electricity and gas tariffs considered to be above affordable levels.

Subsidisation of natural gas can create distortions and discourage development of hydropower and renewables. Generation from geothermal, solar and wind power in Georgia remains marginal, and the review has not identified any subsidies to alternative energy sources or energy efficiency in Georgia. At the same time, Georgia is committed to international climate agreements, the Energy Charter Treaty and the Energy Community Treaty. Under its Intended National Determined Contribution in 2015, Georgia committed unconditionally to reduce its GHG emissions by 2030 to 15% below the business-as-usual scenario.

Georgia does not have an officially approved national energy strategy, although the Ministry of Energy is working on developing such a policy. Meanwhile, the government is pursuing market-oriented policies to increase the country's competitiveness and economic development. Reforms continue in energy sector regulation, market efficiency and transparency. Georgia has made significant progress in deregulating the markets of petroleum products, coal and, to a certain extent, electricity. This experience can help promote further reforms in the electricity and natural gas markets.

Georgia has a solid basis for future rationalisation of energy subsidies and the development of dedicated alternative energy and energy efficiency policies. Increasing transparency on energy subsidies and tariff-setting will be the first step in this direction. Another important area for reform is further targeting the support for social groups that are vulnerable to tariff increases.

Macroeconomic situation and energy sector overview

The breakup of the Soviet Union and the ensuing difficulties in the 1990s severely damaged the Georgian economy.[1] The GDP contracted by 78% from 1988 to 1995. However, Georgia has made substantial economic gains since the mid-1990s, with economic growth rates averaging 6%. The positive dynamic persisted despite the global economic slowdown. The only recent year when Georgia's GDP registered a downturn (-3.8%) was 2009. By 2010-14, its economy was growing again (World Bank, 2015c).

Table 5.1. **Georgia's macroeconomic indicators**

		International statistics		National statistics	
Indicator	**Unit**	**Year**	**Value**	**Year**	**Value**
Population	mln	2014	3.73 (World Bank) 4.50 (IEA)	2015	3.73
GDP, current exchange rate	USD bln	2014	16.51	2014	16.51
GDP per capita, current exchange rate	USD	2014	4 430	2014	4 430
Energy production	mtoe	2014	1.37	2014	1.37
Net imports	mtoe	2014	3.10	2014	3.11
Total primary energy supply (TPES)	mtoe	2014	4.39	2014	4.48
TPES per capita	toe	2014	0.97	2014	1.20
Electricity consumption	TWh	2014	10.02	2014	10.37
Electricity consumption per capita	MWh	2014	2.22	2014	2.78
CO_2 emissions from energy combustion	Mt of CO_2	2014	7.72	2011	8.80
CO_2 per capita (from energy combustion only)	t of CO_2	2014	1.71	2011	2.36

Source: Authors' compilation based on IEA (2015b), World Bank (2015a) and GEOSTAT (2015a).

Table 5.2. **Weighted average exchange rate**

	2012	2013	2014
Weighted average exchange rate, GEL per USD	1.65	1.66	1.77

Source: National Bank of Georgia (n.d.).

Recent policy reforms have liberalised the economy, and Georgia now ranks in 15th place in the World Bank's 2015 "Ease of Doing Business" index. This is the highest ranking of any developing economy globally (World Bank, 2015b). In 2014, Georgia entered into an Association Agreement with the European Union, which included provisions for a Deep and Comprehensive Free Trade Area (EC, 2015). With greater policy certainty, there was an uptake in business and consumer confidence that led to a 4.6% GDP growth in 2014, up from 3.4% in 2013 (GEOSTAT, 2015b). External and internal factors held Georgia's growth at 2.9% and 2.7% in 2015 and 2016, respectively. The economic downturn in the Russian Federation affects both Georgian exports and its remittances (ADB, 2017).

Energy supply

Georgia has a key position at the crossroads of energy trade. Two oil pipelines run through it: Baku-Tbilisi-Ceyhan (BTC, from the Caspian Sea to Turkey) and Baku-Supsa (from the Caspian Sea to the Black Sea). Both transport oil produced by Azerbaijan. The Georgian railway is used to export oil from Kazakhstan that is shipped by tankers to the port of Baku on the Caspian Sea. Parallel to the BTC, from Baku up to Erzurum in Turkey, the South Caucasus Pipeline (SCP) transports gas exports from Azerbaijan's Shah Deniz field. The pipeline that transports Russian gas to Armenia also runs through Georgia. In addition, a high-voltage electricity grid connects Georgia to Turkey, the Russian Federation and Armenia.

Georgia's total primary energy supply (TPES) plummeted after the collapse of the Soviet Union, and the downward trajectory continued until 2002. In 2002, Georgia's TPES fell to just one-fifth of what it was in 1990 (Figure 5.1). The primary reason for this decline was the shrinkage of oil and gas supply.

In 2002, Georgia's TPES started recovering and had increased 76% by 2014, although this was still only a third of its level in 1990 (IEA, 2015a; GEOSTAT, 2015a). Increased domestic demand has been met almost exclusively by imported fossil fuels, with the share of energy imports in TPES increasing from 47% in 2002 to 70% in 2014 (IEA, 2015a). Georgia imported 2.2 bln m^3 of natural gas and 1.1 mtoe of oil products in 2014. About 90% of the country's gas imports and 50% of its oil product imports came from Azerbaijan.

Consequently, the structure of Georgia's TPES has changed fundamentally. In 2002, its energy supply was almost equally distributed among oil, natural gas, hydro electricity, biofuels (fuel wood) and waste (Figure 5.1). Between 2002 and 2014, natural gas supply increased by 170%, making it the country's single most important source of energy (Figure 5.2). Its share in TPES grew from 27% in 2002 to 44% in 2012. In 2014, however, the share of natural gas declined to 41%, due to the increasing use of coal and other renewables, such as hydropower and geothermal (IEA, 2015a).

The supply of oil products almost doubled between 2002 and 2014. Georgia has minor oil-producing fields, with cumulative production of 433 000 tonnes in 2014, and no own refining (though the government has repeatedly announced its plans to find an investor in refining capacity in the port of Poti). All oil refined products are imported. Oil products are the second-largest source of energy in Georgia, at 25% of TPES.

Figure 5.1. **Total primary energy supply, 1990-2014**

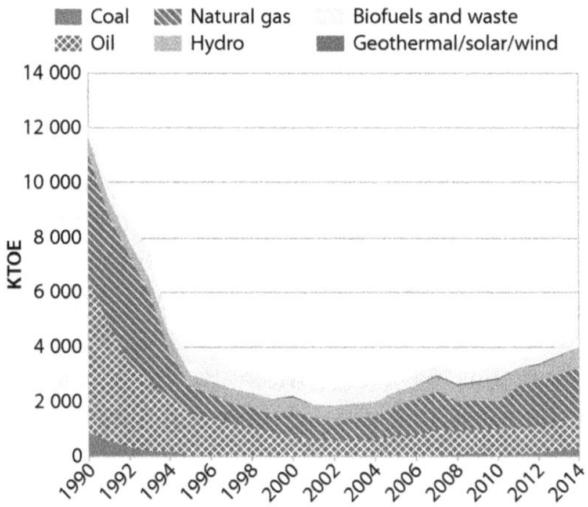

Figure 5.2. **Primary energy supply, 2014, by fuel**

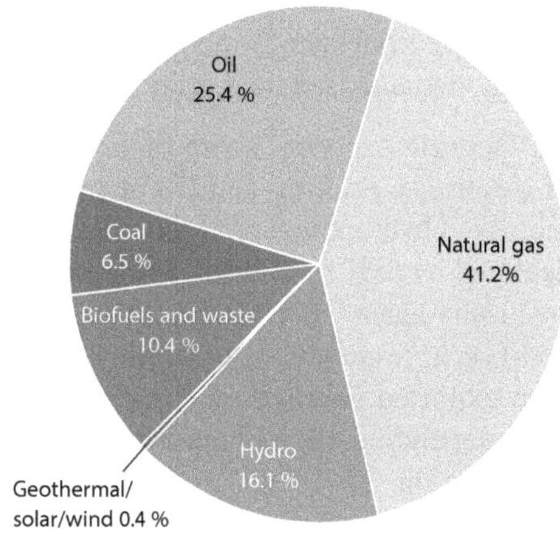

Source: Authors' compilation based on IEA (2015a), GEOSTAT (2015a).

Figure 5.3. **Electricity generation by source**

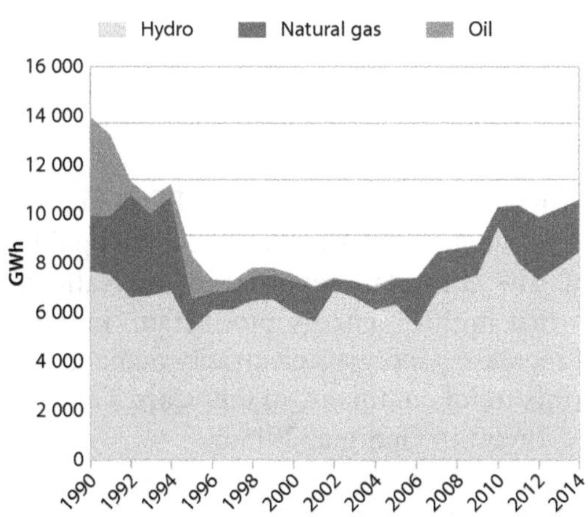

Figure 5.4. **Electricity generation GWh by source, 2014**

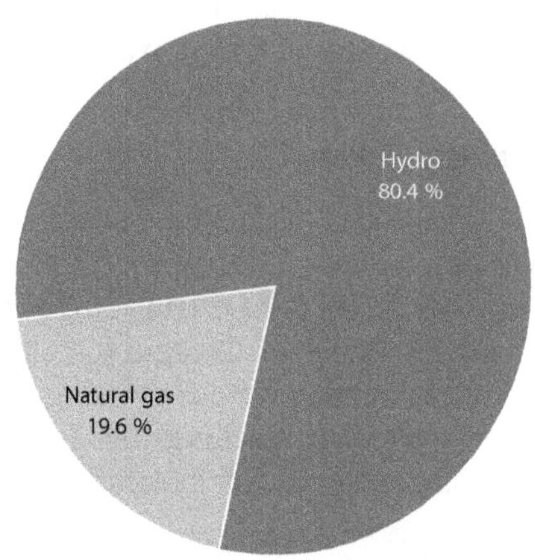

Source: Authors' compilation based on IEA (2015a), GEOSTAT (2015a).

Coal, some of which is mined domestically, played a negligible role in the Georgian energy mix in 2002 (its supply almost zeroed out from 1990 to 1997). However, coal supply increased from 122 ktoe in 2002 to 2 900 ktoe in 2014, accounting for 6.5% of TPES (GEOSTAT, 2015a). Due to shifts in the energy demand structure and increased reliance on natural gas, hydropower's share in TPES decreased and was only 16% of TPES in 2014. Biofuels (mostly fuel wood) and waste contributed 10% of the TPES in 2014 (Figure 5.2).

The overall electricity production increased by 43% between 2002 and 2014. This increase was primarily due to the growth in gas-fired generation. Despite the country's vast and untapped hydropower potential, hydropower generation rose by only 23% over the same period.

In 2014, hydropower accounted for 80% of the country's generation of electricity, while the remainder came from natural gas-fired thermal power plants (Figure 5.4). According to a World Bank report (World Bank, 2015a), only 12% of Georgia's hydropower potential is being utilised. The government is thus focusing on securing private investments for the construction of new hydropower plants. Development of privately owned hydropower is one of the priorities for addressing the anticipated gap in supply, in view of the growing energy demand (see next section).

Georgia exported some of its electricity to neighbouring countries, with net exports of electricity peaking at 12% of production in 2010. High exports were primarily due to increased hydropower production as a result of high precipitation. In 2012, however, exports declined by 65% from 2010, while imports increased, and Georgia became a net importer of electricity again (IEA, 2015a). In 2014, imports and exports of electricity were 853 GWh and 604 GWh, respectively, indicating that imported volumes were approximately 41% higher than exported volumes of electricity. The situation thus varies significantly from year to year, depending upon domestic demand for electricity, availability of fuels and the level of precipitation.

The district-heating network in Tbilisi and the main cities of Georgia collapsed in the 1990s, due to fuel shortages and lack of maintenance of the distribution network. The district-heating is not currently operating, and households commonly use individual heating units (gas heaters and/or electricity and firewood stoves).

Georgia has no nuclear power generation. Substantial potential for solar and geothermal energy exists, but production levels at present are marginal. In October 2016, Georgia's first wind power plant, Qartli, was commissioned.

Energy demand

The shares of the major sectors in the total final energy consumption (TFEC) in 2014 were as follows: industry 15.2%; transport 33%; residential 29.6%; commercial and public services 10.7% (GEOSTAT, 2015a, IEA, 2015a). The latest data reported by the National Statistics Office of Georgia (GEOSTAT) show that in 2015, energy production, imports and consumption were continuing their gradual increase. Georgia's electricity demand has risen with GDP, reaching 10.4 TWt in 2015. If this trend continues, in ten years, Georgia will have a significant generation deficit (GNIA, Invest in Georgia, 2015a).

Energy sector structure, ownership and governance

Georgia does not have an officially approved national energy strategy, although the Ministry of Energy is working on its development. In October 2016, Georgia signed the protocol on the accession to the Treaty establishing the Energy Community, and, pending a relevant procedure, will become an official and fully fledged Contracting Party of the Energy Community. Accession into Energy Community establishes a new framework for the development of Georgia's energy sector, providing for its alignment with the EU standards, including the creation of a competitive market, enhancement of energy security, promotion of the use of renewable energy sources and advancement of energy efficiency and environmental protection (Ministry of Energy, 2016).

The Ministry of Energy (MoE) formulates Georgia's energy policy and has primary responsibility for the energy sector. While the supply of oil, fuels and coal is deregulated, the gas and electricity transportation, distribution and supply are subject to regulation by the Georgian National Energy and Water Supply Regulatory Commission (GNERC) (IEA, 2015b). GNERC is responsible for licencing, and sets producer, network and consumer tariffs for electricity and natural gas. Upstream activities, including oil and gas production and transport through pipelines, are regulated by the National Oil and Gas Agency (NAOG), part of the Ministry of Energy. NAOG is responsible for creating an enabling environment and regulating the oil and gas sector (except gas distribution and consumption) in accordance with the Law on Oil and Gas.

The natural gas and electricity sectors are represented by both government-owned and private players, the latter often being subsidiaries of foreign companies (Figure 5.5). Natural gas is imported by the state-owned company the Georgian Oil and Gas Corporation (GOGC) and SOCAR Georgia Gas, a subsidiary of Azerbaijan's state monopoly, SOCAR. Gas is transported by COGC's subsidiary Georgian Gas Transportation Company (GGTC). The distribution of gas in the capital city of Tbilisi and its surroundings is handled by KazTransGas (owned by Kazakhstan's monopoly KazMunaiGas, but currently operated by the Georgian government, due to a financial dispute). Other parts of the country are served by SOCAR Georgia Gas and SaqOrgGas (both owned by Azerbaijan's SOCAR) and other distribution companies (IEA, 2015b).

Figure 5.5. **Structure of the electricity and gas sectors in Georgia**

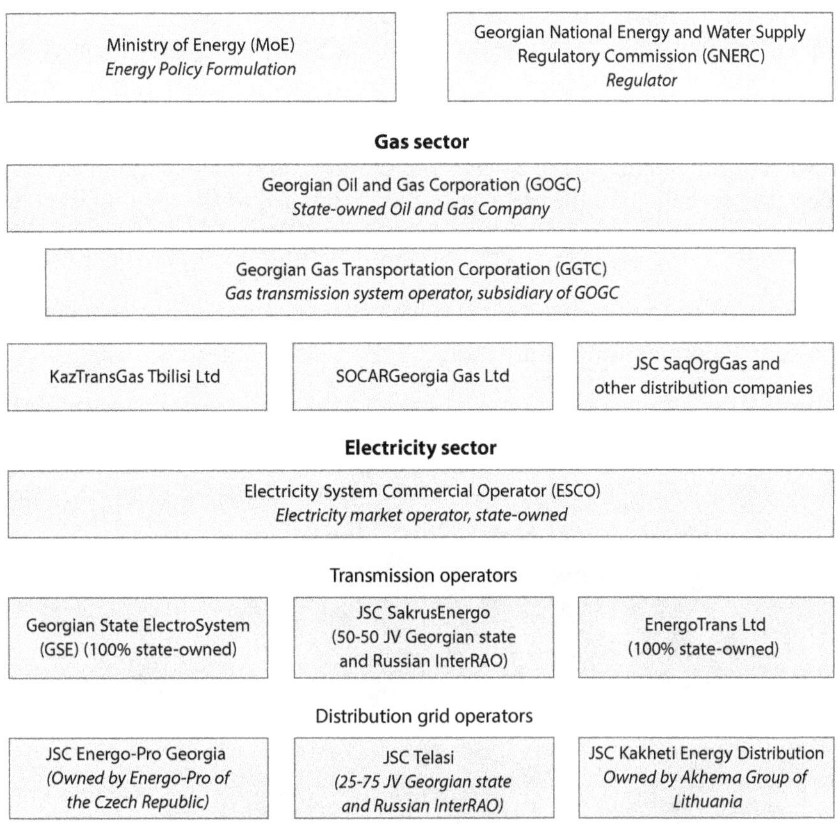

Source: Authors' compilation based on IEA (2015a), ESCO (2014, 2015), GSE (2015), Sakrus (2015), Energotrans (2015), EnergoPro (2015), Telasi (2015), GNERC (2015a; 2015b), GOGC (2015), GGTC (2015), KazTransGas (2015), SGGAS (2015).

As the electricity sector is unbundled, several companies have interests in generation, transmission and distribution (Figure 5.5). The wholesale market operates under bilateral contracts, and the state-owned Electricity System Commercial Operator (ESCO) purchases and sells power not sold through bilateral contracts. ESCO is responsible for balancing and settlement according to market rules, and exports surplus power. About 75% of all electricity generated is sold through bilateral contracts, and the rest through ESCO (IEA, 2015b). The transmission grid operation is managed by three operators. Georgian State Electrosystem (GSE) is a state-owned company, while JSC SakrusEnergo is a partly state-owned proprietor and operator of the 500kV transmission network and the lines connecting Georgia with the Russian Federation and Armenia. The shareholders of the JSC transmission operator are the Georgian state, represented by the Georgian Ministry of Energy, and JSC Federal Grid Company of Unified Energy System (FGC UES) of the Russian Federation. EnergoTrans, the third transmission operator, is state-owned and operates the new Black Sea transmission line and distribution substation connecting Georgia with Turkey (IEA, 2015b).

In the electricity distribution segment, there are three distribution grid operators. As of May 2016, Georgia has 64 hydropower plants (HPP) and 4 thermal power plants (TPPs) with installed capacities of 2 791 MW and 680 MW, respectively. Enguri HPP (1 300 MW) and Vardnili HPP cascade (220 MW) are the largest plants and are state-owned. Other, smaller HPPs and the four TPPs have been privatised. Several new HPPs were under construction.

Power producers of new HPPs and HPPs below 13 MW have the option to sell their power freely through bilateral contracts or sell it to ESCO, which also exports the surplus power.

The import and export of electricity is deregulated and not subject to import or export duties. However, new plants over 13 MW are obliged, under concession agreements, to supply a certain percentage of the electricity they produced to the local market during the three winter months. This commitment varies across different plants both in time and in price.

Mining of coal (lignite) in Georgia is carried out by Saknakhshiri, a subsidiary of the private company Georgian Industrial Group.

Figure 5.6. **Companies' involvement across electricity generation, transmission and distribution**

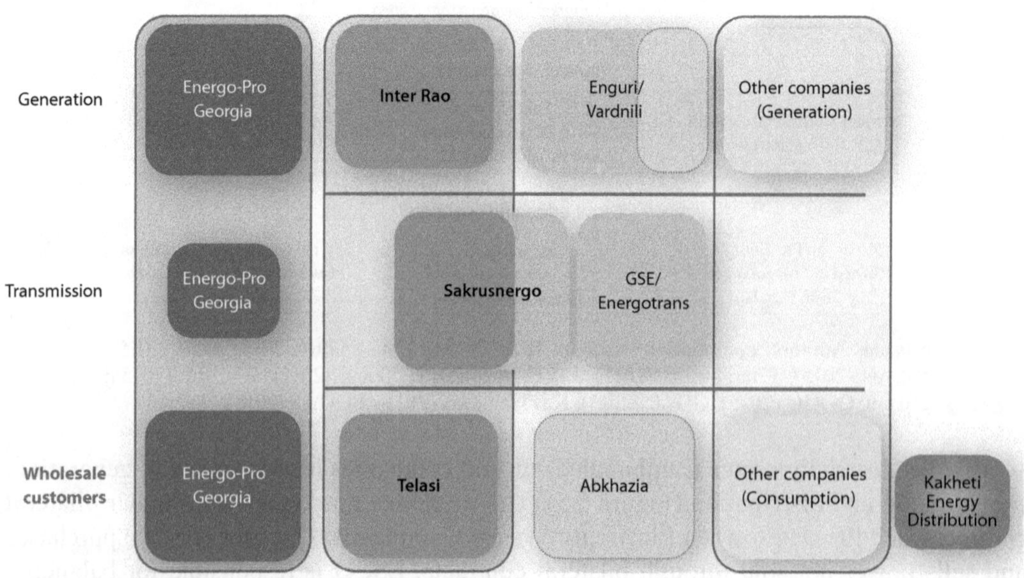

Source: WEG (2012).

Major oil and gas pipelines that transport export gas from Azerbaijan, Central Asia and the Russian Federation through Georgia are mostly owned by consortia of foreign investors. BP is the lead shareholder and operator of both the Baku-Tbilisi-Ceyhan oil pipeline and the Baku-Tbilisi-Erzurum gas pipeline. Petroleum products are supplied by several marketing companies, with SOCAR Georgia playing a prominent role.

Energy pricing policy

Energy markets in Georgia are partially deregulated. Liquid petroleum products and coal are freely traded, while the gas and electricity sectors are subject to some regulation by GNERC. The key principles of regulation are laid out in the Law of Georgia on Electricity and Natural Gas, of 30 April 1999. Table 5.3 provides an overview of both producer and consumer pricing policies by fuel.

Natural gas

According to official estimates, Georgia imported 90% of its gas from Azerbaijan and 10% from the Russian Federation in 2014 (Ministry of Energy, 2014). The total volume of domestic consumption was approximately 2.2 bln cubic metres (bcm), which is partly imported by the GOGC and partly by SOCAR Georgia Gas at undisclosed prices. The imported gas is then sold at regulated prices to distribution operators who in turn sell the gas to residential consumers and TPPs at a price below its market value – a phenomenon known in Georgia as "social gas". Commercial consumers get the so-called "commercial" gas at commercial "market value".

Domestic natural gas tariffs for residential consumers are overseen by GNERC. The residential consumers connected to the gas supply grid before 1 September 2007 (and 1 August 2008 in Tbilisi) pay regulated prices, while remaining consumers may pay unregulated prices. In practice, both pay practically the same tariff, which differs from that of non-residential consumers.

Estimation of the true cost of natural gas and therefore the adequacy of regulated residential tariffs is complicated by the lack of import price transparency. Natural gas from Azerbaijan transits to Turkey via the South Caucasus Pipeline (SCP, Baku-Tbilisi-Erzurum). The international consortium led by BP is in charge of the SCP pipeline and is exempt from corporate income tax in Georgia. Within the framework of the SCP host government agreement, Georgia annually gets 700 mln to 800 mln m^3 of natural gas, the cost of which is as low as around USD 65 per 1 000 m^3. Georgia also sources natural gas from the North-South pipeline that brings Russian gas to Armenia: 10% of the natural gas supplied to Armenia by the Russian Federation (approximately 200 mln m^3) is provided to Georgia as a transit cost (Shelia, 2015; Ministry of Energy, 2014).

According to information provided by the Ministry of Energy in 2012 to the media (http://droni.ge/print.php?m=2&AID=8759), Georgia imports the following amounts of gas from Azerbaijan at the following prices:

- SCP 5% of transited gas – up to 200 mln m^3 at USD 55 USD per 1 000 m^3
- SCP additional gas – up to 500 mln m^3 at USD 65 per 1 000 m^3
- SOCAR (Social Gas) – up to 500 mln m^3 at USD 189 per 1 000 m^3.

Since Georgia receives gas from the Russian Federation, but most importantly also from Azerbaijan, as in-kind payments for transit (Rzayeva, 2015), it is challenging to estimate to what extent the natural gas tariff in the country is cost-reflective. No information on the structure and the level of costs is publicly available for the natural gas supply companies to use as a benchmark.

At the current exchange rate, the sales price to KazTransGas, or, in other words, the wholesale gas tariff for distribution to households, was at USD 143 per 1 000 m^3 in 2015. The gas prices in the regulated residential sector in Georgia were in the range of USD 235-260 per 1 000 m^3 (Table 5.3). Meanwhile, the price of natural gas for commercial consumers was in the range of USD 300-350 per 1 000m^3, which indicates a cross-subsidy to households through a surcharge on the industry and other commercial consumers.

Compressed natural gas (CNG) has become an important transport fuel in Georgia since 2012, due to a combination of competitive market pricing (compared with gasoline and diesel) and behavioural change. Like most of Georgia's natural gas, CNG is imported from Azerbaijan. The consumption of CNG by vehicles has grown to 300 mln to 400 mln m^3 per year. CNG prices are not regulated. The advantageous price level of natural gas compared with other transport fuels suggests that CNG will continue playing a key role in Georgia's transport sector.

Electricity

In the electricity sector, tariffs for generation, dispatch, transmission, distribution and supply have been defined by the independent regulator (GNERC) since 1998. GNERC operates in compliance with the Law of Georgia on Electricity and Natural Gas, of 30 April 1999. Article 43 of the Law lays out the principles of tariff setting in the electricity sector and states that "it shall be prohibited to subsidise tariff privileges for any category of consumers at the expense of a licensee, importer, supplier, the market operator or other categories of consumers" (President of Georgia, 1999), implying that there should be no cross-subsidies between the consumer categories. However, the same Article (point 5) determines that GNERC "may set long-term tariffs taking into account the basic directions of the national policy in the energy sector of the country". In practice, this gives legal permission to the government to set politically defined long-term tariffs.

The tariffs are defined based on the methodologies published by GNERC. GNERC's first electricity tariff formula (GNERC Resolution No. 3, of 1 July 1998) was based on the full-cost principle. However, according to World Bank analysis, electricity and gas prices remained far below the level of cost recovery (World Bank, 2013).

The subsequent methodologies (GNERC Resolution No. 8 of 8 June 2011 and No. 14 of 30 July 2014) were designed to encourage, to a relative extent, investment in new generation capacity in the country. These two latest methodologies rely on price-cap regulation. Resolution No. 14 of 30 July 2014 *On Approving Electricity Tariff Calculation Methodologies* comprises three additional documents:

1. *Tariff-Setting Methodology for Electricity Distribution, Pass-Through and Consumption Tariffs*
2. *Tariff-Setting Methodology for Electricity Generation, Transmission, Dispatch and Electricity Market Operator Service*
3. *Regulated Assets Depreciation/Amortisation Rates of Utilities under Tariff Regulation.*

The abovementioned Resolution is based on two main principles: "incentive-based" and "cost-plus" regulation.

Resolution No. 14 seeks to incentivise investment and follows a "cost-plus" approach (for more detail, see Annex 5.A3). GNERC's previous methodology (GNERC Resolution No. 8, of 8 June 2011) reproduced the clause of the Law of Georgia on Electricity and Natural Gas, on prohibiting tariff subsidisation for any consumer category. However, in the most recent 2014 methodology, this paragraph was removed.

Under GNERC's orders, prices are regulated differently for three categories of producers (GNERC, 2014):

- Regulated prices for thermal power plants (TPPs) that act on the basis of the licences issued by the Commission. In addition, TPPs are guaranteed reserve-capacity payments that constitute a major part of their revenues.
- Partly deregulated prices for seasonal hydropower plants (HPPs) that act on the basis of the licences issued by the Commission and under the upper limit of the tariff set by the Commission. These HPPs are called partly deregulated, as they are subject to price caps.
- Fully deregulated prices for hydropower plants built after 1 August 2008 that require a licence and for small HPPs with installed capacity below 13 MW that do not require a licence.

Uncertainty about the exact costs of generation still makes it difficult to conclude whether the existing tariffs for electricity reflect long-term marginal costs, including the cost of capital required for new investments. Generation costs differ among different plants, while the regulated wholesale price is the average of more expensive thermal power (the TTPs' producer tariff was around GEL 0.12 per kWh in 2015) and cheaper hydropower, especially from large HPPs such as Enguri.

Thermal power plants receive the guaranteed reserve capacity payment paid by all wholesale buyers. The guaranteed payment ranges between tetri 6.7 and 11.3 per kWh for the new TPP This payment can be considered as a subsidy to new TPPs, since all the risk is removed by regulation and the mandatory payment by consumers.

Electricity prices for consumers are regulated, and cross-subsidies are embedded in the tariff for households through a surcharge on industrial and other commercial consumers. In addition, electricity rates vary in relation to electricity consumption and voltage levels. The tariffs for residential consumers are step-wise (a high rate for high electricity consumption), but commercial consumers have to pay a single rate regardless of their power consumption. Consumer prices are differentiated for residential consumers based on consumption levels.[2] In 2015, the consumer tariffs were in the range of GEL 0.13-0.22 per kWh (GNERC, 2014).

The government of Georgia also uses the rate policy to encourage investments in new capacity, though this may or may not deliver the desired activity. An example of a bundled deal between various generators and the cross-subsidy between generation and distribution businesses is the memorandum of understanding between the Georgian government and the Russian company InterRAO that was signed in 2007 and renewed in 2010. The memorandum provided for a long-term increase of consumer tariffs and thus the margin in the distribution segment for InterRAO's subsidiary JSC Telasi. At the same time, the memorandum defined investment obligations of JSC Telasi, including an obligation to build an HPP with 100 MW capacity. GNERC extended the validity of the high distribution margin and consumer tariff through 2015, thereby fulfilling its obligation. However, InterRAO kept the excess profit (GEL 330 mln accumulated between 2006 and 2012), and as of May 2016, still had not invested in a new HPP. The government of Georgia is trying to recover these excess revenues through a reduction in the regulated tariff for consumers.

Petroleum products

Prices of liquid petroleum products (gasoline, diesel, kerosene, LPG, heating fuel, etc.) in Georgia are not regulated. In November 2014, gasoline and diesel prices were USD 1.34 and 1.37 per litre, respectively (GIZ, 2015), which is relatively high by international standards and is at the high end of the range observed in the EaP countries.

Table 5.3. **Price policies for different energy carriers in Georgia**

Energy carrier	Activity subject to price policy	Price policy	Price levels in 2015
Natural gas	Import of natural gas	Bilateral negotiations between foreign suppliers and importers to Georgia	Confidential
	Transport to entry point of distribution networks	Regulated, differentiated by region and gas distributor	GEL 9-13.9 per 1 000 m^3
	Sales to TPPs	Regulated, a cross-subsidy through a surcharge on other consumers	GEL 384 per 1 000 m^3
	Regulated supply tariff component for distribution companies	Regulated, differentiated by gas distributor. Memorandum of Understanding	GEL 243 per 1 000 m^3 to KazTransGas
	Residential consumers connected to the gas grid before 1 September 2007 (1 August in Tbilisi)	Regulated price ceiling. A cross-subsidy through a surcharge on other consumers	GEL 400-446 per 1 000 m^3
	Other residential consumers and commercial sector	Formally deregulated, but getting virtually the same price	For commercial sector, GEL 750 per 1 000 m^3 For residential sector, rates the same as those of regulated consumers or slightly different
	CNG sales	Deregulated	..
Electricity	TPP generation (4 TPPs)	Regulated, guaranteed capacity payments (GEL per day per kW) and generation tariffs (GEL per kWh)	Mtkvari energy: GEL 63 806 per day and GEL 0.109 per kWh Tbilsresi Unit 3: GEL 20 909 per day and GEL 0.102 per kWh Tbilsresi Unit 4: GEL 23 800 per day and GEL 0.102 per kWh G-power: GEL 42 360 per day and GEL 0.075 per kWh Gardabani CCPP (from 2015): GEL 366 173 per day and GEL 0.067 per kWh
	HPP generation with seasonal storage (2 HPPs)	Regulated	Enguri – GEL 0.019 per kWh Vardnili – GEL 0.017 per kWh
	HPP generation commissioned after August 2008, or less than 13 MW	Deregulated	..
	Other HPP generation	Regulated price ceiling	GEL 0.0125-0.0385 per kWh
	Transmission	Regulated, differentiated by operator and voltage	GSE: GEL 0.005 per kWh for 35–110–220 kV SakrusEnergo: GEL 0.0018 per kwh for 500 kV EnergoTrans: GEL 0.0027 and 0.0035 per kWh for 500 and 400 kV

Table 5.3. **Price policies for different energy carriers in Georgia** *(continued)*

Energy carrier	Activity subject to price policy	Price policy	Price levels in 2015
Electricity *(continued)*	Distribution: 35-110, 6-10 and 0.4 kV	Regulated, differentiated by voltage and distributor	EnergoPro: GEL 0.017, 0.022 and 0.069 per kWh Telasi: GEL 0.007, 0.018 and 0.056 per kWh Kakheti: GEL 0.09, 0.026 and 0.062 per kWh
	Market operator fees: GNERC and GSE	Regulated	GEL 0.0002 and 0.00019 per kWh
	Consumption	Regulated, differentiated by region and consumption level. A cross-subsidy for residential consumers within low-consumption bracket by a surcharge on other consumers	GEL 0.08-0.15 per kWh
Liquid petroleum products	Consumption	Deregulated prices for gasoline, diesel, kerosene, heating fuel, LPG, etc.	Gasoline USD 0.6-0.8 per litre, diesel USD 0.6 per litre in 2016
Coal	Deregulated	..	..

Source: Authors' compilation based on GNERC (2015a), GIZ (2015), GNERC (2015c).

Taxation policy

Business entities pay five taxes in Georgia: VAT, profit tax, property tax, import tax and excise tax (GNIA, Invest in Georgia, 2015b). All taxes are national except the property tax (the rate is up to 1% of the value of property), which is local.

The Tax Code of Georgia (President of Georgia, 2010), Article 168, Paragraph 1, provides exemption from VAT without the right to offset the import of natural gas for the production of electricity (thermal power plants). According to Paragraph 3 of the same Article, transactions performed for a targeted purpose pursuant to the certain laws, agreements and treaties shall be exempted from VAT without the right to offset:

a. import, supply of appliances and equipment, means of transport, spare parts and materials intended for the implementation of oil and gas operations according to the Law of Georgia on Oil and Gas, as well as the importation, supply for the investors and operating companies of the goods for the implementation of the agreements set forth under the above-mentioned law and/or the implementation of oil and gas operations in accordance with the issued licences, and/or the provision of services thereof

b. import of goods funded under preferential credit extended by foreign states and/or international organisations under international agreements ratified by the Parliament of Georgia and/or the provision of construction and installation, repair, restoration, experimental constructor, and/or geological-exploratory services for the rehabilitation of the electric energy sector

c. temporary admission of goods to Georgia to facilitate the fulfilment of obligations stipulated under international agreements of Georgia, namely, the construction of the Baku-Tbilisi-Ceyhan and the Baku-Tbilisi-Erzurum pipelines.

In addition to the VAT benefit, the import of appliances and equipment, means of transport, spare parts, and materials designated for the performance of oil and gas transactions envisaged under the Law of Georgia on Oil and Gas is also exempt from import tax (Article 199, Paragraph g), and from the excise tax without the right to offset

(Article 194, Paragraph 5-f). Further, the same oil and gas-related activities specified in the Law on Oil and Gas are exempt from property tax.

Supply of electric energy and guaranteed capacity from 1 January 2011 to 1 January 2015, with the exception of the supply of electric energy to consumers (to the persons determined under the Law of Georgia on Electricity and Natural Gas), as well as the transmission and dispatch operators' services, is exempt from VAT with the offset right (Article 309, Paragraph 6). Electricity lines and land used by electricity plants as water reservoirs are exempt from property tax.

Table 5.4 provides a summary of energy taxation policies in Georgia.

Table 5.4. **Taxation of energy in Georgia**

Activity subject to taxation	Baseline tax system: VAT, profit tax, property tax, import tax	Excise tax
Import of energy-related goods funded under preferential international loans	Exempt from VAT	n.a.
Oil and gas-related activities specified by the Law on Oil and Gas	Exempt from VAT, import tax and property tax	Exempt from excise tax without the right to offset
All other oil and gas-related activities, including import of oil products and natural gas	Applicable as appropriate. Natural gas imported for the production of electricity is exempt from VAT	n.a.
Temporary admission of goods to Georgia to facilitate the construction of the Baku-Tbilisi-Ceyhan and the Baku-Tbilisi-Erzurum pipelines	Exempt from VAT	n.a.
Consumption of petroleum products, coal and natural gas	Applicable as appropriate	Petroleum products and coal are subject to excise tax, no excise tax on natural gas.
Electricity generation and export	Applicable as appropriate. Exempt from VAT. Land used by electricity plants as water reservoirs exempt from property tax	n.a.
Supply of electric energy and guaranteed capacity from 1 January 2011 to 1 January 2015, with the exception of the supply of electric energy to consumers (to the persons determined under the Law of Georgia on Electricity and Natural Gas) as well as transmission and dispatch operators' services	Exempt from VAT with the offset right	n.a.
Electricity transmission and distribution	Electricity lines are exempt from property tax	n.a.
Consumption of electricity	Applicable as appropriate	No excise tax on electricity

Note: **n.a.**: non-applicable.

Source: Authors' compilation based on President of Georgia (2010).

Energy is not subject to any specific taxes, apart from excise taxes on petroleum products and coal. There are no resource rent taxes on the energy sector activities that can generate rents (oil and coal extraction, as well as hydropower). As per the governing laws of the local government, taxes on water consumption can be levied at a rate of GEL 0.1 per 1 000 m^3. At the same time, producer tariffs for a lot of HPPs are kept low, and hydropower is subject to winter supply obligations to the domestic market. The producer tariff and winter export restrictions can be viewed as an implicit tax that reduces the natural-resource rents obtained by investors in Georgian hydropower.

Greenhouse gas emissions and climate policy

Georgia's greenhouse gas (GHG) emissions fell significantly as a result of declining energy consumption, as well as changes in the energy mix after the collapse of the Soviet Union and policy reforms in the early 1990s (MENRP, 2015a). With the support of the Global Environmental Facility (GEF) and UN Development Programme (MENRP, 2015a), Georgia developed and submitted three National Communications to the United Nations Framework Convention on Climate Change (UNFCCC) in 1999, 2009 and 2015, respectively. In 2016, Georgia also submitted its First Biennial Update Report for the UNFCCC, which provides the latest available data on Georgia's GHG emissions for 2013.

In 2013, GHG emissions from all sources in Georgia totalled 16.7 Mt CO_{2eq} (35% of 1990's emissions), without considering the land use, land-use change and forestry (LULUCF) sector, and 12.6 Mt CO_{2eq} when taking this sector into account (MENRP, 2016). In 2013, GHG emissions from the energy sector amounted to 9.4 Mt of CO_{2eq}, about 56% of Georgia's total GHG emissions (excluding LULUCF). This is considerably lower than the contribution of this sector in 1990 (78%). Total GHG emissions from the sector had fallen to one-quarter of 1990 rates, while increasing by 58% relative to 2000. In the energy sector, 80% of emissions come from fuel combustion, and the remaining 20% are fugitive emissions. The transport sector was the largest contributor of CO_2 emissions in 2013, with a share of 33%, followed by manufacturing industries and construction (21%), the gas transmission and distribution subsector (19%) and electricity generation (10%) (MENRP, 2016).

Georgia ratified the UNFCCC in 1994 and joined the Kyoto Protocol in 1999. The country has not so far taken on any quantitative obligations, but Georgia has committed to develop, implement and publish national and regional programmes that would include mitigation measures (MENRP, 2015a).

Since 2013, with the support of the US government, Georgia has been developing a Low-Emission Development Strategy (LEDS), which was expected to be finalised and adopted by the government of Georgia in 2016. A high-level inter-ministerial committee and a LEDS working group have been established under the leadership of the Ministry of Environment and Natural Resources Protection by the Decree of the Government of Georgia of 26 July 2013 (MENRP, 2015a).

Improvements in energy efficiency and environmental protection also form part of the government's agenda after the signing of the protocol on Georgia's accession to the Treaty establishing the Energy Community (MENRP, 2016).

At the local level, eight cities in Georgia have signed the EU Covenant of Mayors initiative, committing to a voluntary reduction of municipal GHG emissions of at least 20% by 2020 compared with a baseline. This holds relevance at the national level, as the eight signatory cities represent 41%-46% of the total population of Georgia, with a large share of GDP (Covenant of Mayors, n.d.).

With the support of the European Union and the government of Germany, Georgia prepared and submitted its Intended Nationally Determined Contribution (INDC) in preparation for the UNFCCC COP21 in Paris. Georgia's INDC largely draws on the outcomes of the LEDS work. The final LEDS and the mitigation actions specified therein will become key instruments in achieving Georgia's mitigation targets (MENRP, 2015b).

Under its INDC, Georgia plans to unconditionally reduce its GHG emissions by 15% by 2030 compared with the business-as-usual (BAU) scenario. The 15% reduction target will be increased up to 25% in a conditional manner, subject to a global agreement addressing the importance of technical co-operation, access to low-cost financial resources and technology transfer. A reduction of 25% below the BAU scenario by 2030 means that Georgia's GHG emissions will remain 40% below the 1990 level.

National definition and discussion of energy subsidies

Georgia joined the World Trade Organization (WTO) in 2000, signing the Agreement on Subsidies and Countervailing Measures (ASCM). Therefore, the ASCM definition of subsidies is fully applicable to Georgia. A further review of the national legislation provides the following example of how subsidies have been codified in Georgia:

> "State aid (a subsidy) is a decision with respect to an economic agent, that includes tax exemption, tax reduction or tax deferral, discharging of debt, restructuring, loan on preferential terms, transfer of operational assets, financial aid, giving assurance of profit, privileges, etc." (President of Georgia, 2010).

As indicated in Figure 5.7 below, with the exception of induced transfers (price regulation), Georgia has incorporated all the main components of the WTO (and OECD) definition in the national legislation. Historically, induced transfers have been widely discussed in Georgia, though under the label of tariff reform and cross-subsidies.

Figure 5.7. **What does Georgia include in the national definition of subsidy?**

Covered by the national definitions of both "subsidy" and "state support" | Covered only by the national definition of "state support" | Not included in the national definition of either "subsidy" or "state support"

Direct budget transfers	Tax expenditures	Induced transfers	Transfer of risk to government	References
				President of Georgia (2010) equates the terms "state aid" and "subsidy"

Source: Authors' compilation.

The IEA has never included Georgia in its published price-gap estimates of consumer subsidies. The most probable reason for this that IEA's price-gap approach does not identify any fossil-fuel subsidies in Georgia (see the section on price-gap estimates below). Not surprisingly, virtually no international publications have examined energy policy in Georgia from the subsidy angle. The only previous report that covers energy subsidies, and specifically consumer subsidies in Georgia, is the "Balancing Act" multi-country analysis on "Cutting Energy Subsidies while Protecting Affordability" by the World Bank (World Bank, 2013). This report mentions, for instance, support for vulnerable customers in the Tbilisi municipality by providing communal vouchers for electricity. The INOGATE project funded by the European Union has further addressed the adequacy of electricity tariffs in the region.

The government of Georgia does provide public information on some of the energy subsidies in the budgetary cycle materials, but information on tax expenditure budgets is not published. Details on pricing and taxation policies are not available in the public domain. At the same time, the Georgian National Investment Agency publishes bilingual information on energy-related investment incentives, that is, subsidies in the WTO-ASCM sense.

Table 5.5 summarises key findings on the legislative basis of different subsidy schemes and data availability by subsidy categories used by the OECD. These serve as the departure point for the rest of the chapter.

Table 5.5. **Subsidy overview**

Energy subsidy	Key findings
Direct transfer of funds and liabilities	• Included in national subsidy definition • Support for vulnerable customers in the Tbilisi Municipality by providing communal vouchers (electricity) (World Bank, 2013) • Reimbursement of the cost of gas supplied to households in the highland Kazbegi and Dusheti municipalities
Tax expenditure (tax revenue foregone)	• Included in national subsidy definition • Tax exemptions stipulated by the Tax Code, Law on Oil and Gas, and some other legislation • Exemptions in the upstream sector discussed by the government as investment incentives
Induced transfers (income or price support provided to producers or consumers through various regulations)	• Not included in national subsidy definitions • Historically discussed under the label of tariff reform and reform of cross-subsidies • "Social gas" provided to TPPs and distribution companies below the market value • Differentiated producer tariffs supporting new hydropower developments • Guaranteed reserve capacity payments to TPPs
Transfer of risk to government	• Included in national subsidy definitions • Little information publicly available

Government support for fossil fuels

To quantify fossil-fuel subsidies in Georgia, the authors have combined a bottom-up approach to subsidy identification with a price-gap analysis. For the price-gap calculations, the authors follow the same logic as the IEA price gap methodology and the analysis of the other EaP countries in this report:

Price gap = Reference price – Net tariff

Subsidy = Price gap × Units consumed

Price-gap estimates of consumer subsidies

For Georgia, as a net importer, the reference price is the price of gas imported from Azerbaijan and the Russian Federation (Table 5.6). The calculations have been adjusted for the VAT exemption for thermal power plants (TPPs) using natural gas as feedstock, because IEA includes VAT in the reference price. However, since the cost of insurance, freight, transport and distribution to end users were not available for all EaP countries, they were excluded from the reference price, which is a simplification of the IEA approach. Therefore, the obtained price-gap estimates of subsidies to natural gas consumers are on the low side.

Table 5.6 summarises the input and the results of the price-gap estimates. The tariff for TPPs and the regulated tariff for households are lower than the import cost, which implies a subsidy to this category of consumers. However, the unregulated price for other consumers is significantly above the import cost, cancelling out subsidies to TPPs and regulated household consumption on the national scale. On the national level, these findings thus correspond to the IEA results, indicating no subsidy to the consumption of natural gas.

Table 5.6. **Price-gap estimates of consumer subsidies in the gas sector of Georgia in 2015, million USD**

Consumer groups	Share	Volume, bln m³	Net tariff per 1 000 m³	Import cost per 1 000 m³	Price gap per 1 000 m³	Subsidy via VAT exemption 1 000 m³	Total subsidy, USD million
TPPs	39%	0.683774	143		19	26 (143 × 18%)	31
Regulated residential tariff[a]	13%	0.23324	143	162	19	0	4
Unregulated price for other consumers	47%	0.82705	282		-120	0	-99
Total		**1.744**					**-64 (no subsidy)**

Note: a. The regulated tariff is applicable only for consumers connected before 2007. Their consumption volumes are assumed at the same level as reported in Georgia's Energy Balance for 2005. Other residential consumers also receive natural gas at almost the same price.

Source: Authors' estimates based on KazTransGgas Tbilisi Ltd (2015), Shelia (2015), GEOSTAT (2015a).

As specified in Table 5.7, purchase costs are assumed to equal USD 162 per 1 000 m³, the average of the price of gas imported from different sources (the Russian Federation and Azerbaijan). Georgia gets some cheap Azerbaijani natural gas from the South Caucasus Pipeline consortium as part of the host government agreement defining the terms of gas transit to Turkey. As mentioned earlier, the cost of this gas is in the range of USD 55-240 per 1 000 m³. Gas from the Russian Federation comes as an in-kind payment for its transit to Armenia and is sold by GOGC for USD 110 per 1 000 m³. A significant volume of gas is imported from Azerbaijan; some of which becomes "social gas", where the price is determined in contracts between TPPs and SOCAR Georgia. The price of this gas is USD 189 per 1 000 m³ and the price of imported commercial gas USD 240 per 1 000 m³.

Table 5.7. **Purchase cost calculations for natural gas imported into Georgia in 2015**

	bcm	USD/1 000m³	Share
Shah-Deniz (5%)	0.25	61	10%
Shah-Deniz additional	0.5	70	21%
Russian transit	0.2	110	8%
Azerbaijan "social gas"	0.5	189	21%
Azerbaijan commercial gas	0.9	240	38%
Sum and weighted average	2.4	162	100%

Source: WEG (2012).

In other words, this price-gap exercise also reveals a cross-subsidy mechanism providing low-cost "social gas" to TPPs and regulated households through a surcharge on other categories of gas consumers. The bottom-up inventory below and Table 5.A1.1 provide further discussion on the mechanism of "social gas" subsidisation in Georgia. While the quantitative estimates obtained by the price-gap and bottom-up inventory methodologies differ, the findings point to the same conclusion: that the cross-subsidy is the most significant form of support for natural gas consumption in Georgia.

Bottom-up inventory of government support for oil and gas

Tables 5.8a and 5.8b list the major subsidies to oil and gas identified in Georgia and discussed above in the sections on energy pricing (page 177) and taxation (page 181).

Annex 5.A1 provides more detailed descriptions of the schemes. No government support for coal has been identified. Broadly, the identified subsidies fall in three categories:

1. support for vulnerable households in the form of direct budget transfers
2. support for TPPs in the form of capacity payments and to distribution companies in the form of price support
3. government revenue foregone from under-taxing oil and gas infrastructure and consumption.

Table 5.8a. **Estimates of major oil and gas subsidies in Georgia, GEL million**

Subsidy	Type of subsidy	2010	2011	2012	2013	2014
Provision of "social gas" below market value to TPPs and distribution companies serving households	Consumer subsidy, induced transfer	206	336	350	314	367
VAT exemption for imported natural gas used by TPPs	Consumer subsidy, government revenue foregone	9	27	30	22	30
Direct subsidies to households in the highland Kazbegi and Dusheti municipalities for gas consumption	Consumer subsidy, direct budget transfers	4.4	5.3	4.3	4.8	6
VAT exemption for import of energy-related goods funded under preferential international loans	General infrastructure subsidy (benefits both producers and consumers), government revenue foregone	n.c.	n.c.	n.c.	n.c.	n.c.
VAT, import tax, property tax and excise tax exemption for oil and gas-related activities specified by the Law on Oil and Gas	General infrastructure subsidy (benefits both producers and consumers), government revenue foregone	n.c.	n.c.	n.c.	n.c.	n.c.
VAT exemption with respect to the admission of goods to Georgia to facilitate the construction of the Baku-Tbilisi-Ceyhan and the Baku-Tbilisi-Erzurum pipelines	General infrastructure subsidy (benefits both producers and consumers), government revenue foregone	n.c.	n.c.	n.c.	n.c.	n.c.
Total for quantified oil and gas subsidies		**219**	**368**	**384**	**341**	**403**

Note: **n.c.**: not calculated.

Source: Authors' compilation and calculations based on Ministry of Finance of Georgia (2014), Ministry of Energy (n.d.), President of Georgia (2010).

Table 5.8b. **Estimates of major oil and gas subsidies in Georgia, USD million**

Subsidy	Type of subsidy	2010	2011	2012	2013	2014
Provision of "social gas" below market value to TPPs and distribution companies serving households	Consumer subsidy, induced transfer	115	199	212	189	208
VAT exemption for imported natural gas used by TPPs	Consumer subsidy, government revenue foregone	5	16	18	13	17
Direct subsidies to households in highland Kazbegi and Dusheti municipalities for gas consumption	Consumer subsidy, direct budget transfers	2	3	3	3	3
VAT exemption for import of energy-related goods funded under preferential international loans	General infrastructure subsidy (benefits both producers and consumers), government revenue foregone	n.c.	n.c.	n.c.	n.c.	n.c.
VAT, import tax, property tax and excise tax exemption for oil and gas-related activities specified by the Law on Oil and Gas	General infrastructure subsidy (benefits both producers and consumers), government revenue foregone	n.c.	n.c.	n.c.	n.c.	n.c.
VAT exemption with respect to the admission of goods to Georgia to facilitate the construction of the Baku-Tbilisi-Ceyhan and the Baku-Tbilisi-Erzurum pipelines	General infrastructure subsidy (benefits both producers and consumers), government revenue foregone	n.c.	n.c.	n.c.	n.c.	n.c.
Total for quantified oil and gas subsidies		**122**	**218**	**233**	**205**	**228**

Note: **n.c.**: not calculated.

Source: Authors' compilation and calculations based on Ministry of Finance of Georgia (2014), Ministry of Energy (n.d.), President of Georgia (2010).

Subsidies to natural gas were quantified at GEL 403 mln (USD 228 mln) in 2014. The beneficiaries of these quantified subsidies are consumers. Government revenue foregone from supporting the upstream oil and gas infrastructure has been more challenging to estimate in monetary terms.

Table 5.9 provides further details on the methodological approaches used to quantify subsidies.

Table 5.9. **Approaches used to quantify oil and gas subsidies in Georgia**

Subsidy scheme	Quantification method
Provision of "social gas" below market value to Thermal Power Plants (TPPs) and distribution companies serving households	Authors' calculations: gas price for TPPs and distribution companies has been deducted from regional wholesale gas price and multiplied by the amount of gas consumed by TPPs and distributors
VAT exemption for imported natural gas used by TPPs	Authors' calculations: gas price for TPP, excluding VAT, multiplied by the VAT rate (18%) and the amount of gas supplied to TPPs
Direct subsidies to households in the highland Kazbegi and Dusheti municipalities for gas consumption	Subsidy estimate has been taken at its face value from the national budget of Georgia for 2014

Source: Authors' summary.

By far the largest scheme (USD 208 mln in 2014) that can be formally qualified as a fossil-fuel subsidy in Georgia is the provision of natural gas below market value to TPPs and distribution companies that serve households. This subsidised gas is called "social gas", which also reveals the nature of the scheme: it is first of all a measure to protect households from tariffs rising beyond the perceived affordability level. With this in mind, the gas price is determined in contracts between TPPs and SOCAR Georgia, the natural gas importer from Azerbaijan and a subsidiary of Azerbaijan's national oil and gas company. According to official sources, distribution companies and thermal power companies receive gas below its market value of USD 143 per 1 000 m^3 (as referenced by Transparency International Georgia, 2015). This is part of undisclosed deal between the government of Georgia and SOCAR, in which the natural gas received as an in-kind payment for transit through the South Caucasus Gas pipeline (from Azerbaijan to Turkey) and the Northeastern Gas pipeline (from the Russian Federation to Armenia) is transferred to SOCAR import-export company by GOGC and its subsidiary. This transit gas is then blended with purchased gas from Azerbaijan and supplied to Georgian consumers in the form of "social gas" (at USD 143 per 1 000 m^3) and gas at commercial rates for all other consumer categories. "Social gas" is funded through cross-subsidisation: there is a surcharge in the tariff for commercial consumers.

As a social protection measure, the government of Georgia also provides direct subsidies to the highland villages of Kazbegi and Dusheti for gas consumption in winter. The allocation is taken from the national budget to improve the socio-economic standards in higher mountain municipalities. This support has been provided since the 1990s, when the Northeastern gas transit pipeline (Russia-Georgia-Armenia) became operational. This pipeline passes though the Kazbegi and Dusheti municipalities. The Georgian government decided to supply gas to the households of these two municipalities free of charge, while the budget transfers go directly to gas suppliers. The subsidy has caused large market distortions. For example, residents have used the free gas to heat their greenhouses and cultivate vegetables in the highlands. Stricter limitations have been imposed in the last few years, but such practices persist, and the burden on the national budget – on the order of USD 3 mln per year – is not declining.

The government provides guaranteed reserve capacity (GRC) payments to gas-based thermal plants in Georgia. The scheme initially designed in 2005-06 to recover the costs of a new gas turbine power plant has now been extended to all gas-based plants. Thermal power plants receive a two-part payment, a guaranteed reserve capacity payment and a generation tariff for electricity supply to the grid. The payment is enshrined in a GNERC resolution, based on the Law on Electricity and Natural Gas and Electricity Market Rules. The GRC payment compensates all fixed operation and maintenance costs, and it also provides a return on the regulated capital base. Since TPPs are compensated in full even without supplying any electricity to the system there is little incentive for them to produce, as it does not bring any additional revenue.

The guaranteed reserve capacity payments are paid by distribution companies, direct consumers and exporters (including new HPPs) on a kWh basis, according to their consumption or export level. The thermal power plants are thus subsidised not only by consumers but also by hydropower plants that are willing to export their electricity to the neighbouring countries (mostly to Turkey). This scheme disincentivises HPP development and diminishes the opportunity for further export of electricity to other countries. Experts argue that schemes that support the development of one kind of capacity only, often employed inefficiently and at the cost of other types of capacity, do not help meet a future increase in domestic electricity demand and prevent the generation of additional revenue from export of electricity. It is recommended that such schemes be discontinued.

This question is debated in many countries, including Canada and the European Union. Such support schemes are considered a subsidy by the government for the development of capacity initially designed to ensure energy security or other grid contingencies, but which, instead, has resulted in idle capacity. This is an issue that requires further scrutiny and is under revision in some of the EU countries that share similar concerns.

Other oil and gas subsidies identified fall into the category of government revenue foregone. In particular, as a measure of social protection against rising energy tariffs, the government of Georgia forgoes revenue due to VAT exemption for imported natural gas for use by TPPs. The value of this subsidy was estimated at USD 17 mln in 2014.

As explained in the energy taxation overview above, there are also a number of tax exemptions that benefit general energy infrastructure, thereby benefitting both producers and consumers. One such category of beneficiaries is the international oil and gas pipeline consortia. VAT, import tax, property tax and excise tax exemptions apply for oil and gas-related activities specified in the Law on Oil and Gas. In addition, there are VAT exemptions for the import of energy-related goods funded under preferential international loans, and with respect to the import of goods to Georgia to facilitate the construction of the Baku-Tbilisi-Ceyhan and the Baku-Tbilisi-Erzurum pipelines. However, due to lack of sufficient data, these forms of government revenue foregone have not been quantified.

Government support for electricity predominantly generated from renewable sources

Several subsidy schemes in Georgia are designed to encourage the production and consumption of electricity in general and can apply to electricity generated both from renewable sources and from gas-fired thermal plants. However, since the bulk of electricity in Georgia is hydropower, including from large hydropower plants, these subsidies are discussed together in this section of the study. It should be noted that it is methodologically challenging to disentangle gas-fired and renewable electricity in Georgia's power mix and policy discussions.

Several subsidy schemes have been designed to benefit electricity consumers. All electricity consumers in Tbilisi receive electricity vouchers to cover their needs. The vouchers can be used for making payments to electricity suppliers, who, upon submission of these vouchers, receive direct transfers from the Tbilisi municipal budget. This subsidy amounted to USD 14 mln in 2014 and is reported at face value, as identified in official sources.

Second, as explained in the energy pricing section above, the residential consumer tariff is differentiated by consumer bracket, and a cross-subsidy for households with low consumption is embedded in the tariff through a surcharge on other consumers of energy. Third, electricity generation and export is exempt from VAT. Fourth, the supply of electric energy and guaranteed capacity from 1 January 2011 to 1 January 2015, with the exception of the supply of electricity to consumers identified in the Law of Georgia on Electricity and Natural Gas, as well as the transmission and dispatch operators' services, were exempt from VAT. Fifth, restrictions on export of hydropower in winter reduce prices for domestic consumers and represent a consumer subsidy. It was impossible to quantify these subsidies, due to lack of data.

The electricity tariff for residential consumers was raised in August 2015, which, on the one hand, increased the payment by consumers but, on the other, increased the government revenue from the VAT tax on the supply of electric energy. The government is planning to offset the increase of the burden on vulnerable residential consumers by allocating 25% of the revenue generated from increased VAT collection back to such consumers. Tariffs are expected to rise further for both residential and industrial consumers, as the cost of generation of the new upcoming plants will be higher. The government is further planning to expand the subsidy to vulnerable groups and allocate up to 40% of the additional VAT-generated revenue for the budget.

In terms of support to electricity producers, the government of Georgia provides incentives for the development of hydro power. One is a producer (feed-in) tariff for the generation of electricity from plants. Support of this kind has been provided to secure investment in the new Khudoni HPP scheduled to begin operating after 2020. The agreement for the construction, operation and ownership of Khudoni was signed between the government of Georgia, Trans Electrica Limited (BVI), Trans Electrica Georgia Ltd., JSC Electricity System Commercial Operator (ESCO) and Energotrans Ltd. The anticipated Khudoni HPP annual generation over the ten years of the Khudoni HPP will be 1.5 TWh, and according to the contract, the producer (feed-in) tariff is set at around 10.5 US cents per kWh. Meanwhile, the anticipated market price is 5.5 US cents per kWh. The estimated annual subsidy to Khudoni HPP will thus be USD 75 mln. Since this subsidy will be provided only after 2020, when the Khudoni HPP becomes operational, this value is not included in Tables 5.10a and 5.10b, but the plan is listed in Table 5.A2.2. The tariff schedule for the Khudoni HPP is provided in Annex 5.A4.

Within the framework of support for electricity producers, electricity lines and land used by electricity power plants for water reservoirs are exempted from property tax. However, due to the lack of sufficient data, this subsidy has not been quantified.

Electricity generation from geothermal, solar and wind energy sources remains marginal in Georgia. The government can potentially use producer (feed-in) tariffs to support these developments. No significant support schemes relevant to alternative energy sources have so far been implemented.

Tables 5.10a and 5.10b list electricity subsidies in Georgia. Annex 5.A2 provides a detailed description of the schemes.

Table 5.10a. **Estimates of major electricity subsidies in Georgia, GEL million**

Subsidy	Type of subsidy	2010	2011	2012	2013	2014
Electricity vouchers for consumers in Tbilisi municipality	Consumer subsidy, direct budget transfers	n.a.	n.a.	6.4	24	25
Cross-subsidy to households with low consumption, embedded in the regulated electricity tariff through a surcharge on other categories of consumers	Consumer subsidy, induced transfers	n.c.	n.c.	n.c.	n.c.	n.c.
VAT exemption for electricity generation and export	Consumer subsidy, government revenue foregone	n.c.	n.c.	n.c.	n.c.	n.c.
VAT exemption for the supply of electric energy and guaranteed capacity from 1 January 2011 to 1 January 2015, with the exception of the supply of electric energy to consumers (to persons determined under the Law of Georgia on Electricity and Natural Gas) as well as the transmission and dispatch operators' services	Consumer subsidy, government revenue foregone	n.c.	n.c.	n.c.	n.c.	n.c.
Winter restrictions on export of electricity	Consumer subsidy, induced transfers	n.c.	n.c.	n.c.	n.c.	n.c.
Property tax exemption for electricity lines and land used by electricity plants as water reservoirs	Producer subsidy, government revenue foregone	n.c.	n.c.	n.c.	n.c.	n.c.
Preferential producer (feed-in) tariff for Khudoni HPP	Producer subsidy, induced transfer	n.a.	n.a.	n.a.	n.a.	n.a.
Total quantified electricity subsidies		**n.c.**	**n.c.**	**6.4**	**24**	**25**

Note: **n.c.**: not calculated; **n.a.**: not applicable.

Source: Authors' summary based on Municipality of Tbilisi Budget Document (2014) and analysis in this report.

Table 5.10b. **Estimates of major electricity subsidies in Georgia, USD million**

Subsidy	Type of subsidy	2010	2011	2012	2013	2014
Electricity vouchers for consumers in Tbilisi municipality	Consumer subsidy, direct budget transfers	n.a.	n.a.	4	14	14
Cross-subsidy to households with low consumption embedded in the regulated electricity tariff through a surcharge on other categories of consumers	Consumer subsidy, induced transfers	n.c.	n.c.	n.c.	n.c.	n.c.
VAT exemption for electricity generation and export	Consumer subsidy, government revenue foregone	n.c.	n.c.	n.c.	n.c.	n.c.
VAT exemption for the supply of electric energy and guaranteed capacity from 1 January 2011 to 1 January 2015, with the exception of the supply of electric energy to consumers (to persons determined under the Law of Georgia on Electricity and Natural Gas), as well as the transmission and dispatch operators' services	Consumer subsidy, government revenue foregone	n.c.	n.c.	n.c.	n.c.	n.c.
Winter restrictions on export of electricity	Consumer subsidy, induced transfers	n.c.	n.c.	n.c.	n.c.	n.c.
Property tax exemption for electricity lines and land used by electricity plants as water reservoirs	Producer subsidy, government revenue foregone	n.c.	n.c.	n.c.	n.c.	n.c.
Preferential producer (feed-in) tariff for Khudoni HPP	Producer subsidy, induced transfer	n.a.	n.a.	n.a.	n.a.	n.a.
Total for quantified electricity subsidies		**n.c.**	**n.c.**	**4**	**14**	**14**

Note: **n.a.**: not applicable; **n.c.**: not calculated.

Source: Authors' summary based on Municipality of Tbilisi Budget Document (2014) and analysis in this report.

Government support for energy efficiency

The energy intensity of the Georgian economy is high, and the energy needed to produce goods and services in Georgia is 2 to 2.5 times higher than in most Western countries. It is estimated that energy efficiency measures can save up to 20% of the energy it uses.

This review of energy subsidies has not identified any measures supporting energy efficiency in Georgia that could be defined as subsidies. This policy direction remains important for Georgia's development, however, in view of commitments to the international climate change agreement (see the section on climate policy above) and international agreements such as the Energy Charter Treaty and Energy Community Treaty.

Annex 5.A1

Fossil-fuel subsidies in Georgia

Table 5.A1.1. **Provision of natural gas at below market value to thermal power plants (TPPs) and distribution companies serving households**

Subsidy category	Income or price support → Market price support and regulation → Regulated prices set at below-market rates
Stimulated activity	Household gas and electricity consumption
Subsidy name	**Provision of natural gas to TPPs and distribution companies at below-market value. The subsidised gas is referred to as "social gas"**
Jurisdiction	National
Legislation/endorsing organisation	Contracts between TPPs and SOCAR Georgia import-export company
Policy objective(s) of subsidy	To make electricity and gas tariffs affordable for residential customers
End recipient(s) of subsidy	All residential customers of electricity and gas in Georgia
Time period	From 2010 to the present
Background	According to official sources, distribution companies and thermal power companies are getting gas below the market value of USD 143 per 1 000 m^3. This subsidised gas is called "social gas", which indicates the purpose of the scheme: a measure to protect households from electricity and tariffs whose rates exceed affordable levels. With this in mind, the gas price is determined in contracts between TPPs and SOCAR Georgia, the natural gas importer from Azerbaijan and a subsidiary of Azerbaijan's national oil and gas company. This is part of the undisclosed deal between the government of Georgia and SOCAR, under which natural gas received as in-kind payment for transit through the South Caucasus Gas pipeline (from Azerbaijan to Turkey) and Northeastern Gas pipeline (from the Russian Federation to Armenia) is transferred to SOCAR import-export company by the Georgian Gas and Oil Company (GOGC) and its subsidiary. This in-kind gas payment is then blended with purchased gas from Azerbaijan and supplied to Georgian consumers in the form of "social gas" (at USD 143 per 1 000 m^3) and gas at commercial rates for all other consumer categories. As detailed below, the value of the subsidy is calculated as follows: the gas price for TPPs and distribution companies is deducted from the regional wholesale gas price and multiplied by the amount of gas consumed by TPPs and distributors. Gas for TPPs is exempt from VAT, and this subsidy is quantified separately. To avoid double-counting, it is assumed here that gas for TPPs is subject to VAT, too.
Amount of subsidy conferred	2010: GEL 206 mln (USD 115 mln) 2011: GEL 336 mln (USD 199 mln) 2012: GEL 350 mln (USD 212 mln) 2013: GEL 314 mln (USD 189 mln) 2014: GEL 367 mln (USD 208 mln)

Table 5.A1.1. **Provision of natural gas below market value to thermal power plants (TPPs) and distribution companies serving households** *(continued)*

Calculations of the value of regulated natural gas tariff for TPPs and distribution companies serving households					
	2010	**2011**	**2012**	**2013**	**2014**
Amount of social gas supplied to TPPs and distributors (mln m³)	644	1 151	1 230	1 080	1 200
Amount of social gas supplied to TPPs (mln m³)	198	629	702	505	650
Amount of social gas supplied to distributors (mln m³)	446	522	528	575	550
Social gas price for TPP, including VAT (USD per 1 000 m³)	169	169	169	169	169
Social gas price for distributors (USD per 1 000 m³)	143	143	143	143	143
Regional wholesale gas price (USD)	330	330	330	330	330
Regional wholesale gas price (GEL)	588	556	545	549	583
Subsidy for TPP (USD)	31 929 480	101 432 540	113 204 520	81 436 300	104 819 000
Subsidy for distributors (USD)	83 402 000	97 614 000	98 736 000	107 525 000	102 850 000
Subsidy for TPP (GEL)	56 917 797	171 019 625	186 930 294	135 462 614	185 095 363
Subsidy for distributors (GEL)	148 673 205	164 581 403	163 038 980	178 859 029	181 618 391
Total subsidy (USD)	**115 331 480**	**199 046 540**	**211 940 520**	**188 961 300**	**207 669 000**
Total subsidy (GEL)	**205 591 002**	**335 601 028**	**349 969 274**	**314 321 643**	**366 713 754**
Exchange rate – GEL/USD	1.78	1.69	1.65	1.66	1.77
Information sources	1. Ministry of Energy of Georgia (Natural Gas Balance). www.energy.gov.ge/legislation.php?id_pages=75&lang=geo 2. Transparency International Georgia (2015), "Negotiations with Gazprom raise questions", 25 November. www.transparency.ge/en/node/5664. 3. Ministry of Energy of Georgia (2007), *On Natural Gas Supply Activities*. Order of the Minister No. 69 of 25 September 2007. (საქართველოს ენერგეტიკის მინისტრის ბრძანება №69, 2007 წლის 25 სექტემბერი. ბუნებრივი გაზის მიწოდების საქმიანობის დერეგულირებისა და ნაწილობრივი დერეგულირების შესახებ). https://matsne.gov.ge/ka/document/view/73006				

Table 5.A1.2. **Direct subsidies to households in highland Kazbegi and Dusheti municipalities for gas consumption**

Subsidy category	Direct and indirect transfer of funds and liabilities → Direct spending → Earmarks
Stimulated activity	Consumption of natural gas (especially for heating) in higher mountain villages of Kazbegi and Dusheti in winter
Subsidy name	**Reimbursement of gas supplied to households of in the highland villages of Kazbegi and Dusheti.** State Budget Code 36 02 (ყაზბეგის მუნიციპალიტეტისა და დუშეთის მუნიციპალიტეტის მაღალმთიანი სოფლების მოსახლეობისათვის მიწოდებული ბუნებრივი აირის ღირებულების ანაზღაურების ღონისძიება 2014 წლის სახელმწიფო ბიუჯეტი, პროგრამული კოდი 36 02)
Jurisdiction	National legislation, but the subsidy is limited to the Kazbegi and Dusheti municipalities
Legislation/endorsing organisation	National budget 2014 of Georgia/Ministry of Energy, Georgia
Policy objective(s) of subsidy	Improve the socio-economic standards in higher mountain villages
End recipient(s) of subsidy	About 3 600 households of the Kazbegi and Dusheti municipalities
Time period	From 1990s to the present

Table 5.A1.2. **Direct subsidies to households in highland Kazbegi and Dusheti municipalities for gas consumption** *(continued)*

Background	This support has been provided since the 1990s, when the Northeastern gas transit pipeline (Russia-Georgia-Armenia), which passes through the Kazbegi and Dusheti municipalities, was first brought online. The Georgian government decided to supply gas free of charge to the households of these two municipalities, while the budget transfers go directly to gas suppliers. The subsidy has caused large market distortions. For example, residents used the free gas to heat their greenhouses and cultivate vegetables in the highlands. Stricter limitations have been imposed in the last few years, but such practices continue, and the burden on the national budget, on the order of USD 3 mln per year, has not diminished. The subsidy estimated is reported at its face value based on the national budget of Georgia.
Amount of subsidy conferred	2010: GEL 4.4 mln (USD 2.47 mln) 2011: GEL 5.3 mln (USD 3.14 mln) 2012: GEL 4.3 mln (USD 2.6 mln) 2013: GEL 4.8 mln (USD 2.89 mln) 2014: GEL 6 mln (USD 3.4 mln)
Information sources	National budget 2014 of Georgia. www.mof.ge/4596

Table 5.A1.3. **VAT exemption for imported natural gas used as feedstock in thermal power plants**

Subsidy category	Government revenue foregone → Tax breaks and special taxes → Tax expenditures
Stimulated Activity	Supporting residential customers
Subsidy name	**VAT exemption for imported natural gas used as feedstock in thermal power plants (TPPs)**
Jurisdiction	National
Legislation/endorsing organisation	Tax Code of Georgia
Policy objective(s) of subsidy	To make tariffs for gas-fired electricity affordable for residential customers
End recipient(s) of subsidy	Consumers of electricity from TPPs
Time period	From 2010 to the present
Background	Article 168, Paragraph 1 of the Tax Code of Georgia provides for exemption from VAT without the right of offset for the import of natural gas for the production of electricity by TPPs. The value of the subsidy is calculated by applying the 18% VAT rate to the gas price for TPP, excluding VAT, and then multiplying by the amount of gas supplied to TPPs.
Amount of subsidy	2010: GEL 9 mln (USD 5 mln) 2011: GEL 27 mln (USD 16 mln) 2012: GEL 30 mln (USD 18 mln) 2013: GEL 22 mln (USD 13 mln) 2014: GEL 30 mln (USD 17 mln)

Calculations of the value of VAT exemption for natural gas used by TPPs

	2010	2011	2012	2013	2014
Amount of social gas supplied to TPPs (mln m^3)	198	629	702	505	650
Gas price for TPP, excluding VAT (USD per 1 000 m^3)	143	143	143	143	143
Gas price for TPP, including VAT (USD per 1 000 m^3)	168.74	168.74	168.74	168.74	168.74
Subsidy-VAT exemption in USD	5 096 520	16 190 460	18 069 480	12 998 700	16 731 000
Subsidy-VAT exemption in GEL	9 085 105	27 297 812	29 837 441	21 622 273	29 544 553
Exchange rate, GEL/USD	1.78	1.69	1.65	1.66	1.77

Information sources	Tax Code of Georgia, Article 168. Ministry of Energy, Georgia (Natural Gas Balance) www.energy.gov.ge/legislation.php?id_pages=75&lang=geo.

Table 5.A1.4. **VAT, import tax, property tax and excise tax exemptions for certain oil and gas-related activities**

Subsidy category	Government revenue foregoforegone → Tax breaks and special taxes → Tax expenditures
Stimulated activity	Construction and maintenance of general oil and gas infrastructure and activities
Subsidy name	**VAT, import tax, property tax and excise tax exemptions for certain oil and gas-related activities**
Jurisdiction	National
Legislation/endorsing organisation	Tax Code of Georgia (2010), Law on Oil and Gas (2001) President of Georgia (2010, 2001)
Policy objective(s) of subsidy	Support for energy companies
End recipient(s) of subsidy	Energy companies in Georgia
Time period	Various periods, depending on exemption. All exemptions were in place for the period reviewed, 2010-14.
Background	The Tax Code of Georgia (President of Georgia, 2010), Article 168 paragraph 3, provides exemption from VAT for transactions performed for a targeted purpose. According to the Tax Code, and in line with the cases identified below, certain imports shall be exempted from VAT without the right to offset: Import, supply of appliances and equipment, means of transport, spare parts and materials intended for the implementation of oil and gas operations according to the Law of Georgia on Oil and Gas, as well as the import, supply for investors and operating companies of the goods for the implementation of the agreements set forth under the above-mentioned law and/or the implementation of oil and gas operations in accordance with the issued licences, and/or the provision of services thereof; Import of goods funded under preferential credit extended by foreign states and/or international organisations under international agreements, ratified by the Parliament of Georgia and/or the provision of construction and installation, repair, restoration, experimental constructor, and/or geological-exploratory services for the rehabilitation of the electric energy sector; Temporary admission of goods to Georgia to facilitate the fulfilment of obligations stipulated under international agreements of Georgia, namely, the construction of the Baku-Tbilisi-Ceyhan and Baku-Tbilisi-Erzurum pipelines. In addition to the VAT benefit, the import of appliances and equipment, means of transport, spare parts and materials designated for the performance of oil and gas transactions, envisaged under the Law of Georgia on Oil and Gas is also exempt from import tax (Article 199, Paragraph g), and from excise tax without the right to offset (Article 194, Paragraph 5-f). Further, the same oil and gas-related activities specified in the Law on Oil and Gas are exempted from property tax. Due to the lack of data, the value of these subsidies has not been calculated.
Amount of subsidy conferred	Not calculated
Information sources	President of Georgia (2010), Tax Code of Georgia, http://rs.ge/4713. President of Georgia (2001), Law on Oil and Gas (with additions and amendments). https://matsne.gov.ge/ru/document/download/18424/22/en/pdf.

Annex 5.A2

Quantification of subsidies to electricity, generated predominantly from renewable sources

Table 5.A2.1. **Electricity vouchers for consumers in Tbilisi municipality**

Subsidy category	Direct and indirect transfer of funds and liabilities → Direct spending → Earmarks
Stimulated activity	Consumption by households in Tbilisi municipality
Subsidy name	**Social Aid Programme** (სოციალური უზრუნველყოფის პროგრამა)
Jurisdiction	Municipal – Tbilisi municipality
Legislation/endorsing organisation	Municipality of Tbilisi Budget Document, Social and Health Service Office of the city (ჯანდაცვისა და სოციალური მომსახურების საქალაქო სამსახური)
Policy objective(s) of subsidy	To support household consumption of electricity and ensure socio-economic standards in Tbilisi
End recipient(s) of subsidy	All customers of electricity in Tbilisi municipality, which has about 410 000 households
Time period	From 2012 to the present
Background	Communal vouchers for electricity have been introduced to support socially vulnerable groups in Tbilisi municipality. However, all customers receive these vouchers. The subsidy amount below is reported at its face value indicated in the Tbilisi municipal budget.
Amount of subsidy conferred	2010: n.a. 2011: n.a. 2012: GEL 6.4 mln (USD 3.88 mln) 2013: GEL 24 mln (USD 14.43 mln) 2014: GEL 25 mln (USD 14.16 mln)
Information sources	Municipality of Tbilisi Budget Document (2014), http://new.tbilisi.gov.ge/news/1500.

Table 5.A2.2. **Government support for hydro power plant developers, producer (feed-in) tariff for Khudoni HPP**

Subsidy category	Income or price support → Market price support and regulation → Feed-in tariff for renewable energy producers
Stimulated activity	Investment in hydro power developments in Georgia
Subsidy name	**Government support for hydro power plant developers, producer (feed-in) tariff for Khudoni HPP**
Jurisdiction	National
Legislation/endorsing organisation	Memorandum of Understanding, Contract between the government of Georgia and Trans Electrica Ltd.
Policy objective(s) of subsidy	Development of renewable energy sources in Georgia
End recipient(s) of subsidy	Trans Electrica Limited, Khudoni HPP
Time period	After 2020, when Khudoni HPP becomes operational
Background	Electricity purchase tariff for Khudoni HPP is defined by the contract. The government of Georgia has provided a special producer (feed-in) tariff to secure investment in the new Khudoni HPP that is scheduled to become operational after 2020. This producer (feed-in) tariff is higher than the current and anticipated market price in Georgia. The agreement for construction, operation and ownership of Khudoni was signed between the government of Georgia, Trans Electrica Ltd (BVI), Trans Electrica Georgia Ltd, JSC Electricity System Commercial Operator (ESCO) and Energotrans Ltd. Given that the anticipated annual electricity generation for ten years of the Khudoni HPP is 1.5 TWh, and according to the contract, the producer (feed-in) tariff is around 10.5 US cent/kWh. Meanwhile, the anticipated market price is 5.5 US cent/kWh. The estimated annual subsidy to Khudoni TPP will thus be USD 75 mln. The tariff schedule for Khudoni HPP is provided in Annex 5.A4.
Amount of subsidy conferred	Estimated annual subsidy in the future (after 2020) is USD 75 mln (GEL 161 mln using an exchange rate of GEL 2.15/USD)
Information sources	Contract between the government of Georgia and Trans Electrica Ltd. www.energy.gov.ge/projects/pdf/pages/Agreement09092015%201169%20eng.pdf.

Annex 5.A3

National methodologies for calculating electricity tariffs in Georgia

In the electricity sector, tariffs for generation, dispatch, transmission, distribution and supply are defined by the independent regulator, the Georgian National Energy and Water Supply Regulatory Commission (GNERC) on the basis of a published tariff methodology. In 2014, the Commission approved new tariff calculation methodologies in the electricity sector. Resolution No. 14 of the Commission "On Approving Electricity Tariff Calculation Methodologies" comprises three annexes:

1. "Tariff-Setting Methodology for Electricity Distribution, Pass-Through and Consumption Tariffs";
2. "Tariff-Setting Methodology for Electricity Generation, Transmission, Dispatch and Electricity Market Operator Service"; and
3. "Regulated Assets Depreciation/Amortisation Rates of Utilities under Tariff Regulation".

The Resolution is based on two main principles: "incentive-based" and "cost-plus" regulation. The methodology is designed with the following objectives of tariff-setting in mind:

- protecting consumers from monopolistic prices
- encouraging utilities to increase their efficiency by optimising costs, with the requirement not to decrease quality of service standards and technical conditions of the utilities
- helping increase the utilities' returns by increasing operational and management efficiency
- promoting the stable and reliable functioning of utilities
- ensuring that tariffs are transparent, stable and fair for utilities
- reflecting the national policy on discounted tariffs, providing that none of the consumer categories receive a discount tariff subsidised by licensee, importer, market operator or any other category
- reflecting different costs between different consumer categories
- covering costs of utilities with funds received from each consumer category, in proportion to the costs incurred for servicing this consumer category.

The Commission sets a Weighted Average Price for Purchased Electricity by the utility for each tariff year, according to the following formula:

$$P_{aver(t+1)} = \frac{COST_{E(t+1)} + COST_{GC(t+1)} + COST_{T(t+1)} + COST_{D(t+1)} + CORR_{EL(t+1)}}{E_{Receiv.(t+1)}} \times 100 \quad (12)$$

where

$P_{aver(t+1)}$	Weighted Average Price for electricity to be purchased for tariff year by the utility (tetri/kWh)
$COST_{E(t+1)}$	Total forecasted cost of electricity to be purchased by the utility for the tariff year (GEL)
$COST_{GC(t+1)}$	Total forecasted cost of guaranteed capacity fee for tariff year (GEL)
$COST_{T(t+1)}$	Total forecasted cost of transmission service provided by transmission licensees (GEL)
$COST_{D(t+1)}$	Total forecasted cost of dispatched service provided by dispatch licensees (GEL)
$CORR_{EL(t+1)}$	Electricity Purchase Correction Factor which ensures the reflection of the difference between planned and actual costs related to the electricity purchase for tariff year
$E_{Receiv.(t+1)}$	Forecasted amount of electricity received (metered) on the delivery points of the utility for the tariff year (kWh)

Regulatory Cost Base for the tariff year is calculated according to the following formula:

$$RCB(t+1) = CAPEX(t+1) + cOPEX(t+1) + ncOPEX(t+1) + CNL(t+1) + CORR(t+1)$$

where

RCB(t+1)	Regulatory Cost Base for the tariff year (GEL)
CAPEX(t+1)	Capital Expenses for the tariff year (GEL)
cOPEX(t+1)	Controllable Operational Expenses for the tariff year (GEL)
ncOPEX(t+1)	Non-controllable Operational Expenses for the tariff year (GEL)
CNL(t+1)	Cost of Normative Losses in distribution networks for the tariff year (GEL)
CORR(t+1)	Cost correction factor, which provides the reflection of the difference between factual and planned costs of Tariff Year in the Regulatory Cost Base of the Tariff Year, and also received income from nonoperational activity envisaged in sub-paragraph "e" of Paragraph 1 of Article 19 of this Methodology, based on the principles defined in the Methodology (GEL).

More details on the electricity tariff calculation methodologies can be accessed from Resolution No. 14 of the Georgian National Energy and Water Supply Regulatory Commission (GNERC, 2014).

Annex 5.A4

Producer (feed-in) tariff for Khudoni HPP

Year from the commencement of the operation of facility	US cents per kWh
1st year	10.5
2nd year	10.5
3rd year	10.5
4th year	10.5
5th year	10.5
6th year	10.25
7th year	10.25
8th year	10.25
9th year	9.75
10th year	9.75
11th year	9.5
12th year	6
13th year	5
14th year	5
15th year	5

Source: Government of Georgia, Khudoni HPP Agreement (2015).

Notes

1. In the interest of inter-country comparability, this section builds on data from international sources such as the World Bank and the International Energy Agency. These data, however, have certain discrepancies with Georgia's own statistics, primarily the data of the National Statistics Office of Georgia (GEOSTAT). In some instances, national sources provide more recent data. Therefore, for all key indicators, the chapter seeks to provide references for both national and international statistics.

2. From 1 August 2015, consumers are subject to a new electricity price, increased by 3.348 tetri (without VAT). Consumer tariffs differ according to the consumption level: GEL 0.13 per kWh for less than 101 kWh; GEL 0.17 per kWh for 101-301 kWh; GEL 0.215 per kWh for more than 301 kWh.

References

ADB (2017), *Asian Development Bank: Country Overview Georgia*, Asian Development Bank, Tbilisi. www.adb.org/countries/georgia/economy.

Covenant of Mayors (n.d.), *Covenant of Mayors for Climate and Energy*, Brussels.

EBRD (2013), *Strategy for Georgia*, European Bank for Reconstruction and Development, Tbilisi. www.ebrd.com/downloads/country/strategy/georgia.pdf.

EC (2015), *Trade, Countries and Region, Georgia*, European Commission, Brussels. http://ec.europa.eu/trade/policy/countries-and-regions/countries/georgia/.

EnergoPro (2015), *Energo-Pro Georgia,* EnergoPro, Tbilisi. www.energo-pro.ge.

Energotrans (2015), *Energotrans – About Us*, Energotrans, Tbilisi. http://energotrans.com.ge/?lang=en.

ESCO (2015), *JSC Electricity System Commercial Operator "ESCO"*, Electricity System Commercial Operator, Tbilisi. http://esco.ge/index.php?article_id=1&clang=1.

ESCO (2014), *Energy Balance of Georgia*, Electricity System Commercial Operator, Tbilisi. http://esco.ge/index.php?article_id=111&clang=1.

Gazprom (2015), *Gazprom in Numbers – Databook*, Gazprom, Moscow.

GEOSTAT (2015a), *Energy Balance of Georgia*, National Statistics Office of Georgia, Tbilisi. www.geostat.ge.

GEOSTAT (2015b), *Gross Domestic Product,* National Statistics Office of Georgia, Tbilisi. http://geostat.ge/index.php?action=page&p_id=119&lang=eng.

GGTC (2015), *Georgian Gas Transport Corporation*. http://ggtc.ge.

GIZ (2015), *International Fuel Prices 2014: Data Preview, Deutsche Gesellschaft für Internationale Zusammenarbeit*, Berlin. Available at: https://www.giz.de/expertise/downloads/giz-2015-en-ifp2014.pdf.

GNERC (2016), *Annual Report 2015,* Georgian National Energy and Water Supply Regulatory Commission, Tbilisi. http://gnerc.org/ge/public-information/reports/tsliuri-angarishi.

GNERC (2015a), *About GNERC*, Georgian National Energy and Water Supply Regulatory Commission, Tbilisi. http://gnerc.org.

GNERC (2015b), *Annual Report 2014*, Georgian National Energy and Water Supply Regulatory Commission, Tbilisi. http://gnerc.org/files/wliuri%20angariSi/Anual_Report_Eng_opt.pdf.

GNERC (2015c), *Resolution No. 33 of 4 December 2008, Last Updated July 2015*, Georgian National Energy and Water Supply Regulatory Commission, Tbilisi.

GNERC (2014), *Resolution No. 14 of 30 July 2014 on Approving Electricity Tariff Calculation Methodologies*, Georgian National Energy and Water Supply Regulatory Commission, Tbilisi. http://gnerc.org/files/Acts%20in%20english/Tariff%20Setting%20%20Methodology%20for%20Electricity_opt.pdf.

GNIA (2015a), *Invest in Georgia – Energy,* Georgian National Investment Agency, Tbilisi. www.investingeorgia.org/en/keysectors/energy.

GNIA (2015b), *Invest in Georgia – Taxation,* Georgian National Investment Agency, Tbilisi. http://investingeorgia.org/en/georgia/taxation.

GOGC (2015), *Georgian Oil and Gas Corporation*. www.gogc.ge/en/home.

Government of Georgia (2015), *Khudoni HPP Agreement*, Government of Georgia, Tbilisi. www.energy.gov.ge/projects/pdf/pages/Agreement09092015%201169%20eng.pdf.

GSE (2015), *Georgian State Electrosystem*, Tbilisi. www.gse.com.ge/new/?lang=en.

IEA (2015a), *Country Report Georgia*, International Energy Agency, Paris. www.iea.org/countries/non-membercountries/georgia/.

IEA (2015b), *Eastern Europe, Caucasus and Central Asia: Energy Policies beyond IEA Countries*, OECD/International Energy Agency, Paris. https://www.iea.org/publications/freepublications/publication/IDR_EasternEuropeCaucasus_2015.pdf.

IEA (n.d.), *Georgia Balance for 2014*, OECD/International Energy Agency, Paris. www.iea.org/statistics/statisticssearch/report/?year=2014&country=Georgia&product=Balances.

IGU (2015), *Wholesale Gas Price Survey – 2015 Edition,* International Gas Union.

KazTransGas Tbilisi Ltd (2015), *Distribution Tariffs,* KazTransGas Tbilisi Ltd, Tbilisi. https://www.ktg-tbilisi.ge.

MENRP (2016), *First Biennial Update Report of Georgia to the UNFCCC*, Ministry of Environment and Natural Resources Protection, Tbilisi. http://unfccc.int/files/national_reports/non-annex_i_parties/ica/application/pdf/first_bur_-_georgia.pdf.

MENRP (2015a), *Georgia's Third National Communication to the UNFCC,* Ministry of Environment and Natural Resources Protection of Georgia, Tbilisi. www.ge.undp.org/

content/georgia/en/home/library/environment_energy/third-national-communication-of-georgia-to-the-un-framework-conv0.html.

MENRP (2015b), *Intended Nationally Determined Contribution of the Republic of Georgia,* Ministry of Environment and Natural Resources Protection of Georgia, Tbilisi.

Ministry of Energy (2016), *Protocol Concerning the Accession of Georgia to the Treaty Establishing the Energy Community was Signed*, Ministry of Energy of Georgia, Tbilisi. www.energy.gov.ge/show%20news%20mediacenter.php?id=633&lang=eng.

Ministry of Energy (2014), *Projected Gas Balance 2015,* Ministry of Energy of Georgia, Tbilisi.

Ministry of Energy (2007), *Order of the Minister of Energy No. 69 of 25 September 2007 on Natural Gas Supply Activities,* Ministry of Energy of Georgia, Tbilisi. (საქართველოს_ენერგეტიკის_მინისტრის_ბრძანება №69, 2007 წლის 25 სექტემბერი. ბუნებრივი გაზის მიწოდების საქმიანობის დერეგულირებისა და ნაწილობრივი დერეგულირების შესახებ). https://matsne.gov.ge/ka/document/view/73006.

Ministry of Energy (n.d.), *Natural Gas Balance,* Ministry of Energy of Georgia, Tbilisi. www.energy.gov.ge/legislation.php?lang=eng&id_pages=75.

Ministry of Finance of Georgia (2014), Tbilisi. www.mof.ge/4596.

Municipality of Tbilisi (2014), *Budget Document*, Municipality of Tbilisi.

National Bank of Georgia (n.d.), Tbilisi. https://www.nbg.gov.ge/index.php?m=2.

President of Georgia (2014), *Law No. 2 159 of 21 March 2014 "On Competition"*, President of Georgia, Tbilisi. https://matsne.gov.ge/ka/document/download/1659450/4/en/pdf.

President of Georgia (2010), *Law of Georgia No. 3591– II S of 17 September 2010 on Tax Code of Georgia,* President of Georgia, Tbilisi.

President of Georgia (2001), *Law of Georgia No. 1 892 – IIs of 2 March 2001 on Oil and Gas (with Additions and Amendments),* President of Georgia, Tbilisi. https://matsne.gov.ge/ru/document/download/18424/22/en/pdf.

President of Georgia (1999), *Law of Georgia No. 1 934 of 30 April 1999 on Electricity and Natural Gas (with Additions and Amendments)*, President of Georgia, Tbilisi. https://matsne.gov.ge/en/document/download/31744/29/en/pdf.

Rzayeva, G. (2015), *The Outlook for Azerbaijani Gas Supplies to Europe: Challenges and Perspectives*, Oxford Energy Institute. https://www.oxfordenergy.org/wpcms/wp-content/uploads/2015/06/NG-97.pdf.

Sakrusenergo (2015), *Sakrusenergo JSC United Energy System,* Tbilisi. http://sakrusenergo.ge/new/index.php?action_skin_change=yes&skin_name=english.

SGGAS (2015), *SOCAR Georgia Gas,* Tbilisi. http://sggas.ge.

Shelia, R. (2015), "What will higher gas tariffs bring us?" 12 February, *Georgian Journal*, Tbilisi. https://www.georgianjournal.ge/business/29634-what-will-higher-gas-tariffs-bring-us.html.

Telasi (2015), *About Telasi*, Joint-Stock Company Telasi, Tbilisi. www.telasi.ge/en.

Transparency International Georgia (2015), "Negotiations with Gazprom raise questions", Transparency International Georgia, Tbilisi. www.transparency.ge/en/node/5664.

WEG (2012), *Competition and Monopoly in Internal Energy Markets,* World Experience for Georgia, Tbilisi.

World Bank (2015a), *Country Overview Georgia*, World Bank, Tbilisi. www.worldbank.org/en/country/georgia/overview.

World Bank (2015b), *Ease of Doing Business Index*, World Bank, Washington, DC. www.doingbusiness.org/rankings.

World Bank (2015c), *World Development Indicators*, World Bank, Washington, DC. http://data.worldbank.org/country/georgia.

World Bank (2013), *Balancing Act: Cutting Energy Subsidies while Protecting Affordability*, World Bank, Washington, DC. https://openknowledge.worldbank.org/bitstream/handle/10986/12296/9780821397893.pdf?sequence=7.

Chapter 6

Republic of Moldova's energy subsidies

This chapter identifies, documents and provides estimates of the various subsidies in Moldova that relate to the production or use of coal, oil and related petroleum products, natural gas, and electricity and heat generated on the basis of these fossil fuels. The chapter also briefly looks at the subsidies benefiting energy-efficiency measures and renewable energy sources. An overview of the country's energy sector is first given to place the measures listed into context. In addition, the chapter discusses pricing and tax policies in the energy sector in Moldova. The analysis summarises the context, the state of play, and the mechanics of the complex and evolving landscape of energy subsidies in the country.

Key findings

The Republic of Moldova, which has few fossil-fuel resources, is totally dependent on imported energy. In fact, Moldova imports around 90% of its energy needs. The cost of energy imports amounted to about USD 1.3 bln, equivalent to 18.1% of GDP, or 23.9% of total imports in 2014.

Being a net energy importer largely determines the structure of Moldova's energy subsidies. Most government support goes to consumers. The only support scheme designed to support energy producers is related to the "green" (feed-in) tariff introduced in 2013.

Analysis of energy subsidies shows that Moldova has eliminated direct consumer subsidies and does not pursue a pro-subsidy policy. Total government support for consumption of fossil fuels (natural gas, electricity, heat, petroleum products) from 2011 to 2015 amounted to about USD 0.7 bln. Unlike in the other European Union Eastern Partnership (EaP) countries, most government support in Moldova in the energy sector is the result of reduced taxes and tax exemptions. In 2015 only, mostly due to reduced taxation, the state budget failed to collect an estimated USD 48.2 mln, or 0.7% of GDP.

Moldova provides subsidies through different channels. In addition to tax exemptions and tax rate reductions, the Moldovan government supports consumers by making direct transfers to disadvantaged people and by keeping energy utility prices below cost-recovery levels. The government assumes the risk of covering losses of indebted energy companies.

The largest government support scheme, which accounts for most of the fossil-fuel consumer subsidies (60%) in Moldova, is a reduced VAT rate on natural gas, electricity and heat consumption for domestic users. The estimated revenue foregone for the government as a result of the reduced VAT rate in 2015 was USD 41 mln.

Like other EaP countries, energy subsidy reform in Moldova is discussed in the context of energy utility tariffs and energy sector reforms more broadly. The National Energy Regulatory Agency regulates energy utility tariffs for gas, electricity and heat. While gas and electricity tariffs were increased significantly in July 2015 (by 37% for electricity and 15.4% for gas) they still remain below cost-recovery levels. Tariffs were basically frozen for several years, which led to rising intercompany payment arrears, debts and losses for energy companies in the country. Accumulated losses of utility companies were estimated to be around MDL 2 bln in 2014. Regulated prices for end users limit the opportunities that energy companies in Moldova have to recover their costs through adequately set tariffs. Subsidies for gas consumption that resulted from tariffs set below cost-recovery levels in 2015 amounted to USD 7 mln.

Government support for energy efficiency and renewable energy producers is fragmented and inconsistent. As a result, the government relies on donor funds to finance investments. Over the period 2010-15, the government of Moldova, supported by donors and international finance instutitions (IFIs), is estimated to have spent about USD 107 mln on energy efficiency and renewable energy. This is far from sufficient to cover urgent investment needs in energy infrastructure and clean energy.

Governments that have taken up the challenge of launching energy subsidy reforms know it is not an easy task. Such reforms require additional research and their social cost needs to be carefully assessed.

As a follow-up to this inventory, the Moldovan government requested that the OECD analyse the impact of reforming the two largest government support schemes, the reduced VAT rate on natural gas consumption and the VAT exemption on electricity and heat consumption by domestic users. Reforming these subsidy schemes means increasing VAT rates to the standard 20%. In turn, this implies higher prices for gas, electricity and heat for Moldovan households, a major concern for the government. Without proper policy measures to support the poor, such a reform may be socially difficult to undertake. The OECD study analyses five different protection measures (five scenarios) and estimates their costs for the national budget.

Moldovan authorities are fully aware of these challenges and of the need to rationalise the spending on energy subsidies. At the last COP21, held in Paris in 2015, Moldova signed the Communiqué of the Friends of Fossil Fuel Subsidy Reform, calling for accelerated action to eliminate inefficient fossil fuel subsidies in a transparent and efficient manner, as part of a major contribution to climate change mitigation. Such politically important commitments need to be translated into practical measures. Reforming energy subsidies can help reduce Moldova's energy consumption and energy dependence, making it more energy efficient and competitive, increasing fiscal space in the state budget and improving the country's environment.

Macroeconomic situation and energy sector overview

Moldova has a population of 3.6 mln, with a GDP of USD 7.96 bln (in 2014).[1] After the disintegration of the Soviet Union in the early 1990s, its economy suffered significant economic losses, and GDP fell at an average rate of 9.4% between 1990 and 1999. In 2000, Moldova began to recoup some of these losses and real economic growth averaged about 4.6% per year. However, growth was volatile, due to the global financial crisis in 2009 and climatic conditions (drought) in 2012. In 2015, GDP declined by 0.5% as a result of vicissitudes in the banking sector, with strong repercussions on the national economy, and a reduction in the demand for domestic products on traditional markets. The GDP per capita at purchasing power parity remains among the lowest in Europe, at USD 4 743 in 2014 (World Bank, 2016).

Table 6.1. **Moldova's macroeconomic indicators**

Key indicators	Year and unit	International statistics[a]	National statistics
Population	*2014, mln*	3.6	3.557634
GDP	*2014, USD bln*	7.96	7.98
GDP per capita	*2014, USD*	2 239	2 243
Energy production	*2014, mtoe*	0.33	0.303
Net imports	*2014, mtoe*	2.99	1.8
Total primary energy supply (TPES)	*2014, mtoe*	3.3	2.31
TPES per capita	*2014, toe*	0.93	0.6493
Electricity consumption	*2014, TWh*	4.93	4.256
Electricity consumption per capita	*2014, MWh*	1.39	1.196
CO_2 emissions	*2014, Mt of CO_2*	7.25	.
CO_2 emissions	*2010, Mt of CO_2*		13.276
CO_2 emissions per capita	*2014, t of CO_2*	2.04	.

Notes: **n.a.**: not available.

a. International statistics include Transnistria, but national statistics do not.

Source: IEA (2016), World Bank (2016), NBS (2015).

Moldova's GDP is heavily dependent on services (68.4% of GDP), including transport and financial services (especially related to expatriate remittances). Agriculture and industry contribute a limited share to the national economy, 14.9% and 16.7% of GDP, respectively. Remittances are a key source of national GDP and have sustained private consumption and overall economic growth since 2000. Remittances expanded from 11.5% of GDP in 2000 to 30% in 2008. Although they collapsed in 2009, they started rising again, reaching 26.2% of GDP in 2015. The drop in remittances was offset by an improvement in the trade balance, mostly due to lower energy (gas import) prices (IMF, 2016).

Table 6.2. **Weighted average exchange rate**

	2011	2012	2013	2014	2015
Weighted average exchange rate USD/MDL	11.74	12.11	12.59	14.04	18.82
Weighted average exchange rate EUR/MDL	16.34	15.56	16.72	18.63	20.90

Source: National Bank of Moldova (2016).

In 2014, Moldova signed the Association Agreement with a view to the political association and economic integration of Moldova with the European Union (EU). European integration policy anchors the government's reform agenda, but political tensions and weak governance have put these reforms at risk.

With few fossil-fuel resources, Moldova depends on imported energy, importing 90% of its energy. In 2014, its energy imports were about USD 1.3 bln, equivalent to 18.1% of GDP, or 23.9% of total imports.

Energy supply

The total primary energy supply (TPES) in Moldova (excluding Transnistria) in 2014 was 2.3 mln tonnes of oil equivalent (mtoe). Imported natural gas and petroleum products dominate the energy balance (36.5% and 35%, respectively, of total primary energy supply); electricity and biofuels account for about 12%-13%.

Figure 6.1. **TPES, ktoe, 1990-2014**

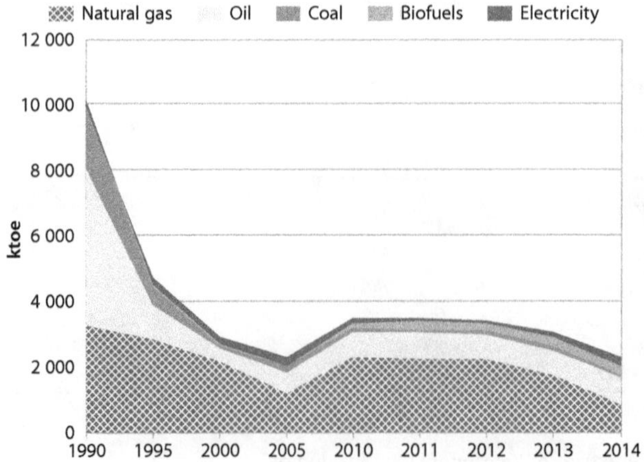

Figure 6.2. **TPES structure by fuel type, 2014**

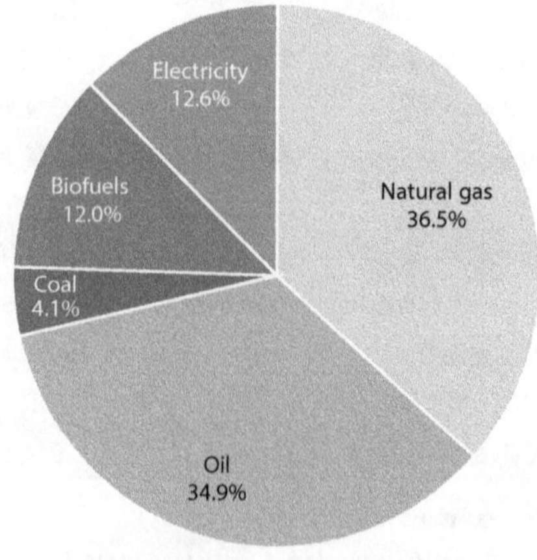

Source: NBS (2015).

Natural gas is exclusively imported from the Russian Federation (via Ukraine until the end of 2014) and is the main fuel for electricity generation and district heating (about 43% of the country's total gas consumption excluding Transnistria (World Bank, 2015a). The annual volume of gas imported is about 2 bln m^3. According to the National Energy Regulatory Agency (ANRE), 53.3% of settlements are linked to the central gas supply network. In towns, the gas network covers about 99% of households. In 2015, the average tariff for gas purchased from the Russian concern Gazprom was USD 256 per 1 000 m^3, 32.1% less than in 2014.

Moldova's government is making efforts to diversify the country's energy supply sources. The Ungheni-Iasi gas interconnector between Romania and Moldova was commissioned in 2014 and has been operational since 2015, when 1 mln m^3 was imported from OMV Petrom (Nutu and Cenusa, 2016). Once at full capacity, the pipeline is expected to supply a third of Moldova's gas.

Electricity generation in Moldova is basically gas-fired, and in 2015, stood at about 995 mln kWh. Electricity is generated by three Combined Heat and Power (CHP) Plants: CHP1, CHP2 and CHP North, all natural-gas fired. The three CHPs cover 91%-95% of the electricity generation in Moldova. The rest is provided by a hydro plant in Costesti.

Figure 6.3. **Electricity generation and import, million kWh, 1997-2013**

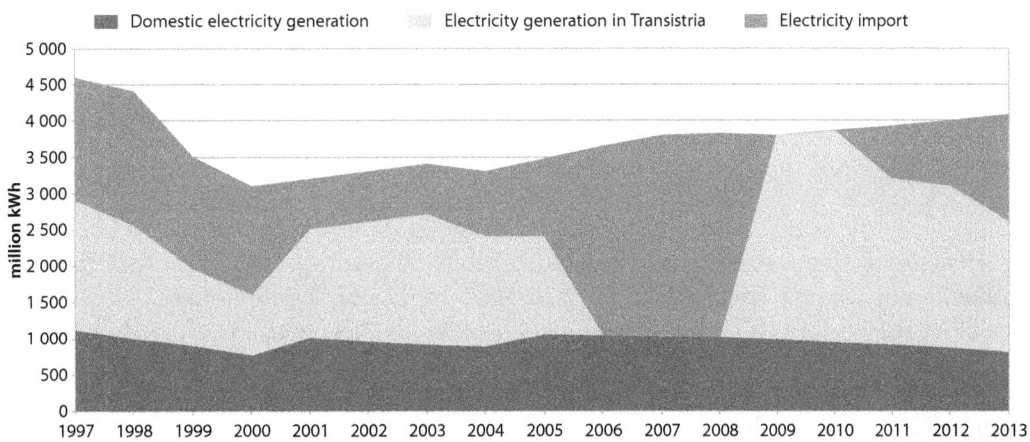

Source: World Bank (2015a).

Figure 6.4. **Structure of electricity generation and import in 2013**

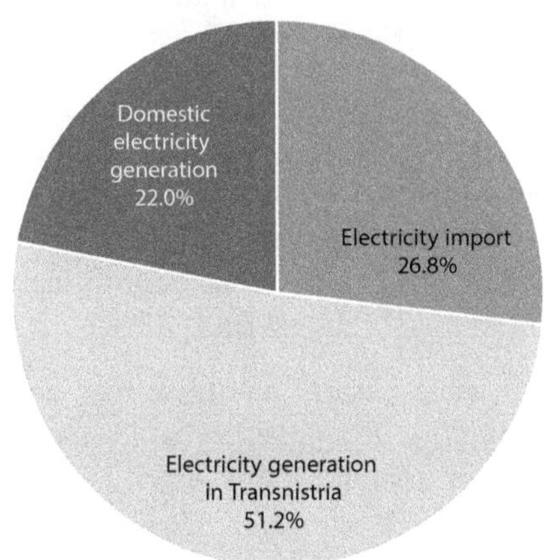

Source: World Bank (2015a).

Moldova's most important power plant (Moldova GRES) is located in Transnistria. Its installed capacity constitutes about 90% of the country's total generating capacity. Due to difficult relations with Transnistria and the deterioration of generating capacities, Moldova imports electricity from Ukraine and Romania. Domestic electricity generation (excluding Transnistria) covers less than 23% of domestic demand and was 3.7 mln kWh in 2015. The prices for imported electricity are lower than electricity produced domestically.

Figure 6.5. **Electricity production in Moldova, 2001-15, million kWh**

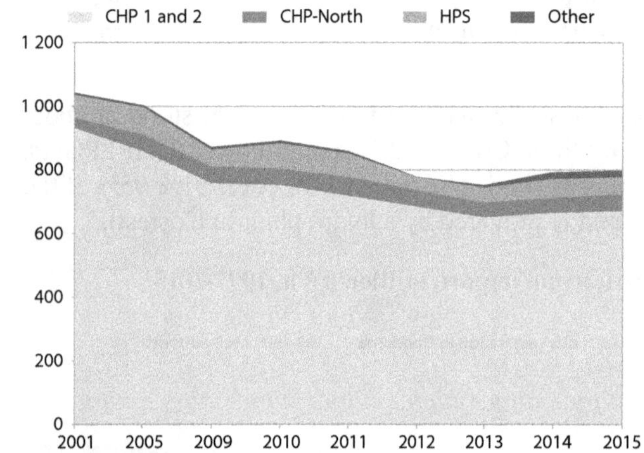

Figure 6.6. **Structure of electricity generation in Moldova in 2015**

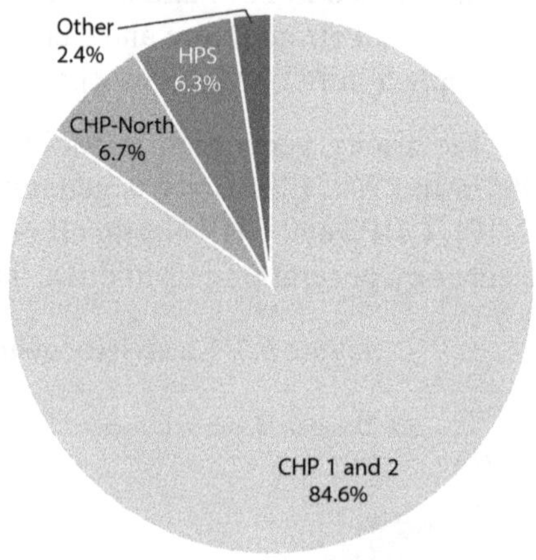

Source: ANRE (2016).

Heat production is mainly gas-fired, using heavy oil (*mazut*) as a reserve fuel. In 2015, production (excluding Transnistria) reached 1.875 mln Gcal, less than half 1990s levels. The chief reason for this drop is the decline in industrial heat consumption. Most heat is produced and consumed in urban areas, where there are 12 operating district heating (DH) systems. The largest DH systems are operated in the two main cities: Chisinau (CHP1, CHP2) and Balti (CHP North).

The district heating sector faces a number of significant challenges in Moldova. These include issues related to the low efficiency of the system, disconnection of customers, and non-payment of bills. One significant challenge is the accumulated debt in the sector, especially by the distribution company in Chisinau. These debts accumulated due to the increase in gas prices, as well as tariffs set below cost-recovery levels.

Moldova's oil reserves are low and located in the southern Cahul and Cantemir districts. The Cahul reserve is in operation, but the Cantemir reserves have not yet been exploited. To satisfy demand, Moldova imports oil products from Romania, Belarus and the Russian Federation. Imports have fallen sharply since 1991, from 2.9 mln tonnes (mt) to about 0.7 mt in 2015, including 1.607 mln tonnes of gasoline; 743 000 tonnes of liquefied petroleum gas; and 4.876 mln tonnes of diesel fuel (ANRE, 2016).

Moldova has also some modest natural gas resources concentrated in the village of Victorovca, in the Cantemir region. These reserves are estimated at about 346 mln m^3 (UNDP, 2009), but possibilities of exploiting this deposit are limited (UNDP, 2002).

Energy demand

Total final energy consumption (TFEC) in Moldova (excluding Transnistria) was 2.3 mtoe in 2014, almost 10% lower than in 2005. The residential sector is the largest consumer (41.5% of TFEC in 2014), while in other sectors, consumption was 13.8% for industry, 29.7% for transport and 15% for the commercial/services sector. The residential and commercial sectors mainly consume natural gas, electricity and oil. The transport sector is reliant on oil and some electricity, while TFEC in industry is mostly natural gas and electricity (ANRE, 2016).

Figure 6.7. **Total final energy consumption, ktoe**

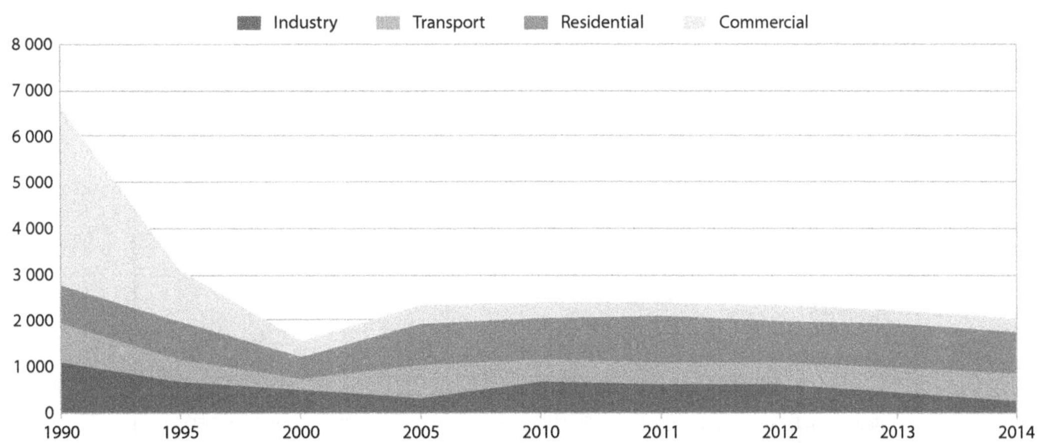

Source: NBS (2015).

Energy sector structure, ownership and governance

The current energy sector structure features partial unbundling and privatisation. Moldova separated generation from the transmission and distribution systems for both natural gas and electricity. The electricity distribution system is privatised, while generation and transition remain under state ownership.

Moldova's energy sector is overseen by the Ministry of Economy and the Ministry of Environment. While the gas and power (electricity) markets are partially unbundled, they are subject to regulation by the National Energy Regulatory Agency (ANRE). The supply of oil, petroleum fuels and coal is deregulated (OECD/IEA, 2015).

In the electricity sector, the transmission system operator (TSO) and distribution system operators (DSOs) are legally unbundled. DSOs also acted as retailers of last resort. MoldElectrica is the state-owned TSO and also the central dispatcher for the Transnistria region. There are three DSOs on the right bank of the Dniester River (Moldovan territory), including RED Nord (state-owned), RED Nord-Vest (state-owned) and RED Union Fenosa, privately owned and covering two-thirds of the country. As of 1 January 2015, the DSOs unbundled the distribution activity from the universal service supply and supply of last resort. Currently, in Moldova, universal service supply is provided by two entities: Gas Natural Fenosa Furnizare Energie and Furnizarea Energiei Electrice Nord. Electricity distribution in the Transnistria region is carried out by two DSOs, RED Est and RED Sud-Est, both of which operate under the Transnistrian authorities. There are six electricity generation operators in Moldova, four on the right bank of the Dniester River and two in the Transnistria region. Figure 6.8 schematically shows the electricity market in Moldova.

The power generation market in Moldova is not regulated, except with regard to the three Combined Heat and Power Plants (CHP) and the hydro plant. The Power Market Rules limit regulated electricity generation to four sources, all owned by the state. The main electricity generators include: CHP-1 (66 MW), CHP-2 (240 MW), both located in Chisinau, CHP North (20.4 MW) and the Costesti hydro plant (16 MW). Electricity production in 2015 generally declined compared to the early 2000s (by about 25%), particularly in Chisinau. This is closely related to the increase in gas prices.

Figure 6.8. **Structure of the energy sector in Moldova**

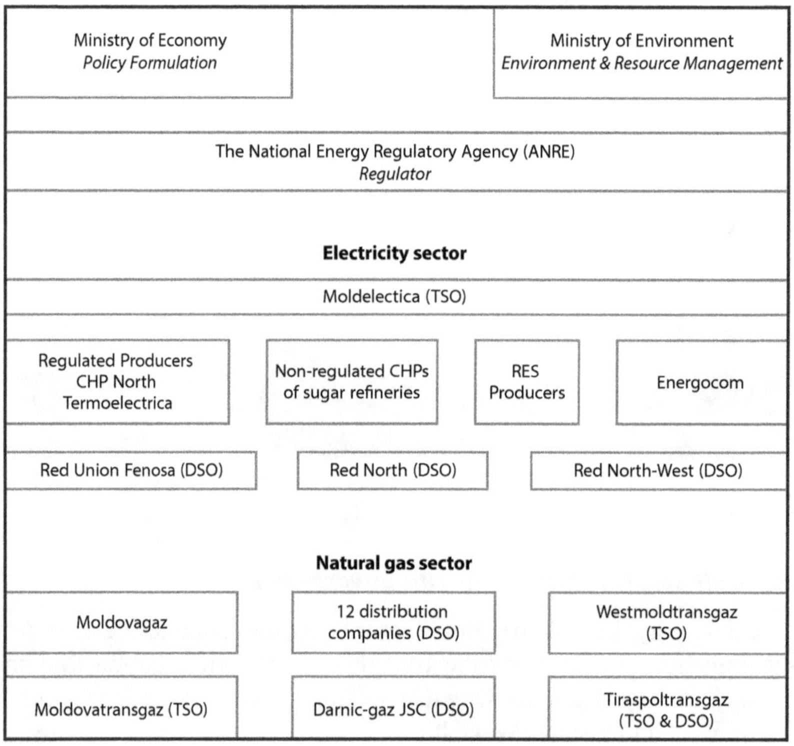

Source: Energy Community (2015).

Moldova's electricity system is interconnected with Ukraine's, and the two systems operate in parallel. Energocom is a state-owned company and acts as a single buyer at nonregulated prices for imported electricity from Ukraine as well as from Transnistria. Energocom sells to RED Nord and RED Nord-Vest, or directly to eligible customers (Ener2i, 2014).

Moldova's heat supply and district heating companies are being restructured. This includes the merger of the two operators of combined heat and power plants CHP-1 and CHP-2, with Termocom, the state-owned company that owns and operates the district heating network in Chisinau.

In the natural gas sector, the vertically integrated Moldovagaz, which is owned by Gazprom (50%), the Moldovan government (36.6%) and the Transnistria administration (13.4%), performs the majority of the functions, including transmission, distribution and retail. The company is legally unbundled, while the DSO Westmoldtransgaz is a state-owned company that has been operating Moldova's section of the new Ungheni-Iasi gas

Figure 6.9. **Electricity market scheme for Moldova**

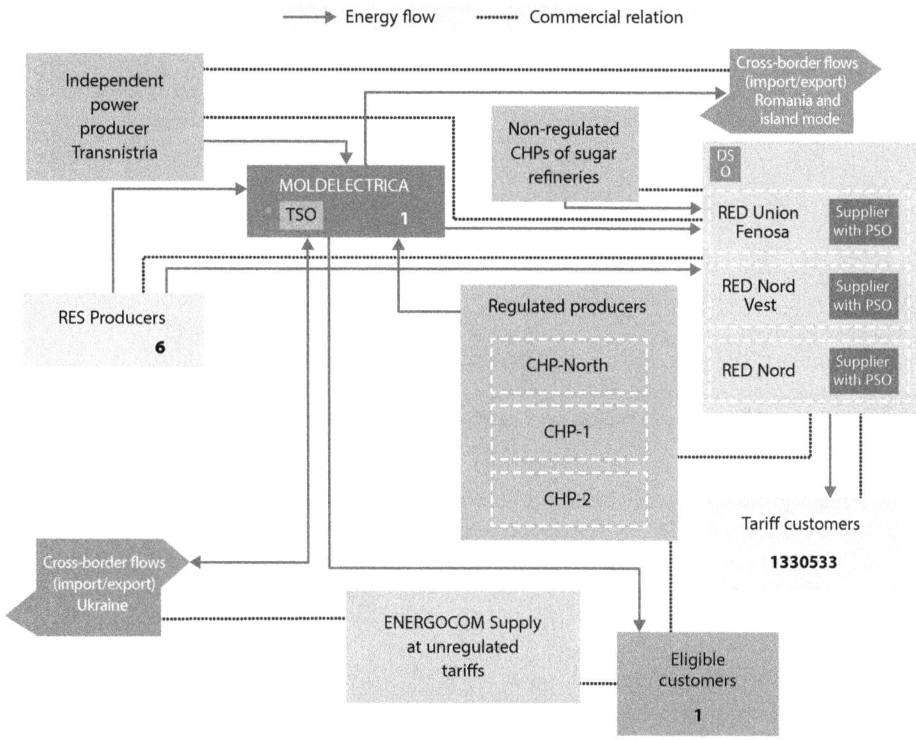

Note: PSO, as in "Supplier with PSO", stands for Public Service Obligation. This means that the company may be private, but has some additional social obligations. For example, it is subject to certain restrictions on cutting supply to customers in case of non-payment of bills by customers.

Source: Energy Community (2015).

Figure 6.10. **Natural gas market scheme for Moldova**

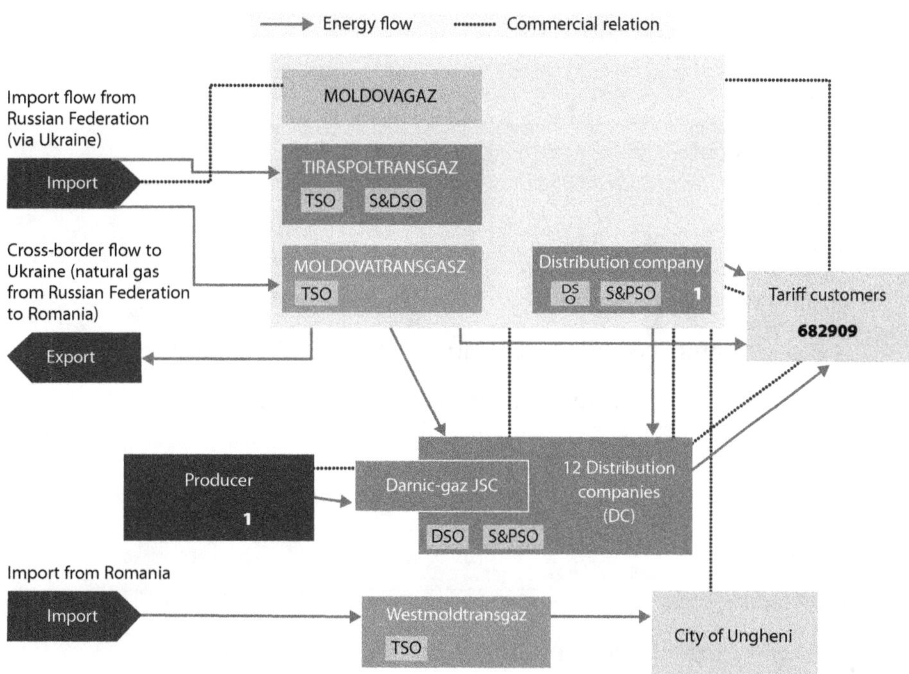

Source: Energy Community (2015).

interconnector pipeline since 2015. The main gas DSOs in Moldova are 12 of Moldovagaz's subsidiaries, and 11 other, smaller, DSOs, which cover less than 2% of gas distribution. Tiraspoltransgaz, also a subsidiary of MoldovaGaz, is the TSO, DSO and retailer in the region of Transnistria.

Box 6.1. **MoldovaGaz's debt to Gazprom**

MoldovaGaz operates as a subsidiary of the Russian Company Gazprom. Gazprom supplies natural gas to Moldova and Transnistria, which is delivered to both by MoldovaGaz. Transnistria's contract is with MoldovaGaz, not Gazprom. However, for more than 26 years, Tiraspol-Transgaz (the Transnistrian gas supplier) has failed to pay MoldovaGaz for the gas supplied. Tiraspol-Transgaz resells the gas to local Transnistrian households and enterprises at low prices, including to the Moldovskaya GRES power plant (which has been owned, since 2005, by the Russian Inter RAO UES energy holding company).

Transnistria's debt amounts to 89% of the whole of Moldova's debt to Gazprom, which in 2016 amounted to about USD 5.8 bln, a figure that approaches that of Moldova's GDP in 2016, USD 6.65 bln. MoldovaGaz's debt to Gazprom is a major energy security issue for Moldova, and the Moldovan government is discussing with the Russian Federation, hoping that it will approve a proposal to restructure its historic debt to Gazprom.

Source: Sputnik International (2016); Tulyev, M. (2017).

Energy pricing policy

ANRE regulates and approves electricity, gas and heat tariffs in Moldova. Tariff methodologies vary across the distribution system operators (DSOs). Due to sector unbundling, ANRE regulates tariffs for the energy sector, including the following (ANRE, 2015):

- Natural gas tariffs for:
  - supply
  - transmission
  - distribution
  - end users
- Electricity tariffs for:
  - electricity produced by co-generation (combined heat and power) plants
  - electricity generated from renewable energy sources
  - transmission
  - distribution
  - end users
- Heating tariffs for:
  - heat energy produced at power plants
  - tariffs for public services for heat supply through district heating systems.

Tariffs are based on specific technical characteristics of each distribution company and the number of customers per kilometre of line. One exception is Energocom, a state-owned monopoly for electricity imports, which supplies electricity directly to free-market consumers at unregulated prices.

Companies submit to ANRE their annual tariff calculations for the next year, based on a methodology approved by ANRE. Tariff calculations include planned operational costs and capital investments for new lines, as well as for modernisation, rehabilitation and loss reduction. ANRE then reviews the tariff proposal, approves it or makes recommendations for adjustment.

Tariffs and methodologies are transparent and are published in the Official Monitor. ANRE organises public hearings before tariff approvals to ensure transparency of the approval process.

Regulated electricity tariffs include the costs of metering and investments in the SCADA (Supervisory Control and Data Acquisition) system, which has been completed in the electricity sector. Individual meters have been installed for all end users.

Natural gas and district heating

Due to the unbundling of the sector, the end-consumer price is not the only one regulated by ANRE. ANRE also regulates intermediate categories for each company, such as import price, transport to entry point of the distribution network, sale to the distribution network and end-user price for different categories of consumers.

After the drop in world prices, the gas import price, set through bilateral negotiations, was reduced in 2015 from USD 377 per 1 000 m^3 in 2014 to USD 256 per 1 000 m^3 in 2015. The price for transport to the entry point of the distribution network was set at USD 17 per 1 000 m^3 in 2015, and the price of gas sold to distribution networks at USD 54 per 1 000 m^3.

End-user prices for residential consumers are differentiated by consumption level (lower than 30 m^3/month and above) and ranged between USD 348 per 1 000 m^3 (for consumption below 30 m^3/month) and USD 363 per 1 000 m^3 (for consumption above 30 m^3/month) in 2015.

Tariffs for other end users (industry, service sector, budgetary organisations) vary on the basis of the level of pressure at which gas is delivered to them: high, medium or low. In 2015, tariffs for these customers were respectively set at USD 327 (high), USD 341 (medium) and USD 363 (low) per 1 000 m^3.

The highest tariffs for gas are paid by residential users who consume more than 30 m^3/month and other users who consume gas delivered at low pressure. In 2015, this tariff was the same for both categories, set at USD 363 per 1 000 m^3. The three co-generators (CHP plants) and individual District Heating plants benefit from the lowest tariffs, paying USD 304 per 1 000 m^3 of gas delivered to them in 2015. These companies pay lower tariffs because they are Moldova's largest consumers, and as such, have lower distribution costs.

In the gas sector, all industrial and commercial customers are metered, and 93% of households have individual meters. The rest have a common meter for multi-residential properties. Moldovagaz is progressively switching all consumers to individual meters.

In 2012, ANRE approved a new methodology for district heating tariffs, to attract investment to the sector. Moldova's district heating network is considered to be highly inefficient, and significant funding is needed to rehabilitate and modernise the existing systems, as well as for new development. Under the new Law on Heat and Cogeneration (Law No. 92, 2014), ANRE is required to issue licences and set tariffs for new entrants in the district heating sector. Tariffs include weighted average cost of capital (WACC) calculations as a mechanism to encourage investment.

Electricity

Electricity prices are differentiated by generation, transmission, distribution and consumption. Each of the four power generators (three co-generators and one hydro) gets an individual tariff approved by ANRE. Tariffs for co-generators range from USD 0.011 per kWh to USD 0.088 per kWh. CHP1 in Chisinau gets the highest tariff (USD 0.088 per kWh) and the Costesti Hydropower Plant gets the lowest (USD 0.011 per kWh), due to its relatively low operation and maintenance costs.

Both transmission and distribution tariffs are differentiated by operator and voltage levels. The average transmission tariff in 2015 stood at USD 0.008 per kWh. Depending on the distribution company and the voltage at which electricity is delivered, tariffs for electricity distribution range from USD 0.008 per kWh to USD 0.044 per kWh. RED Union Fenosa offers competitive prices in Moldova's electricity market.

Tariffs for electricity consumption are also differentiated by operator and consumption levels. All consumers with low voltage pay the same price. Higher voltage is for industrial consumers. Tariffs range from USD 0.089 per kWh to USD 0.124 per kWh.

On average, electricity tariffs in Moldova are the highest in the EaP region and comparable to or higher than the tariffs of southeastern European countries such as Kosovo, Serbia, Albania or Macedonia. According to Eurostat, electricity prices for households in 2015 in Moldova were EUR 0.088 per kWh (or USD 0.098 per kWh). In Kosovo, rates were EUR 0.061 per kWh (USD 0.068 per kWh), in Serbia EUR 0.065 per kWh (USD 0.072 per kWh), in Albania EUR 0.082 per kWh (USD 0.091 per kWh) and in Macedonia EUR 0.084 per kWh (USD 0.093 per kWh).

Petroleum products

Petroleum product prices (gasoline, diesel, liquefied petroleum gas (LPG) (as well as coal prices) are deregulated in Moldova. In 2015, gasoline, diesel and LPG average prices were USD 0.918, 0.810 and 0.507 per litre, respectively (ANRE, 2015).

According to amendments to the Law on the Petroleum Products Market (Law No. 460, 2001) passed in 2015, ANRE is required to apply a new methodology for petroleum product prices based on international quotations (using Platts and Argus price quotations). The new regulation prohibits commercialisation of petroleum products at a price that exceeds the price ceiling set and published by ANRE.

Table 6.3 provides a summary of the pricing policies in Moldova for natural gas, electricity, (liquid) petroleum products and coal. It contains basic information on tariff-setting/pricing policy for different price categories.

Table 6.3. **Price policies for different energy carriers in Moldova, 2015**

Energy carrier	Price category		Pricing policy	Price levels, MDL	Price levels, USD
Natural gas	Import price		Bilateral negotiations		Average: USD 256 per 1 000 m³ (2015), USD 377 per 1 000 m³ (2014)
	Transport to entry point of distribution network		Regulated, "cost-plus" methodology	MDL 324.75 per 1 000 m³	USD 17 per 1 000 m³
	Sales to distribution networks			MDL 1 010.22 per 1 000 m³	USD 54 per 1 000 m³
	End-user price	Residential sector, differentiated by consumption (lower for those who use less than 30 m³/month)		MDL 6 556 per 1 000 m³ (<30m³) MDL 6 830 per 1 000 m³ (>30m³)	USD 348 per 1 000 m³ (<30m³) USD 363 per 1 000 m³ (>30m³)
		Combined heat and power (CHP) and district heating (DH) plants		MDL 5 712 per 1 000 m³	USD 304 per 1 000 m³
		Other consumers differentiated by high, medium and low pressure		MDL 6 157 per 1 000 m³ (H) MDL 6 418 per 1 000 m³ (M) MDL 6 830 per 1 000 m³ (L)	327 USD per1 000 m³ (H) USD 341 per 1 000 m³ (M) USD 363 per 1 000 m³ (L)
Electricity	CHP generation		Regulated, "cost-plus" methodology	CHP1 – MDL 1.6614 per kWh	CHP1 – 0.088 USD per kWh
				CHP2 – MDL 1.5863 per kWh	USD CHP2 – 0.084 per kWh
				CHP Nord – MDL 1.3711 per kWh	USD CHP Nord – 0.073 per kWh
	HPP generation			HPP Costesti – MDL 0.2064 per kWh	USD HPP Costesti – 0.011 per kWh
	Transmission		Regulated, differentiated by operator and voltage, "cost plus" methodology	MDL 0.145 per kWh (average)	USD 0.008 per kWh (average)
	Distribution: 35-110, 6-10 and 0.4 kV		Regulated, differentiated by voltage and operator, "cost-plus" methodology	RED UF: MDL 0.15, 0.42, 0.63 per kWh	USD RED UF: 0.008, 0.022, 0.033 per kWh
				RED Nord: MDL 0.50 (6-10), 0.61 (0.4) per kWh	USD RED Nord: 0.027 (6-10), 0.032 (0.4) per kWh
				RED Nord Vest: MDL 0.56 (6-10), 0.82 (0.4) per kWh	USD RED Nord Vest: 0.030 (6-10), 0.044 (0.4) per kWh
	Consumption		Regulated, differentiated by operator and consumption level, "cost-plus" methodology	MDL 1.68-2.33 per kWh	USD 0.089-0.124 per kWh
Liquid petroleum products	Gasoline		Deregulated	Average: MDL 17.28 per litre	Average: USD 0.918 per litre
	Diesel			MDL 15.24 per litre	USD 0.810 per litre
	LPG			MDL 9.54 per litre	USD 0.507 per litre
Coal			Deregulated	.	

Note: All prices as of end of 2015, unless otherwise indicated. Prices are exclusive of VAT.

Source: ANRE (2015).

The tariff-setting methodology for heating and electricity has been analysed by the World Bank (World Bank, 2015a). While the general conclusion is that tariff regulation is mainly well-defined and based on global good practices, several shortcomings were noted. The financial status of the energy sector is not robust, and in 2013-14, all companies generated losses after a significant cost increase, as a result of the latest tariff approval. Only Union Fenosa increased its receivables. The general conclusion of the report is that ANRE did not ensure tariffs set at cost-recovery levels in 2012-14, and that losses had accumulated as a result. Based on a scenario analysis, the report estimates that the increase in electricity tariffs by 2020 will be 73%-113%, and the heat tariff 30%-78%. The analysis also assumes a 50% increase in gas tariff by 2020.

The most important shortcomings in tariff-setting noted in the World Bank report are:

- No rate of return is established in the methodology for electricity supply,[2] and no detailed definition is given for heat and electricity generation. WACC (weighted average cost of capital) and asset valuation need to be determined based on a clearer and more consistent method. This flaw in the methodology limits operators' investment, because they need to account for the risk that these investments may not be profitable and may not even cover the costs of capital. Also, there is a need to set asset value based on economic and not on accounting value, which in the case of old assets has a significant effect on the capacity of the operator to replace assets.
- The timeline of tariff setting has not been defined clearly in the methodology, and certain terms lack detailed clarifications.

Figure 6.11. **Electricity and heat tariffs based on specific regulations**

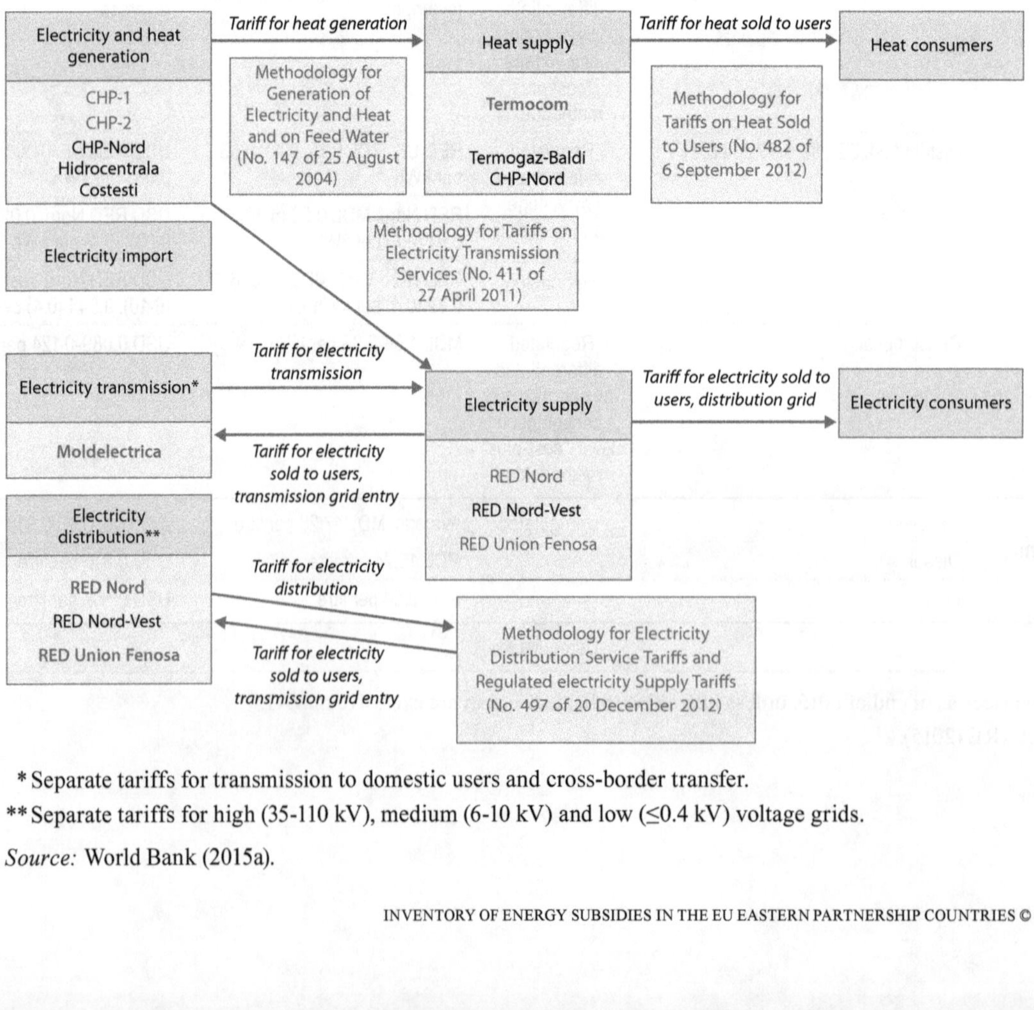

* Separate tariffs for transmission to domestic users and cross-border transfer.

** Separate tariffs for high (35-110 kV), medium (6-10 kV) and low (≤0.4 kV) voltage grids.

Source: World Bank (2015a).

Without a defined tariff-setting timeline, ANRE was unable to adjust tariffs for several years. Due to fluctuations in operating costs, especially related to the costs of natural gas and exchange rates, this had an adverse effect on cost recovery. For gas, tariffs were not adjusted between 2011 and 2015, and for electricity, over a period of three years, 2012-15, tariffs were not adjusted. To address mounting debts and losses in the energy sector, ANRE only recently (at the end of 2015) increased electricity and gas tariffs. According to ANRE, however, the tariffs approved in 2015 cover all the current costs of the energy providers (including return on investment). The only elements tariffs did not include were the losses supported by the companies in the period prior to tariff approval. These losses will be returned to the energy companies in the 2017-20 period (according to ANRE Decision No. 201/2016 of 15 July 2016).

Taxation policy

Moldova's taxation system includes 6 general state taxes (value added tax, or VAT, excise tax, corporate income tax, personal income tax, custom tax and road tax) and 14 local taxes (property tax, land tax, natural resources taxes, etc.). Energy production is not subject to any specific taxation beyond the taxes levied on commercial activities.

Consumption of gasoline and diesel, as well as liquefied petroleum gas (LPG), is subject to excise tax. Natural gas, compressed natural gas, electricity and heat production are not subject to excise tax. The Moldova Tax Code (Law No. 1 163 XIII, 1997) sets a reduced VAT (8%) for the delivery of natural gas and LPG, and no (0%) VAT for the delivery of electricity and heat to households where the standard VAT rate is set at 20%.

Table 6.4. **Taxation of energy in Moldova**

Baseline tax system	**VAT, profit tax, private tax, property tax, land tax**		
Specific taxes	**Excise tax**		
Energy sector taxation	**Upstream**	**Midstream**	**Downstream**
Natural gas	n.a.	No specific taxes	Natural gas not subject to excise tax Compressed natural gas subject to excise tax
Electricity	No specific taxes	No specific taxes	No specific taxes
Liquid petroleum products	n.a.	n.a.	Excise tax for gasoline, diesel, crude oil and other petroleum products, diesel fuel, petroleum gases and other gaseous hydrocarbons, with the exception of natural gas Gasoline (petrol): MDL 3 714 per 1 000 l (2015), USD 197.38 per 1 000 l Diesel: MDL 1 544 per 1 000 l (2015), USD 82 per 1 000 l
Coal	No specific taxes	No specific taxes	No specific taxes

Note: **n.a.**: not applicable.

Source: Tax Code (1997).

Greenhouse gas emissions and climate policy

Moldova's main environmental problems are soil degradation, surface water pollution, lack of sustainable waste management (both solid and liquid), and increased groundwater pollution due to poor manure management in rural communities. Moldova has made significant progress in protecting the environment, but it remains vulnerable to changes in climate.

Moldova's economy is both energy- and carbon-intensive. In 2013, its energy intensity was 139 koe/USD 1 000 (purchasing power parity, or PPP, adjusted) (Energy Community, 2015), which is higher than the average energy intensity of the EU countries. The average for EU countries in 2014, stood at 121.7 koe/USD 1 000 (PPP adjusted) (Eurostat, 2016). Moldova's carbon intensity (measured in kilogrammes of CO_2 from energy use per USD of GDP, in 2010 prices) has significantly declined, from 3.43 in the early 1990s to 1.03 in 2014. Its carbon intensity is nevertheless higher than most other countries in Eastern Europe, Caucasus and Central Asia (IEA, 2016). With the growth of the economy, domestic demand for energy will rise, and related greenhouse gas (GHG) emissions will further increase. Meanwhile, the country's aging energy infrastructure needs substantial modernisation. Most of Moldova's power-generating plants are more than 30 to 40 years old. The transmission network is also run-down and needs significant rehabilitation, and obsolete energy technologies need replacement. The government is concerned that Moldova's high energy intensity is a major impediment to improving the competitiveness of its economy.

To combat climate change and increase economic competitiveness, the government of Moldova has made a number of important political decisions. In its Energy Strategy to 2030 (GoM, 2013b, Decree No. 102), the government has set ambitious targets. Given Moldova's orientation to the EU, these are closely aligned with the EU energy strategy objectives. Specifically, Moldova has committed to:

- reduce primary energy consumption by 20% until 2020
- reduce GHG emissions by 20% until 2020
- increase the use of energy produced from renewable sources in relation to the total internal gross consumption by 20% by 2020.

Moldova ratified the UN Framework Convention on Climate Change (UNFCCC) in 1995 and the Kyoto Protocol in 2003. As a non-Annex I country under the Kyoto Protocol, Moldova has no legal commitments to reduce GHG emissions. However, it has committed to work towards a low-carbon economy. The Ministry of Environment has developed the Low-Emission Development Strategy (LEDS) to 2030 (Ministry of Environment, 2016) and a National Climate Change Adaptation Strategy (GoM, 2014a, Decree No. 1 009). The development of renewable energy and increased energy efficiency in the residential and industrial sectors, transport and agriculture are among Moldova's priorities. An adequate legal framework has also been established with the Law on Renewable Energy (Law No. 160, 2007), the Law on Energy Efficiency (Law No. 142, 2010) and the National Energy Efficiency Programme 2011-2020 (GoM, 2011, Decree No. 833). A gradual approximation of the national legislation with the relevant EU *acquis* is under way.

Moldova prepared its Intended Nationally Determined Contribution for UNFCCC negotiations during the COP21 meeting in Paris in 2015. In the document, Moldova committed to "an unconditional target of a 64%-67% reduction of its GHG emissions by 2030 compared to 1990 levels". Moldova further commits to up to a 78% decrease if a global agreement can be reached on low-cost financial resources, technology transfers, and technical co-operation accessible to all at a scale commensurate with the challenge of global climate change (GoM, 2015; COP21). Implementing the "conditional" targets will take an estimated USD 4.9 bln-USD 5.1 bln (about USD 327 mln-340 mln per year) until 2030. Although the costs of the scenarios vary, low-carbon economic growth will require significant domestic resources, as well as international support.

National definition and discussion of energy subsidies

Moldova has adopted the World Trade Organization (WTO) definition of subsidies, as specified in the WTO Agreement on Subsidies and Countervailing Measures. In addition, every year, after the adoption of the annual Budget Law, the Ministry of Agriculture prepares a Regulation on the Use of Agricultural Subsidies, which further specifies what constitutes an agricultural subsidy in the country. In its report for the WTO of 27 October 2015, Moldova is mentioned as a country with a "no notification has been submitted" label to the Committee on Subsidies and Countervailing Measures regarding any subsidies.

Moldovan legislation does not provide any comprehensive national definition of a subsidy. However, straightforward narrow definitions of subsidies are found in some governmental normative acts. For instance, in the Law on Anti-Dumping, Countervailing and Safeguard measures (Law No. 820, 2000), subsidies are defined as "public authorities granting, direct or indirect, financial contributions for traders in order to capitalise export activity". Addressing agriculture support, the government of Moldova Decree on the Distribution of the Fund for Subsidising Farmers (Decree No. 135, 2014) defines a subsidy as an "aid and non-taxable cash grant of subsidy fund for farmers in order to support investments made by farmers who meet the eligibility criteria". This is a budget line in the state budget, and not a separate fund.

Figure 6.12. **What does Moldova include in the national definition of subsidy?**

(dark shading)	(light shading)	(no shading)
Covered by the national definitions of both "subsidy" and "state support"	Covered only by the national definition of "state support"	Not included in the national definition of either "subsidy" or "state support"

Direct budget transfers	Tax expenditures	Induced transfers	Transfer of risk to government	References
(dark shading)				Ministry of Finance of Moldova, Reports on State Budget Execution for 2011-2014, www.mf.gov.md/reports. Tax Code No. 1 163-XIII of 24 April 1997 Article 96, Article 104. Chisinau Municipal Council Decree 8/9 of 20 December 2012, www.chisinau.md/libview.php?l=ro&idc=408&id=4907.

Table 6.5 summarises the main findings of the previous research and the knowledge frontier by subsidy type. These serve as a point of departure for the discussion in the subsequent sections.

Table 6.5. **Subsidy overview**

Energy subsidy	Key findings
Direct budget transfer of funds and liabilities	• Partially included in national subsidy definitions (except liabilities) • Compensation to households for high energy prices
Tax expenditures (tax revenue foregone)	• Not included in national subsidies definitions • No tax expenditure published by the government of Moldova • Reduced VAT rate for electricity (0%), heating (0%) and for natural gas (8%) for domestic users • Low gasoline and diesel excise tax rate • Exemption from environmental charges • Tax exemption for Moldovagaz (discontinued as of 2014)

Table 6.5. **Subsidy overview** *(continued)*

Energy subsidy	Key findings
Induced transfers (income or price support provided to producers or consumers through various regulations)	• Not included in the national subsidy definition • No price-gap estimates available from IEA or other international sources • Induced subsidy by not applying a proper tariff calculation and by not adjusting tariffs for a long time
Transfer of risk to government	• Not included in the national subsidies definition • No significant discussion of the issue (except in terms of public investment in gas and electricity grids)

Government support for fossil fuels

Energy subsidies in Moldova are limited compared with some peer-countries in the EaP region. Moldova has eliminated direct consumer subsidies and does not pursue a pro-subsidy policy, either in relation to consumption or production. However, a combination of the bottom-up approach to subsidy identification and price-gap analysis has revealed several fossil fuel subsidy schemes in Moldova.

It is important to note that some numbers in this study, in particular the sum of intermediate and final calculations included in the summary tables, have been rounded. The numbers given as the sum or the intermediate sums in the tables and those in the text may thus not always correspond to the arithmetical sum.

Price-gap estimates of consumer subsidies

While the International Energy Agency (IEA) provides price-gap estimates of subsidies to end consumers of fossil fuels and electricity in many countries, no such estimates exist for Moldova. Applying this methodology to Moldova did not identify any subsidies in the natural gas sector. The price-gap approach applied in Moldova[3] follows the same logic as in the analysis of the other EaP countries.

Price gap = Reference price – End-user Price

Subsidy = Price gap × Units consumed

Price-gap estimates of consumer subsidies for natural gas

When using a price-gap approach, the key issue is to choose the proper reference price. For net energy importers – as in the case of Moldova – reference prices are based on the import parity price: the price of a product at the nearest international hub, adjusted for quality differences of the fuel imported, if necessary, plus the cost of transport and insurance to the net importer, plus the cost of internal distribution, plus VAT. For natural gas and coal, transport and internal distribution costs are estimated on the basis of available shipping data.

For Moldova, as a net importer, the reference price is the price of imported gas plus the costs of transport and distribution, and VAT. On balance, the price-gap method does not reveal natural gas subsidies to consumers.

To calculate the subsidy to consumers of natural gas, we need to know the price gap and the amount of gas consumed in a given year. In 2015, data from ANRE show that Moldovan consumers (residential and industry and transport sector) used a total of 0.93 bln m^3 of natural gas. The price gap is calculated as the difference between the reference price for gas and the net tariff for end users.

Table 6.6. **Price-gap estimates of consumer subsidies for natural gas**

Consumer groups	Share	Average net tariff, USD per 1 000 m³	Average gross tariff, USD per 1 000 m³	Natural gas consumed, bln m³	Purchase cost, USD per 1 000 m³	Price gap, USD per 1 000 m³	Subsidy MDL million	Subsidy USD million
Residential	29%	331	357.48 (331 + 8%)	0.27	307 (256 +20% VAT)	-24	-122	-6
Industry and transport	71%	331	397.2 (331 + 20%)	0.66	307 (256 +20% VAT)	-24	-298	-16
Total				**0.93**			**-420**	**-22**
Weighted average			**386**		**307**	**-77.64**		

Source: Authors' calculations based on data from ANRE (2015, 2016).

The reference price is the cost of purchasing gas on the border, which is USD 307 per 1 000 m^3 (or USD 256 per 1 000 m^3 + 20% VAT). The net tariff is established by ANRE on an annual basis for different consumer groups and is estimated at USD 331 per 1 000 m^3. The price gap becomes -24 (USD 307-331). When we multiply the price gap for each consumer category by the amount of gas consumed (and adjusted for the difference in measure units), we obtain a negative subsidy, which amounts to -6 (residential) and -16 (industry and transport), or in total, USD 22 mln. In other words, our calculations confirm that there are no consumer subsidies in Moldova in the gas sector.

Bottom-up inventory of government support for fossil fuels

Government support measures in the natural gas sector

The analysis of natural gas and electricity subsidies in Moldova reveals two main types of subsidies. These are: support measures that result from reduced taxes (aka tax expenditure) and price support for consumers by keeping end-prices below cost-recovery levels (aka induced transfers). The two main types of subsidies are:

- reduced VAT rate for electricity and natural gas for domestic users
- induced subsidy through not applying a proper tariff calculation (described in the previous section).

Moldova has regulated prices for gas, electricity, heat and other utilities, but by comparison with other EaP countries, it has a more liberal pricing policy. Rates for households are similar to but just below those paid by business. Although the prices (see the section entitled "Energy pricing policy" on page 216) are close to cost-recovery levels, the government supports households in several ways by:

- establishing a lower rate for households that consume less than 30 m^3 of natural gas per month[4]
- setting a 8% VAT rate on natural gas instead of the standard 20% rate
- giving a tax exemption to Moldovagaz
- setting tariffs below full-cost recovery by not adjusting them for extended periods, as was the case for natural gas tariffs between 2011 and 2015. These subsidies affect the financial performance of gas distributors and have a significant impact on investments made in the sector.

Reduced VAT rate on natural gas consumption for domestic users

The standard VAT rate in Moldova is 20%. For the reduced VAT tax rate, the number was calculated by multiplying the average net price for households by the amount sold annually and by the VAT reduction (20%-8%, or 12%). The results of this estimate are presented in Table 6.7 below.

Table 6.7. **Estimates of consumer subsidies in the natural gas sector of Moldova in 2011-15 (nominal 2015 million USD) resulting from a reduced VAT rate**

	Average tariff (VAT 8%)	Reference price (VAT 20%)	Amount of natural gas sold	Price gap	Subsidy in MDL	Subsidy in USD
Year	*MDL/1 000 m³*	*MDL/1 000 m³*	*bcm*	*MDL/1 000 m³*	*MDL mln*	*USD mln*
2011	4 966.92	5 518.80	0.28	551.88	153.48	13.07
2012	5 294.16	5 882.40	0.28	588.24	163.59	13.51
2013	5 294.16	5 882.40	0.28	588.24	163.59	12.99
2014	5 294.16	5 882.40	0.28	588.24	163.00	11.61
2015	6 719.76	7 466.40	0.27	746.64	202.79	10.78

Source: Authors' own calculations based on ANRE reports (ANRE, 2012, 2013, 2014, 2015, 2016).

Our calculations show that the reduced VAT rate on gas consumption in the period 2011-15 resulted in foregone government revenue of about USD 62 mln.

Import tax exemption for Moldovagaz

The tax exemption for Moldovagaz was USD 4 per 1 000 m^3 of natural gas, which was in effect from 2004 to 2013. It was then discontinued, when the government of Moldova redeemed bills issued by the Ministry of Finance for JSC Gazprom. Table 6.8 presents the calculation of the subsidy for 2011-13.

Table 6.8. **Estimates of subsidies by tax exemption to Moldovagaz (nominal 2015 USD million)**

	Amount of natural gas sold by Moldovagaz	Unit subsidy	Subsidy in MDL	Subsidy in USD
Year	*BCM*	*USD/1 000 m³*	*MDL mln*	*USD mln*
2011	1.02	4	47.82	4.07
2012	0.97	4	47.07	3.89
2013	0.95	4	47.61	3.78
2014	0.96	0	0.00	0.00
2015	0.93	0	0.00	0.00

Source: Authors' own calculations, based on ANRE reports (ANRE, 2012, 2013, 2014, 2015, 2016).

Induced subsidy by price regulation

Tariffs in Moldova are approved by ANRE. The general principles of tariff calculation are appropriate, and tariffs are set on the basis of good practices. Heat and electricity tariff-setting is based on a global good practice using rate-of-return methodology. The electricity and heat generation tariff-setting methodology is not as well-defined, and lacks a definition of the rate of return. Every sector – heat, electricity and gas distribution – has high investment needs, and therefore, attracting capital with a fair return is necessary.

Through ANRE, Moldova has several possibilities for allowing for subsidies, by:

- not adjusting tariffs for an extended period, as was the case with natural gas tariffs between 2011 and 2015
- approving district heating and natural gas tariffs separately, which carries the risk that increasing heat tariffs may lead to disconnections from the district heating system
- setting distribution costs below full-cost recovery.

Analysis of the tariffs approved by ANRE indicates that transport and internal distribution costs vary. For example, in 2015, ANRE approved transport and internal distribution costs of natural gas at MDL 1 551.00 per 1 000 m^3, as compared with MDL 616.92 per 1 000 m^3 in 2011. This threefold increase in the costs of transport and internal distribution in the span of four years is significant (inflation in the period was only 27.12%) and suggests that in 2011, transport and internal distribution costs were set at a level that did not allow for proper cost recovery and an appropriate rate of return.

According to ANRE, however, this threefold increase was caused mostly by changes in the natural gas tariff-setting methodology for gas transport and distribution to end users. In 2014, ANRE adopted a new methodology, in which the cost of the natural gas losses in the distribution network is included in the tariff for distribution. Until then and under the old methodology, this cost was included in the end-user supply tariff.

The reason for the sharp increase in the gas transmission tariff was Parliament's amendment to the Law on Natural Gas. The amendment ended ANRE's regulation of natural gas transit, so that most of the transmission costs will be linked only to actually transported natural gas volumes (around 1 bln m^3) and not to transported and transit gas volumes (around 18 bln m^3), as was the case earlier.

In 2015, the reallocation of the cost of losses from the end-user supply tariff to the distribution tariff coincided with changes related to the gas transmission tariff and a drop in the cost of natural gas imports. This made it possible to set tariffs at an appropriate level, covering costs, while keeping end-user prices stable.

Despite the changes in the tariff-setting methodology, not adjusting the tariff in the period 2011-15[5] still constituted a subsidy. A discussion of the proper level of tariffs for transport and internal distribution of natural gas is beyond the scope of this study, but a simplified estimation approach was used.

In estimating the amount of the subsidy incurred in Moldova by not adjusting the tariff, the methodology was to use the average annual costs of import.[6] For the costs of internal distribution, it was assumed that the tariff was properly calculated in 2015, and that amount was adjusted for previous years (2012-14). Although this is only an approximation, it gives some idea of the magnitude of the subsidy.

The results of these estimates are presented in Table 6.9. Our estimates show a significant reduction of subsidies to gas consumers in Moldova in 2015 by comparison with previous years. In 2015, consumer gas subsidies were about USD 7 mln.

Table 6.9. **Induced subsidy estimates in the natural gas sector of Moldova in 2011-15 (nominal 2015 USD million) imposed by tariff setting**

Year	Weighted average end-user tariff	Annual cost of import (purchase cost)	Assumed costs of transport and internal distribution	Reference price	Amount of natural gas sold	Price gap	Subsidy in MDL	Subsidy in USD
	MDL/1 000 m³	*MDL/1 000 m³*	*MDL/1 000 m³*	*MDL/1 000 m³*	*bcm*	*MDL/1 000 m³*	*MDL mln*	*USD mln*
2011	4 599.00	3 983.73	1 551.00	5 534.73	1.02	935.73	952.80	81.16
2012	4 902.00	4 770.98	1 551.00	6 321.98	0.97	1 419.98	1 379.95	113.95
2013	4 902.00	4 779.16	1 551.00	6 330.16	0.95	1 428.16	1 350.04	107.23
2014	4 902.00	5 294.48	1 551.00	6 845.48	0.96	1 943.48	1 863.70	132.74
2015	6 222.00	4 816.92	1 551.00	6 367.92	0.93	145.92	135.36	7.19

Note: **Reference price** = Purchase cost + Assumed costs of transport and internal distribution
Price gap = Reference price – Weighted average end-user tariff
Subsidy = Price gap × Amount of natural gas sold

Source: Authors' own estimates based on ANRE reports (ANRE, 2012, 2013, 2014, 2015, 2016).

Exemption from environmental (air pollution) charges

Whereas emissions of large combustion plants in Moldova (such as NO_x) are subject to pollution charges, small plants and individual boilers are exempted. This puts centralised production of heat and electricity at a disadvantage compared to small-scale boilers. Since the average emissions per unit of useful energy produced are generally lower in centralised production, this exemption from pollution charges can be considered an environmentally harmful subsidy.

The environmental charge is MDL 18 per conventional tonne,[7] and the exemption can be estimated by multiplying the consumption of gas for small heating systems (107 mln m^3 per year), by the charge (MDL 18) and by the unit emission. The standard coefficient for natural gas emissions is 0.4855608 kg per 1 000 m^3). The total amount of the charge, if imposed, would thus be MDL 932 (USD 49). This is the government's opportunity cost of exempting small plants and individual boilers from air pollution charges.

Table 6.10 presents the calculation of the subsidy resulting from the exemption from environmental charges.

Table 6.10. **Estimate of consumer subsidies through exemption from environmental charges in 2015 (nominal 2015 USD million)**

Year	Amount of gas sold for heating purposes	Average pollution	Subsidy in MDL	Subsidy in USD
	mln m³	*Conventional tonne from 1 000 m³*	*MDL*	*USD*
2015	107	0.4855608	932	49

Source: Authors' own calculations based on ANRE reports (ANRE, 2012, 2013, 2014, 2015, 2016).

Total estimate of consumer subsidies in Moldova's natural gas sector\

The total estimate of consumer subsidies in the natural gas sector of Moldova is presented in Table 6.11 (it also includes the induced subsidies for natural gas described in the previous section).

Table 6.11. **Estimates of consumer subsidies in Moldova's gas sector, 2011-15 (nominal 2015 million USD)**

	Induced by tariff	Reduced VAT rate	Tax exemption for Moldovagaz	Exemption from environmental charges	TOTAL	
Year	*MDL mln*	*MDL mln*	*MDL mln*	*MDL mln*	*MDL mln*	*USD mln*
2011	952.80	153.48	47.82	0.00	1 154.10	98.30
2012	1 379.95	163.59	47.07	0.00	1 590.62	131.35
2013	1 350.04	163.59	47.61	0.00	1 561.24	124.01
2014	1 863.70	163.00	0.00	0.00	2 026.71	144.35
2015	135.36	202.79	0.00	0.00	3 38.14	17.97
Total	5 681.00	846.00	142.00	0.00	6 670.00	515.98

Source: Authors' own calculation.

In the period 2011-15, total government support for consumers in the natural gas sector, through reduced taxes and induced prices, was about USD 515 mln. Of this, the opportunity fiscal cost for the government (the budget revenue foregone) from not collecting the relevant taxes was USD 73.70 mln.

Government support measures in the electricity sector

VAT exemption for electricity consumers (domestic users)

Moldova's electricity sector imports almost half of its electricity from Transnistria. This subsidy is the result of a reduced taxation level: the VAT tax rate on electricity is set at 0%. Table 6.12 below presents the calculation of the subsidy granted through the reduced VAT rate to domestic users of electricity.

Table 6.12. **Estimate of consumer subsidies in Moldova's electricity sector, 2011-15 (nominal 2015 USD million)**

	Average tariff for households (VAT 0%)	Reference price (VAT 20%)	Electricity sold to domestic users	Subsidy in MDL	Subsidy in USD
Year	*Bani [a]/kWh*	*Bani/kWh*	*kWh mln*	*MDL mln*	*USD mln*
2011	142.75	171.30	1 542.80	264.28	22.51
2012	152.60	183.12	1 574.90	288.40	23.81
2013	156.81	188.17	1 605.20	302.05	23.99
2014	156.86	188.23	1 656.20	311.75	22.20
2015	167.76	201.31	1 663.30	334.85	17.80
Total				1 501.00	110.32

Note a. 100 bani make one Moldovan leu.

Source: Authors' own calculations based on ANRE reports (ANRE, 2012, 2013, 2014, 2015, 2016).

The increase in electricity tariffs for households has led to an increase in the level of subsidy in domestic prices. However, increased exchange rates reduced the value of these subsidies in 2015, compared to previous years. The subsidy was a total of USD 110.3 mln from 2011 to 2015, which is the actual fiscal cost of the subsidy to the state budget.

Tariff support for renewable electricity producers

A feed-in tariff for renewable energy producers was introduced in Moldova in 2013. According to Law No. 160 of 2007, the so-called "green" tariff for renewable energy producers is set based on the special methodology approved by ANRE. The methodology assumes the recovery of investments in renewable energy production for a period of up to 15 years, provided that the prescribed rate of return does not exceed twice the corresponding rate in the traditional energy sector.

The value of the induced transfer to renewable energy producers was estimated based on the weighted average "green" tariff for production of electricity from renewable energy sources (biogas, solar, wind energy), using the data provided in 2015 ANRE Annual Report (ANRE, 2015). The reference price is the price of importing 1 kWh of electricity from Ukraine.

Table 6.13. **Estimate of subsidies for renewable-energy producers in Moldova's electricity sector, 2011-15 (nominal 2015 USD million)**

	Average "green" tariff for renewable energy producers	Reference price (import)	Electricity sold to domestic users	Subsidy in MDL	Subsidy in USD
Year	*Bani/kWh*	*Bani/kWh*	*M kWh*	*MDL mln*	*USD mln*
2013	1.80	0.87	1.91	1.76	0.14
2014	1.76	0.96	3.10	2.50	0.80
2015	1.72	1.29	17.20	7.35	0.39

Source: Authors' own calculations (ANRE, 2014, 2015, 2016).

Although the "green" tariff has been decreasing in absolute terms since it was introduced, the total subsidy to electricity producers for producing clean energy in the period 2013-15 has been steadily increasing when calculated in local currency. In dollar terms and on an annual basis, however, due to the devaluation of the MDL, the amount has fallen. The subsidy to energy producers through the "green tariff" in the period 2013-15 amounted to USD 1.33 mln.

Government support measures in the heating sector

The subsidy to consumers in the heating sector is the result of a reduced taxation level: the VAT tax rate for heat is set at 0%. Table 6.14 presents calculations for the subsidy resulting from this reduced VAT rate.

The annual subsidy to heat consumers, calculated in national currency, remained stable in the period from 2011 to 2015, but declined in USD terms. In total, due to this subsidy scheme, the state budget lost an additional USD 85 mln in foregone revenue between 2011 and 2015.

Table 6.14. **Estimate of consumer subsidies in the heating sector of Moldova, 2011-15 (nominal 2015 USD million)**

Year	Average tariff for households (VAT 0%) *MDL/Gcal*	Reference price (VAT 20%) *MDL/Gcal*	Heat sold to domestic users *mln/Gcal*	Subsidy in MDL *MDL mln*	Subsidy in USD *USD mln*
2011	923.43	1 108.11	1.268	234.31	19.96
2012	995.24	1 194.29	1.206	240.08	19.83
2013	996.92	1 196.30	1.089	217.19	17.25
2014	998.46	1 198.15	1.092	217.98	15.53
2015	999.14	1 198.97	1.171	234.12	12.44
Total				1 143.00	85.01

Source: Authors' own calculations based on ANRE reports (ANRE, 2012, 2013, 2014, 2015, 2016).

Targeted subsidies to low-income households in Chisinau

Several government programmes provide energy subsidies to vulnerable groups, although they reach only a limited number of people, and limits on consumption levels apply. The most significant is in Chisinau, where city residents at or below a minimum income level receive compensation for 40% of their heating bills. The subsidy totals MDL 52 mln-77 mln annually, taken at face value from the city's budget expenses.

Summary of energy subsidy estimates

Tables 6.15 and 6.16 and Figure 6.13 below provide summary information on the magnitude of energy subsidies for the period 2011-15 in Moldova, in both Moldovan lei and US dollars.

Table 6.15. **Estimates of consumer energy subsidies in Moldova in 2011-15 (million MDL)**

Year	Natural gas *MDL mln*	Electricity *MDL mln*	Heating *MDL mln*	Total *MDL mln*
2011	1 154.10	264.28	234.33	1 652.71
2012	1 590.62	288.40	240.14	2 119.15
2013	1 561.24	302.05	217.18	2 080.47
2014	2 026.71	311.75	218.04	2 556.50
2015	338.14	334.85	234.07	907.06
Total	6 670.80	1 501.33	1 143.76	9 315.89

Source: Authors' own calculations.

Generally, the amount of subsidies in USD has remained stable (with some fluctuations), except in 2015, when a drop in import prices for natural gas reduced the induced subsidy for the gas sector, by allowing a higher share of the costs for transport and distribution to be reflected in the tariff.

Total government support for consumption of fossil-fuel subsidies in Moldova in the period 2011-15 totals about USD 711 mln, which is low compared with the other EaP countries. This amount excludes support for producers of green energy (feed-in tariff) and targeted subsidies to low-income households in Chisinau.

Table 6.16. **Estimates of consumer energy subsidies in Moldova in 2011-15 (nominal 2015 million USD)**

Year	Natural gas *USD mln*	Electricity *USD mln*	Heating *USD mln*	Total *USD mln*
2011	98.30	22.51	19.96	140.78
2012	131.35	23.81	19.83	174.99
2013	124.01	23.99	17.25	165.25
2014	144.35	22.20	15.53	182.09
2015	17.97	17.80	12.44	48.21
Total	515.98	110.32	85.01	711.31

Source: Authors' own calculations.

Figure 6.13. **Summary of estimated consumer energy subsidies in Moldova**

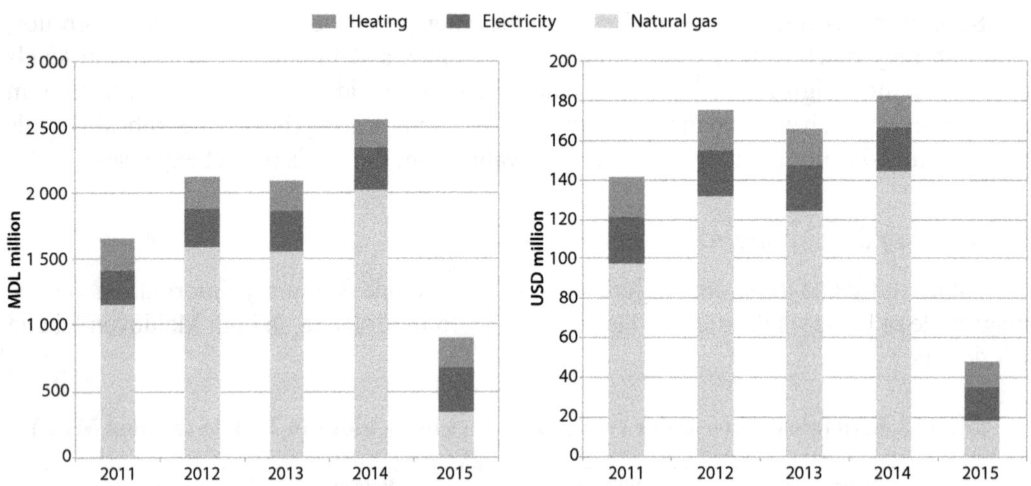

Source: Authors' own calculations.

Government support for energy efficiency and renewable energy producers

Moldova is a full member of the Energy Community and has committed to implementing the Energy Community *acquis.* Energy efficiency and renewable energy play a major role in achieving energy and climate-related objectives in the EU member states. Given that Moldova's economy and welfare are vulnerable to changes in climate, the government has set ambitious climate-related targets.

Energy efficiency in buildings is of particular concern in Moldova. The legislation that regulates energy efficiency in buildings in the EU and that guides Moldova's policy in this regard is the Directive on Energy End-Use Efficiency and Energy Services and Energy Performance (EU, 2006).

The National Development Strategy Moldova 2020 (Law No. 166, 2012) establishes the specific objective of renovating 10% of the total stock of public buildings by 2020 and achieving a 10% reduction in energy use in public buildings by the same date. Under the Modernisation of Local Public Services (MLPS) project,[8] German Technical Assistance (GIZ) assisted the government of Moldova through the Ministry of Regional Development and Construction (MRDC) to translate these targets into action on the regional level in Regional Sector Programmes (RSP) for Energy Efficiency in Public Buildings. The estimated total investment cost in Moldova for 100% refurbishment of education and health care institutions (excluding other public buildings) is about EUR 760 mln and EUR 135 mln, respectively, excluding Chisinau. For comparison, the third call for proposals of the Energy Efficiency Fund had a budget of EUR 5.7 mln, and a World-Bank financed school refurbishment programme had a budget of around EUR 25 mln.

Government support for energy-efficiency measures

The main institutions involved in the financing of energy efficiency are the Energy Efficiency Agency, the Energy Efficiency Fund, the National Environmental Fund, the Social Investment Fund, and the National Fund for Regional Development. Of these, however, the National Fund for Regional Development has not yet financed an energy efficiency project.

The Energy Efficiency Agency, with an annual budget ranging from MDL 1 mln to 25 mln, aims to supervise and monitor state policy and implementation of energy efficiency measures. In 2012, funding from the state budget was only MDL 1.2 mln; in 2013, MDL 7.9 mln; in 2014, MDL 25.7 mln, and in 2015, MDL 14.5 mln. In addition, in 2014, EUR 5.8 mln from local budgets was used to finance energy efficiency measures (EEA, 2015).

The Energy Efficiency Fund (EEF) finances projects in:

- energy-saving measures such as thermal insulation of walls and roofs, replacement of windows and exterior doors
- rehabilitation of heating and domestic hot water source and distribution systems
- renewable energy resources
- public lighting.

The EEF operates based on calls for proposals rather than annual investment programmes. To date, there have been three calls. The first, in 2013, was launched for public institutions (including schools and hospitals), resulting in the selection of 86 projects worth a total of MDL 135 mln (about EUR 78 000 per project on average). A second call focused on the private sector, but ultimately no projects were implemented. The third call in 2014 was launched again for public institutions, which resulted in the selection of 92 projects worth a total of MDL 114 mln (about EUR 62 000 per project on average). The EEF offers financing in the form of grants, credits, leasing and guarantees (EEF, 2015). In 2014 and 2015, MDL 172 mln and MDL 125 mln, respectively were planned for allocation but were not transferred from the state budget due to insufficient resources.

In 2013-14, the Social Investment Fund of Moldova (FISM) implemented projects worth MDL 30 mln, including local budget contributions worth MDL 3.4 mln and MDL 5.2 mln through the National Environmental Fund (state budget). FISM also manages a grant programme worth EUR 20 mln for the government of Romania, which includes energy efficiency projects. Local contributions, typically 15% of total costs, are expected for FISM-financed projects.

Donor support for energy-efficiency measures

In addition to the projects discussed in the previous section, the Moldova Biomass and Energy Project (MEBP), funded by the EU and UN Development Programme, financed 144 energy efficiency public projects worth about EUR 14 mln, of which MDL 28.3 mln were contributions from local governments (EC/UNDP, 2015). The project focuses on improving heating comfort levels in rural public sector buildings (schools, kindergartens, etc.) by using readily available biomass supplied from local agricultural enterprises. The project was topped up with EUR 9.4 mln. The "top-up" includes geographical extension of the project (including to Transnistria, Gagauzia and Taraclia) and reinforcement of sustainability of the biomass market in Moldova.

In the period 2016-18, the EU plans EUR 10 mln of energy efficiency investments in schools and hospitals developed by the MLPS project mentioned earlier. Under this project, nine priority school and three priority hospital thermal renovation projects were developed to an advanced stage (feasibility study and conceptual design). A further 20 projects were developed to the project fiche stage, and roughly 30 more were identified in the Regional Sector Programmes for Energy Efficiency in Public Buildings as priority projects.

In addition, the EU started three projects in early 2015 supported by the Sustainable Urban Demonstration Projects. Of their total cost of EUR 2.7 mln, the EU contribution is EUR 2 mln and the rest is contributed by the communities concerned. The projects will support investments in energy efficiency and renewable energy in five municipalities: the towns of Ungheni, Orhei, Ocnita, Soroca and Cantemir.

The EBRD has opened a credit line of EUR 42 mln, which, combined with a 5%-20% grant component, is provided for on-lending to both Moldovan companies and households through local partner banks. Two special Sustainable Energy and Energy Efficiency Financing Facilities (MoSEFF and MoREEF) provide technical assistance to the projects. The financing is bound to investments in sustainable energy and production of renewable energy. Up to 2014, about 2 150 loans were made, for a total of EUR 8.66 mln. The government of Moldova has not made any expenditures on these projects.

Table 6.17. **Public support for energy efficiency and renewable energy sources**

	Projects supported in 2010-15	Estimated amount in MDL or EUR	Estimated amount in USD
	Government support		
1.	Energy Efficiency Agency	MLD 49.3 mln	USD 2.62 mln
2.	Energy Efficiency Fund	MLD 249 mln	USD 13.23 mln
3.	Social Investment Fund	MLD 30 mln	USD 1.59 mln
4.	National Environmental Fund (EE)		
	• Energy efficiency	MLD 5.2 mln	USD 0.276 mln
	• Renewable energy	MLD 16.3 mln	USD 0.866 mln
5.	Local budgets	MLD 37.5 mln	USD 1.99 mln
	Donor support		
6.	World Bank Refurbishment Programme	EUR 25 mln	USD 28 mln
7.	Government of Romania	EUR 20 mln	USD 22.42 mln
8.	EU and UNDP Moldova Biogas and Energy Project	EUR 23.4 mln	USD 26.24 mln
9.	EBRD	EUR 8.6 mln	USD 9.71 mln
			USD 106.942 mln

Note: Data in this table exclude support for the "green" tariff.

Source: Authors' own compilations.

Government support for renewable energy producers

The players involved in renewable energy are also involved in energy efficiency. In general, energy efficiency and renewable energy projects are reported by these institutions in a single category. According to its annual reporting, the National Environmental Fund financed ten projects worth a total of MDL 16.3 mln for the development of renewable energy sources in the period 2011-13.

As discussed earlier, government support for renewable energy producers is also provided through the "green" tariff first introduced in Moldova in 2013. This subsidy amounted to USD 1.33 mln in the period 2013-15.

Detailed description of the subsidy schemes in Moldova is provided in Annex 6.A1 and Annex 6.A2.

Annex 6.A1

Fossil-fuel subsidies in Moldova

Table 6.A1.1. **Compensation of the Chisinau population for prices on energy resources**

Subsidy category	Direct transfer
Stimulated activity	Consumption of heat energy
Subsidy name	**Compensation of the Chisinau population for prices on energy resources**
Jurisdiction	Municipal level
Legislation/endorsing organisation	• Article 131 (5) of the Tax Code (Tax Code, 1997) • Article 14 (2) and 19 (4) of the Law of Local Public Administration (Law No. 436, 2006) • Decree 8/9 of 20 December 2012 of the Chisinau Municipal Council
Policy objective(s) of subsidy	To provide compensation to vulnerable people for energy consumption payments
End recipient(s) of subsidy	Households (vulnerable people)
Time period	2012-15
Background	In recent years, energy prices in Moldova have increased significantly, and the government provides compensation schemes to protect the most vulnerable segments of the population. Such schemes exist both at the national and local levels. At the national level, compensation schemes pay fixed amounts (e.g. per family or person), regardless of the amount of energy used. However, some local schemes (e.g. the compensation paid in Chisinau to low-income families) provide payment as a percentage of the energy bills. The latter type of support is potentially environmentally harmful (to the extent that energy bills are proportional to actual energy use). Since 2012, according to the Chisinau Municipal Council Decree 8/9 of 20 December 2012, residents of the city of Chisinau with a minimum income level (established annually at MDL 2 500 per per person per month in 2015) receive compensation for payments for energy resources (heating, electricity, gas, wood and coal) in the amount of 40% of the bills. The subsidy is estimated at MDL 52 mln-MLD 77 mln (USD 4 mln-USD 6 mln) annually, taken at face value from the Chisinau city expenditure budget.
Amount of subsidy conferred	2012: MDL 77.1 mln (USD 6.37 mln) 2013: MDL 74.3 mln (USD 5.9 mln) 2014: MDL 52.5 mln (USD 3.74 mln)
Information sources	CMC (2012) Decree 8/9 of 20 December 2012, CMC (2013) Report on the Progress of the Heating Season 2012-2013, DHP (2014), Annual Reports for 2013 and 2014

Table 6.A1.2. **Reduced VAT rates for natural gas consumption by households**

Subsidy category	Tax revenue foregone
Stimulated activity	Households consumption of natural gas
Subsidy name	**Reduced VAT rates for natural gas consumption by households**
Jurisdiction	National level
Legislation/endorsing organisation	Article 96 of the Tax Code No. 1 163-XIII of 24 April 1997 (Tax Code, 1997)
Policy objective(s) of subsidy	The primary objective of the subsidy is to decrease the burden on individual households that pay natural gas bills
End recipient(s) of subsidy	Households through natural gas bills Private and public institutions through natural gas bills
Time period	From 1997 until now
Background	Under Moldovan VAT rules, supplies of natural gas and LPG are taxed at the reduced rate of 8%, while the standard VAT rate in Moldova is 20%. Whereas this reduced rate does not affect the energy price for business purposes (since most companies can deduct the VAT paid), it does imply a lower energy price for households, not-for-profit institutions and public institutions. The authors estimate the value of the tax revenue foregone based on the average tariff and households consumption of heat, based on the data provided in ANRE Annual Reports.
Amount of subsidy conferred	2011: MDL 1 154 mln (USD 98.30 mln) 2012: MDL 1 590 mln (USD 131.35 mln) 2013: MDL 1 561 mln (USD 124.01 mln) 2014: MDL 2 026 mln (USD 144.35 mln) 2015 MDL 338 mln (USD 17.97 mln)
Information sources	Tax Code (1997), ANRE (2013, 2014, 2015, 2016) Annual Reports for 2012, 2013, 2014, 2015

Table 6.A1.3. **Reduced VAT rates for electricity consumption by households**

Subsidy category	Tax revenue foregone
Stimulated activity	Household consumption of electricity
Subsidy name	**Reduced VAT rates for electricity consumption by households**
Jurisdiction	National level
Legislation/endorsing organisation	Article 104 of the Tax Code 1 163-XIII of 24 April 1997 (Tax Code, 1997)
Policy objective(s) of subsidy	The primary objective of the subsidy is to decrease the burden on individual households that pay electricity bills
End recipient(s) of subsidy	Households through electricity bills
Time period	From 1997 until now
Background	Under Moldovan VAT rules, electricity supply is taxed at 0%. The standard VAT rate is 20%. This reduced rate does not affect the energy price for business purposes (since most companies can deduct the VAT paid), but it does imply a lower energy price for households, not-for-profit institutions and public institutions. The authors estimate the value of the tax revenue foregone based on the average tariff and households consumption of electricity based on the data provided in ANRE Annual Reports.
Amount of subsidy conferred	2011: MDL 264 mln (USD 22.51 mln) 2012: MDL 288 mln (USD 23.81 mln) 2013: MDL 302 mln (USD 23.99 mln) 2014: MDL 311 mln (USD 22.2 mln) 2015: MDL 334 mln (USD 17.8 mln)
Information sources	Tax Code (1997), ANRE (2013, 2014, 2015, 2016) Annual Reports for 2012, 2013, 2014, 2015

Table 6.A1.4. **Reduced VAT rates for household heat consumption**

Subsidy category	Tax revenue foregone
Stimulated activity	Households consumption of heat
Subsidy name	**Reduced VAT rates for heat consumption by households**
Jurisdiction	National level
Legislation/endorsing organisation	Article 104 of the Tax Code 1 163-XIII of 24 April 1997
Policy objective(s) of subsidy	The primary objective of the subsidy is to decrease the burden on individual households that pay heat bills
End recipient(s) of subsidy	Households through heat bills
Time period	From 1997 until now
Background	Under Moldovan VAT rules, heating supply is taxed at 0%. The standard VAT rate in Moldova is 20%. This reduced rate does not affect the energy price for business purposes (since most companies can deduct the VAT paid), but it does imply a lower energy price for households, not-for-profit institutions and public institutions. The authors estimate the value of the tax revenue foregone based on the average tariff and households consumption of heat based on the data provided in ANRE Annual Reports.
Amount of subsidy conferred	2011: MDL 234 mln (USD 19.96 mln) 2012: MDL 240 mln (USD 19.83 mln) 2013: MDL 217 mln (USD 17.25 mln) 2014: MDL 218 mln (USD 15.53 mln) 2015: MDL 234 mln (USD 12.44 mln)
Information sources	Tax Code (1997), ANRE (2013, 2014, 2015, 2016) Annual Reports for 2012, 2013, 2014, 2015

Table 6.A1.5. **Induced subsidy from not applying an appropriate tariff calculation for natural gas**

Subsidy category	**Induced transfer**
Stimulated activity	Households consumption of natural gas
Subsidy name	**Induced subsidy by not applying a proper tariff calculation for natural gas**
Jurisdiction	National level
Legislation/endorsing organisation	ANRE regulation
Policy objective(s) of subsidy	The primary objective of the subsidy is to decrease the burden on individual consumers of natural gas
End recipient(s) of subsidy	Natural gas consumers
Time period	From 2000 onwards
Background	The general principles of tariff calculation are correct and defined according to good practices. Heat and electricity tariff-setting is based on a global good practice using rate-of-return methodology. The electricity and heat generation tariff-setting methodology is not as well defined and does not include a definition of the rate of return. Every sector, whether heat, electricity or gas distribution, has high future investment needs, which makes it important to attract capital with a fair return. Through ANRE, the government of Moldova has several options for inducing subsidies: • not adjusting tariffs for an extended period, as was the case with natural gas tariffs between 2011 and 2015 • approving district heat and natural gas tariffs separately, which carried the risk that increased heat tariffs might lead to disconnections from the district heating system • approving the tariff using a weak definition of the rate of return.
Amount of subsidy conferred	2011: MDL 952 mln (USD 81.16 mln) 2012: MDL 1 379 mln (USD 113.95 mln) 2013: MDL 1 350 mln (USD 107.23 mln) 2014: MDL 1 863 mln (USD 132.74 mln) 2015: MDL 135 mln (USD 7.19 mln)
Information sources	Tax Code (1997), ANRE (2013, 2014, 2015, 2016) Annual Reports for 2012, 2013, 2014, 2015

Table 6.A1.6. **Exemption from environmental (air pollution) charges**

Subsidy category	Tax revenue foregone
Stimulated activity	Households and small business using fossil fuels and natural gas for heating
Subsidy name	**Exemption from environmental (air pollution) charges**
Jurisdiction	National level
Legislation/endorsing organisation	Law on Environment Pollution Payment, No. 1 540 of 25 February1998
Policy objective(s) of subsidy	The primary objective of the subsidy is to decrease the burden on owners of individual heating systems
End recipient(s) of subsidy	Households and small business
Time period	1998
Background	Whereas large combustion plants in Moldova are subject to pollution charges on their emissions (such as NO_x), small plants and individual boilers are exempted. This puts centralised production of heat and electricity at a disadvantage compared to small-scale boilers. Since the average emissions per unit of useful energy produced are generally lower in centralised production, the exemption from pollution charges can probably be considered an environmentally harmful subsidy. The environmental charge is MDL 18 per conventional tonne, and the exemption can be estimated by multiplying consumption of gas for small heating systems (107 mln m^3 per year) by the charge (MDL 18) and by the unit emission. The standard coefficient for natural gas emissions is 0.4855608 kg/1 000 m^3, so the total charge would be MDL 932.
Amount of subsidy conferred	2015: MDL 932 (USD 49.53)
Information sources	Law No. 1 540 (1998), ANRE (2016, 2016) Annual Reports 2015 and 2016

Table 6.A1.7. **Tax exemption for Moldovagaz**

Subsidy category	Tax revenue foregone
Stimulated activity	Households and public and private institutions using natural gas
Subsidy name	**Tax exemption for Moldovagaz**
Jurisdiction	National level
Legislation/endorsing organisation	The Budget Law for 2013, Article 13 (Law No. 249, 2012)
Policy objective(s) of subsidy	The primary objective of the subsidy is to decrease Moldovagaz debt and help improve its financial health
End recipient(s) of subsidy	Moldovagaz
Time period	2012-13
Background	Since 2004, ANRE has authorised the inclusion in the gas tariff of a charge (USD 4 per 1 000 m^3) which was collected by Moldovagaz and then transferred to the state budget. Article 13 of the Budget Law for 2013 provides that the revenue obtained should be exempt from revenue tax.
Amount of subsidy conferred	2011: MDL 47 mln (USD 4.07 mln) 2012 (MDL 47 mln/USD 3.89 mln) 2013: MDL 47 mln (USD 3.78 mln)
Information sources	Law No. 249 (2012)

Table 6.A1.8. **Public investment in natural gas and electricity grids**

Subsidy category	Direct transfer of funds
Stimulated activity	Consumption of natural gas and electricity
Subsidy name	**Public investment in natural gas and electricity grids**
Jurisdiction	National level
Legislation/endorsing organisation	• National Development Strategy "Moldova 2020" (Law No. 166, 2012) • Energy Strategy of the Republic of Moldova until 2030 (Government Decree No. 102 of 5 February 2013) • Ministry of Economy
Policy objective(s) of subsidy	To extend the natural gas and electricity infrastructure
End recipient(s) of subsidy	Households, public and private institutions
Time period	2014-20
Background	The Energy Strategy of the Republic of Moldova until 2030 (approved by Governmental Decree No. 102 of 5 February 2013) lists as a national energy priority reinforcing the power and natural gas transit, by extending interconnectors (additional 139 km of power grid/40 km of natural gas pipelines by 2020). The new Iasi-Ungheni gas interconnector pipeline has been operational since 2015. Government expenditure for this project was MDL 141.8 mln. The next Ungheni-Chisinau gas pipeline connection is planned to be under construction until 2020, with an estimated investment of EUR 92 mln. The feasibility study for building new interconnectors, connected to the ENTSO-E system, was developed with a government contribution of MDL 18.5 mln in 2014. This subsidy scheme is not reflected in the total amount of subsidy in Moldova, as the project is ongoing, state support is as yet incomplete and the full subsidy not yet realised.
Amount of subsidy conferred	2012: MDL 2.6 mln (USD 0.215 mln) 2013: MDL 29.6 mln (USD 2.35 mln) 2014: MDL 128.1 mln (USD 9.12 mln)
Information sources	MoF (2014)

Table 6.A1.9. **Debt restructuring of energy companies**

Subsidy category	Transfer of risk to government
Stimulated Activity	Consumption of natural gas and electricity
Subsidy name	**Debt restructuring of energy companies**
Jurisdiction	National level
Legislation/endorsing organisation	• Government Decree No. 318 of 7 May 2014 • CMC Decree No. 9/53 of 18 December 2013 • Termoelectrica SA
Policy objective(s) of subsidy	To reduce fiscal payments of Termoelectrica SA to the state budget
End recipient(s) of subsidy	Households, public and private institutions
Time period	2001-15
Background	One of the most significant challenges in the energy sector is the large historic debts accumulated by the heating company Termocom, of MDL 2.3 bln (or 3.5% GDP). These debts were the result of the increase in the price of imported gas, but also due to tariffs set at below cost-recovery levels. In 2011, the Moldovan government approved a decision that addresses the problem through: an improved legal framework (promotion of co-generation); institutional and corporate restructuring (a merger of three companies: CHP-1, CHP-2 and Termocom); and debt restructuring (asset evaluation, sale of unused assets and forgiveness of historical debts accumulated until 2002). The institutional and corporate restructuring plan has been implemented (with a new company, Thermoelectrica, established in 2015), but the final resolution of debt restructuring is pending.
Amount of subsidy conferred	2015: MDL 1 285 mln (USD 68.29 mln)
Information sources	Government Decree No. 318 (2014)

Annex 6.A2

Government support for energy efficiency and renewable energy sources

Table 6.A2.1. **Government support (co-financing) to domestic and international sources providing financing to energy efficiency and renewables**

Subsidy category	Direct transfer
Stimulated activity	Energy efficiency and production of renewable energy
subsidy name	**Government support to energy efficiency (EE) and renewable energy sources (RES)**
Jurisdiction	National level
Legislation/endorsing organisation	**Legislation** • National Development Strategy "Moldova 2020", approved by Law No. 166 of 11 July 2012 • Energy Strategy of the Republic of Moldova until 2030, approved by Government Decree No. 102 of 5 February 2013 • Law on Renewable Energy No. 160-XVI of 12 July 2007 • Amendments to Law on Renewable Energy, approved on 27 February 2014 in a Government meeting • National Renewable Energy Action Plan 2013-2020, approved by Government Decree No. 1 073 of 27 December 2013 • National Energy Efficiency Programme 2011-2020, approved by Government Decree No. 833 • Law No. 92 on Thermal Energy and Promotion of Cogeneration of 29 May 2014 • Law No. 151 on Eco Design Requirements for Energy-Related Products of 17 July 2014 • Law No. 86 on Environmental Impact Evaluation of 29 May 2014 • Law No. 128 on Energy Performance of Buildings of 11 July 2014 • Law No. 44 on Labelling of Energy-Related Products of 27 March 2014 **Endorsing organisations** • Energy Efficiency Agency • Energy Efficiency Fund • National Environmental Fund • Moldova Social Investment Fund
Policy objective(s) of subsidy	To stimulate energy efficiency and the production of renewable energy by providing co-financing to other domestic and international sources
End recipient(s) of subsidy	Renewable energy producers
Time period	From 2011 onward
Background	Since 2011, the Government has initiated programmes to promote energy efficiency and the use of renewable energy resources. Several governmental agencies were involved in the implementation of EE and RES projects. Government support for EE allocated through the Energy Efficiency Fund amounted to MDL 100 mln in 2012 and MDL 192.5 mln in 2013. In 2013-14, the Moldova Social Investment Fund implemented projects worth over MDL 30 mln. Through the Moldova Biomass Energy Project, 144 public projects involving renewables were implemented. Also, local governments contributed to the implementation of local public projects, usually at a rate of 15%-20% of the total cost. Generally, this type of expenditure is intended to be environmentally benign. In some cases, however, there may be environmentally harmful side effects (e.g. related to land use for biomass cultivation).
Amount of subsidy conferred	2011-15: USD 106.94 mln
Information sources	EEA (2015), EEF (2014)

Table 6.A2.2. **Feed-in tariff for renewable energy producers**

Subsidy category	Induced transfer
Stimulated activity	Production of renewable energy
subsidy name	**Feed-in tariff for renewable energy producers**
Jurisdiction	National level
Legislation/endorsing organisation	Article 12.a of the Law on Renewable Energy (Law No. 160, 2007)
Policy objective(s) of subsidy	To stimulate the development of the renewable energy sector
End recipient(s) of subsidy	Renewable energy producers
Time period	Staring from 2013
Background	The feed-in tariff for renewable energy producers was introduced in Moldova in 2013. According to Law No. 160 of 2007, the so-called "green" tariff for renewable energy producers is set based on a special methodology approved by ANRE. The methodology assumes the recovery of investments in renewable energy production for a period of up to 15 years, providing that the prescribed rate of return does not exceed twice the corresponding rate in the traditional energy sector. The tariff is set and approved at the request of the producer. The authors estimate the value of the induced transfer to renewable energy producers, based on the weighted average "green" tariff for production of electricity from renewable energy sources (biogas, solar, wind energy), using data provided in the ANRE Annual Reports.
Amount of subsidy conferred	2013: MDL 1.76 mln (USD 0.15 mln) 2014: MDL 2.5 mln (USD 0.20 mln) 2015: MDL 37.35 mln (USD 2.66 mln)
Information sources	ANRE (2015) Annual Report 2015

Notes

1. The breakaway territory of Transnistria, located between the Dniester river and Ukraine, is not included in the analysis of this report.

2. ANRE does not fully agree with this assessment. According to ANRE, tariff methodologies specify the formula and all components included in the formula (including the sources where all the components can be found) and it is clear to all regulated utilities what level of rate of return they can expect during the regulatory period.

3. Unlike oil, gas and coal, electricity is not extensively traded over national borders, so there is no reliable international reference price used by the IEA. IEA electricity reference prices were thus based on annual average-cost pricing for electricity in each country (weighted according to output levels from each generating option). In other words, electricity reference prices were set to account for the cost of production, transmission and distribution, but no other costs, such as allowances for building new capacity. They were determined using reference prices for fossil fuels and annual average fuel efficiencies for power generation. An allowance of USD 15/MWh and USD 40/MWh was added to account for transmission and distribution costs for industrial and residential uses, respectively. To avoid over-estimation, electricity reference prices were capped at the levelised cost of a combined-cycle gas turbine (CCGT) plant.

4. It was not possible to estimate this subsidy, due to lack of precise household gas consumption data.

5. ANRE has made the decision to compensate the energy companies for their losses between 2011 and 2015 by adjusting the tariff gradually over the period 2017-20. However, given that it is not clear how this will be achieved and whether the financial losses will be adjusted for inflation for the period analysed in this study (2011-15), not adjusting the gas tariff is considered a subsidy.

6. The annual cost of import instead of import parity price is used here in order to capture the annual cost of imports, which generally does not include transport costs.

7. A specific indicator calculated in the emission of pollutants (such as SO_2, NO_2, CO) is used to calculate environmental fees.

8. The project has received financing from the governments of Germany, Sweden, Switzerland, Romania and the EU.

References

ANRE (2016), *Annual Report for 2015*, National Energy Regulatory Agency, Chisinau.

ANRE (2015a), *Annual Report for 2014*, National Energy Regulatory Agency, Chisinau.

ANRE (2015b), *Tariff Model and Regulatory Incentives in the Republic of Moldova*, National Energy Regulatory Agency, Chisinau.

ANRE (2014), *Annual Report for 2013*, National Energy Regulatory Agency, Chisinau.

ANRE (2013), *Annual Report for 2012*, National Energy Regulatory Agency, Chisinau.

ANRE (2012), *Annual Report for 2011*, National Energy Regulatory Agency, Chisinau.

CMC (2013), *Report on the Progress of the Heating Season 2012-2013 in the Municipality of Chisinau*, Chisinau Municipal Council, Chisinau. www.chisinau.md/pageview.php?l=ro&idc=462&id=5393.

CMC (2012), *Decree No. 8/9 of 20 December 2012 on the Compensation to Disadvantaged People for Payments for Energy Resources for the Heating Season 2012-2013*, Chisinau Municipal Council, Chisinau. www.chisinau.md/libview.php?l=ro&idc=408&id=4907.

Coady, D. et al. (2015), "How Large are Global Energy Subsidies?", *IMF Working Paper* WP 15/105, May 2015, Fiscal Affairs Department, International Monetary Fund, Washington, DC. https://www.imf.org/external/pubs/ft/wp/2015/wp15105.pdf.

DHP (2014), *Annual Reports for 2013 and 2014*, Department for Housing and Planning, Chisinau Municipal Housing, Chisinau.

EBRD (2011), *The Low Carbon Transition*, European Bank for Reconstruction and Development, London. www.ebrd.com/news/publications/special-reports/special-report-on-climate-change-the-low-carbon-transition.html.

EC/UNDP (2015), *Final Report of the Moldova Energy and Biomass Project 2011-2014*, European Commission/United Nations Development Programme, Chisinau.

EEA (2015), *Annual Report for 2014*, Energy Efficiency Agency, Chisinau.

EEF (2015), *Annual Report for 2014*, Energy Efficiency Fund, Chisinau.

EEF (2014), *Annual Report for 2013*, Energy Efficiency Fund, Chisinau.

Ener2i (2014), *Reinforcing Co-operation with ENP Countries on Bridging the Gap between Energy Research and Energy Innovation, Energy Research to Innovation Project*. https://ener2i.eu/object/news/50/attach/cross-countries_report_pre_final_version_18_11_2014.pdf.

Energy Community (2015), *Energy Community Web-Page – Moldova Overview*, Energy Community, Brussels.

EU (2006), *Directive 2006/32/EC on Energy End-Use Efficiency and Energy Services and Repealing Council Directive 93/76/EEC and Directive 2010/31/EU on the Energy Performance of Buildings*, European Commission, Brussels.

Eurostat (2016), *Eurostat Web-Page*, Eurostat, Brussels. http://ec.europa.eu/eurostat/tgm/refreshTableAction.do?tab=table&plugin=1&pcode=tsdec360&language=en.

GoM (2015), *Republic of Moldova's Intended National Determined Contribution, Submitted at COP21, United Nations Framework Convention on Climate Change*, Bonn. http://www4.unfccc.int/submissions/INDC/Published%20Documents/Republic%20of%20Moldova/1/INDC_Republic_of_Moldova_25.09.2015.pdf.

GoM (2014a), *Decree No. 1 009 on National Climate Change Adaptation Strategy*, Government of Moldova, Chisinau.

GoM (2014b), *Decree No. 318 on Measures Concerning the Procedure for Restructuring JSC Termocom*, Government of Moldova, Chisinau.

GoM (2014c), *Decree No. 135 on the Distribution of the Fund for Subsidising Farmers*, Government of Moldova, Chisinau.

GoM (2013a), *Decree No. 1 073 on National Renewable Energy Action Plan 2013-2020*, Government of Moldova, Chisinau.

GoM (2013b), *Decree No. 102 on Energy Strategy of the Republic of Moldova until 2030*, Government of Moldova, Chisinau.

GoM (2011), *Decree No. 833 on National Energy Efficiency Programme for 2011-2020*, Government of Moldova, Chisinau.

GSI (2014), *Comparison of Fossil-Fuel Subsidy and Support Estimates,* Global Subsidies Initiative, Geneva. www.iisd.org/gsi/sites/default/files/ffs_methods_estimationcomparison.pdf.

IEA (2016), *World Energy Balances*, Organisation for Economic Co-operation and Development/International Energy Agency, Paris.

IEA (2014), *Energy Balances of Non-OECD Countries*, International Energy Agency, Paris.

IEA (2013), *CO_2 Emissions from Fuel Combustion*, International Energy Agency, Paris.

IMF (2016), *The Republic of Moldova, Staff Report for the 2015 Article IV Consultation and Third Post-Progress Monitoring Discussions – Press Release; Staff Report; and Statement by the Executive Director for the Republic of Moldova*, IMF Country Report No. 16/19, January 2016, International Monetary Fund, Washington, DC. www.imf.org/external/pubs/ft/scr/2016/cr1619.pdf.

MoE (2016), *Low-Emission Development Strategy of the Republic of Moldova to the Year 2030*, Ministry of Environment of the Republic of Moldova, Chisinau.

MoF (2014), *Reports on State Budget Execution for 2012, 2013, 2014*, Ministry of Finance of the Republic of Moldova, Chisinau.

NBM (2016), *National Bank of Moldova Web-Page – Official Exchange Rates*, National Bank of the Republic of Moldova, Chisinau.

NBS (2015), *Energy Balance – Energy and Fuel Resources*, National Bureau of Statistics of the Republic of Moldova, Chisinau. www.statistica.md/category.php?l=en&idc=128.

Nutu, A.O. and D. Cenusa (2016), *Interconnecting Moldova's Gas Market: The Iasi-Ungheni Case,* February 2016, Expert Grup, Centru Analitic Independent, Chisinau. www.expert-grup.org/ro/biblioteca/item/download/1511_d3527cd3fb892d86a39ec496490692c0.

OECD/IEA (2015), *Eastern Europe, Caucasus and Central Asia – Energy Policies beyond IEA Countries*, OECD/International Energy Agency, Paris. https://www.iea.org/publications/freepublications/publication/IDR_EasternEuropeCaucasus_2015.pdf.

OECD (2013), *Analysing Subsidies in the Countries of Eastern Europe, Caucasus and Central Asia*, Organisation for Economic Co-operation and Development, Paris. https://www.oecd.org/env/outreach/EHS%20report_20%20August%202013_ENG.pdf.

PoM (2014a), *Law on Environmental Requirements for Designing Eco-Friendly Energy-Consuming Buildings, No. 151*, Parliament of the Republic of Moldova, Chisinau.

PoM (2014b), *Law on Energy Performance of Buildings, No. 128*, Parliament of the Republic of Moldova, Chisinau.

PoM (2014c), *Law on Environmental Impact Evaluation, No. 86*, Parliament of the Republic of Moldova, Chisinau.

PoM (2014d), *Law on Labelling of Energy-Related Products, No. 44*, Parliament of the Republic of Moldova, Chisinau.

PoM (2014e), *Law on Thermal Energy and Promotion of Cogeneration, No. 92*, Parliament of the Republic of Moldova, Chisinau.

PoM (2012a), *Law on the 2013 State Budget, No. 249*, Parliament of the Republic of Moldova, Chisinau.

PoM (2012b), *Law on the National Development Strategy "Moldova 2020"*, No. 166, Parliament of the Republic of Moldova, Chisinau.

PoM (2010), *Law on Energy Efficiency, No. 142*, Parliament of the Republic of Moldova, Chisinau.

PoM (2007), *Law on Renewable Energy, No. 160,* Parliament of the Republic of Moldova, Chisinau.

PoM (2006), *Law on Local Public Administration, No. 436-XVI*, Parliament of the Republic of Moldova, Chisinau.

PoM (2001), *Law on the Petroleum Products Market, No. 460 (with Amendments of 2015)*, Parliament of the Republic of Moldova, Chisinau.

PoM (2000), *Law on Anti-Dumping, Countervailing and Safeguard Measures, No. 820*, Parliament of the Republic of Moldova, Chisinau.

PoM (1998), *Law on Environment Pollution Payment, No. 1 540,* Parliament of the Republic of Moldova, Chisinau.

PoM (1997), *Law on the Tax Code, No. 1 163 XIII,* Parliament of the Republic of Moldova, Chisinau.

Sputnik International (2016), "Going Halves: Moldova Blames Transnistria for Unpaid Russian Gas Debt", Sputnik, Sputnik International, Moscow, 9 January. http://sptnkne.ws/dH3q.

Tulyev, M. (2017), "Russian Gas for Moldova: Who Will Pay the Debts?", *EurAsia Daily*, 13 February. https://eadaily.com/en/news/2017/02/13/russian-gas-for-moldova-who-will-pay-the-debts.

UNDP (2009), *Republic of Moldova: National Energy Policy Information for Regional Analysis*, United Nations Development Programme, Chisinau.

UNDP (2002), *Technology Needs Assessment, Report Elaborated under the United Nations Framework Convention on Climate Change*, United Nations Development Programme, Chisinau.

World Bank (2016), *Moldova Overview*, World Bank website, www.worldbank.org/en/country/moldova/overview.

World Bank (2015a), *District Heating and Electricity Tariff and Affordability Analysis Report No: ACS 13855,* World Bank, Chisinau.

World Bank (2015b), *World Development Indicators*, World Bank, Washington, DC. http://data.worldbank.org/country/moldova.

WTO (1996), *Agreement on Subsidies and Countervailing Measures*, World Trade Organization, Geneva. https://www.wto.org/english/docs_e/legal_e/24-scm_01_e.htm.

Chapter 7

Ukraine's energy subsidies

This chapter identifies, documents and provides estimates of the various subsidies in Ukraine that relate to the production or use of coal, oil and related petroleum products, natural gas, and electricity and heat generated on the basis of these fossil fuels. The chapter also briefly looks at the subsidies benefiting energy-efficiency measures and renewable energy sources. An overview of the country's energy sector is first given to place the measures listed into context. In addition, the chapter discusses pricing and tax policies in the energy sector in Ukraine. The analysis summarises the context, the state of play, and the mechanics of the complex and evolving landscape of energy subsidies in the country.

Key findings

Among the countries of the EU's Eastern Partnership (EaP), Ukraine stands out as having both significant energy subsidies and an active programme for their reform. The reform is subject to discussion and action by several important government actors and other stakeholders.

Over the years, various strategic documents and state programmes included plans to reform energy subsidies, but the government of Ukraine had long been trying to postpone these politically sensitive decisions. Electricity, gas and heat tariffs for households were kept frozen for years, despite increasing international prices and production costs of utility suppliers. As a result, the government developed a plethora of support measures to compensate for the resulting losses to utility providers. This led to increased government spending in the energy sector, augmented state debt or, in the case of electricity, shifted the costs to industrial consumers, reducing their competitiveness.

This detailed bottom-up inventory of energy subsidies in Ukraine suggests that government support for both the production and consumption of fossil fuels peaked at UAH 202.8 bln (USD 17 bln) in 2014. However, as a result of the set of comprehensive measures put in place by the government, energy subsidies in Ukraine declined to UAH 153.2 bln (USD 7 bln) in 2015. In 2016, the total number of subsidies was expected to drop even further, as the result of phasing out of several major subsidy schemes.

The exceptionally difficult economic and political situation over the past few two years has made it difficult for Ukraine to cope with the increasing burden of energy subsidies, and the government has had no choice but to undertake some radical energy-subsidy reform measures. Utility tariffs were increased substantially in 2014, 2015 and 2016. Gas prices for households reached market levels in 2016, which effectively eliminated all direct and indirect consumer subsidies. Cross-subsidisation in the electricity sector is planned to be phased out by 2017. At the same time, the government has reinforced targeted support schemes to the most vulnerable groups.

Given that the increase of utility tariffs is a politically sensitive issue, there are certain risks of a reform's rollback. In all countries, such risks also typically increase before elections. Hence, for the longer-term success of the reform, it is essential to depoliticise energy tariff setting, to make it as much of a technocratic issue as possible. In this respect, the successful experience of other countries with fossil-fuel reforms shows that the introduction of an automatic pricing mechanism can help. In Ukraine, the government can approve a special mechanism or formula that will enable a regular automatic revision of utility tariffs to reflect fluctuations in the international energy market, regardless of the political agenda.

Another important issue to consider is how to ensure that targeted subsidies can be allocated most efficiently. The burden of increased utility tariffs on low-income households could be eased not only by providing subsidies to the poor to help them make utility payments but by encouraging full metering, and incentivising energy saving. This will require the installation of building-level heat meters, which have not yet been installed in about half of households. These now pay for consumption based on normative values, which in some cases, is considerably higher than properly metered consumption volumes.

Although the existing targeted subsidy scheme provides an essential lifeline for vulnerable groups, it could also act as a disincentive to energy saving at the household level. This is particularly true given that about 1 in 3 households receive partial compensation for the payment of utility services within normative consumption volumes. This, in turn, could impede the long-awaited modernisation of the housing sector. One way of addressing this problem could be by providing low-income households subsidies in the form of conditional cash transfers (i.e. providing cash transfers only after utility bills are fully paid). This can create incentives to cut expenditure on utility bills and spend the savings elsewhere, which could be restricted to energy-efficiency measures. However, this step requires detailed analysis and planning, both to address the risk of nonpayment and to design a policy simple enough to administer.

The Ukrainian government has recently made considerable efforts to reform fossil-fuel subsidies, which has helped reduce both the budget deficit and the national debt. At the same time, generated savings were partially rechannelled to targeted subsidies for low-income groups and the energy-efficiency programme in the residential sector. Overall, Ukraine has all the prerequisites for a successful reform of energy subsidies if the government delivers on its commitments on the energy sector reform and if appropriate safeguards are in place to prevent a rollback. The short-term effects of higher utility tariffs are always difficult to cope with, but the reform is likely to deliver multiple benefits in the medium and long term in terms of macroeconomic stabilisation, reduced energy consumption and thus less dependence on energy imports. Improved environmental quality and associated health benefits are also likely to be significant.

Macroeconomic situation and energy sector overview

Since its independence in 1991, Ukraine has undergone significant political and economic changes. Soon after the most recent political events of 2014, the Ukrainian government started working on its reform agenda, which largely focused on deregulation, decentralisation, demonopolisation and privatisation of state-owned enterprises (SOEs), energy sector and financial market reforms.

Table 7.1. **Key macroeconomic indicators**

	International statistics		National statistics	
Population	*million, 2015*	45.2	*million, December 2015*	42.8
GDP	*2015 USD bln*	90.6	*2015 UAH bln*	1 979.5
GDP/per capita	*2015 USD*	2 115	*2015 UAH*	46 201
GDP growth	*2015 yoy %*	-9.9%	*2015 yoy %*	-9.9%
Energy production	*mtoe 2013*	85.93	*mtoe 2014*	76.93
Net energy imports	*mtoe 2013*	31.68	*mtoe 2014*	27.47
Total primary energy supply (TPES)	*mtoe 2013*	116.14	*mtoe 2014*	105.68
TPES/per capita	*toe 2013*	2.55	*toe 2014*	2.47
Electricity consumption	*TWh 2013*	163.77		
Electricity cons./capita	*MWh/capita 2013*	3.6		
CO_2 emissions[a]	*Mt of CO_2 2013*	265.05		
CO_2/capita	*t of CO_2 2013*	5.83		
Total GHG emissions			*Mt of $CO_{2eq.}$ excl. LULUCF, 2014*	385.9

Note: a. CO_2 emissions from fuel combustion only.

Source: Authors' compilation based on IEA (2016), World Bank (2016), State Statistics Service (2016a), Ministry of Ecology and Natural Resources (2016).

After the collapse of the Soviet Union, Ukraine's economy faced a severe crisis. In the 1990s, its GDP was shrinking and in 1994, in particular, it decreased by as much as by 22% year over year. The economy started to recover in 2000, and a peak of annual GDP growth of 12% was reached in 2004, but it was hard-hit by the global economic depression in 2009 (with a drop in GDP of 15%) and it has not fully recovered since then (World Bank, 2016). Ukraine faces a multidimensional crisis due to the military conflict in its eastern region. However, the four-year USD 17.5 bln Extended Fund Facility (EFF) provided by the International Monetary Fund (IMF) accelerated the long-awaited macroeconomic reforms, leading to some stabilisation in 2015 and a slow recovery, with GDP growth of 1.6% forecast for 2016 and 3.3% for 2017 (IER, 2016).

Table 7.2. **Weighted average exchange rate**

	2012	2013	2014	2015	2016 (July)
Weighted average exchange rate USD/UAH	8.0	8.0	11.9	21.8	24.8

Source: National Bank of Ukraine (2016).

The Ukrainian government has made multiple commitments to liberalise the energy market, including tariff reform, in the next few years, after joining the Energy Community Treaty and signing the EU-Ukraine Association Agreement. These commitments are also reflected in the Coalition Agreement signed by five political parties (Parliament of Ukraine, 2014) and Government Action Plan of Priority Measures for 2016 (Cabinet of Ministers Order No. 418-p, 2016). The resolution of the conflict in the East and the effectiveness of the reforms that have been announced will determine Ukraine's future economic outlook.

Energy supply

The total primary energy supply (TPES) fell by 46% from 1990 to 1998 (Figure 7.1). It rose slightly only in 2003, and has continued to decline since, given the restructuring of the economy, after a considerable decline in manufacturing and a rise in the share of services. In 2013, TPES was at 116 mtoe, still 14% lower than 2008 levels. Domestic production covered 74% of TPES, with the largest shares accounted for by coal (40.7 mtoe), nuclear (21.8 mtoe), natural gas (16 mtoe). The contribution of other energy sources is marginal (crude oil 3.2 mtoe; biofuels 1.9 mtoe; hydro 1.2 mtoe) (IEA, 2016).

Figure 7.1. **Total primary energy supply, 1990-2013**

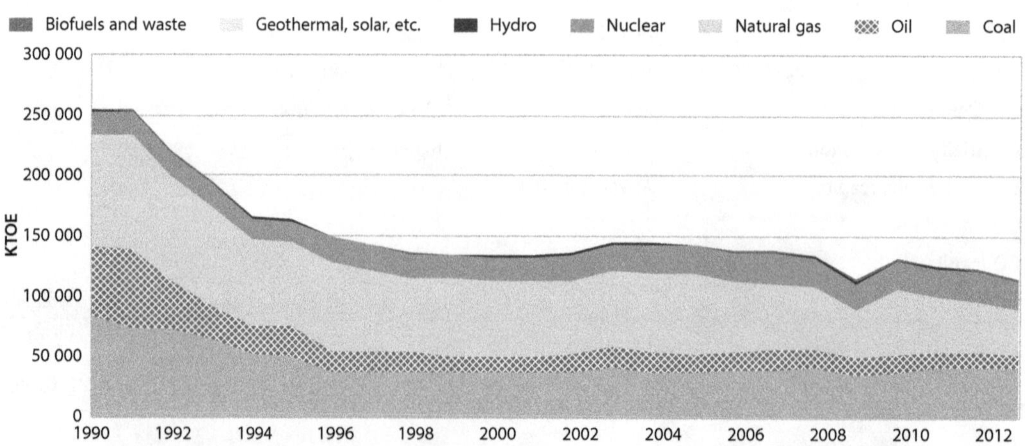

Source: Authors' compilation based on IEA (2016).

As illustrated in Figure 7.1, coal and natural gas have historically been the key sources of TPES, and each accounted for over a third of supply in 1990. The share of natural gas increased to 50% in 1996, while coal dropped to 26%. The economic downturn in 2009, and increased prices of imported gas, stimulated policies aimed at substituting gas for coal. As of 2013, natural gas and coal accounted for 34% and 36% of Ukraine's energy balance, respectively (see Figure 7.2). However, the production and supply of coal, the most critical domestic energy source for meeting internal demand, decreased by 22.4% in 2014 (64.9 Mt) due to the military operations in the Donbass region, where the main coal deposits are located (IEA, 2015a). The contribution of nuclear energy in TPES gradually expanded, from 8% in the 1990s to 19% in 2013, while the share of oil and oil products shrank from 23% to 8% in the same period. The contribution of biofuels and other renewable energy sources slightly increased but is still marginal, according to the available statistics.

Figure 7.2. **Primary energy supply in 2013 by fuel**

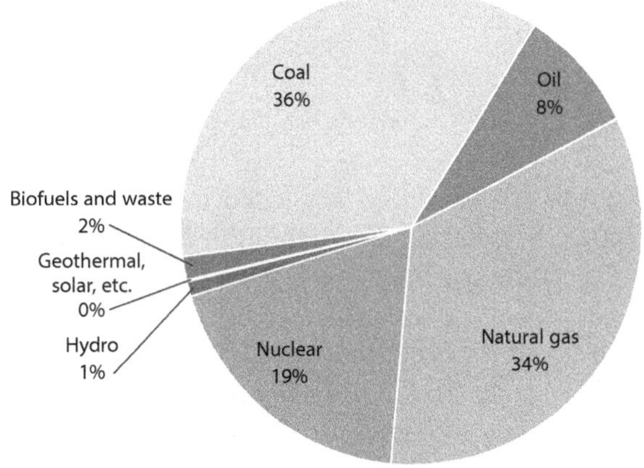

Source: Authors' compilation based on IEA (2016).

In 2013, total electricity production was 194 TWh, at 65% of the 1990 levels. However, it was trending upward, thanks to increased generation at nuclear and coal-fired power plants (Figure 7.3). Nuclear energy accounts for 43% of total electricity production in

Figure 7.3. **Electricity generation by source, 1990-2013**

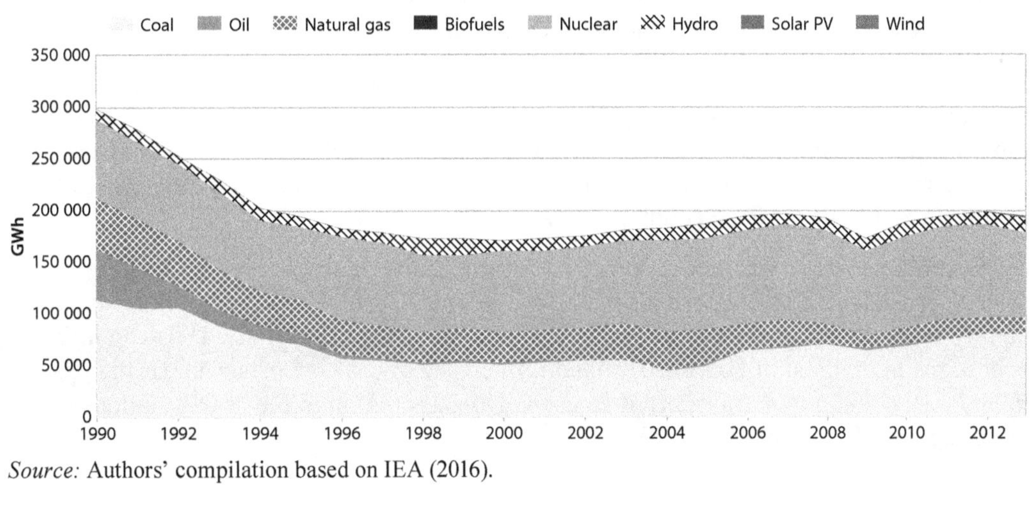

Source: Authors' compilation based on IEA (2016).

Ukraine, while the share of coal-fired electricity is 42% lower (Figure 7.4). The share of hydropower has remained largely stable over the last ten years, while the contribution of other renewables is negligible.

Figure 7.4. **Electricity generation GWh by fuel in 2013**

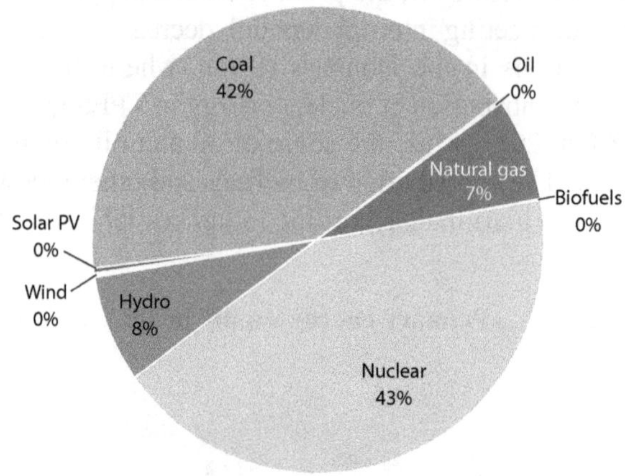

Source: Authors' compilation based on IEA (2016).

The district heating network is widely developed in Ukraine and covers over 40% of households (Energy Charter Secretariat, 2013). In 2013, heat production was at 586.2 PJ, or 66% below the 1990 level. Natural gas is the main fuel for heat generation, accounting for over 70%, and coal accounts for about 22%, while only 1.9% is attributed to biofuels. Although, in absolute terms, the use of gas for heat production has fallen by 70% to 427 PJ since 1990, its share remained relatively stable (IEA, 2016). In recent years, the government of Ukraine introduced several initiatives to incentivise heat production from solid biomass (IEA, 2015a).

Ukraine is a net energy importer, but the share of net imports in TPES decreased considerably, from 43.6% in 2002 to 27.3% in 2013, and continues to decline, due to reduced consumption caused by the economic crisis. In 2013, Ukraine imported 27.5 bcm of gas (15% less than in 2012), 92% of which came from the Russian Federation, while the rest was purchased from Germany, Hungary, Austria and Poland. However, the increasing use of reverse flow imports has changed the situation considerably: in 2014 Ukraine imported 5.1 bcm (26%) of natural gas from the European Union (EU), while imports from the Russian Federation declined to 14.3 bcm (74%) (IEA, 2015a). In 2015, gas imports were diversified further. More than 10 European companies supplied 10.3 bcm, while imports from the Russian Federation dropped to 6.1 bcm (Naftogaz, 2016a).

In 2013, crude oil imports were at 0.8 mtoe (50% below 2012 levels) with the Russian Federation (67%) and Kazakhstan (33%) being the main supplier countries. At the same time, oil product imports increased fivefold compared to 2002. Oil products are largely sourced from Belarus (36%) and the Russian Federation (31.2%) and the rest comes from European and Central Asian countries (IEA, 2015a).

Even though domestic production of coal is high, since Ukraine has plentiful resources of coal, it is also a net importer of coal. In 2013, 10.1 mtoe of hard coal were imported mainly from the Russian Federation (70.2%) and the United States (22.4%). The military operations in the East of Ukraine resulted in increase of coal imports even further, as the mined coal could not be transported from the Donbass region to the power stations in the other regions of Ukraine (IEA, 2015a).

Energy demand

In 2013, total final consumption (TFC) of energy was at 70.1 mtoe, the lion's share of which was used by industry (31.2%), while households accounted for over 33.4%. Contrary to the decline of energy demand from industry and the residential sector in the last ten years, energy consumption by the transport and commercial sectors increased, accounting for 16.9% and 8.2% of TFC, respectively, in 2013 (IEA, 2016). The annual thermal energy demand fluctuates at 130 mln-140 mln Gcal/year. Gas consumption has declined to a historic low of 42.4 bcm in 2014 (7.8% below 2013), which can be explained by the drop in demand due to the economic crisis, gas substitution policies and loss of control over Crimea and the territory in the military conflict in the east (IEA, 2015a).

Energy sector structure and ownership

Ukraine's energy sector has gone through several stages of reform and several rounds of privatisation since 1990. The electricity sector consists of separate generation and a wholesale market, while the transmission system is bundled together with the distribution and retail market. The wholesale electricity market (WEM), created in 1996, is operated by the state-owned company Energorynok, under a single-buyer model. All market players are required to join the WEM, which had over 370 participants by the end of 2014. The United Energy System of Ukraine, including transmission networks and interconnections with neighbouring countries, is owned and operated by the state company UkrEnergo (Ukrainian National Power Company). The majority of thermal generation plants are either partially or completely in private ownership, and the largest share of the market is controlled by the private company DTEK. Regional distribution and retail companies (*oblenergos*) were created in each administrative region in 1995, which have been subject to several waves of privatisation since then (IEA, 2015a).

Ukraine has over 8 000 heat-producing companies. About 22% of all heat is provided by combined heat and power (CHP) plants, while heat-only plants account for about 60% of all heat produced. The National Joint Stock Company (NJSC) Naftogaz has shares in both large and small CHP plants. The latter are often controlled by *oblenergos* or industrial companies. There are also around 900 local heat supply companies (*teplokomunenerhos* – TKEs), which are owned and controlled by local governments. TKEs operate their own heat plants and district heating networks and are responsible for supplying heat to end consumers (IEA, 2012).

Oil and gas exploration activities are performed by the state company NJSC Nadra Ukrayiny, which was established in 2000 by merging 13 geological and specialised mining enterprises (IEA, 2012). NJSC Naftogaz is the largest state-owned vertically integrated company which performs a full cycle of operations from exploration and exploitation of oil and gas to refining and supply of natural gas and liquefied petroleum gas (LPG) to consumers. The company and its subsidiaries account for over 90% of oil and gas production in Ukraine (Naftogaz, 2015a). The company is supervised by the Ministry of Economic Development and Trade. A number of private oil and gas companies are operating in Ukraine, but their share of total production was less than 10% in 2013 (IEA, 2015a).

Coal extraction is carried out at about 300 mines. The profitable ones were privatised largely by DTEK, while unprofitable mines remain in state ownership and are heavily reliant on state subsidies. The largest coal deposits are located in the Donbass region, parts of which are severely affected by the military activities, leading to disruptions in coal production and supply (IEA, 2015a). In 2013, 53 private mines (39.3% of the total number) extracted 60.2 mln tonnes of coal out of 84.3 mln tonnes produced in Ukraine in a given year. The share of thermal coal constituted 68.9% (43.6 mln tonnes) of marketable coal production, while coking coal accounted for 31% as of 2013 (NISS, 2014).

Energy sector governance

A number of government agencies are involved in the regulation of the energy market. The Ministry of Energy and Coal Industry is responsible for general policy-setting and co-ordination across the government. It is also in charge of regulating the downstream oil sector and setting a price range ("corridor") in which retailers set prices for oil products. Setting prices outside of the corridor could attract the attention of the Anti-Monopoly Committee or the state tax administration, but it is not restrictive, and prices are market-driven (IEA, 2015a). In 2014, the National Commission for State Regulation of Energy and Public Utilities (NCSREPU) replaced two commissions that had been in charge of energy markets and communal services. The new commission is responsible for the oversight of natural gas and electricity markets, as well as the district heating sector and other communal services. The commission is accountable to the Parliament and reports to the President of Ukraine.

Energy pricing policy

Natural gas

Until recently, price-setting policy in the gas sector was characterised by differentiation of gas suppliers and tariffs depending on the origin of gas, i.e. whether it was produced domestically or imported. According to the Cabinet of Ministers' Resolution No. 1 729 of 27 December 2001 (with amendments), domestically produced gas was supplied to the residential sector (a requirement applied to companies with more than 50% shares in state ownership), while imported gas was delivered to all other consumers. This resolution was cancelled on 16 July 2016.

Prior to 1 October 2015, natural gas prices for all consumer groups, as well as tariffs on its transport, distribution, storage and supply were subject to state regulation following procedures defined in NCSREPU Resolution No. 466 of 2011. End-user gas prices covered the weighted average price of gas as commodity (purchased from state-owned domestic producers), operational costs, special surcharge, transport and supply tariffs and VAT. Marginal (highest) prices for industrial consumers and publicly funded institutions were defined based on the prices of imported gas and costs incurred by Naftogaz, and were revised regularly (NCSREPU, 2015a).

Procedures on tariff setting were modified considerably when Law No. 329-VIII (2015) on the Gas Market came into effect on 1 October 2015 (Parliament of Ukraine, 2015b). On the one hand, the law envisions government regulation of monopolistic markets (transport, distribution, storage, services of liquefied natural gas installation) and, on the other hand, the development of fair competition in the commodity market of natural gas. Liberalisation of prices in the wholesale and retail gas market (except for cases when the Cabinet of Ministers assigns special responsibilities to the gas market players) and free choice of gas suppliers are anticipated.

In the transition period from 1 October to 30 April 2016, gas prices for households and heat supply companies (TKEs) providing heat for household needs were defined by the Cabinet of Ministers (Cabinet of Ministers Resolution No. 758, 2015a) "On approval of the assigning of special responsibilities of the natural gas market players to ensure interests of the general public". Gas prices for industrial and other consumers, which are not covered by the above resolution, are defined and established by gas market players independently.

For many years, gas prices for residential consumers were considerably lower than for industrial consumers, but recent price amendments have reduced this gap to a certain extent. In April 2015, the NCSREPU roughly tripled gas tariffs for households, differentiating them depending on consumption volumes and the time of the year (NCSREPU Resolution No. 583, 2015d). Gas prices for heat supply companies were also increased considerably in April 2015, by a factor of 2.3, to UAH 2 994 per 1 000 m^3 (NCSREPU Resolution No. 584, 2015c).

On 27 April 2016, the Cabinet of Ministers approved amendments to Resolution No. 758 of 1 October 2015, which effectively established a gas price for households at the market level (import parity approach). Starting on 1 May 2016, the wholesale gas price was set at UAH 4 942 per 1 000 m^3, which includes the forecast gas price at the German gas hub NCG (according to Platt's European Gas Daily) and transport costs to the border of Ukraine. This is now the price of gas supplied by the NJSK Naftogaz for heat and hot water generation installations (excluding VAT, transport and distribution tariffs). The marginal level of retail prices is established at UAH 6 879 (246 EUR) per 1 000 m^3, which is based on the wholesale price, weighted average transport costs within the country and distribution tariffs, as well as the trade margin of the supplier. The wholesale gas price for domestic producers (with 50% of shares in state ownership) was also tripled to market level, at UAH 4 849 (EUR 173) per 1 000 m^3 as of 1 May 2016. Notably, 50% of the gas price for domestic producers will be recycled back in the form of rent to the budget and will be used for social support of vulnerable groups. This decision will also help to boost investments and increase domestic gas extraction by 30% by 2020 (Ministry of Economic Development and Trade, 2016).

Heat

Tariffs for heating and hot water supply as well as other utilities are set by the NCSREPU and local authorities, according to the procedures described in NCSREPU Resolution No. 377 (2016) and Resolution No. 528 (2016). Heat supply companies calculate their costs and submit their estimates for approval to the NCSREPU. End-user prices depend on the cost structure (including primary fuel used) of a particular heat supply company, and vary from region to region. As noted above, until recently, TKEs purchased natural gas from Naftogaz at below-market prices for heat supply to the residential sector. Other consumers, such as public institutions and industry, were subject to much higher tariffs, based on the price of imported gas. An increase in the gas price for TKEs, in April 2015, triggered an increase of heating rates for households by 67%. Further revision of gas prices for TKEs to market levels resulted in an increase of heating rates by 75%-90%, depending on the fuel mix used by heat producers (coal-based generation is cheaper).

Although tariffs are supposed to cover depreciation, expenditures on repair and improvement of fixed assets and allow for marginal profits, they were set too low for decades, and it became impossible to collect sufficient funds for the modernisation and rehabilitation of the system network. According to a World Bank study (World Bank, 2012), expenditures on depreciation account for about 3% of the total TKEs' costs, which is lower by five to eight times than what is required to provide satisfactory services. As a result, district heating assets are often close to or beyond the end of their design life, which poses serious risks of system collapse and disruptions in the heating supply. One worrisome example was a system collapse in Alchevsk in midwinter in 2006, during which residents had to be evacuated from the city.

The majority of households still do not have building-level heat meters installed. It is estimated that households without meters pay on average 30% more (for services they do not consume) than households where meters are installed (Shlapak, 2015).

Electricity

Wholesale electricity tariffs for producers selling electricity on WEM (particularly nuclear, large hydro and cogeneration plants) are set by the NCSREPU on the basis of the cost-plus methodology. While the wholesale price for thermal power plants is defined daily on a largely competitive basis at the wholesale market (generators submit bids to the market operator) NCSREPU could introduce a ceiling on certain price components, for example, on fuel cost).

The wholesale price for electricity suppliers and distribution companies is defined as a weighted average of the cost of electricity bought from all producers, outlays on dispatching and maintenance of the main and interstate electricity networks, operational expenditures of the Wholesale Energy Market (WEM) and additional state charges (e.g. special surcharge and "subsidy certificates" to compensate for reduced prices, largely to households). The wholesale electricity price is formed at the WEM and approved by the NCSREPU each month. The percentage of the wholesale electricity price in the structure of retail tariffs is about 80% (NCSREPU, 2015a).

Table 7.3. **Price policies**

Energy carrier	Pricing policy	Price categories	Price levels
Natural gas	Marginal prices were set for households, religious organisations, and regulated price for district heating companies for the transition period (1 May 2016-31 March 2017) according to Cabinet of Ministers Resolution No. 758, 2015a Tariffs for industrial consumers and public institutions are deregulated	Differentiated by consumer groups (households, public institutions, religious organisations, etc.)	Marginal price (including all tariffs and taxes) for households – UAH 6 879 UAH per 1 000 m^3, for religious organisations – UAH 3 913 per 1 000 m^3. Regulated tariff (excluding gas transport and distribution tariffs and taxes) for district heating companies supplying heat and hot water for households – UAH 4 942 per 1 000 m^3 and for religious organisations UAH 2 471 per 1 000 m^3. Tariffs for other consumers (industries and public institutions) are defined and established by market players independently. Tariffs are revised on a monthly basis. Current information is available from Naftogaz (2016a).
Electricity	"Cost plus" methodology, but cross-subsidisation is embedded in the tariff.	Highly differentiated rates, depending on the consumer group, consumption volume and time of day, etc.	As of August 2016, tariffs for non-residential consumers (without VAT) are the following: first class, UAH 1. 44 per kWh; second class, UAH 1.8 per kWh (NCSREPU Resolution No. 1 309, 2016e); tariffs for households (including VAT) UAH 0.57-1.56 (NCSREPU, 2016b).
Heat	"Cost plus" methodology; tariffs have fully recovered costs since July 2016	Differentiated by consumer groups (households, public institutions, religious organisations, etc.). The tariffs for households are differentiated depending on the availability of meters	Different tariffs are approved for 169 TKEs providing services to the residential sector. Current tariffs for households are available from NCSREPU (2016c) and for state institutions, religious organisations and other consumers from NCSREPU (2016b)
Liquid petroleum products	Prices and marketing of products are fully liberalised (IEA, 2015a)		
Coal	Prices are not regulated, but state-owned coal mines receive compensation from the budget to cover their production costs if they are higher than the sale price		

Source: Authors' compilation based on IEA (2015a), NCSREPU (2015a).

Retail prices are also set based on the cost-plus methodology, which takes into account the wholesale electricity price at WEM, the electricity transmission tariff of local networks, the supply tariff and normative losses in local networks. Electricity tariffs for industrial consumers are uniform across Ukraine and differentiated depending on the voltage class of electricity (the first class is at 27.5 kV and higher, and the second class below 27.5 kV).

At the same time, certain categories of consumers (primarily households, but also coal mining enterprises, municipal electric transport, etc.) enjoy fixed preferential tariffs, which are well below cost-recovery levels. As a result, energy supply companies incur losses that are compensated through "subsidy certificates" incorporated into the wholesale electricity price. Consequently, electricity prices for industry are significantly higher than for residential consumers (see Table 7.3 for comparison).

Over an extended period, electricity tariffs for households remained unchanged. In 2006, electricity tariffs for households were revised upwards twice by 25%, and the next revision of tariffs took place during 2011-12 (tariffs were differentiated depending on consumption volumes). In June 2014, tariffs for households were increased by 14% on average (10%-40%, depending on consumption volumes) (NCSREPU, 2015c). On 26 February 2015, NCSREPU approved Resolution No. 220 which increased tariffs for households by 45.2% on average (compared with previous levels) in April 2015, and laid out a plan for a step-wise tariff increase to market levels by March 2017, when tariffs for households were to reach 0.9-1.68 UAH/kWh.

Taxation policy

The 2015 tax reform reduced the previously large number of taxes and charges to only 7 at the national level (corporate profit tax, personal income tax, VAT, excise tax, environmental tax, resource rent and customs duty) and 4 at the local level (property tax, unified tax, parking charge, tourist charge). Ukraine does not have any additional taxes specific to the energy sector, but there was a special surcharge incorporated in the end-use tariff for gas (cancelled as of 1 January 2016). Table 7.4 provides a schematic illustration

Table 7.4. **Taxation of energy**

Activity subject to taxation	Baseline tax system: VAT, corporate profit tax, personal income tax, environmental tax, customs duty (national level) and property tax (local level)	Resource rent	Excise
Companies extracting and refining oil and gas	Applicable as appropriate	Rent differentiated depending on the depth of deposits, and corrective coefficient applied in certain cases	Applicable as appropriate
Companies extracting coal	Applicable as appropriate	Rent differentiated depending on the coal type; corrective coefficient applied in certain cases	n.a.
Consumers of liquid petroleum products and liquefied petroleum gas (LPG)	Applicable as appropriate	n.a.	Excise tax differentiated depending on the product, 0% excise tax is applied for bioethanol use
Companies generating electricity	Applicable as appropriate	n.a.	n.a.
Consumers of electricity	Applicable as appropriate	n.a.	n.a.

Note: **n.a.**: not applicable.

Source: Authors' compilation based on Tax Code (Parliament of Ukraine, 2010c).

of how energy is taxed in Ukraine. The Tax Code of Ukraine (issue of 13 August 2015) provides a number of incentives (e.g. corporate income tax benefits, VAT and excise tax exemptions) to support capital investments in the development and modernisation of infrastructure, and in energy-saving projects, as well as to encourage the development of renewables.

Greenhouse gas emissions and climate policy

As a result of the post-Soviet economic downturn, Ukraine's GHG emissions dropped from 912.7 mln t $CO_{2\text{-eq}}$ in 1990 to 408.6 mln t $CO_{2\text{-eq}}$ in 2000. Although the economy started to recover after 2000 and annual GDP growth rates were considerable, the GHG emissions took a different trajectory. After having peaked at 451.6 mln t $CO_{2\text{-eq}}$ in 2007, Ukraine's GHG emissions declined and have since fluctuated at around 400 mln t $CO_{2\text{-eq}}$ (Ministry of Ecology and Natural Resources of Ukraine, 2016). This is due to the fact that Ukraine's economy has been going through substantial structural changes, and the inefficient energy-intensive sectors were partially replaced by services and agriculture. Moreover, the energy efficiency of the economy has also been improving, as outdated assets are gradually modernised.

Current (as of 2014) GHG emissions of Ukraine are 62.7% below 1990 levels (Ministry of Ecology and Natural Resources of Ukraine, 2016). The energy sector is the largest contributor to the national GHG emissions and accounts for 67.7% of the total. Industrial processes and agriculture are responsible for 16.7% and 12.6%, respectively. According to the Intended Nationally Determined Contribution (INDC) submitted to the UNFCCC before its Conference of the Parties in Paris at the end of 2015, Ukraine "will not exceed 60% of 1990 GHG emissions level in 2030" (Ministry of Ecology and Natural Resources of Ukraine, 2015).

There have been several attempts in recent years to develop a national low-carbon strategy, but to date, no such strategy has been officially adopted by the Ukrainian government.

National definition and discussion of energy subsidies

There is no comprehensive definition of subsidies in Ukraine, though different terms are used in the legislation on budget policy and state support. These terms are comparable to components of much wider definitions used by international organisations (Figure 7.5). A straightforward narrow definition of subsidies can be found in the "Instruction on the use of economic classification of expenditures" approved by Decree No. 333 of 12 March 2012 by the Ministry of Finance of Ukraine. According to the Instruction, subsidies are defined as:

> "all current payments to companies that do not envision compensation in the form of special payments due or goods and services in exchange for payments made and also expenditures related to compensation of losses of state enterprises".

However, budget laws of Ukraine contain a range of terms, such as subventions, grants and other transfers (State Treasury Service, 2011-2016), which are not classified as subsidies according to national legislation, but are *de facto* subsidies by international definitions. In addition, the term "subsidy" is not used for tax expenditures, but the government of Ukraine considers certain cases of tax benefits as revenue foregone (State Fiscal Service, 2015) and the Ministry of Finance estimates such losses to the budget.

Moreover, given that Ukraine has been a member of the World Trade Organization (WTO) since 16 May 2008 (Parliament of Ukraine Law No. 250-VI, 2008), the definition of "subsidy" stipulated in the *Subsidies and Countervailing Measures Agreement (SCMA)* automatically applies to state regulations in Ukraine. SCMA notifications are regularly submitted by Ukraine, which *inter alia*, cover support provided to coal mining (WTO, 2015).

Figure 7.5. **What does Ukraine include in the national definition of subsidy?**

- Covered by the national definitions of both "subsidy" and "state support"
- Covered only by the national definition of "state support"
- Not included in the national definition of either "subsidy" or "state support"

Direct budget transfers	Tax expenditures	Induced transfers	Transfer of risk to government	References
				Decree No. 333 of 2012 by the Ministry of Finance of Ukraine contains a very narrow definition of subsidies (direct transfers only). Other government documents recognise tax expenditures as state support. Induced transfers in the form of cross-subsidised tariffs are also widely discussed, including by the Regulator.

Reports of the Treasury of Ukraine are a primary source of information (State Treasury Service, 2011-2016) on direct transfers. The State Fiscal Service of Ukraine publishes the handbook on tax expenditure, which covers all effective tax benefits each year but does not estimate the revenue foregone due to such measures (State Fiscal Service, 2015). Annual reports of the Regulator provide detailed information on energy pricing policy, including data on cross-subsidisation and feed-in tariffs for renewables (NCSREPU, 2015a, NERC, 2014). Loan guarantees and equity injections are usually specified in the budget planning documents authorised by resolutions of the Cabinet of Ministers. At the same time, there is no nationwide inventory of all energy subsidies in Ukraine.

At the level of international organisations, Ukraine regularly submits its communication to the WTO Committee on Subsidies and Countervailing Measures (WTO, 2015). The dataset supporting the IEA's World Energy Outlook 2014 includes estimates of fossil-fuel consumer subsidies in Ukraine at USD 6.4 bln for all types of fossil fuels in 2014 (IEA, 2015b).

Moreover, two relevant studies have recently been published. The first is an in-depth analysis of various forms of state support for companies (including those in the energy sector) by Hölzler et al. (2015). This was prepared within the EU-funded Project: *Harmonisation of Public Procurement System in Ukraine with EU Standards.* The second study, by Oharenko and Denysenko (2015) reviewed budget spending in the energy sector of Ukraine, revealing the huge amount of funds provided to subsidise unprofitable state-owned coal mines and to compensate for below cost-recovery heat tariffs for households, in contrast with the limited budget support for incentivising energy-efficiency projects.

Following the OECD (2013) methodology, Table 7.5 presents an overview of key data and information sources on the different types of energy subsidies in Ukraine.

Table 7.5. **Subsidy overview**

Energy subsidy	Key findings
Direct transfer of funds and liabilities	• Included in the national definition of subsidies (except liabilities) • Various forms of direct budget transfers were identified in the Budget Laws of Ukraine • Reports of the Treasury of Ukraine serve as a primary source of information on direct transfers (State Treasury Service, 2011-16) • Estimates are available in Oharenko and Denysenko (2015), WTO (2015), Hölzler et al. (2015)
Tax expenditure (tax revenue foregone)	• Several tax benefits relevant to the energy sector are mentioned in the Tax Code of Ukraine • The State Fiscal Service of Ukraine (State Fiscal Service, 2015) publishes the Handbook on tax privileges, which covers all effective tax benefits for a particular year, but does not estimate the revenue foregone due to such measures • Estimates of the value of tax benefits for all economic sectors, including energy, are provided by the Ministry of Finance (cited in Hölzler et al., 2015)
Induced transfers (income or price support provided to producers or consumers through various regulations)	• Below cost-recovery energy pricing is widespread, e.g. cross-subsidisation of electricity tariffs for households by industry. "Green" feed-in tariffs for renewable electricity producers is another example of induced transfer • Annual reports of the regulator provide detailed information on energy pricing policy, including data on cross-subsidisation and feed-in tariffs for renewables (NCSREPU, 2015a, NERC, 2014)
Transfer of risk to government	• Loan guarantees and equity injections are usually specified in the budget planning documents, authorised by the resolutions of the Cabinet of Ministers and reported by the Ministry of Finance (2015) • Equity injections to JSC Naftogaz are briefly mentioned in Oharenko and Denysenko (2015); quasi-fiscal activities of Naftogaz and loan guarantees are described in detail by Hölzler et al. (2015)

Government support for fossil fuels

Price-gap estimates of consumer subsidies

IEA's price-gap approach quantifies subsidies to end consumers of fossil fuels and electricity by comparing average end-user prices with reference prices. In the case of Ukraine, a net energy importer, subsidies in the gas sector are estimated based on the import gas price at the nearest international hub, plus transport and distribution costs and value-added tax (VAT). Quantification of fossil-fuel subsidies embedded in electricity, which is not widely traded across borders, is based on the annual average-cost pricing of combined-cycle gas turbine (CCGT) plants. This covers production, transmission and distribution costs, but no allowance for building new capacities is included (IEA, 2015b).

Table 7.6 illustrates the most recent estimates of fossil-fuel subsidies in Ukraine calculated by the IEA's *World Energy Outlook 2015* (IEA, 2015c). According to the IEA estimates, consumer subsidies to gas and electricity totalled USD 10 bln and USD 4.2 bln, respectively, in 2012. The total amount of subsidies decreased more than by half by 2014, which is explained not so much by energy policy reforms, but by the sharp decline of international gas prices that IEA uses as a benchmark. Although the Ukrainian government started revisions of energy tariffs for households in 2014, these adjustments were not significant enough to explain such a dramatic decline in consumer subsidies.

Given that prices for oil and oil products are liberalised in Ukraine, the IEA does not identify any subsidies in the oil sector. Table 7.6 also shows that there are no consumer subsidies in the coal sector, because the price-gap approach captures only those government interventions that impact the price for end users. However, producer subsidies are granted to state-owned coal mines in Ukraine, as discussed in detail below.

Table 7.6. **IEA estimates of fossil-fuel consumer subsidies in Ukraine based on the price-gap approach (real 2013 USD billion)**

Subsidised fossil-fuel type	2012	2013	2014
Oil	-	-	-
Electricity	4.2	4.4	2.7
Gas	10.0	8.0	3.7
Coal	-	-	-
Total	**14.1**	**12.4**	**6.4**

Source: IEA (2015c).

The project team has developed its own price-gap estimate of consumer subsidies in Ukraine's gas sector in 2015. The estimate is based on the weighted average import gas price (estimated based on Naftogaz, 2016c) as a benchmark, as well as on Naftogaz's forecast of gas consumption values for 2015 (Naftogaz, 2015a). Table 7.7 presents the results obtained for 2015. These findings suggest a further decline in subsidies to about USD 3.1 bln, compared with IEA's figures for 2014, which could be explained both by the sharp increases of gas and heat tariffs for households as well as further depreciation of gas prices in the international market in 2015.

Table 7.7. **Price-gap estimates of consumer subsidies in the gas sector in Ukraine in 2015 (nominal 2015 billion USD)**

Tariffs based on consumer groups	Net tariff/1 000 m³[a]	bcm[b]	Opportunity cost/1 000 m³	Price gap/1 000 m³	Subsidy in USD million
Full tariff for households (primarily for cooking)	231.2	5.8	277	46	264
Reduced tariff for households (for use in individual heating systems within certain limits)	99.3	8.7	277	178	1 551
Tariff for the district heating units serving households	82.7	6.8	277	194	1 322
Industry and state-funded institutions[c]	255.0	7.1	277	22[d]	157[d]
Total					**3 137**

Notes: a. Net of taxes and cost of transport and distribution, purchase cost also net of VAT and transport.

b. Naftogaz's 12-month estimate starting from 1 May 2015.

c. 2014 volumes for lack of 2015 estimates; applied maximum tariff in April 2015; net tariff calculated using average mark-up for household tariff groups.

d. This could be explained by data discrepancy, rather than mispricing. The price gap for industry should be zero, as gas tariffs for industry and state-funded institutions fully reflect import gas prices and are revised regularly. Hence, it is not included in the total.

Source: Authors' estimates based on Naftogaz (2015a, 2015c, 2016b).

Ukraine is a net gas importer but also has domestic production at 13-15 bcm annually, which is mandated for household consumption (a requirement for producers with 50% or more shares in state ownership). The price-gap estimates described above thus reflect both explicit measures, such as direct transfers and other measures needed to compensate the losses of the energy suppliers (providing services to households at regulated below cost-recovery tariffs), as well as implicit subsidies in the form of opportunity cost for domestic producers.

Bottom-up inventory of government support for fossil fuels

Overview of bottom-up estimates of government support for fossil fuels

Tables 7.8a and 7.8b summarise the detailed bottom-up analysis of government support measures in Ukraine's energy sector. The largest group of subsidies constitute explicit measures to compensate losses of energy companies for supplying gas and heat to households at regulated tariffs, which amounted to UAH 109 bln (USD 9.2 bln) in 2014. Implicit subsidies, in the form of the opportunity cost for domestic producers, fluctuated from USD 5.4 bln in 2012 to USD 2.5 bln in 2014, depending on world market prices.

The next largest government support measure is cross-subsidisation in the electricity sector, which has increased considerably since 2012 in terms of UAH values (the currency depreciation decreased the USD value). Ukraine does not provide support for coal consumers (with the exception of targeted subsidies for households), but direct budgetary transfers to the coal sector have been a heavy burden on the budget. However, these transfers have been steadily decreasing in the recent years, due partly to the fact that most coal mines are located in the area of the military conflict. Neither consumer nor producer subsidies were identified in the transport fuel sector, since it is fully liberalised.

Government support in the form of tax benefits (only two measures were identified) was limited in 2012 and 2013, and no data are available for subsequent years. The first tax expenditure measure was a VAT exemption on imported gas for the needs of industrial consumers, which was applied from 6 August 2011 until 1 July 2012. This was introduced to boost the competitiveness of domestic industries at a time of increasing import gas prices. The Ministry of Finance estimated that the revenue foregone as a result of this tax benefit was about UAH 1.5 bln in 2012 (quoted in Hölzler et al., 2015).

Another relevant tax expenditure policy is the corporate income tax relief for expenditures of energy enterprises for investment programmes approved by the NCSREPU. These programmes could include capital investment (reconstruction, modernisation) of international, trunk and distribution (local) electricity networks, thermal power plants (TPPs), CHPs, trunk gas networks, etc. and for the repayment of loans financing the objectives specified above. The Ministry of Finance (quoted in Hölzler et al., 2015) reported revenue foregone as a result of this measure in 2012 and 2013 at UAH 975 mln and UAH 761 mln respectively, but this scheme was cancelled at the beginning of 2015.

The amount of funds spent on direct transfers for low-income households increased in 2015 when the government started raising utility tariffs for consumers and partly rechannelling support measures to compensate energy companies' losses in order to provide direct support for vulnerable groups. Specific government support measures are discussed in detail below (see Table 7.A2.1 on methodological approaches used for the quantification of key energy subsidies).

Although care was taken to collect the most accurate data and avoid double-counting, the price-gap estimates described in the previous section did not fully match the results obtained from the bottom-up analysis of government support measures. This might be explained by remaining data discrepancies and a possible time-lag in the compensation of losses to Naftogaz payable for the provision of gas for household needs at regulated tariffs.

Table 7.8a. **Summary of major energy subsidies in Ukraine, UAH million**

	2012	2013	2014	2015	2016p[a]
Explicit subsidies to gas consumers	24 342.8	10 052.5	109 032.7	34 385.1	0
Implicit subsidies to gas consumers	43 168.1	44 493.0	36 678.7	54 141.6p	.
Subsidies to electricity consumers	34 466.5	37 557.1	40 824.6	43 848.0	.
Producer subsidies to state-owned coal mines	12 998.2	15 290.3	9 405.4	1 998.0	1 345.6
Targeted subsidies to households	7 455.8	6 779.0	6 887.5	19 116.0	41 474.2
Revenue foregone	2 438.6	761.0	.	.	.
Total	**124 870.0**	**114 932.9**	**202 828.9**	**153 488.6**	**.**

Notes: a. **p**: provisional.

Source: Authors' estimates based on State Treasury Service (2011-2016), NCSREPU (2015a), NERC (2014), Ministry of Finance quoted in Hölzler et al. (2015), Naftogaz (2015c) and Resolutions of the NCSREPU.

Table 7.8b. **Summary of major energy subsidies in Ukraine, USD million**

	2012	2013	2014	2015	2016p[a]
Explicit subsidies to gas consumers	4 284.5	2 201.0	9 752.1	1 577.3	0
Implicit subsidies to gas consumers	5 402.1	5 566.5	3 085.7	2 483.6p	.
Subsidies to electricity consumers	4 313.2	4 698.8	3 434.5	2 011.4	.
Producer subsidies to state-owned coal mines	1 626.6	1 913.0	791.3	91.6	54.3
Targeted subsidies to households	933.0	848.1	579.4	876.9	1 672.3
Revenue foregone	305.2	95.2	.	.	.
Total	**15 626.3**	**14 379.2**	**17 063.5**	**7 040.8**	**.**

Notes: a. **p**: provisional.

Source: Authors' estimates based on State Treasury Service (2011-2016), NCSREPU (2015a), NERC (2014), Ministry of Finance quoted in Hölzler et al. (2015), Naftogaz (2015c) and Resolutions of the NCSREPU.

Government support measures in the gas sector

Gas, heat and other utilities were traditionally supplied to households at well below cost-recovery levels (see the section on energy pricing policy), while companies providing services to households operated at huge losses. For example, the cumulative deficit of Naftogaz from selling gas to the distribution companies serving households at regulated prices amounted to about USD 20 bln in the last ten years (2005-14). In 2014, the difference between the gas purchase cost (including imported and domestically produced gas) and the value of its sales to households was UAH 18.7 bln (Naftogaz, 2015c).

The government developed various support schemes to compensate utility providers for accumulated losses due to inefficient energy pricing policy. In particular, budget transfers were made to Naftogaz either directly (by 2012) or indirectly covered by local budgets, which received transfers (referred to as "subventions" in the legislation) from the national budget (Figure 7.6, Tables 7.9a and 7.9b). The latter mechanism is rather complicated. Administered by the Ministry of Regional Development, Construction and Utilities, it is intended to settle the arrears accumulated as a result of the difference between the actual costs of central heating and services of centralised water supply and wastewater treatment, on the one hand, and regulated tariffs on the other (see Table 7.A2.3 for details).

Direct budgetary transfers were not always provided on time and were not sufficient to fully cover the deficit Naftogaz accumulated from selling imported gas to households at regulated prices. For this reason, Naftogaz had to take on loans to cover liquidity gaps and ensure timely payments for imported gas. The company had to pay back a considerable share of these loans in 2014. Overall, payments to creditors amounted to 21% (UAH 39 bln) of the total company's expenditures in 2014 (Naftogaz, 2015c). However, Naftogaz would not have been able to pay back the loans without additional government support measures, as described below.

Figure 7.6. **Budget transfers to compensate for losses of energy and utilities providers**

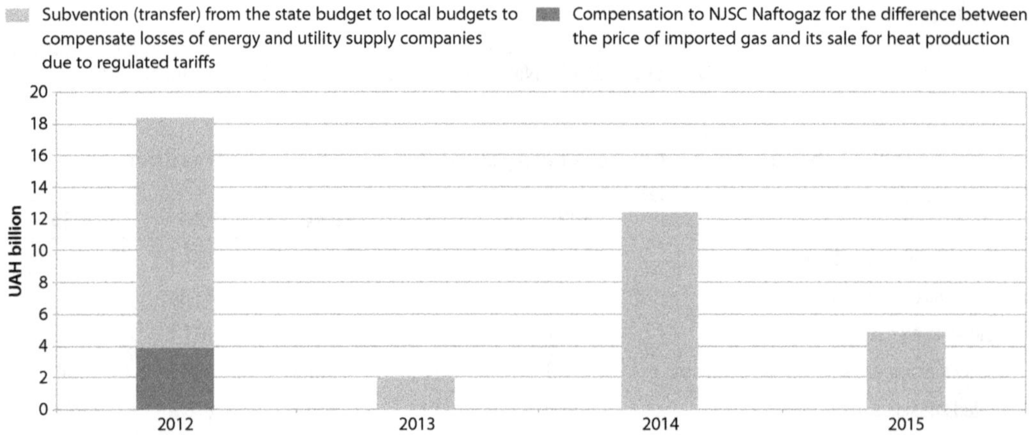

Source: Authors' compilation based on State Treasury Service (2011-2016).

The Cabinet of Ministers developed yet another complex mechanism to cover the deficit of Naftogaz indirectly without adding to the budget deficit. It chose to authorise the issue of special state bonds to recapitalise Naftogaz, and, thus, provide it with the capital to finance the deficit (this led to the increase in domestic debt). Figure 7.7 illustrates this mechanism. For the period 2012-15, the Ministry of Finance issued state bonds to cover

Figure 7.7. **Increasing statutory capital of the National JSC Company Naftogaz by issuing state bonds to cover its deficit**

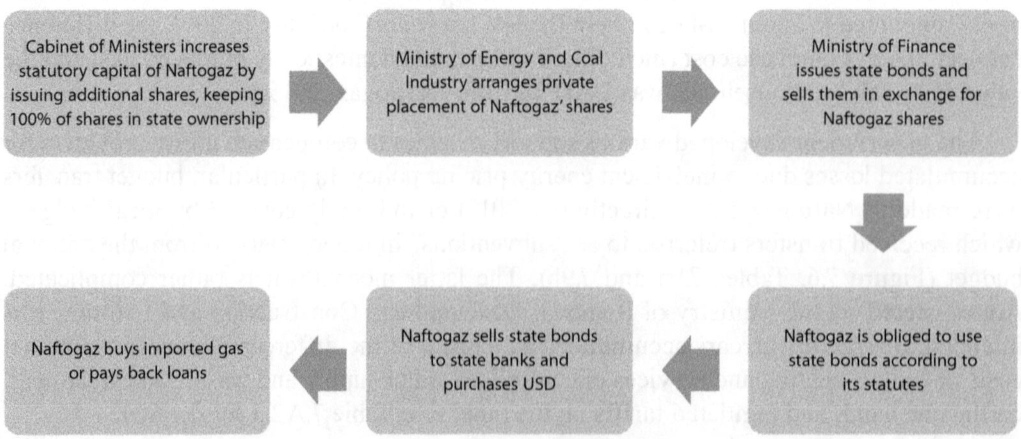

Source: Authors' presentation based on Cabinet of Ministers Resolution No. 13 (2015c).

Naftogaz's deficit. The value of the bonds was UAH 142.1 bln with a 3- to 10-year maturity period at 9.95%-14.5% annual interest rate (see Figure 7.8 and Table 7.A2.1 for more details). The bonds typically appeared in the portfolio of the National Bank of Ukraine (through state-owned banks) the next day after issuance due to insufficient demand from other players.

Figure 7.8. **Capital injection into NJSC Naftogaz**

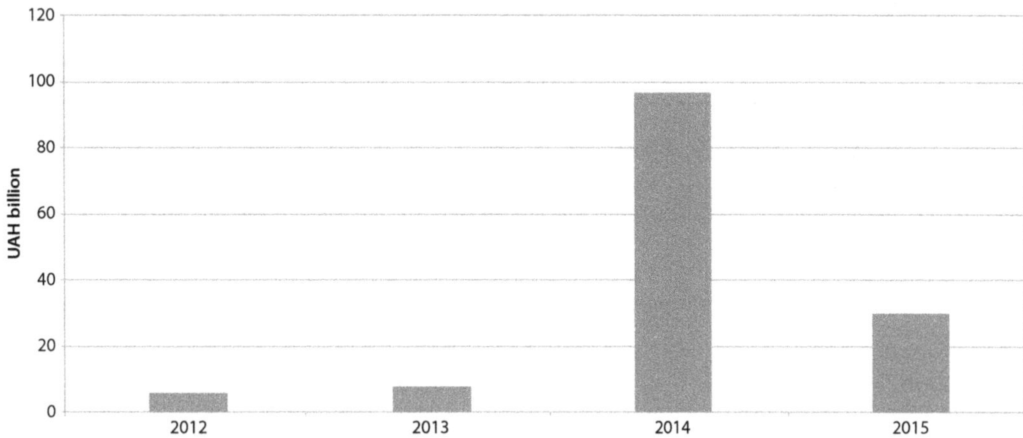

Source: Authors' compilation based on Resolutions of the Cabinet of Ministers.

The government designed these support measures to compensate Naftogaz for the difference between regulated sales prices for households, on the one hand, and the much higher price paid for imported gas. In addition, the requirement for state-owned domestic gas producers (with 50% or more shares in state ownership) to sell gas to households for domestic needs at regulated tariffs established by the NCSREPU is *de facto* an implicit subsidy to households. For domestic producers, the sales prices covered the costs but did not allow for investments in modernisation and exploration of new deposits. In particular, such upstream companies as *Ukrgasvydobuvannya* and *Chornomornaftogaz* were required to sell gas at about USD 45 per 1 000 m^3 (weighted average estimate), while in the EU gas market, the price was over USD 400 per 1 000 m^3 in 2012-13 (see Figure 7.9 on opportunity cost for domestic gas producers).

Figure 7.9. **Opportunity cost for domestic gas producers**

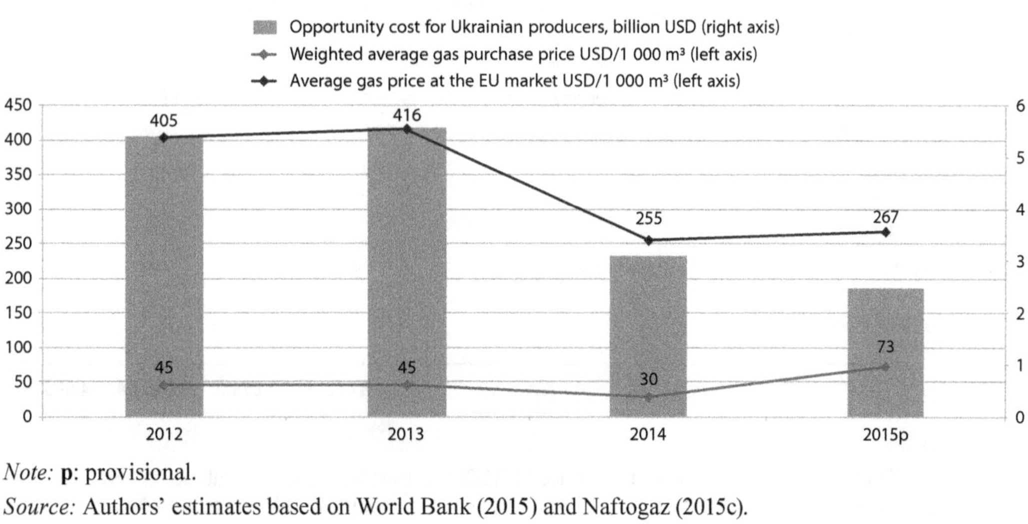

Note: **p**: provisional.

Source: Authors' estimates based on World Bank (2015) and Naftogaz (2015c).

In 2015, the NCSREPU increased tariffs for domestic producers to USD 73 per 1 000 m^3, while gas prices at the EU market dropped to USD 270 per 1 000 m^3. As the government made the decision to increase wholesale gas price for domestic producers to market levels (based on import parity) starting in May 2016, the price gap between domestically produced and imported gas is now closed (see Tables 7.9a and 7.9b and Table 7.A2.2 for more details). However, requirement for *Ukrgasvydobuvannya* to sell produced gas for household needs is still valid, as specified in Cabinet of Ministers Resolution No. 758 of 1 October 2015.

Table 7.9a. **Major government support measures in the gas sector, UAH million**

	Type of subsidy	2012	2013	2014	2015	2016p[a]
Increasing the statutory capital of Naftogaz via the mechanism of issuing state bonds to cover its deficit	Consumer subsidy, transfer of risk to government	6 000	8 000	96 609.6	29 700	0
Requirements for domestic gas producers (more than 50% owned by the state) to sell gas for household needs at regulated tariffs	Consumer subsidy, induced transfer	43 168.1	44 493.0	36 678.7	53 893	.
Subvention (transfers) from the national budget to local budgets to settle the arrears due to the difference between the actual cost of central heating and services of centralised water supply and wastewater treatment, on the one hand, and regulated tariffs on the other	Consumer subsidy, direct transfer	14 442.8	2 052.5	12 423.1	4 685	n.a.
Compensation to Naftogaz for the difference between the purchase prices of imported natural gas and the regulated price of its sale for district heating purposes	Consumer subsidy, direct transfer	3 900	n.a.	n.a.	n.a.	n.a.
Total		**67 511**	**54 545**	**145 711**	**88 526.7**	**.**

Notes: a. **p**: provisional.

Source: Authors' compilation based on State Treasury Service (2011-2016), Resolutions of the Cabinet of Ministers. Opportunity cost for domestic producers is estimated based on data from World Bank (2015), Naftogaz (2015c) and Resolutions of the NCSREPU.

Table 7.9b. **Major government support measures in the gas sector, USD million**

	Type of subsidy	2012	2013	2014	2015	2016p[a]
Increasing the statutory capital of Naftogaz by issuing state bonds to cover the deficit	Consumer subsidy, transfer of risk to government	750.8	1 000.9	8 127.5	1 362.4	0.0
Requirement for domestic gas producers (more than 50% owned by the state) to sell gas for household needs at regulated tariffs	Consumer subsidy, induced transfer	5 402.1	5 566.5	3 085.7	2 483.6	.
Subvention (transfer) from the national budget to local budgets to settle the arrears due to the difference between the actual costs of central heating and services of centralised water supply and wastewater treatment, on the one hand, and regulated tariffs on the other	Consumer subsidy, direct transfer	1 807.4	256.8	1 045.1	214.9	0.0
Compensation to Naftogaz for the difference between the purchase prices of imported natural gas and the regulated price of its sale for district heating purposes	Consumer subsidy, direct transfer	488.0	n.a.	n.a.	n.a.	n.a.
Total		**8 448.4**	**6 824.2**	**12 258.4**	**4 068.8**	.

Notes: a. **p**: provisional.

Source: Authors' compilation based on State Treasury Service (2011-2016), Resolutions of the Cabinet of Ministers. Opportunity cost for domestic producers is estimated based on data from World Bank (2015), Naftogaz (2015c) and Resolutions of the NCSREPU.

Recent government decision to increase gas prices for households to market levels effectively eliminated all explicit and implicit subsidies in the gas sector described above. The Ministry of Economic Development and Trade (2016) has announced there will no longer be direct and indirect compensations of losses of NJSC Naftogaz and heat-generating companies.

Government support measures in the electricity sector

The difference between regulated tariffs for households and other preferential consumers, on the one hand, and electricity production costs on the other, are compensated for by subsidies incorporated in the tariff for industry, railway transport and state-funded institutions. These three categories of consumers pay, on average, 26% higher electricity prices due to this cross-subsidisation (see Table 7.A2.8 for details). At the same time, households consume electricity at a price that covered only 21% of the cost of generation, transmission and supply of electricity as of January 2015. The total value of cross-subsidies increased by about 7.6 times, from UAH 5.4 bln in 2006 to UAH 43.8 bln in 2015 (NCSREPU, 2015b, 2016a). Tables 7.10a and 7.10b below provide more detail.

Figure 7.10. **Cross-subsidisation in the electricity sector**

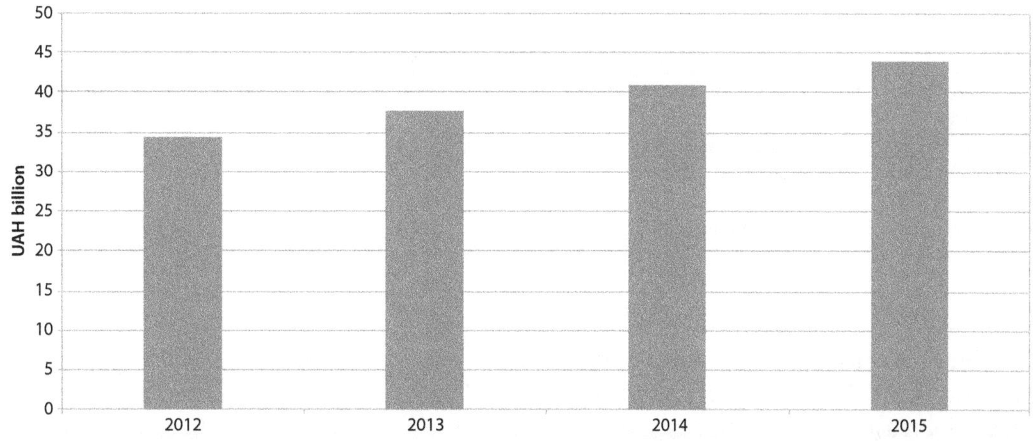

Source: Authors' compilation based on NCSREPU (2015a, 2016a), NERC (2014).

Electricity suppliers are compensated for providing services at regulated tariffs for up to 10 categories of consumers (the number varies from year to year), but more than 90% of the subsidies benefit households (UAH 40.3 bln in 2015). Subsidies to consumers paying a differentiated tariff constituted 5% of the total value (UAH 2.2 bln), subsidies to electric municipal transport amounted to 1.8% (UAH 0.8 bln), and about 1% of the subsidies was provided to other categories of preferential consumers (street lighting, companies implementing innovative projects, etc.). Ore mining and chemical enterprises also benefited from preferential tariffs until 2010, when this policy was discontinued (NERC, 2014, NCSREPU, 2015a). Reduced tariffs to coal-mining enterprises and economic entities implementing innovation projects were cancelled in 2015. These decisions helped to reduce cross-subsidisation by about UAH 2.8 mln (excluding VAT) compared to 2014 (NCSREPU, 2016a).

Like coal subsidies, cross-subsidies in the electricity sector have frequently been declared a target for reform, but so far, this reform has been poorly implemented. Ukraine's current Energy Strategy of Ukraine aimed to phase out cross-subsidies by 2014, but failed to achieve this objective (Cabinet of Ministers Resolution No. 1 071, 2013). The Coalition Agreement plans for elimination of cross-subsidisation by 2017. The agreement also introduces a moratorium on establishing new preferential prices (Parliament of Ukraine, 2014).

The most recent policy changes finally indicate a step towards implementing these commitments. Most significant have been the recent revisions of the electricity tariffs for households and the approval of the step-wise tariff increase to full cost recovery by March 2017.

Table 7.10a. **Cross-subsidisation in the electricity sector, UAH million**

Subsidy	Type of subsidy	2012	2013	2014	2015	2016p[a]
Compensating energy supply companies for losses supplying electricity to certain categories of consumers through a system of subsidy certificates (cross-subsidisation)	Consumer subsidy, induced transfer	34 467	37 557	40 825	43 848	.

Notes: a. **p**: provisional.

Source: Authors' compilation based on NCSREPU (2015a, 2016a), NERC (2014).

Table 7.10b. **Cross-subsidisation in the electricity sector, USD million**

Subsidy	Type of subsidy	2012	2013	2014	2015	2016p[a]
Compensating energy supply companies for losses supplying electricity to certain categories of consumers through a system of subsidy certificates (cross-subsidisation)	Consumer subsidy, induced transfer	4 313	4 699	3 434	2 011	.

Notes: a. **p**: provisional.

Source: Authors' compilation based on NCSREPU (2015a, 2016a), NERC (2014).

Government support measures in the coal sector

The majority of state-owned coal mines face exceptionally difficult geological conditions. Coal seams have gradually been depleted, requiring extraction at far deeper levels, increasing production costs dramatically in the past ten years. In 2005, state-owned mines spent, on average, UAH 274 to extract each tonne of marketable coal, at a sale price that was only UAH 219. In 2013, prices for coal covered only 36% of production costs (UAH 1 352/t). Unlike publicly owned mines, mines belonging to private, vertically integrated steel and power companies are economically viable and do not receive any direct transfers from the government. Privately owned mines outperform state-owned mines by production capacity use (on average, more than 90%), labour productivity (two to three times higher compared with state-owned mines) and salary (20%-25% higher than at state-owned mines) (NISS, 2014).

The number of state-owned mines fell from 145 in 2005 to 82 in 2013. In the same period, their output dropped from 46.1 mln tonnes to 24.1 mln tonnes, but budget transfers to the sector grew annually, as shown in Figure 7.11. State support in the form of compensation of losses to unprofitable mines increased from UAH 0.9 bln in 2005 (NISS, 2014) to UAH 13.3 bln in 2013 and UAH 8.7 bln in 2014 (State Treasury Service, 2011-2016). The allocation of budget funds for the partial compensation of costs incurred by public mines is regulated by Resolution of the Cabinet of Ministers No. 153 of 23 February 2011. Under this Resolution, the funds could be spent to cover expenditures on wages and electricity consumed (see Table 7.A2.4 for more details). State support was also provided for the construction of coal and peat mining facilities and technical re-equipment, a total of UAH 1.7 bln from 2012 to 2014. Public expenditures on safety measures at mining enterprises (e.g. installation of modern equipment to control air parameters at mines and devices to control degassing parameters) totalled UAH 80 mln, while more than UAH 1 bln was spent on rescue operations from 2012 to 2014. Budget funding was also provided for various measures for the restructuring of the coal and peat industry (see Table 7.A2.5 for details).

The total amount of direct government spending on the coal sector peaked in 2013, at UAH 15.3 bln, which constituted 3.8% of budget outlays. In 2014, UAH 9.4 bln was allocated in budget programmes to support state-owned mines (2.2% of budget expenditures). In 2015, however, state support to cover losses of state-owned mines fell to UAH 1.2 bln (State Treasury Service, 2011-2016), since the majority of unprofitable mines in the Donbass region were idled by the military conflict. The Ukrainian government controls only 35 state-owned mines, and the rest (about 55) are located in the occupied territory in Donbass (Koval, 2015). In 2015, expenditures on the restructuring programme totalled UAH 206 mln, while UAH 234 mln was allocated for rescue measures. In addition, UAH 146 mln was set aside for the construction of the No. 10 Novovolynska mine and UAH 200 mln for capital injections into state-owned mines, to settle the arrears of wages to employees. In the 2016 budget, UAH 1.4 bln is set aside for state support of the coal sector as of February 2016 (State Treasury Service, 2011-2016).

Figure 7.11. **Government support measures in the coal sector**

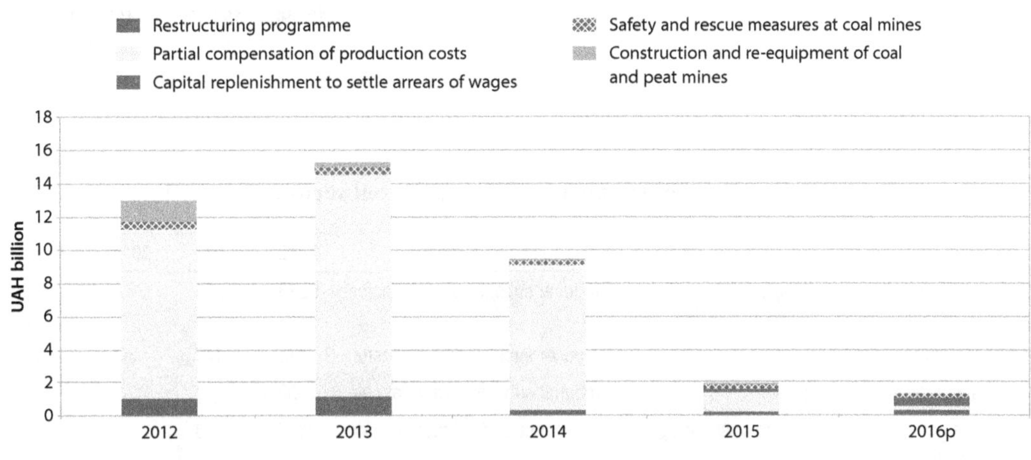

Note: **p**: provisional.

Source: Authors' compilation based on State Treasury Service (2011-2016).

Over the years, various strategic documents and state programmes of the Ukrainian government have included plans for a gradual phaseout of subsidies in the coal sector and decommissioning of unprofitable mines, together with social programmes for ex-miners. The pace of the reform has been slow. The five elected parties' Coalition Agreement of 2014 declared that all potentially viable coal enterprises should be privatised by 2016 and the rest either decommissioned or conserved by 2019, while reinforcing social support for ex-miners. State support programmes are to be fully rolled out by 2020, including phasing out all state support for the coal industry but drainage and environmental measures (Parliament of Ukraine, 2014).

In 2015, the Cabinet of Ministers approved a list of mines for privatisation (Resolution No. 271, 2015b). The deposits of 11 remaining mines are considered to be exhausted (with 6 mines planned for conservation and 5 for decommissioning) (Koval, 2015). Table 7.11a and 7.11b below summarise the reported figures for government support for coal mining.

Table 7.11a. **Government support for Ukraine's coal sector, UAH million**

Subsidy	Type of subsidy	2012	2013	2014	2015	2016p[a]
State support for coal mining enterprises for partial compensation of production costs of finished marketable coal	Producer subsidy, direct transfer	10 172	13 302	8 705	1 212	250
Restructuring of coal and peat industry	Producer subsidy, direct transfer	1 078	1 178	355	206	306
Rescue measures at coal mining enterprises	Producer subsidy, direct transfer	414	430	288	234	290
State support for the construction of coal and peat mining facilities, technical re-equipment of these enterprises	Producer subsidy, direct transfer	1 293	343	54	n.a.	n.a.
Measures to improve safety measures at mining enterprises, such as installation of modern equipment to control air parameters at mines and devices to control degassing parameters	Producer subsidy, direct transfer	40	37	3	n.a.	n.a.
Replenishment of current capital, or increasing statutory funds of coal mines, to settle arrears in employee wages as of 1 January 2015	Producer subsidy, direct transfer	n.a.	n.a.	n.a.	200	500
State support for the construction of the No. 10 Novovolynska mine	Producer subsidy, direct transfer	n.a.	n.a.	n.a.	146	n.a.
Total		**12 998**	**15 290**	**9 405**	**1 998.0**	**1 345.6**

Notes: a. **p**: provisional.
Source: State Treasury Service (2011-2016).

Table 7.11b. **Government support for Ukraine's coal sector, USD million**

Subsidy	Type of subsidy	2012	2013	2014	2015	2016p[a]
State support for coal mining enterprises for partial compensation of production costs of finished marketable coal	Producer subsidy, direct transfer	1 273	1 664	732	56	10
Restructuring of coal and peat industry	Producer subsidy, direct transfer	135	147	30	9	12
Rescue measures at coal mining enterprises	Producer subsidy, direct transfer	52	54	24	11	12
State support for the construction of coal and peat mining facilities, technical re-equipment of these enterprises	Producer subsidy, direct transfer	162	43	5	n.a.	n.a.
Measures to improve safety measures at mining enterprises, such as installation of modern equipment to control air parameters at mines and devices to control degassing parameters	Producer subsidy, direct transfer	5	5	0.2	n.a.	n.a.
Replenishment of current capital or increase statutory funds of coal mines to settle arrears in employee wages as of 1 January 2015	Producer subsidy, direct transfer	n.a.	n.a.	n.a.	9	20
State support for the construction of the No. 10 Novovolynska mine	Producer subsidy, direct transfer	n.a.	n.a.	n.a.	7	n.a.
Total		**1 627**	**1 913**	**791**	**91.6**	**54.3**

Notes: a. **p**: provisional.
Source: State Treasury Service (2011-2016).

Targeted subsidies to low-income households

Targeted subsidies to vulnerable groups have been provided since the early 1990s. In addition to low-income households eligible for partial compensation for utility payments, under procedures defined in Resolution of the Cabinet of Ministers No. 848 of 21 October 1995, many preferential categories of consumers have been able to apply for substantial discounts on utility payments, of 25% to 100%. The legal underpinnings of such benefits are supported by a large body of legislation. Such benefits are granted, for example, to citizens affected by the Chernobyl disaster, participants in military actions and disabled persons after World War II, persons with such awards as Hero of the USSR, former prisoners of concentration camps, retired workers of the Security Service of Ukraine, families with three or more kids, etc. (for a full list see Article 102, Paragraph 3-4 of the Budget Code, Parliament of Ukraine, 2010a). Until recently, all these consumers were eligible for discounts regardless of their income. The procedures for allocating benefits to these groups were amended by Law No. 76-VIII of 28 December 2014 (Parliament of Ukraine, 2015a). Since July 2015, the average monthly household income has been taken into account when granting discounts on apartment rent, utility payment and purchase of fuel for individual heating to most of the consumer categories listed above, in accordance with the procedures defined in the Cabinet of Ministers Resolution No. 389 of 4 June 2015. Nevertheless, quite a few categories are still not required to submit their income declarations in applying for a discount on utility payments (104.ua, 2016). Targeted subsidies to low-income households and benefits to certain categories of consumers are arranged via subvention (transfer) from the national budget to local budgets, in line with the procedures defined in the Cabinet of Ministers Resolution No. 256 of 4 March 2002 (Cabinet of Ministers, 2002).

Considering that utility tariffs were traditionally kept relatively low (well below cost-recovery levels) and the procedure of application for targeted support was quite complicated, the number of subsidy beneficiaries was not large, at 1.2 mln households in 2014 (Voitko, 2015). Hence, the overall burden of these targeted subsidies on the national budget was lower, for example, than that of transfers to the coal sector. In particular, the Ukrainian government allocated UAH 6 bln to UAH 6.7 bln for partial compensation to low-income households for utility payments and UAH 715-738 mln for the purchase of LPG, solid and liquid furnace fuel each year in the period 2012-14 (see Figure 7.12).

Figure 7.12. **Targeted subsidies to low-income households and benefits to certain categories of consumers**

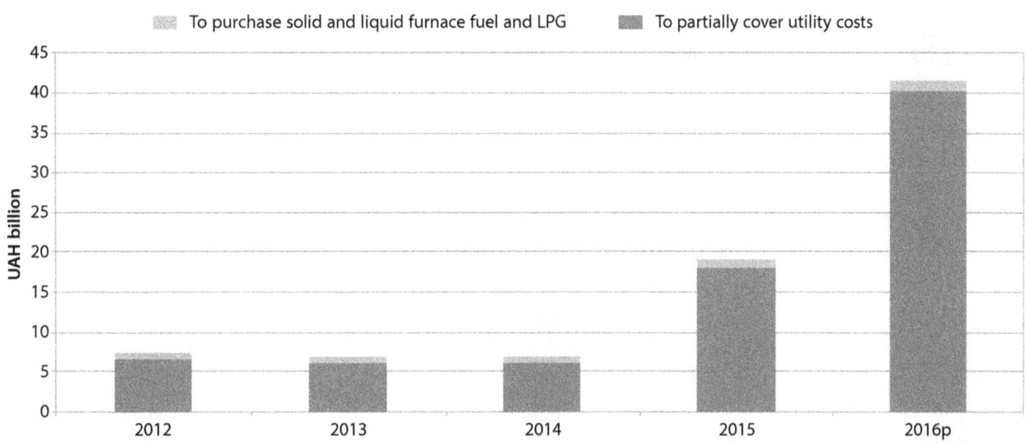

Note: **p**: provisional.

Source: Authors' compilation based on State Treasury Service (2011-2016).

Utility tariffs were substantially increased at the beginning of 2015, and the funds allocated for targeted subsidies to low-income households and benefits to certain categories of consumers were repeatedly increased, to UAH 19.1 bln (State Treasury Service, 2011-2016). The government also simplified the procedures for allocating subsidies and reduced the number of documents required for submission. Several eligibility requirements were also cancelled, dramatically increasing the number of applications for subsidies.

In the first 11 months of 2015, about 5.1 mln households (out of 15 mln) applied for targeted subsidies for utility payments, and 4.6 mln were awarded compensation, four times more than in the same period in 2014. As of November 2015, UAH 14.8 bln was provided in subsidies to low-income households, 66% of them in urban areas. Additionally, 4.84 mln households (78% of applicants) received subsidies in monetary form for partial compensation of expenditures for the purchase of LPG, solid and liquid furnace fuel; these recipients were largely in rural areas (80%) (Voitko, 2015). The budget allocated UAH 1.1 bln for this programme (State Treasury Service, 2011-2016). Tables 7.12a and 7.12b report the targeted subsidy allocations.

Table 7.12a. **Targeted subsidies to low-income households, UAH million**

Subsidy	Type of subsidy	2012	2013	2014	2015	2016p[a]
Subvention (transfer) from the state budget to local budgets to provide benefits and housing subsidies to low-income households for electricity, natural gas, heat, water supply and wastewater treatment, rent (maintenance of houses and buildings and areas adjacent to houses), removal of domestic waste and liquid sewage	Consumer subsidy, direct transfer	6 718	6 046	6 173	17 995	40 269
Subvention (transfer) from the state budget to local budgets to provide benefits and housing subsidies to low-income households to purchase solid and liquid household furnace fuel and liquefied gas	Consumer subsidy, direct transfer	738	733	715	1 121	1 205
Total		**7 456**	**6 779**	**6 888**	**19 116**	**41 474**

Notes: a. **p**: provisional.

Source: State Treasury Service (2011-2016).

Table 7.12b. **Targeted subsidies to low-income households in Ukraine, USD million**

Subsidy	Type of subsidy	2012	2013	2014	2015	2016p[a]
Subvention (transfer) from the state budget to local budgets to provide benefits and housing subsidies to low-income households for electricity, natural gas, heat, water supply and wastewater treatment, rent (maintenance of houses and buildings and areas adjacent to houses), removal of domestic waste and liquid sewage	Consumer subsidy, direct transfer	841	756	519	825	1 624
Subvention (transfer) from the state budget to local budgets for benefits and housing subsidies to low-income households to purchase solid and liquid household furnace fuel and liquefied gas	Consumer subsidy, direct transfer	92	92	60	51	49
Total		**933**	**848**	**579**	**876.9**	**1 672.3**

Notes: a. **p**: provisional.

Source: State Treasury Service (2011-2016).

The recent government decision to increase household gas prices to market levels almost doubled the price households paid for central heating and hot water, depending on the region and particular fuel mix used in generation. The number of households that will require subsidies for utility payments is expected to increase, the social support programme was further reinforced and the amount of funds planned in the budget for this purpose was raised from UAH 36.2 bln to UAH 40.3 bln. As of June 2016, UAH 21 bln has been allocated for this programme (State Treasury Service, 2011-2016).

Government support for energy efficiency measures

Government support for energy-efficiency measures was limited until recently (Figure 7.13). Although the State Targeted Economic Programme on Energy Efficiency and Development of Renewable Energy Sources was approved as early as 2010 (Cabinet of Ministers Resolution No. 243, 2010) it did not operate effectively due to the lack of incentives encouraging energy efficiency projects and constant underfinancing. Tables 7.13a and 7.13b provide the officially reported values of support under this scheme.

Table 7.13a. **Government support for energy efficiency measures, UAH million**

Subsidy	Type of subsidy	2012	2013	2014	2015	2016p[a]
Implementation of the State Targeted Economic Programme on Energy Efficiency for 2010-16	Consumer subsidy, direct transfer	57	0	2	302	790

Notes: a. **p**: provisional.

Source: State Treasury Service (2011-2016).

Table 7.13b. **Government support for energy efficiency measures, USD million**

Subsidy	Type of subsidy	2012	2013	2014	2015	2016p[a]
Implementation of the State Targeted Economic Programme on Energy Efficiency for 2010-16	Consumer subsidy, direct transfer	7	0	0.2	14	32

Notes: a. **p**: provisional.

Source: State Treasury Service (2011-2016).

Many legislative changes have been approved since 2014, however. In particular, the State Energy Efficiency Programme was reinforced in 2015. This provides soft loans to households willing to implement specific measures. It is intended to reimburse 20% of the loan principal (capped at UAH 12 000) for replacing gas boilers with electric or solid fuel boilers; 30% for individual households implementing energy efficiency measures (capped at UAH 14 000) and 40% for condominiums (capped at UAH 14 000 per flat) (Cabinet of Ministers Resolution No. 1 056, 2011a). Recent amendments to the State Programme introduced additional incentives for recipients of targeted subsidies partially compensating for utility costs. Such households could obtain up to a 70% compensation of the loan principal (from 40% to 70% for condominiums, depending on the number of residents receiving targeted subsidies).

According to Ukraine's State Agency of Energy Efficiency and Energy Saving, about 80 000 loans worth UAH 1.3 bln were made in 2015, UAH 302 mln of which was underwritten by the budget (SAEEES, 2015). About UAH 790 mln is to be allocated for this programme in 2016. As of June 2016, 38.7% of this amount was already spent (State Treasury Service, 2011-2016).

Government support for electricity produced from renewable energy sources

Feed-in tariffs (FITs) (aka green tariffs, according to the Ukrainian legislation) for electricity producers from renewable energy sources (for small hydro, wind, bio and solar energy) have been the main policy incentive for developing the sector. FITs were introduced in 2009 and have boosted electricity production from renewables from just 51.8 mln kWh in 2009 to over 1.8 bln kWh in 2015. The share of renewables in total power generation remains marginal (about 1%) (NCSREPU, 2015a, 2016a). The renewables sector has been growing rapidly, and total induced transfers increased from UAH 1.7 bln in 2009 to UAH 6 bln in 2015 (see Table 7.A3.1 for details).

Figure 7.13. **Government support for electricity producers using renewable energy sources**

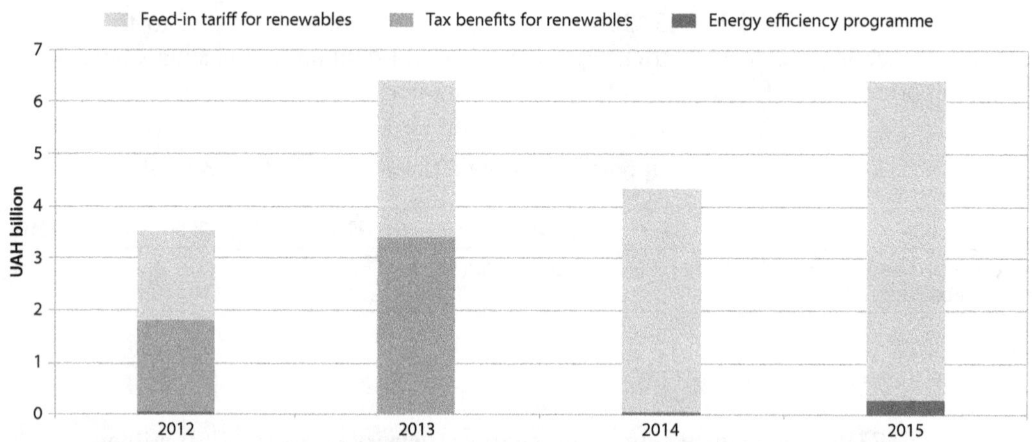

Source: Authors' estimates and compilation based on NCSREPU (2015a), Ministry of Finance (cited in Hölzler et al., 2015), State Treasury Service (2011-2016).

Renewable energy producers also enjoyed a corporate profit tax exemption. The foregone revenue to the government was estimated at UAH 752 mln and UAH 2 773 mln in 2012 and 2013, respectively (Ministry of Finance, quoted in Hölzler et al., 2015). Corporate profit tax relief was also applied to the income of biofuel producers, as well as to the income of combined heat and power plants using biofuels, and thermal power plants using biofuels. Corporate tax benefits for renewables were cancelled as of January 2015, however. The only remaining tax benefit is the zero excise tax rate on 100% bio-based ethanol. Overall, the total value of government support for the renewable energy sector amounted to UAH 3.5 bln in 2013 and UAH 6 bln in 2015 (see Figure 7.13, Tables 7.14a and 7.14b for details). This figure is low compared to subsidies provided to conventional energy sources, as noted earlier.

Table 7.14a. **Government support for electricity producers using renewable energy sources, UAH million**

Subsidy	Type of subsidy	2012	2013	2014	2015
Feed-in tariff for electricity from renewable energy projects (wind, solar, biomass, small hydro, etc.)	Induced transfer, producer subsidy	1 700	3 029	4 322	6 095
Zero excise tax rate applied per litre of 100% bio-based ethanol	Tax revenue foregone, producer subsidy	752	2 773	.	.
Corporate profit tax exemption on the profit of power producers that generate electricity exclusively from renewable energy sources	Tax revenue foregone, producer subsidy	454	594	.	n.a.
Corporate profit tax exemption for income of biofuel producers from sales of biofuels	Tax revenue foregone, producer subsidy	15	18	.	n.a.
Corporate profit tax exemption on the income of combined heat and power plants using biofuels, and thermal energy using biofuels	Tax revenue foregone, producer subsidy	548	0.01	.	n.a.
Total		**3 470**	**6 414**	**4 322**	**6 095**

Notes: **n.a.**: non-applicable.

Source: Authors' estimates of induced transfer to renewables based on data from NCSREPU (2015a), Ministry of Finance, quoted in Hölzler et al. (2015).

Table 7.14b. **Government support for electricity producers using renewable energy sources, USD million**

Subsidy	Type of subsidy	2012	2013	2014	2015
Feed-in tariff for electricity from renewable energy projects (wind, solar, biomass, etc.)	Induced transfer	213	379	364	279.6
Zero excise tax rate applied per litre of 100% bio-based ethanol	Tax revenue foregone, producer subsidy	94	347	.	.
Corporate profit tax exemption on the profit of power producers that generate electricity exclusively from renewable energy sources	Tax revenue foregone, producer subsidy	57	74	.	n.a.
Corporate profit tax exemption on the income of biofuel producers obtained from the sales of biofuels	Tax revenue foregone, producer subsidy	2	2	.	n.a
Corporate profit tax exemption on the income of combined heat and power plants using biofuels, and thermal energy using biofuels	Tax revenue foregone, producer subsidy	69	0.001	.	n.a.
Total		**434**	**802**	**364**	**279.6**

Notes: **n.a.**: non-applicable.

Source: Authors' estimates of induced transfer to renewables based on data from NCSREPU (2015a), Ministry of Finance quoted in Hölzler et al., 2015.

Annex 7.A1

Methodological approaches used for the quantification of key energy subsidies in Ukraine

Subsidy scheme	Quantification method
Increase in the statutory capital of the National joint-stock company Naftogaz	Subsidy estimate is taken at face value from government sources: resolutions of the Cabinet of Ministers ("On increasing statute capital of the NJSC Naftogaz") No. 139 of 22 February 2012, No. 12 of 9 January 2013, No. 302 of 4 January 2014, No. 151 of 29 May 2014, No. 40 of 12 February 2014, No. 13 of 23 January 2015
Requirement for state-owned domestic gas producers to sell gas for household needs at regulated tariffs	Authors' calculations: average gas price at the EU market (World Bank, 2015) compared with purchase prices for gas extracted by *Ukrgasvydobuvannya* and *Chornomornaftogaz* approved by the NCSEPU and multiplied by the amount of domestically produced gas (Naftogaz, 2015c)
Compensation for the losses of utility supply companies	Subsidy estimate is taken at face value from government sources: State Treasury Service (2011-2016)
State support for coal mining enterprises for partial compensation of the production costs of finished marketable coal	Subsidy estimate is taken at face value from government sources: State Treasury Service (2011-2016)
State support for the restructuring of coal and peat industry	Subsidy estimate is taken at face value from government sources: State Treasury Service (2011-2016)
Targeted subsidy scheme to support low-income households (partial compensation of utility payments)	Subsidy estimate is taken at face value from government sources: State Treasury Service (2011-2016)
Targeted subsidy scheme to support low-income households (partial compensation for purchasing of solid and liquid household furnace fuel and liquefied gas)	Subsidy estimate is taken at face value from government sources: State Treasury Service (2011-2016)
Cross-subsidisation in the electricity sector	Subsidy estimate is taken at face value from official sources: NERC (2014), NCSREPU (2015a), NCSREPU (2016a)
Feed-in tariff for electricity producers from renewable energy sources	Authors' calculations: weighted average "green" tariff compared with average tariff for electricity-generating companies (thermal power plants) and multiplied by the amount of electricity produced from renewable energy sources and based on the data provided in the report of NCSREPU (2015a)

Annex 7.A2

Fossil-fuel subsidies in Ukraine

Table 7.A2.1. **Increase in the statutory capital of the National JSC Naftogaz**

Subsidy category	Transfer of risk to government
Stimulated activity	Consumption of natural gas
Subsidy name	**Increase in the statutory capital of the National Joint-Stock Company Naftogaz via the mechanism of issuing state bonds to cover its deficit**
Jurisdiction	National level
Legislation/endorsing organisation	Resolutions of the Cabinet of Ministers No. 139 of 22 February 2012, No. 12 of 9 January 2013, No. 302 of 4 January 2014, No. 151 of 29 May 2014, No. 40 of 12 February 2014, No. 13 of 23 January 2015
Policy objective(s) of subsidy	To decrease the deficit of the NJSC Naftogaz accumulated due to selling gas for household needs at regulated prices
End recipient(s) of subsidy	NJSC Naftogaz receives compensation for the losses, but the final beneficiaries are households
Time period	2009-15
Background	The NJSC Naftogaz has accumulated a significant deficit by selling natural gas to both households and heat-supply companies, serving households at prices lower than the import price. A complex, multi-step mechanism has been designed to cover this deficit. First, the Cabinet of Ministers increases the statutory capital of NJSC Naftogaz by issuing additional shares while maintaining their 100% ownership. Then, the Ministry of Energy and Coal Industry arranges a private placement of these shares. At the same time, the Ministry of Finance issues state bonds and sells them on behalf of the state for additional shares of NJSC Naftogaz. Naftogaz is obliged to use the state bonds according to its statute, and in particular, to use the funds obtained from selling state bonds for payments for imported natural gas. As the government increased all gas prices to households to market level starting in May 2016, there will no longer be a need for this measure.
Amount of subsidy conferred	2012: UAH 6 bln (USD 750.8 mln) 2013: UAH 8 bln (USD 1 bln) 2014: UAH 96.6 bln (USD 8.1 bln) 2015: UAH 29.7 bln (USD 1.4 bln)
Information sources	Resolutions of the Cabinet of Ministers ("On increasing statute capital of the NJSC Naftogaz") No. 139 of 22 February 2012, No. 12 of 9 January 2013, No. 302 of 4 January 2014, No. 151 of 29 May 2014, No. 40 of 12 February 2014, No. 13 of 23 January 2015

Table 7.A2.2. **Requirement for state-owned domestic gas producers to sell gas for household needs at regulated tariffs**

Subsidy category	Income or price support → Market price support and regulation → Regulated prices set at below-market rates for households
Stimulated activity	Consumption of natural gas
Subsidy name	**Requirement for state-owned domestic gas producers to sell gas for household needs at regulated tariffs**
Jurisdiction	National level
Legislation/endorsing organisation	Artcle No. 10 of Law No. 2 467-VI, 2010 (Parliament of Ukraine, 2010b)
Policy objective(s) of subsidy	To ensure reliable gas supply and keep tariffs for households low
End recipient(s) of subsidy	Households
Time period	At least from 2001 by 2016
Background	Under Law No. 2 467-VI (Parliament of Ukraine (2010b) on the Principles and Functioning of the Natural Gas Market, state-owned enterprises (50% and more shares in state ownership) were required to sell all domestically produced gas for the needs of households at regulated tariffs established by the NCSEPU. This law was replaced by the new Law No. 329-VIII (Parliament of Ukraine, 2015b) on the Gas Market, starting from October 2015. The government increased the wholesale gas price for domestic producers to market levels (based on import parity) starting in May 2016. However, the requirement for *Ukrgasvydobuvannya* to sell produced gas for household needs is still valid, as specified in Cabinet of Ministers Resolution No. 758 of 1 October 2015 (Cabinet of Ministers, 2015a). The value of this implicit subsidy for households is estimated as an opportunity cost for domestic producers (i.e. the sales price that could be recovered in a fully liberalised market). Calculations are based on the annual average gas price at the EU market, purchase prices for gas extracted by *Ukrgasvydobuvannya* and *Chornomornaftogaz* approved by the NCSEPU, and the amount of domestically produced gas.
Amount of subsidy conferred	2012: UAH 43.2 bln (USD 5.4 bln) 2013: UAH 44.5 bln (USD 5.6 bln) 2014: UAH 36.7 bln (USD 3 bln) 2015 provisional: UAH 53.9 bln (USD 2.5 bln)
Information sources	World Bank (2015), Naftogaz (2015c) and Resolutions of the NCSEPU establishing purchase prices for gas produced domestically by *Ukrgasvydobuvannya* and *Chornomornaftogaz*

Table 7.A2.3. **Compensation for the losses of utility supply companies**

Subsidy category	Direct and indirect transfer of funds and liabilities → Direct spending → Earmarks
Stimulated activity	Energy and other utility consumption
Subsidy name	**Subvention (transfer) from the national budget to local budgets to settle the arrears accumulated due to a difference between the actual costs of central heating and services of centralised water supply and wastewater treatment and tariffs that were approved and/or agreed by the government or local government**
Jurisdiction	National and/or local level
Legislation/endorsing organisation	Budget Code of Ukraine, Article 2, Paragraph 48 (Parliament of Ukraine, 2010a) and budget laws passed by Verkhovna Rada (Parliament) of Ukraine; Resolution of the Cabinet of Ministers No. 692-p of 1 August 2012; Resolutions of the Cabinet of Ministers No. 517 of 11 June 2012, No. 375 of 20 March 2013; No. 30 of 29 January 2014, No. 375 of 4 June 2015
Policy objective(s) of subsidy	To keep utility tariffs for households low
End recipient(s) of subsidy	Utility supply companies are compensated for losses, but the final beneficiaries are households
Time period	Start date is unclear, phased out in 2016

Table 7.A2.3. **Compensation for the losses of utility supply companies** *(continued)*

Background	Providers of utility services received compensation for the difference between the actual cost of central heating and the services of centralised water supply and wastewater treatment, on the one hand, and actual tariffs, on the other, via a subvention (transfer) from the national budget to local governments. Regulation No. 692-p by the Cabinet of Ministers of 1 August 2012 categorises provision of heat and water supply services to households at prices (tariffs) lower than economically justified production costs as "a quasi-fiscal operation". The Cabinet of Ministers would approve the procedures for this subvention on an annual basis. The responsibility for the administration of this programme lay with the Ministry of the Regional Development, Construction and Utilities. As the government increased all gas prices to households to market level starting from May 2016, there will no longer be a need for this measure.
Amount of subsidy conferred	2012: UAH 14.4 bln (USD 1.8 bln) 2013: UAH 2.1 bln (USD 256.8 mln) 2014: UAH 12.4 bln (USD 1 bln) 2015: UAH 4.7 bln (USD 214.9 mln)
Information sources	Treasury reports on budget execution (State Treasury Service, 2011-2016); Cabinet of Ministers Resolution No. 692-p of 1 August 2012 "On the approval of the list of quasi-fiscal operations and authorities responsible for the assessment of possible impact of such transactions on budget indicators" (Cabinet of Ministers, 2012a; Cabinet of Ministers, 2012b) and similar Resolutions of the Cabinet of Ministers approved in subsequent years (No. 375 of 20 March 2013; No. 30 of 29 January 2014, No. 375 of 4 June 2015)

Table 7.A2.4. **State support for coal mining enterprises for partial compensation of the production costs of finished marketable coal**

Subsidy category	Direct and indirect transfer of funds and liabilities → Direct spending → Earmarks
Stimulated activity	Coal production
Subsidy name	**State support for coal mining enterprises for partial compensation of the production costs of finished marketable coal**
Jurisdiction	National level
Legislation/endorsing organisation	Budget Code of Ukraine (Law No. 2456-VI of 8 July 2010, Article 20, Paragraph 7) and budget laws passed by Verkhovna Rada (Parliament) of Ukraine; Resolution of the Cabinet of Ministers No. 153 of 23 February 2011
Policy objective(s) of subsidy	To provide state support for unprofitable state-owned coal mines
End recipient(s) of subsidy	State enterprises and economic operators 100% owned by the state or enterprises operating under concession or lease agreements registered by the Ministry of Energy and Coal Industry
Time period	Starting in the early 2000s, planned to be phased out by 2020
Background	According to Resolution of the Cabinet of Ministers No. 153, budget funds are used for financial rehabilitation of coal mining enterprises via partial compensation of the costs, which are included in the production cost of finished marketable coal products, and can be used to cover expenditures for the payment of wages and the cost of electricity consumed. Coal mining enterprises prepare estimates of forecast technical and economic performance indicators and submit them for consideration of the Ministry of Energy and Coal Industry. The minstry is responsible for the allocation of the national budget funds to coal mines if the forecast prices for coal do not cover the estimated production costs. The ministry also approves monthly performance indicators of coal mines (including their output amounts) and defines production costs and losses for each coal mining enterprise depending on its product range as well as quality indicators and forecast prices.
Amount of subsidy conferred	2012: UAH 10.2 bln (USD 1.3 bln) 2013: UAH 13.3 bln (USD 1.7 bln) 2014: UAH 8.7 bln (USD 732 mln) 2015: UAH 1.2 bln (USD 56 mln) 2016 provisional: UAH 250 mln (USD 10 mln)
Information sources	Treasury reports on budget execution (State Treasury Service, 2011-2016); Resolution of the Cabinet of Ministers No. 153 of 23 February 2011 "On the approval of the procedure on the use of national budget funds to provide partial compensation for costs of coal mining enterprises, which are included in the prime cost of finished marketable coal" (Cabinet of Ministers, 2011c)

Table 7.A2.5. **State support for the restructuring of coal and peat industry**

Subsidy category	Direct and indirect transfer of funds and liabilities → Direct spending → Earmarks
Stimulated activity	Decommissioning of coal mines
Subsidy name	**State support for the restructuring of coal and peat industry**
Jurisdiction	National level
Legislation/endorsing organisation	Budget Code of Ukraine (Law No. 2 456-VI of 8 July 2010, Article 20, Paragraph 7) and budget laws passed by Verkhovna Rada (Parliament) of Ukraine; Resolution of Cabinet of Ministers No. 236 of 11 March 2011
Policy objective(s) of subsidy	To increase the efficiency of the coal industry in preparation for the liquidation of coal extracting, coal processing and peat mining enterprises, measures for liquidation (legal, physical) of such enterprises and ensuring safe maintenance of drainage facilities
End recipient(s) of subsidy	State-owned coal and peat mining enterprises that are being prepared for liquidation
Time period	Starting at least in the early 2000s, planned to be phased out by 2020
Background	According to the procedure on the use of the national budget funds on the restructuring of the coal and peat industry (Cabinet of Ministers Resolution No. 236, 2011b), these funds could be allocated for the preparation of the coal-mining enterprises for liquidation (e.g. preparation for the transfer or write-off of coal stock and equipment; reducing the number of employees; settling arrears of wages and social payments; development of the documentation for liquidation and government inspections, etc.), liquidation of coal-extracting, coal-processing and peat-mining enterprises (physical liquidation, environmental protection measures, measures ensuring hydrological safety of coal mines and their surroundings), safe maintenance of drainage facilities, settling arrears for the electricity consumed in the previous years. The list of works (services) and expenditures applicable to the liquidation of coal extracting, coal processing and peat mining enterprises is approved by the Ministry of Energy and Coal Industry, Ministry of Economic Development and Trade and Ministry of Finance. The Ministry of Energy and Coal Industry of Ukraine is the main administrator of the budget funds and the main implementer of the national programme on the restructuring of the coal and peat industry.
Amount of subsidy conferred	2012: UAH 1.1 bln (USD 135 mln) 2013: UAH 1.2 bln (USD 147 mln) 2014: UAH 355 mln (USD 30 mln) 2015: UAH 206 mln (USD 9 mln) 2016 provisional: UAH 306 mln (USD 12 mln)
Information sources	Treasury reports on budget execution (State Treasury Service, 2011-2016). Cabinet of Ministers Resolution No. 236 (2011b)

Table 7.A2.6. **Targeted subsidy scheme to support low-income households**

Subsidy category	Direct and indirect transfer of funds and liabilities → Direct spending → Earmarks
Stimulated activity	Consumption of energy and other utilities
Subsidy name	**Subvention (inter-budget transfer) from the national budget to local budgets to provide benefits and housing subsidies to households for electricity, natural gas, heat, water supply and wastewater treatment, rent (maintenance of houses and buildings and areas adjacent to houses), removal of domestic waste and liquid sewage**
Jurisdiction	National level
Legislation/endorsing organisation	Budget Code of Ukraine (Law No. 2 456-VI of 8 July 2010, Article 2, Paragraph 48, Article 102, Paragraph 3) and budget laws passed by the Verkhovna Rada (Parliament) of Ukraine; Resolutions of Cabinet of Ministers No. 256 of 4 March 2002, No. 848 of October 1995 and No. 1 156 of July 1998
Policy objective(s) of subsidy	To provide targeted support for low-income households (mostly in cities) and benefits on utility payments to certain categories of consumers
End recipient(s) of subsidy	Low-income households and a range of beneficiary groups of consumers listed in Article 102 (Paragraph 3) of the Budget Code of Ukraine
Time period	At least from 1995 until the present

Table 7.A2.6. **Targeted subsidy scheme to support low-income households** *(continued)*

Background	Means-tested households are eligible for a nonmonetary subsidy for partial compensation of utility bills according to the procedures defined in Resolution of Cabinet of Ministers No. 848 of 21 October 1995. Means-testing is based on a formula taking into account the household's income and the minimum cost of living (Resolution No. 1 156, 1998). In addition to low-income households, certain categories of consumers listed in Article 102, Paragraph 3 of the Budget Code could apply for a 25%-100% discount on apartment rent, utility payments and purchase of fuel for individual heating, in accordance with procedures defined in the Resolution of Cabinet of Ministers No. 389 of 4 June 2015. Financing of local budgets' expenditures related to the implementation of the national social programmes is undertaken through subventions (transfers) from the national budget for a given year, in line with Resolution of Cabinet of Ministers No. 256 of 4 March 2002. Decisions on the allocation of subsidies to households and monitoring of the earmarked funds are a responsibility of the social protection departments of regional authorities. Personified accounting for subsidy beneficiaries and settling up compensation for utility companies (based on their monthly reports on services eligible for subsidies) are also undertaken at a local level.
Amount of subsidy conferred	2012: UAH 6.7 bln (USD 841 mln) 2013: UAH 6 bln (USD 756 mln) 2014: UAH 6.2 bln (USD 519 mln) 2015: UAH 18 bln (USD 825 mln) 2016 provisional: UAH 40.3 bln (USD 1.6 bln)
Information sources	Treasury reports on budget execution (State Treasury Service, 2011-2016), Cabinet of Ministers Resolutions (Resolution No. 256, 2002; Resolution No. 848, 1995; Resolution No. 1 156, 1998)

Table 7.A2.7. **Targeted subsidy scheme to support low-income households**

Subsidy category	Direct and indirect transfer of funds and liabilities → Direct spending → Earmarks
Stimulated activity	Consumption of energy
Subsidy name	**Subvention (inter-budget transfer) from the national budget to local budgets to provide benefits and housing subsidies for the purchase of solid and liquid household furnace fuel and liquefied gas**
Jurisdiction	National level
Legislation/endorsing organisation	Budget Code of Ukraine (Law No. 2 456-VI of 8 July 2010, Article 2, Paragraph 48, Article 102, Paragraph 3) and budget laws passed by the Verkhovna Rada (Parliament) of Ukraine; Resolutions of Cabinet of Ministers No. 256 of 4 March 2002, No. 848 of October 1995 and No. 1 156 of July 1998
Policy objective(s) of subsidy	To provide targeted support for low-income households (mostly in villages) and benefits on utility payments to certain categories of consumers
End recipient(s) of subsidy	Low-income households and a range of beneficiary groups of consumers listed in Article 102 (Paragraph 4) of the Budget Code of Ukraine
Time period	At least from 1995 until present
Background	Subsidies and benefits to certain categories for partial compensation of expenditures for the purchase of solid and liquid furnace fuel and liquefied gas are provided to low-income households if their houses are not equipped with electricity, heat and gas for heating. Procedures for defining the eligibility of households and allocation of subsidies are similar to those for the targeted subsidies programme for utility payments defined by Cabinet of Ministers' Resolutions No. 256 of 4 March 2002, No. 848 of October 1995 and No. 1 156 of July 1998. However, subsidies for solid and liquid furnace fuel and liquefied gas are provided in a monetary form and on an annual basis.
Amount of subsidy conferred	2012: UAH 737.6 mln (USD 92 mln) 2013: UAH 733 mln (USD 92 mln) 2014: UAH 714.7 mln (USD 60 mln) 2016: UAH 1.1 bln (USD 51 mln) 2016 provisional: UAH 1.2 bln (USD 49 mln)
Information sources	State Treasury Service (2011-2016); Resolution of Cabinet of Ministers No. 256 of 4 March 2002 "On the approval of the procedure of funding expenditures by local budgets for the implementation of state social protection programmes via subventions from the state budget" Resolution of Cabinet of Ministers No. 848 of October 1995 "On the simplification of the procedure of allocation of subsidies to households for the reimbursement of the costs of housing and communal services, LPG and solid and liquid furnace fuel"; Resolution of Cabinet of Ministers No. 1 156 of 27 July 1998 "On the new amount of payment for housing and utility services, purchase of LPG, solid and liquid furnace fuel in the case housing subsidies are provided"

Table 7.A2.8. **Cross-subsidisation in the electricity sector**

Subsidy category	Income or price support → Market price support and regulation → Regulated prices set at below-market rates for households
Stimulated activity	Consumption of electricity
Subsidy name	**Cross-subsidisation of households by industrial consumers**
Jurisdiction	National level
Legislation/endorsing organisation	Resolutions of the National Electricity Regulatory Commission No. 184 of 26 February 2001, No. 1 487 of 16 November 2006, No. 27 of 18 January 2007, No. 198 of 21 February 2008, No. 996 of 26 July 2007, No. 387 of 2 April 2009, No. 408 of 11 April 2013
Policy objective(s) of subsidy	To keep electricity prices for all households at an affordable level regardless of their income
End recipient(s) of subsidy	Preferential groups of consumers (up to 10 different groups)
Time period	At least since 2001, planned to be phased out by 2019
Background	Cross-subsidisation of preferential consumers at the expense of industrial consumers is designed via the system of so-called "subsidy certificates". To compensate the losses of energy companies, which supply electricity to preferential categories of consumers at regulated tariffs (well below cost-recovery levels), the value of "subsidy certificates" is incorporated into the structure of the wholesale market price of electricity. The share of "subsidy certificates" in the electricity price was about 30.5% (0.25 UAH/kWh) in 2014. Overall, the volume of cross-subsidisation increased from UAH 18 bln in 2009 (NCSREPU, 2015a) to UAH 43.8 bln in 2015 (NCSREPU, 2016a), despite the fact that certain preferential groups were cancelled year by year. For example, preferences for ore mining and chemical companies were cancelled in 2011 (NERC, 2014) and preferences to coal mining enterprises and economic entities that implement innovation projects were cancelled in 2015. By the end of 2015, only six preferential groups of consumers remained (NCSREPU, 2016a).
Amount of subsidy conferred	2012: UAH 34.5 bln (USD 4.3 bln) 2013: UAH 37.7 bln (USD 4.7 bln) 2014: UAH 40.8 bln (USD 3.4 bln) 2015: UAH 43.9 bln (USD 2 bln)
Information sources	Resolution of National Electricity Regulatory Commission No. 184 of 26 February 2001 "On Approval of the procedure for compensation of losses to licensees for electricity supply at regulated tariffs for households" (Resolution No. 184, 2001) and similar resolutions for other preferential groups of consumers (No. 1 487 of 16 November 2006, No. 27 of 18 January 2007, No. 198 of 21 February 2008, No. 996 of 26 July 2007, No. 387 of 2 April 2009, No. 408 of 11 April 2013); Resolution of the NCSERPU No. 971 of 31 March 2015 "On the results of activities of NCSEPPU in 2014" (NCSREPU, 2015a); Resolution of NERC No. 348 of 27 March 2014 " On the approval of activities of NERC in 2013" (NERC, 2014)

Annex 7.A3

Government support for renewable energy sources

Table 7.A3.1. **Feed-in tariff for electricity producers from renewable energy sources**

Subsidy category	Income or price support → Market price support and regulation → Feed-in tariff for renewable energy producers
Stimulated activity	Production of renewable energy
Subsidy name	**Feed-in tariff for renewable energy producers**
Jurisdiction	National
Legislation/endorsing organisation	Article 17.1 of Law "On electric power industry" (Parliament of Ukraine, Law No. 575/97-BP, 1997)
Policy objective(s) of subsidy	To stimulate the development of the renewable energy sector
End recipient(s) of subsidy	Renewable energy producers
Time period	Staring from 2009
Background	A feed-in tariff for renewable energy producers was introduced in Ukraine in 2009. According to Law No. 575/97-BP (1997), the so-called "green" tariff for renewable energy producers is set based on the retail tariff for consumers of the second voltage class, as of January 2009, multiplied by the "green" coefficient approved for each type of renewable energy (Article 17.1). The same law provides that "green" tariffs should be revised by the NCSREPU each month, taking into account the official UAH/EUR exchange rate, defined by the National Bank of Ukraine. The authors estimate the value of the induced transfer to renewable energy producers based on the weighted average "green" tariff, average tariff for electricity generating companies (thermal power plants) and electricity produced from renewable energy sources based on the data provided in the NCSREPU report (2015b).
Amount of subsidy conferred	2012: UAH 1.7 bln (USD 213 mln) 2013: UAH 3 bln (USD 379 mln) 2014: UAH 4.3 bln (USD 364 mln) 2015: UAH 6.1 bln (USD 280 mln)
Information sources	Annual reports of the National Commission for State Regulation of Energy and Public Utilities (NCSREPU, 2015a)

References

104.ua (2016), *New Amendments to Calculation of Subsidies and Benefits,* 104.ua. https://104.ua/ua/news/id/informacija-dlja-pilgovikiv-18319#sub18320.

Cabinet of Ministers (2016), *Order No. 418-p of 27 May 2016 on the Approval of the Government Action Plan of Priority Measures for 2016,* Cabinet of Ministers of Ukraine, Kyiv.

Cabinet of Ministers (2015a), *Resolution No. 758 of 1 October 2015 on Approval of the Assigning of Special Responsibilities of the Natural Gas Market Players to Ensure Interests of the General Public,* Cabinet of Ministers of Ukraine, Kyiv.

Cabinet of Ministers (2015b), *Resolution No. 271 on Conducting a Transparent and Competitive Privatisation in 2015,* Cabinet of Ministers of Ukraine, Kyiv.

Cabinet of Ministers (2015c), *Resolution No. 13 of 23 January 2015 on Increasing Statutory Capital of the NJSC Naftogaz,* Cabinet of Ministers of Ukraine, Kyiv.

Cabinet of Ministers (2013), *Resolution No. 1 071 of 24 July 2013 on the Approval of the Energy Strategy of Ukraine by 2030,* Cabinet of Ministers of Ukraine, Kyiv.

Cabinet of Ministers (2012a), *Resolution No. 692-p of 1 August 2012 on the Approval of the List of Quasi-Fiscal Operations and Authorities (Governance) Responsible for Assessment of Possible Impact of Such Transactions on Budget Indicators,* Cabinet of Ministers of Ukraine, Kyiv.

Cabinet of Ministers (2012b), *Resolution No. 517 of 11 June 2012 on the Approval of Procedures and Conditions for Allocation of Subvention from the State Budget to Local Budgets to Settle the Arrears Accumulated Due to Differences between the Actual Costs of Central Heating and Services of Centralised Water Supply,* Cabinet of Ministers of Ukraine, Kyiv.

Cabinet of Ministers (2011a), *Resolution No. 1 056 of 17 October 2011 Concerning Some Issues on the Use of Funds on Energy Efficiency and Energy Saving (with Amendments),* Cabinet of Ministers of Ukraine, Kyiv.

Cabinet of Ministers (2011b), *Resolution No. 236 on Approval of the Procedure on the Use of Funds Provided in the State Budget for the Restructuring of the Coal and Peat Industry*, Cabinet of Ministers of Ukraine, Kyiv.

Cabinet of Ministers (2011c), *Resolution No. 153 on the Approval of the Procedure on the Use of State Budget Funds to Provide Partial Compensation for Costs of Coal Mining Enterprises, Which Are Included in the Prime Cost of Finished Marketable Coal,* Cabinet of Ministers of Ukraine, Kyiv.

Cabinet of Ministers (2010), *Resolution No. 243 of 1 March 2010 on the Approval of the State Target Economic Programme on Energy Efficiency and Development of Renewable Energy Sources and Alternative Fuels for the Period 2010-2016,* Cabinet of Ministers of Ukraine, Kyiv.

Cabinet of Ministers (2002), *Resolution No. 256 of 4 March 2002 on the Approval of the Procedure on Funding of Expenditures of Local Budgets on Implementation of State Social Protection Programmes by Subventions from the State Budget,* Cabinet of Ministers of Ukraine, Kyiv.

Cabinet of Ministers (2001), *Resolution No. 1 729 of 27 December 2001 on Supplying Consumers with Natural Gas (with Amendments),* Cabinet of Ministers of Ukraine, Kyiv.

Cabinet of Ministers (1998), *Resolution No. 1 156* of *27 July 1998 on the New Amount of Payment for Housing and Utilities, Purchase of LNG, Solid and Liquid Furnace Fuel in the Case Housing Subsidies are Provided,* Cabinet of Ministers of Ukraine, Kyiv.

Cabinet of Ministers (1995), *Resolution No. 848 of October 1995 on the Simplification of the Procedure of Allocation of Subsidies to the Population on the Reimbursement for Housing and Communal Services, LPG and Solid and Liquid Furnace Fuel,* Cabinet of Ministers of Ukraine, Kyiv.

Energy Charter Secretariat (2013), *In-Depth Review of Energy Efficiency Policy of Ukraine,* 2013, Energy Charter Secretariat, Brussels.

Hölzler, H. et al. (2015), *Harmonisation of Public Procurement System in Ukraine with EU Standards. Study on State Support for Undertakings in Ukraine*, Crown Agents. www.amc.gov.ua/amku/doccatalog/document?id=120933&schema=main.

IEA (2016), *Ukraine: Indicators for 2013,* International Energy Agency, Paris. www.iea.org/statistics/statisticssearch/report/?country=Ukraine&product=indicators&year=2013.

IEA (2015a), *Eastern Europe, Caucasus and Central Asia: Energy Policies Beyond IEA Countries,* Organisation for Economic Co-operation and Development/International Energy Agency, Paris. https://www.iea.org/publications/freepublications/publication/IDR_EasternEuropeCaucasus_2015.pdf.

IEA (2015b), *Fossil-Fuel Subsidies: Methodology and Assumptions,* International Energy Agency, Paris. www.worldenergyoutlook.org/resources/energysubsidies/methodology.

IEA (2015c), *World Energy Outlook 2015,* International Energy Agency, Paris. www.worldenergyoutlook.org/weo2015/.

IEA (2012), *Ukraine 2012: Energy Policies Beyond OECD Countries,* Organisation for Economic Co-operation and Development/International Energy Agency, Paris. https://www.iea.org/publications/freepublications/publication/Ukraine2012_free.pdf.

IER (2016), *Macroeconomic Forecast Ukraine: Positive Signs Emerge,* Institute for Economic Research, Kyiv. www.ier.com.ua/en/publications/regular_products/forecast?pid=5310.

Koval, I. (2015), "Sale of Mines: The Conditions Will Dictate Buyers" (in Ukrainian). http://forbes.ua/ua/nation/1397002-rozprodazh-shaht-umovi-budut-diktuvati-pokupci.

Ministry of Ecology and Natural Resources (2016), *National Inventory of GHG Emissions in Ukraine, 1990-2014,* Ministry of Ecology and Natural Resources of Ukraine, Kyiv.

Ministry of Ecology and Natural Resources (2015), *Intended Nationally Determined Contribution of Ukraine,* Ministry of Ecology and Natural Resources of Ukraine, Kyiv. http://www4.unfccc.int/submissions/INDC/Published%20Documents/Ukraine/1/150930_Ukraine_INDC.pdf.

Ministry of Economic Development and Trade (2016), *Why and How Gas and Heat Prices Will Change Starting from 1 May 2016?,* Ministry of Economic Development and Trade, Kyiv. https://issuu.com/mineconomdev/docs/ministrypresentation11-2.

Ministry of Finance (2015), *Loans under State Guarantees,* Ministry of Finance of Ukraine, Kyiv. www.minfin.gov.ua/control/uk/publish/archive/main?cat_id=74685.

Ministry of Finance (2012). *Decree No. 333 of 12 March 2012 on Approval of Instruction on the Use of Economic Classification of Expenditures (with Amendments),* Ministry of Finance of Ukraine, Kyiv.

Naftogaz (2016a), *Gas Prices,* Naftogaz, Kyiv. www.naftogaz.com/www/3/nakweb.nsf/0/D71B09681A380951C2257F48004BF67B?OpenDocument.

Naftogaz (2016b), *In 2015, Ukraine Covered 63% of Demand for Imported Gas from Europe.* Naftogaz, Kyiv. www.naftogaz.com/www/3/nakweb.nsf/0/DDF058F6412F06C8C2257F4900584C01?OpenDocument.

Naftogaz (2016c), *Statistics on the Gas Import Prices in 2015,* Naftogaz, Kyiv. http://naftogaz.com/www/3/nakweb.nsf/0/553F49E6579520EDC2257F5300371CCE?OpenDocument.

Naftogaz (2015a), *Annual Report 2014* (in Ukrainian), Naftogaz, Kyiv. www.naftogaz.com/files/Zvity/Naftogaz%20Annual%20Report%202014.pdf.

Naftogaz (2015b), *Company,* Naftogaz, Kyiv. www.naftogaz.com/www/3/nakweben.nsf/0/3A25D65C2606A6C9C22570D800318869?OpenDocument.

Naftogaz (2015c), *Why Should Gas Prices Be Increased?* (in Ukrainian), Naftogaz, Kyiv. www.naftogaz.com/files/Information/Tariffs.pdf.

National Bank of Ukraine (2016), *Official UAH Exchange Rate, National Bank of Ukraine, Kyiv.* http://bank.gov.ua/files/Exchange_r.xls.

NCSREPU (2016a), *Annual Report for 2015,* National Commission for State Regulation of Energy and Public Utilities of Ukraine, Kyiv.

NCSREPU (2016b), *Electricity Tariffs,* National Commission for State Regulation of Energy and Public Utilities of Ukraine, Kyiv. www.nerc.gov.ua/?id=15011.

NCSREPU (2016c), *Heat Tariffs for Households,* National Commission for State Regulation of Energy and Public Utilities of Ukraine, Kyiv. www.nerc.gov.ua/?id=19309.

NCSREPU (2016d), *Heat Tariffs for Legal Persons,* National Commission for State Regulation of Energy and Public Utilities of Ukraine, Kyiv. www.nerc.gov.ua/?id=19599.

NCSREPU (2016e), *Resolution No. 1 309 of 22 July 2016 on the Establishment of Retail Tariffs for Non-Residential Consumers for August 2016,* National Commission for State Regulation of Energy and Public Utilities of Ukraine, Kyiv.

NCSREPU (2016f), *Resolution No. 528 of 31 March 2016 on the Approval of Procedures on Tariffs Setting for Thermal Energy, its Production, Transportation and Supply,* National Commission for State Regulation of Energy and Public Utilities of Ukraine, Kyiv.

NCSREPU (2015a), *Annual Report for 2014,* National Commission for State Regulation of Energy and Public Utilities of Ukraine, Kyiv.

NCSREPU (2015b), *NCSREPU Communication to Local Authorities on the Utility Tariffs Setting,* National Commission for State Regulation of Energy and Public Utilities of Ukraine, Kyiv. www.nerc.gov.ua/data/filearch/Zvernennya_rad.pdf.

NCSREPU (2015c), *Resolution No. 584 of 3March 2015 on Approval of Marginal Prices for Gas for Heat Generation Entities,* National Commission for State Regulation of Energy and Public Utilities of Ukraine, Kyiv.

NCSREPU (2015d), *Resolution No. 583 of 3 March 2015 on Setting Retail Prices for Natural Gas Used for the Needs of the Population,* National Commission for State Regulation of Energy and Public Utilities of Ukraine, Kyiv.

NCSREPU (2015e), *Resolution No. 220 on the Establishment of the Electricity Tariffs for the Population,* National Commission for State Regulation of Energy and Public Utilities of Ukraine, Kyiv.

NCSREPU (2011), *Resolution No. 466 of 31 March.2011 on Approval of the Procedure for the Establishment of Retail Prices on Natural Gas for Households (with Amendments),* National Commission for State Regulation of Energy and Public Utilities of Ukraine, Kyiv.

NERC (2014), *Annual Report for 2013,* National Electricity Regulatory Commission of Ukraine, Kyiv.

NERC (2001), *Resolution No. 184 of 26 February 2001 on Approval of the Procedure for Compensation of Losses to Licensees for Electricity Supply at Regulated Tariffs for Households,* National Electricity Regulatory Commission of Ukraine, Kyiv.

NISS (2014), *Priorities and Modernisation Leverage of the Coal Industry in Ukraine,* National Institute for Strategic Studies, Kyiv. www.niss.gov.ua/articles/1495/#_ftn1.

OECD (2013), *Analysing Energy Subsidies in the Countries of Eastern Europe, Caucasus and Central Asia,* OECD Publishing, Paris. https://www.oecd.org/env/outreach/EHS%20report_20%20August%202013_ENG.pdf.

Oharenko, Y. and A. Denysenko (2015), *Government Spending and Cross-Subsidisation in the Energy Sector of Ukraine 2009-2015,* National Ecological Centre of Ukraine, Kyiv.

Parliament of Ukraine (2015a), *Law of Ukraine No. 80-VIII of 28 December 2014 on the Budget of Ukraine for 2015 (with Amendments),* Parliament of Ukraine, Kyiv.

Parliament of Ukraine (2015b), *Law of Ukraine No. 329-VIII of 9 April 2015 on the Gas Market,* Parliament of Ukraine, Kyiv.

Parliament of Ukraine (2014), *Coalition Agreement of Deputies "European Ukraine",* Parliament of Ukraine, Kyiv.

Parliament of Ukraine (2010a), *Budget Code of Ukraine No. 2 456-VI of 8 July 2010 (with Amendments),* Parliament of Ukraine, Kyiv.

Parliament of Ukraine (2010b), *Law of Ukraine No. 2 467-VI of 8 July 2010 on Principles and Functioning of the Natural Gas Market (with Amendments),* Parliament of Ukraine, Kyiv.

Parliament of Ukraine (2010c), *Tax Code of Ukraine No. 2 755-VI of 2 December 2010 (with Amendments),* Parliament of Ukraine.

Parliament of Ukraine (2008), *Law of Ukraine No. 250-VI of 10 April.2008 on Ratification of the Protocol of Accession of Ukraine to the World Trade Organization,* Parliament of Ukraine, Kyiv.

Parliament of Ukraine (1997), *Law No. 75/97-BP of 16 October 1997 on Electric Power Industry (with Amendments),* Parliament of Ukraine, Kyiv.

SAEEES (2015), *Implementation of the Key Objectives of the SAEEES in 2015,* State Agency on Energy Efficiency and Energy Saving of Ukraine, Kyiv.

Shlapak, M. (2015), "Ukrainians Are Cheated with Heat Bills" (in Ukrainian). http://gazeta.dt.ua/energy_market/ukrayinciv-nagrivayut-rahuyuchi-teplo-na-oko-_.html.

State Fiscal Service (2015), *Reference Book of Tax Privileges,* State Fiscal Service of Ukraine, Kyiv.

State Statistics Service (2016a), *Energy Balance of Ukraine for 2014,* State Statistics Service of Ukraine, Kyiv. www.ukrstat.gov.ua/.

State Statistics Service (2016b), *Express Issues of Statistical Information of the State Statistics Service of Ukraine,* State Statistics Service of Ukraine, Kyiv. www.ukrstat.gov.ua/.

State Treasury Service (2016), *Reports on the Execution of State Budget 2011-2016,* State Treasury Service of Ukraine, Kyiv. www.treasury.gov.ua/main/uk/doccatalog/list?currDir=146477.

Voitko, A. (2015), "Spending This Year on Subsidies 'Exceeded' the Billions Spent Last Year". http://statistic.jkg-portal.com.ua/ua/publication/one/vitrati-u-comu-roc-na-subsidji-objshli-minulorchn-na-mljardi-45933.

World Bank (2016), *World Development Indicators,* World Bank, Washington, DC. http://data.worldbank.org/country/ukraine.

World Bank (2015), *Commodity Markets Monthly Data,* World Bank, Washington, DC. www.worldbank.org/en/research/commodity-markets.

World Bank (2012), *Modernization of the District Heating Systems in Ukraine: Heat Metering and Consumption-Based Billing,* World Bank, Washington, DC, http://hdl.handle.net/10986/17147.

WTO (2015), *Ukraine: New and Full Notification Pursuant to Article XVI:1 of the GATT 1994 and Article 25 of the Agreement on Subsidies and Countervailing Measures,* WTO Committee on Subsidies and Countervailing Measures, World Trade Organisation, Geneva.

ORGANISATION FOR ECONOMIC CO-OPERATION AND DEVELOPMENT

The OECD is a unique forum where governments work together to address the economic, social and environmental challenges of globalisation. The OECD is also at the forefront of efforts to understand and to help governments respond to new developments and concerns, such as corporate governance, the information economy and the challenges of an ageing population. The Organisation provides a setting where governments can compare policy experiences, seek answers to common problems, identify good practice and work to co-ordinate domestic and international policies.

The OECD member countries are: Australia, Austria, Belgium, Canada, Chile, the Czech Republic, Denmark, Estonia, Finland, France, Germany, Greece, Hungary, Iceland, Ireland, Israel, Italy, Japan, Korea, Latvia, Luxembourg, Mexico, the Netherlands, New Zealand, Norway, Poland, Portugal, the Slovak Republic, Slovenia, Spain, Sweden, Switzerland, Turkey, the United Kingdom and the United States. The European Union takes part in the work of the OECD.

OECD Publishing disseminates widely the results of the Organisation's statistics gathering and research on economic, social and environmental issues, as well as the conventions, guidelines and standards agreed by its members.

OECD PUBLISHING, 2, rue André-Pascal, 75775 PARIS CEDEX 16
(97 2017 72 1 P) ISBN 978-92-64-28430-2 – 2018

www.ingramcontent.com/pod-product-compliance
Lightning Source LLC
Chambersburg PA
CBHW061203240926
51846CB00006B/1099